Historical Dictionary
of
COSTA RICA

second edition

by
Theodore S. Creedman

Latin American Historical Dictionaries, No. 16

The Scarecrow Press, Inc.
Metuchen, N.J., & London
1991

British Library Cataloguing-in-Publication data available

Library of Congress Cataloging-in-Publication Data

Creedman, Theodore S.
    Historical dictionary of Costa Rica / by Theodore S. Creedman.
-- 2nd ed.
        p.   cm. -- (Latin American historical dictionaries ; no. 16)
    Bibliography: p.
    ISBN 0-8108-2215-6
    1. Costa Rica--Dictionaries and encyclopedias. I. Title.
II. Series.
F1542.C7   1991
972.86'003--dc20   89-6210

CONTENTS

EDITOR'S FOREWORD

The 1977 edition of this work was dedicated "to those who will now never read it." Unhappily, this has now become apposite for the author himself. Dr. Creedman died soon after sending me the first draft of the new manuscript. In accordance with his last instructions, I then approached Professor Gary Kuhn of the University of Wisconsin-La Crosse. He most generously agreed, not only to answer all my subsequent queries, but also to read and carefully check the entire manuscript. My transfer from Ohio State to the University of Minnesota made it possible for us to meet and consult with some regularity. In the process, I made a few revisions and additions of my own. All entries that have been substantially affected by our revisions are accordingly labelled with Gary's initials or my own, as appropriate. We were also most fortunate in having Rosa Maria de la Cueva de Peterson to convert the whole into the final manuscript: she drew our attention to a number of minor errors and inconsistencies we had both overlooked.

Dr. Theodore S. Creedman was born in Brooklyn, N.Y. He studied at the University of Kentucky, Columbia University, the University of Madrid, and in Mexico. His interest in Costa Rica led to an Organization of American States fellowship there from 1965 to 1967, which enabled him to prepare his doctoral dissertation, "The Political Evolution of Costa Rica, 1936-1964." He obtained his PhD from the University of Maryland in 1971 and subsequently taught in high schools in New York City, at Beloit College in Wisconsin, at the University of Maryland, and in Costa Rica. Immediately before his final illness he was a bilingual professor of history at the Inter-American University in Puerto Rico.

The only connection I can myself claim with Costa Rica is the accident of having obtained my PhD in the same year

and from the same English university (Essex) as ex-President
Arias. Working with the present book over a 3½-year period,
however, has taught me a great deal and awakened my interest
in this most fascinating of countries. I hope it will serve as
a similar introduction to many of those who will read it.

Among Dr. Creedman's papers at his death was an ac-
knowledgments page of the first edition heavily annotated with
many new names. It has not, alas, proved possible to decipher
all of these notes. Those I could read are listed in alphabetical
order: Rigoberto Araya; Carla Araya Guillén (INDEP); Carlos
Araya Pochet; Ricardo Blanco Segura; John and Mavis Biesanz
and family; Mario Camacho; Alfonso Chase (Ministerio de Cultura); Robert Claxton; Alberto Corballo Q.; Ben Crosby;
Duria Díaz; Dr. and Col. Heath; Dr. R. Hunter; Vladimir de
Icarus; Edgar Mayorga; Carlos Meléndez; Rafael Obregon Loría;
Victor Julio Peralta; Olger Ruiz; Flora Villalobos Montero
(Biblioteca Nacional).

We regret it was not typographically practicable to indicate accents (including the tilde) over capital (upper case)
letters. So, although (e.g.) "peña" is distinguished from
"pena" in the text, both appear as "PENA" in the headings.

Laurence Hallewell
University of Minnesota

PREFACE: A PERSONAL NOTE

From our mother's father, my brother inherited a knack for language ... a talent to talk about what was really happening with all kinds of people from Rumania to Brazil and from Russia to Israel.

From our mother, he was endowed with a generous spirit and hearty sense of humor.

Our father passed along toughness that allowed him to endure research in remote regions.

And from a source I cannot identify, Ted Creedman was born with the spirit of adventure. He was a meddler who possessed a keen intelligence, a quick wit, and a habit for never quite taking himself seriously.

One thing he did take seriously was the worth and fascination of history. As a boy, I remember him spending endless hours poring over baseball statistics. He made up elaborate tables and schemes to keep track of the players and the teams in all the leagues. Although I found it terribly boring at the time, I see now that his play established a foundation for the methods and attitudes employed in his life's work--the field of Latin American history.

That same meticulous concern with details, coupled with an insatiable curiosity and craving for adventure, is what led him to write this historical dictionary of Costa Rica. Although Ted was teaching at a University in Puerto Rico when he died at age 54, his heart was always in Costa Rica.

He lived in San Jose for many years while researching his first book and maintained a house in the country, a place where he eventually planned to retreat after a career in education. He wanted, in Costa Rica, to devote himself to writing, talking, cooking, and finding new ways to get himself and his friends into delightful trouble.

That unerring ability to be in the midst of the action allowed Ted to personally experience many of the people and situations described in this book. Always willing to introduce himself to strangers, he knew well the leaders of Costa Rica, both the public figures and those who moved behind the scenes.

He always sought information directly from the source and he set down his perceptions with absolute honesty, just as he perceived the truth. That insistence on telling the story as he saw it got him into trouble occasionally. But because he was dealing with the truth, the troubles never lasted long.

This book was important to him. He was still working on the revisions before his death in the summer of 1985. I want to thank his editor, Laurence Hallewell, and his friend, Professor Gary G. Kuhn of the University of Wisconsin-La Crosse, for their efforts to assure completion of this edition. It was an eloquent statement of their friendship for Ted and their respect for his work.

His friends miss him as much his family. It is my hope that this book will prove useful and productive in increasing the understanding of peoples for one another. I believe that was Ted's desire, too.

Michael Creedman
Sausalito, California

INTRODUCTION

The history of Costa Rica has been one of the most unusual in Latin America. In its uniqueness and seeming simplicity lies the enigma as to what is its true national character.

During the colonial period, this country was left largely to its own devices, principally because its lack of natural resources and small indigenous population made it unattractive to Spanish exploitation. Land, therefore, was more evenly distributed, and a class of yeoman farmers emerged, which was important in the future development of Costa Rica's democratic tradition. However, it should be remembered that there was an aristocracy which exerted considerable influence, and democratic practices were more myth than reality.

After the vacillations of the independence period, the Costa Ricans had a disappointing experience with the short-lived Central American Federal Republic. Costa Rica became somewhat isolated from the rest of the isthmus and looked toward Europe for cultural inspiration. Attention was focused on increasing the production of coffee and on internal affairs rather than in participation in Central American affairs. Towards the end of the nineteenth century, the railroad to the Atlantic coast was inaugurated, bananas began to supplement coffee as the chief cash crop, and, in turn, European influence was displaced by United States trade.

The first half of the twentieth century was dominated by a liberal semi-democracy in which the ruling class usually won, although several elections were most questionable. It was not until after the 1948 Civil War that genuinely free elections were institutionalized.

Compared to its turbulent Central American neighbors, the development of Costa Rica has been somewhat--but not

ix

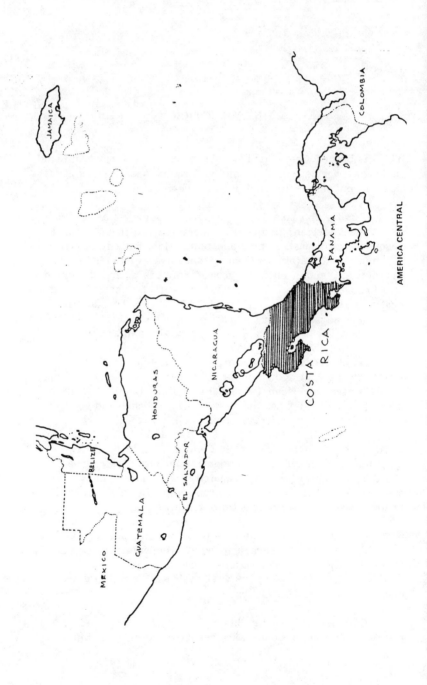

AMERICA CENTRAL

completely--different. What has happened is that a "white myth" (leyenda blanca) has evolved which portrays Costa Rica as an idyllic democracy without violence or poverty, a so-called "Switzerland of Central America."

Actually, some elements of the myth are true. Nonetheless, Costa Rica has had its share of civil wars, revolutions, and similar upheavals. These problems have been as serious as those of the neighboring republics, but they have usually been handled with a bit less bloodshed and civil disorder. Possibly the benign climate, small population, availability of land, and even the desire to live in accordance with the "white myth" have helped to maintain something of this legend.

From a scholarly point of view, researchers are handicapped because there is no complete critical history of the country, and the casual tourist or the scholar who comes on a short junket often falls prey to the superficialities of the country. The realities, which lie somewhere between the idyllic democratic legend and the stereotyped picture of a banana republic, can only be understood by a long immersion

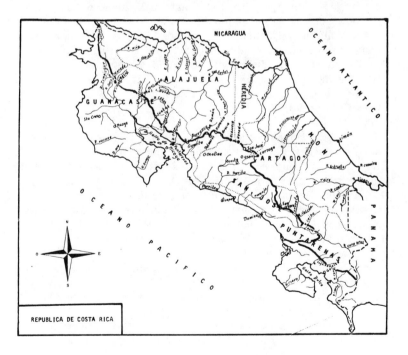

REPUBLICA DE COSTA RICA

in the Costa Rican environment. This is, of course, difficult
because of lack of time and inadequate reference tools. Possibly this work will do something to help fill the great lack
of basic books on this attractive country.

[T.C.]

The alphabetical arrangement of entries is that followed by
other volumes in this series. English order is used (ch follows
cg, ll follows lk, ñ is treated as n), on the word-by-word
principle (MORA VALVERDE before MORACIA). Acronyms
(e.g., ANDE), being pronounced as words, are filed as such.
The abbreviations St. (for "Saint") and Mc (for "Mac") are
treated as if spelled out. Initial articles are ignored in
alphabetizing, with the traditional exception of surnames of
French origin (e.g., LE LACHEUR).

Hispanic personal names are made up of three elements:
the baptismal (one or more given names), the patronymic,
and a third which is either the maternal surname (traditionally,
but now seldom, preceded by "y"), or, in the case of a married
woman, the marital surname (preceded by "de"). The patronymic determines the filing order; thus the entry for President
Tomás Guardia Gutiérrez will be found among the "Guardias";
that for his wife, Emilia Solórzano de Guardia, is under
"Solórzano." Prefixes are ignored, so Juan de la Cruz Zumbado files under "Cruz."

Internationally known events, places, persons, and
institutions can generally be found under the name by which
they are generally referred to in English (Columbus, Christopher; Inter-American Institute of Agricultural Sciences;
Inquisition; Jesuits). Although the Spanish name has been
mostly preferred for Costa Rican institutions, organizations,
and places (Ferrocarril del Norte; Partido Liberación Nacional;
Universidad Nacional de Costa Rica), exceptions have been
made whenever it was thought that the Anglophone reader
might be more likely to know the English form (banana strike,
national anthem, University of Costa Rica). Cross-references
from the form not adopted have been liberally provided.

An asterisk marks any word used elsewhere in the
dictionary as an entry heading. Thus, a mention of

xii

Comandante Eden *Pastora Gómez indicates the existence of an entry headed PASTORA GOMEZ.

This new edition of the dictionary is followed by an updated bibliography. A new feature, which has been appreciated by users of other dictionaries in the series, is a brief chronology (compiled by the editor). This can be supplemented by the various specialized chronological listings in the dictionary itself (e.g., under EARTHQUAKES; ELECTIONS; GOVERNORS; PIRATES; PRESIDENTS AND CHIEFS OF STATE; and REVOLUTIONS, WARS, CIVIL WARS, AND MAJOR UPRISINGS).

[L.H.]

CHRONOLOGY

1502	September 17: Christopher Columbus lands at Cariary, modern Puerto Limón
1510	Diego de Nicuesa explores Caribbean coast
1513	September 9: Vasco Núñez de Balboa crosses Isthmus of Panama and discovers the South Seas (i.e., the Pacific Ocean)
1513-1531	Pedrarias governor of the Duchy of Veragua
1526	Villa de Bruselas founded
1534-1536	Felipe Gutiérrez second governor of Veragua
1539	April-November: Alonso Calero descends the Desaguadero, modern Rio San Juan
1541-1544	Diego de Gutiérrez first governor of Nuevo Cartago, (i.e., Costa Rica)
1543	Santiago founded on the banks of the Suerre, modern Reventazón river
1561-1562	Expedition of Juan de Cavallón
1562	Juan Vázquez de Coronado alcalde mayor of Costa Rica and Nuevo Cartago
1563	Original founding of Cartago
1566	Perafán governor of Costa Rica
1568	Costa Rica made part of the Audiencia of Guatemala

1572	Cartago refounded in new site
1574	Cartago moved a second time; Esparza founded; borders of the Gobernación of Costa Rica defined
1601	Camino de Mulas from Caldera to Chiriqui opened
1605	Santiago de Talamanca founded by Diego de Sojo
1610	Santiago burned and Spaniards obliged to evacuate Talamanca, which is left to its Indians
1633	English occupation of Providence Island (now Isla de Providencia) marks beginning of English piracy in Western Caribbean
1666	April 8: Raid on Costa Rica by Captain Mansfield and the future Sir Henry Morgan
1676	June 30: English pirate raid on Matina driven off
1678	Cacao plantations estimated at 130,000 trees
1681	Nicoya burned by pirates
1685–1686	Two pirate raids on Esparza
1693	Slaving raids by English in Talamanca
1709	Insurrection by Indians in Talamanca
1736	Foundation of Villanueva, now San José
1741–1742	Building of Fuerte de San Fernando to protect Caribbean coast against English and Zambo-Mosquitos
1747	August 13: English destroy Fuerte de San Fernando

1782	Alajuela founded
1787-1792	Attempt to aid colony's development by granting it exclusive right to provide tobacco for the estanco of Guatemala
1810-1814	Liberal Cortes de Cadiz attempts far-reaching reform of way Spain and its empire are administered
1814	Casa de Enseñanza de Santo Tomás established; Port of Puntarenas officially inaugurated
1820	October 12: First recorded export of coffee (to Perico, Panama)
1821	September 9: Acta de Guatemala proclaims Central America independent September 27: Effective independence of Mexico September 28: Acta de los Nublados October 25: Junta set up in Costa Rica, chaired by Juan Manuel de Cañas
1822	May 18: Iturbide proclaimed Emperor Agustín I of Mexico
1823	April: First Costa Rican Civil War June: National Constituent Assembly of the United Provinces of Central America
1824	May 25: Slavery abolished in Costa Rica July 25: Cabildo Abierto of Nicoya seeks the transfer of its province of Guanacaste from Nicaragua to Costa Rica November 22: United Provinces of Central America become the Federation of Central America
1825	January 26: Ley fundamental del Estado Libre de Costa Rica December 9: Federal Congress sanctions Costa Rican annexation of Guanacaste
1830	Arrival of Costa Rica's first printing press

1832	First export of coffee by Jorge Stiepel to Valparaíso
1835	Election of Braulio Carrillo as Head of State September 26: Outbreak of the War of the League
1838	November 14: Costa Rica withdraws from Central American Federation
1841	March 8: Carrillo promulgates Ley de Bases y Garantías September 2: Earthquake destroys Cartago
1842	April: President Francisco Morazán invades Costa Rica and incorporates it back into his Central American Federation September 15: Morazán having been defeated and Costa Rican independence recovered, he is publicly shot in San José
1843	Casa de Enseñanza de Santo Tomás made a university
1844	William Le Lacheur begins coffee export trade to England
1847	May 8: José María Castro Madriz elected Head of State November: French intervention in Central America (to mid-1848)
1848	First Protestant church August 31: Castro Madriz proclaims Costa Rica a republic and himself its first President November 30: "Reformed" Constitution
1850	San José made an archdiocese April 19: Clayton-Bulwer Treaty
1855	March: Outbreak of Campaña del Tránsito (war with William Walker)

1856	April 11: Victory of Rivas over Walker; his defeat is followed by a devastating cholera outbreak
1860	August 14: President Juan Rafael Mora Porras deposed September 30: Mora executed in Puntarenas
1863	Banco Anglo-Costarricense (first bank) founded; currency decimalized; first postage stamps
1869	New constitution declares education shall be free, obligatory, and tax supported
1870	General Tomás Guardia Gutiérrez seizes power in a military coup d'état: first President not representative of traditional oligarchy
1871	New constitution; inception of Ferrocarril del Norte
1881	First banana exports to New York
1882	Death penalty abolished
1884	Jesuits expelled
1885	March: Declaration of war on Guatemala
1886	February 26: Ley general de educación común
1888	New civil code; Universidad de Santo Tomás closed
1889	November 7: President Bernardo Soto Alfaro accepts electoral defeat
1890	Ferrocarril del Norte completed
1893	Tobacco estanco abolished; gold standard enacted

1896-1898	New attempts at Central American federation prove abortive.
1899	United Fruit Company formed
1903	Colombia ceases to be Costa Rica's southern neighbor with the independence of Panama
1908-1918	Central American Court of Justice
1910	May 4: Cartago again destroyed by earth-quake June 23: Ferrocarril del Pacífico completed
1911	British loans renegotiated
1913	Peak banana export year: 11,170,152 branches; introduction of direct elections
1917	January 27: Coup d'état to prevent intro-duction of income tax
1918	May: Declaration of war on Germany
1919	August 12: President Federico Tinoco Granados abdicates after his brother Joaquín is murdered August 30: United States demands Francis-co Aguilar Barquero be given presidency of Costa Rica
1921	March: Coto War with Panama
1923	Pan American Congress accepts idea of Pan American Highway
1929	Pan American Airways starts international flying boat service to Chaves.
1931	Bellavistazo coup attempt
1932	Empresa Nacional de Transportes Aéreos established; Costa Rica suspends payment on foreign loans

1934	Communist Party leads banana workers' strike
1937	Inception of construction of Interamerican Highway in Costa Rica.
1939	September: U.K. entry into World War Two leads to end of British market for Costa Rican coffee
1940	May 8: Rafael Angel Calderón Guardía elected a conservative reformer President with Church and Communist Party support August 26: Universidad de Costa Rica founded
1941	May 1: Echardi-Fernández Treaty with Panama December: Costa Rica anticipates the United States in declaring war on Japan
1942	September 25: Alien Property Law allows takeover of properties owned by German and Italian residents October 7: Creation of Interamerican Institute of Agricultural Sciences
1948	April: Civil War overthrows Calderón government; the new regime abolishes the Armed Forces, reestablishes the Catholic Church, nationalizes the banks, and becomes one of the first nations to follow Chile's 1947 example of claiming a 200-nautical-mile zone of exclusive economic exploitation beyond its shoreline
1957	October: Fundamental Education Law
1960	December 13: Creation of Central American Common Market
1971	Creation of National Parks
1972	Entry of Robert Vesco

1979	Coming to power of Sandinistas in Nicaragua
1982	Caribbean Basin Initiative
1984	May 30: La Penca attempt on life of Edén Pastora Gómez
1987	August 7: Arias Plan October 13: President Arias awarded Nobel Peace Prize in face of U.S. opposition to his Peace Plan
1989	January 13: John Hull arrested for drug-running and spying for C.I.A. October: Hurricane Joan kills 27 in Costa Rica November 7: Costa Rica admitted to GATT
1990	February 2: PUSC wins 51.4% of vote, and 29 of the 57 seats in the Legislative Assembly May 8: Rafael Angel Calderón Fournier succeeds Arias as President June 8: Death of José María Hipolito Figueres Ferrer

[L.H.]

THE DICTIONARY

ABACA. (Manila hemp). See: FIBER.

ABANGARES. *Canton in *Guanacaste Province, which was established June 4, 1915. Its *cabecera is Las Juntas and the total population is 12,575. Abangares was noted for gold mining, particularly from 1884 to 1930. More important today are *cattle and grains.

ABATE, John de (1929-). Scientist, writer and theatrical producer. He wrote under the pseudonym of Pablo Ariel. In addition to producing several theatrical works he wrote Mi amigo Pedro (1964) and the prize-winning El angelito que se quedó perdido (1963). Partially because of problems with his life style, Abate left the country and now resides in Venezuela.

ACADEMIA DE GEOGRAFIA E HISTORIA DE COSTA RICA. A learned organization founded July 10, 1940 under the guidance of Secretary of Education, Luis Demetrio Tinoco Castro. The Academy has a permanent office, a small research library, and functions as a center for encouraging and disseminating historical investigation. It publishes a journal (Anales) about every two years. In addition, it has published books and sponsored conferences, such as one for the 150th anniversary of Central American Independence (1971) and one to commemorate the 500th anniversary of Gonzalo *Fernández de Oviedo (1978). The Academia was instrumental in bringing the remains of several distinguished people like Braulio *Carrillo Colina and Florencio del *Castillo Solano back to Costa Rica. Other activities are erecting commemorative plaques and making pronouncements on historical questions. The current members of the Academy are:

> Oscar *Aguilar Bulgarelli
> Alejandro *Aguilar Machado
> Carlos H. Aguilar Piedra
> Carlos Araya Pochet
> Mario Barrantes Ferrero
> Ricardo Blanco Segura
> María Eugenia Bozzoli de Wille
> Oscar Castro Vega
> Ligia Cavallini de Arauz
> Luz Alba Chacón de Umaña

1

José Luis Coto Conde
Marco A. Fallas Barrantes
Rosa Greñas Morales
Carolyn Hall de Saborio
Otón Jiménez Luthmer
Carlos Meléndez Chaverri
María Molina de Lines
Francisco María Núñez Monge
Francisco Picado Soto
Enrique Roberto Luján
Jorge Enrique Romero Pérez
Carlos A. Serrano
Samuel Stone
Emmanuel Thompson Quirós
Luis Demetrio Tinoco Castro
Gabriel Ureña Morales
Macabeo Vargas Castro
Edwin León Villalobos
Marco Tulio Zeledón Matamoros
Chester Zelaya Goodman

ACADEMIC GENERATION. School of painters trained in a classical approach in the early years of the *Escuela Nacional de Bellas Artes, c. 1900-1920. See: PAINTING.

ACCION DEMOCRATA. A wing of the Democratic Party (*Partido Demócrata) of León *Cortés Castro principally composed of young men who wanted a more democratic electoral process and who vigorously opposed Rafael *Calderón Guardia. Two of its most important members were future presidents José *Figueres Ferrer and Francisco J. *Orlich Bolamacich. Acción Demócrata merged with the *Centro para el Estudio de Problemas Nacionales (Center for the Study of National Problems) in March 1945 to form the Social Democratic Party (*Partido Social Demócrata), forerunner of the current National Liberation Party (*Partido Liberación Nacional). Consult Carlos Araya, Historia de los partidos políticos: Liberación Nacional and Burt English, Liberación Nacional de Costa Rica.

ACOSTA. *Canton in *San José Province about eight miles south of the capital. Its *cabecera is San Ignacio and it was established October 27, 1910. It produces *coffee, grains and timber, and has a population of 14,853.

ACOSTA, Tomás de (1747-1821). *Governor (1797-1810) and considered one of the most capable and beloved of colonial governors. Cuban by birth, his era established a Costa Rican national sense on the eve of independence. It may have been during his administration that *coffee was first cultivated in Costa Rica. He left to become governor of Santa Marta (Colombia) but returned in 1812 as a brigadier in the royal army. He died in *Cartago.

Consult Ligia Estrada Molina, La Costa Rica de Don Tomás de Acosta.

ACOSTA GARCIA, Julio (1872-1954). The many offices held by Acosta included the presidency of the Republic 1920-1924 and the foreign ministry, 1915-1916 and 1944. He was a leader of the revolution that drove Federico *Tinoco Granados from power; as president he sought to unite the country by conciliatory government. In the 1940s he was selected as president of the new Social Security system (*Caja Costarricense de Seguro Social). He represented Costa Rica at the San Francisco Conference and was one of the original signers of the United Nations Charter. He was declared *Benemérito de la Patria in 1954.

ACTA DE GUATEMALA. The act signed in Guatemala City, September 15, 1821, which declared the Captaincy General of Guatemala (Capitanía General de Guatemala) independent of Spain. This act automatically made Costa Rica independent, because it was a political subdivision of the Captaincy General. The date of the signing of this act is a national *holiday throughout Central America. See: ACTA DE LOS NUBLADOS; INDEPENDENCE.

ACTA DE LOS NUBLADOS. (The Act of the Clouds, September 28, 1821). When word reached León, Nicaragua, that Guatemala had declared independence, the *Diputación Provincial (a combined government of the provinces of Costa Rica and Nicaragua) declared provisional independence. Because of the many uncertainties, they would not commit themselves further, preferring to "remain on the margin of events until the clouds of the day clear up." This curious act set the stage for later conflict because it did not settle the question whether Costa Rica would join the *Central American Federation or Agustín de *Iturbide's Mexican Empire. See: INDEPENDENCE: CIVIL WARS (1823); and consult Ricardo Fernández Guardia, Historia de Costa Rica: La independencia.

ACTIVISTAS. A group within the Church which favored the implementation of social reformist policies along the lines of the encyclicals Rerum Novarum and Quadragesimo Anno. Consult James Backer, La iglesia y el sindicalismo en Costa Rica (1978).

ACUNA, José Basilio (1897-). Writer and dramatist. One of the most important Costa Rican writers of this century. He studied psychology and philosophy in both Costa Rica and France. During the First World War he fought with the French Foreign Legion, and after coming back to Costa Rica was professor of education. Among his most important stage plays are a trilogy of Inca themes called Intiada: "La ciudad de las puertas de oro," "Entreacto fantástico," and "El imperio Incaica." He was awarded a National Theatre prize in 1970. Other notable plays are "Máscaras y candilejas," and "El pequeño Napoleón." Acuña has also written poetry and novels. Some of the more noteworthy are: Quetzal-cóatl (1947), Proyecciones (1953), Rapsodia de América (1962), Campanas de medianoche (1968), El soneto interminable (1971), and Entre dos mundos (1971). He won the Magón Prize in 1983 (the highest national award for literature).

ACUNA DE CHACON, Angela. Pioneer feminist, and Costa Rica's first woman lawyer. She founded the national feminist journal Fígaro in 1915 the year before she graduated, and formed a national feminist group in 1923, two years before obtaining her licenciatura. A lifetime of political writing and speaking helped achieve votes for women in 1949. [L.H.]

ADELANTADO. A title granted for life (and sometimes hereditary) to those who led expeditions to the New World in the first part of the colonial period. This title gave the right to govern and populate a given territory. It also granted the adelantado a virtual economic monopoly over the area except for the *quinto real and taxes imposed by the *Consejo de Indias. In Costa Rica this title was held by Juan *Vázquez de Coronado, his son Gonzalo *Vázquez de Coronado, and Juan *Fernández de Salinas (among others).

AEROVIAS NACIONALES DE COSTA RICA. Pioneer airline founded by Costa Rican pilot Ramón Macaya in January 1934. Taken over by the Compañia *TACA de Costa Rica in 1940. See also: AVIATION. [L.H.]

AFECTOS DE ODIO Y AMOR. A theatrical work performed in the patio of the governor's palace on January 30, 1725. It is said to be the first theatrical piece presented in Costa Rica.

AFRICAN PALM OIL. The traditional Spanish olive is unsuited to Costa Rican climate, and although the country has always had appreciable numbers of pigs (see: LIVESTOCK), no local lard-making industry has developed. Coconuts have always been grown but not in sufficient quantity. There has been therefore a long standing dependence on imports for all edible oils and fats. An attempt to remedy this began in 1949 when the Banana Company began planting the African oil palm (a native of West Africa well suited to lowland Costa Rica) on abandoned banana lands near Puerto Quepos. The fruit of this palm can provide oil for cooking, margarine and soap, and the inner nut is suitable for livestock feed. By 1968 production reached 20,000 tonnes, and an export surplus was predicted within twenty years. Profits have been restricted however by governmental fixing of domestic prices and 1983 production was still only 24,000 tonnes. [L.H.]

AFRO-AMERICANS. See: BLACKS.

AGRICULTOR COSTARRICENSE, El. See: GRANJA NACIONAL DE AGRICULTURA.

AGRICULTURE. See: ECONOMY, The; EXPORTS; FERTILIZERS; HACIENDA; INSTITUTO INTERAMERICANO DE CIENCIAS AGRO-PECUARIAS; SOCIEDAD ITALIANA DE COLONIZACION AGRI-COLA: QUAKERS; UNITED FRUIT COMPANY; and individual crops: AFRICAN PALM OIL; BANANAS; CACAO; CATTLE; COFFEE; DRUGS; FIBER; FRUIT; LIVESTOCK; RICE; SARSA-PARILLA; SUGAR; TOBACCO; WHEAT.

AGUA DULCE. Beverage made from TAPA DE DULCE, q.v. See also: GUARO.

AGUACATE. See: MONTE DE AGUACATE.

AGUARDIENTE. Any distilled liquor, but particularly aniseed-flavored rum from sugarcane. Its sale was made a government monopoly (the *estanco) in 1783. [L.H.] See also: LIQUOR.

AGUERDO, Diego de. Franciscan priest who accompanied Gil *González de Avila expedition in 1522. He is considered the first priest to have visited Costa Rica, and is said to have baptized over 10,000 Indians.

AGUERO, Juan de. Interim *governor (1634-36) of Costa Rica. In addition, he served as governor of Nicaragua in 1627.

AGUERO CHAVES, Arturo (1907-). Folklore poet whose most important work is Romancero tico (collection of ballads) (1953).

AGUILAR, Diego de. Sexton (sacristán) of the church in *Cartago. He is said to have been the first teacher in Costa Rica. In 1594 he founded a school or "tutorial institution" which operated until 1623.

AGUILAR, Marco (1944-). Poet born in *Turrialba. Most notable works: Raigambres (1961) and Cantos para la semana (1962).

AGUILAR BARQUERO, Francisco (1857-1924). Lawyer and professor of law. He served as minister of war in the government of Bernardo *Soto Alfaro. After the fall of the *Tinoco Granados government, and at the insistence of the United States government, Aguilar was selected by a Committee of Notables to serve as acting president of the Republic (September 2, 1919 to May 8, 1920). He conducted a conciliatory government and helped the country return to civilian government by calling and supervising honest elections in 1920. Declared *Benemérito de la Patria in 1923.

AGUILAR BULGARELLI, Oscar (1944-). Received a doctorate in

Spain and he has taught in the local universities. He has written
several books of Costa Rican history. Of late he has turned
more to politics, elected to the Legislative Assembly in 1982.
He is a major power in the *Partido Unidad Social Cristiano.

AGUILAR CHACON, Manuel (1797-1846). Lawyer and president of
the Republic. He studied law in León, Nicaragua, and later
served as member of the Constituent Assembly 1824-25, *deputy
1828-31 and 1835-37, and president of the country from September
2, 1837, until he was overthrown by Braulio *Carrillo Colina
May 27, 1838. During his term of office the capital was moved
from *Murciélago (San Juan Tibás) and encouragement was given
to building roads. After his overthrow, Aguilar was exiled
to El Salvador. While there he served as Costa Rican representative
to the Dieta Centroamericana in Sonsonate in 1846. See:
GUERRA DE LA LIGA; LEY DE AMBULANCIA.

AGUILAR MACHADO, Alejandro (1897-). Educator, politician,
orator and writer. An ultra conservative, who has written on
law, history, philosophy, and politics. In 1931 he helped negotiate
the surrender of the insurgents in the *"Bellavistazo."
He was also director of the *Liceo de Costa Rica and was named
*Benemérito de la Patria in 1980.

AGUILERA GARRAMUNO, Marco Tulio (1949-). Novelist born in
Colombia. A naturalized Costa Rican (1968). His most important
work published in Costa Rica and which won the Aquileo Eheverría
prize in 1975 was Breve historia de todas las cosas (1973),
which deals fictionally with the history of San Isidro del General.

AGUINALDO. A Christmas bonus which ranges from two weeks'
salary to one month's salary and which is usually paid at the
end of November. It is sometimes referred to as the "thirteenth
month's salary." In legal existence since about 1960.

AGUIRRE. A *canton of *Puntarenas Province, whose *cabecera
is Quepos. This canton was established October 30, 1948, and
until 1985 was a major center for the *United Brands plantations.
Its population is 13,319. It also produces *African palm (for
vegetable oil), grains and is developing into an important tourist
center because of its attractive beaches.

AIR TRANSPORT. See: AVIATION.

ALAJUELA (canton). Formed December 7, 1848. It comprises
the city of Alajuela and some of the surrounding territory.
Its population is 127,472. The Juan *Santamaría international
airport is located in this *canton.

ALAJUELA (city). City in central Costa Rica at 10°N, 84°12'W,
altitude 952 meters. It was officially founded October 12, 1782

as an oratory out of a nucleus of small settlement by people who
had migrated from the *Barva Valley. The creation of this small
church in a place called La Lajuela served as an impetus for
future growth. Today the city of Alajuela is the capital of the
province of the same name and it is the distribution and commercial center of the province. Population has grown from 3,828
in 1892 to 4,860 in 1904, 8,496 in 1927, 19,620 in 1963, 33,929
in 1984, 34,556 (est.) in 1987.

ALAJUELA (province). The second largest province in Costa Rica
whose population has grown from 118,497 in 1910 to 430,634
in 1984. Although most of the province is in the highlands,
it also has extensive lowland areas which reach all the way to
the Nicaraguan border. For this reason Alajuela produces a
variety of products, the most important of which are hardwoods,
grains, fruits, sugar, *coffee, and *cattle. In addition there
are some industries which produce vegetable oils, fabrics, and
processed foods. Juan *Santamaría, the national hero, is from
Alajuela.

ALAJUELITA. A *canton in *San José Province about three miles
from the capital city. It was chartered July 4, 1909, and has
a population of 31,390. Its *cabecera is Alajuelita, where each
January is celebrated the festival of *Santo Cristo de Esquipulas.
Unlike the Guatemalan celebration, this one has become more
civic than religious. *Coffee and truck farm crops are produced. [G.K.]

ALAS, Paralonso de (b. ca. 1536). One of the conquistadors who
accompanied Juan *Vázquez de Coronado on an expedition in
1563. Alas was procurador of *Garcimuñoz, and in 1562 served
as *Alcalde ordinario of *Cartago.

ALBAN, Laureano (b. 1942). Poet born in *Turrialba. He was
one of the leading figures in the *Círculo de Poetas Costarricenses (Costa Rican Circle of Poets) in the 1960s. He has
lived in Spain the past several years and has won awards both
in Costa Rica and in Europe. His most important works are:
Poema en cruz (1961), Este hombre (1967), and two anthologies:
Poesía contra poesía (1970) and Manifiesto transcendentalista y
poesía de sus autores (1977). His latest work: Viaje interminable (1982) has won several awards in Europe.

ALBERTAZZI AVENDANO, José (1892-1967). Poet, lawyer, and
politician. He was a *deputy 1926-34 and 1938-48. Albertazzi
served as president of Congress 1944-45. He had a great fame
as a political orator and helped Dr. *Calderón Guardia in his
political campaigns. Some people criticized his overly inflammatory
discourses. After the 1948 *civil war Albertazzi went into exile,
where he wrote an anti-Figueres Ferrer book called La tragedia
de Costa Rica (1951). His most important literary works are

"Cromo," a sonnet, and the novels Bajo el azul (1918) and Pala-
bras al viento.

ALCABALA. A tax of Roman origin of 2 percent (increased to 6
percent in the 18th century) on the value of goods sold. It
was enacted in 1592 and abolished by the *Cortes de Cádiz in
1812.

ALCALDE MAYOR. Officer of a subdivision of a large Spanish
colony or viceroyalty. In the *Kingdom of *Guatemala there
existed eight alcaldes mayores, generally in areas where there
was not enough population to warrant a *governor, but with
greater emphasis on the military.

ALCALDE ORDINARIO. Colonial magistrate and municipal clerk,
performing functions within the municipality subordinate to the
*Alcalde mayor. [L.H.]

ALCOA. See: ALUMINUM COMPANY OF AMERICA.

ALFARO, Anastasio (1865-1951). An investigator in the fields of
archeology, geology, ethnology, and zoology. He wrote several
books, the most celebrated of which are El delfín de Corobicí,
Arqueología criminal americana, and Mamíferos de Costa Rica.

ALFARO, Francisco. Member of the *Junta Superior Gubernativa
from January to March 1823. He was also a *deputy 1826-28,
1846; and a member of the Supreme Court in 1830.

ALFARO ARIAS, Luciano (d. 1838). *Deputy 1830-32 and president
of Congress March-May 1832. He was a member of the conservative wing of the Congress. Alfaro Arias was also Costa Rican
representative to the Central American Federal Congress in 1824.

ALFARO COOPER, José María (1861-1939). Poet. He studied in
Costa Rica and France. His most important works include Al
margen de la tragedia (1923), and a two-volume epic poem, La
epopeya de la cruz (1921).

ALFARO GUELL, Mario. Composer and musician. He studied in
the Conservatorio de Castella and in Europe. He writes chamber
and modern music. He shared the *Ancora music prize in 1974.
Most notable composition is "Fantasía impromptu."

ALFARO RUIZ. A *canton in *Alajuela Province situated about
six miles from *Naranjo. Its *cabecera is Zarcero, and it was
chartered June 21, 1915. Its most important products are potatoes, peaches, *cattle, and truck farm crops. Present population is 7,005.

ALFARO ZAMORA, José María (1799-1856). Alfaro Zamora was

interim Chief of State from September 27, 1842 to November 29, 1844. After the overthrow of the *Gallegos y Alvarado government he returned to be Chief of State, June 7, 1846 to May 8, 1847. He also was a *deputy on several occasions and president of the Congress in 1847.

ALFEREZ REAL. A royal official. He was the standard-bearer on ceremonial occasions and substituted for the mayor of the city when the mayor could not fulfill his functions. In addition he had a great deal of unofficial powers since he was a royal appointee.

ALGUACIL MAYOR. A functionary of the *Audiencia in charge of executing the edicts of the audiencia and watching over the morals of the city.

ALIANZA NACIONAL DEMOCRATICA. An uneasy alliance between Manuel *Mora V. of the Communist Party (*Partido Comunista) and Ricardo *Jiménez Oreamuno in which it was agreed that they would work for Jiménez's candidacy in the 1940 presidential elections. This alliance lasted from June to November 1939, with Mora the Chief of Staff for the group. It disintegrated because of Manuel Mora's refusal to criticize Russia's signing a non-aggression pact with Germany, and Jiménez's continued reluctance to pursue an electoral campaign at an advanced age in the face of strong governmental pressure against him.

ALIEN PROPERTY LAW. Enacted June 24, 1946. It gave the government the right to confiscate, manage or sell all enemy alien property; some of its actions were later challenged. See: JUNTA DE CUSTODIA DE LA PROPIEDAD ENEMIGA.

ALMATICAZO. First attempt at revolution by the opposition to *Calderón Guardia (June 24, 1946). A group of men were to take over the radio station, Alma Tico, and have other groups capture strategic points in the capital. Plan failed and its principal authors were arrested but soon released.

ALMEIDA, Matalicia (b. 1937). *Arte Nuevo artist born in Mexico who later became a Costa Rican citizen. She has had shows of her work in Central America, Mexico, and the United States.

ALMOJARIFAZGO. A colonial port tax of 5 percent on merchandise brought into the market and 2 percent on merchandise taken out of the colony.

ALTAMIRANO, Carlos Luis (b. 1934). Poet born in *Alajuela City. Most important works are: Funeral de un sueño (1958) and Enlace de gritos (1962).

ALUMINUM COMPANY OF AMERICA (ALCOA). Signed contracts with the Costa Rican government in 1964 and 1970 in which

ALCOA received concessions to exploit lignite deposits in the
*Pérez Zeledón area. After public demonstrations, the contract
was not ratified.

ALVARADO. A *canton located on the slopes of the volcanoes
*Irazú and *Turrialba about 12 miles from *Cartago City. Its
*cabecera is Pacayas and it was chartered July 9, 1908. Al-
varado has a population of 8,338 and is a *coffee, *cattle and
potato producing area.

ALVARADO, Gina (b. 1956). *Arte Nuevo painter who also does
interior decorating and architectural drawing.

ALVARADO, José Antonio [Father]. A liberal priest who opposed
annexation by Mexico. He was one of the representatives sent
by Costa Rica to the Constituent Congress in Guatemala in 1823.

ALVARADO ABELLA, José Francisco (1929-). Artist and illustra-
tor. Born in *Limón he studied in Costa Rica, Italy, and Mexico.
He has done oil paintings and has illustrated various books.
In 1980 he had a successful exhibit of his works.

ALVARADO ALVARADO, Manuel (b. 1771). Member and president
of the Constituent Assembly (March to April 14, 1825). He
was also the national treasurer in 1825.

ALVARADO BARROETA, Manuel (1820-1889). President of the
Chamber of Justice 1866, member of the Constituent Assembly
of 1859. Negotiated treaty of friendship with Chile and Peru
1870 and arranged for Minor Cooper *Keith to come to Costa
Rica to build the Atlantic Railroad (*Ferrocarril del Norte).
He was also the Costa Rican representative who negotiated
the unfortunate *British loans in the 1870s. He exiled himself
permanently from the country after a disagreement with General
Tomás *Guardia Gutiérrez, and died in Paris in 1889. See also:
BRITISH LOANS.

ALVARADO BONILLA, Pablo (1785-1850). A physician and liberal
politician. Alvarado started his political career while a student
in Guatemala. He wrote a pro-independence tract called El Hispano-
Americano, for which the governor jailed him for a short time.
During the independence period he favored association with
Guatemala. He was sent as a Costa Rican representative to
the 1823 Constituent Assembly in Guatemala City and also served
in the Central American Federal Congress where he helped press
for the abolition of *slavery. In 1971 Alvarado was declared
"Precursor y Prócer de la Independencia." Consult Anales (1977-
78), and Ligia Caravini de Arauz in Revista de Costa Rica,
No. 2 (1921).

ALVARADO GARCIA, Alejandro (1839-1922). President of the

Supreme Court (1904). He also served as rector of the *Universidad de Santo Tomás and minister of the interior (gobernación).

ALVARADO HIDALGO, Manuel [Father] (1775-1836). Politician and priest. Father Alvarado was a staunch defender of republican principles and served in many posts. He was head of the *Casa de Enseñanza de Santo Tomás (1818-21), first president of the *Junta de Legados (1821), member of the first *Junta Superior Gubernativa (1822), and president of the Third Junta (May 1823 to September 1824). He was a member and president of Congress on several occasions. Alvarado suggested that the problem of the location of the capital might be solved by establishing it at El Ingenio (near city of *Alajuela).

ALVARADO QUIROS, Alejandro (1876-1945). First rector of the *Universidad de Costa Rica. *Deputy (1926-30), and president of Congress (1929-30). Foreign minister in the 1920s. Alvarado supported non-intervention, particularly at the Central America Conference (1920-21). In the 1923 Conference he proposed a Pan American Court, but it was defeated because the U.S. refused to accept compulsory arbitration. Writer in the French tradition. Most important works are: Piedras preciosas (1903) and Lilias resedas (1912), both of which are translations of French stories. Consult Richard V. Salisbury, "The Anti-Imperialistic Career of Alejandro Alvarado" in Hispanic American Historical Review (Nov. 1979).

ALVARADO DE OSORIO, Diego (d. 1536). Canon of the cathedral in Panama and protector of the *Indians in Nicaragua. Elected first bishop of León, Nicaragua (which at that time also included Costa Rica) in 1532 but that election was never ratified by the Vatican.

AMAPALA (Honduras), Pact of (1896). Honduran President Policarpo Bonilla sponsored a conference in this Honduran port to try to promote Central American unionism. Out of this conference an agreement was signed which established the República Mayor de Centro América (Greater Republic of Central America). It established a type of confederation in which each member state would have internal autonomy, but conduct common foreign policy, and be governed by a Central American Diet. It met in 1896. This arrangement was accepted by Honduras, El Salvador, and Nicaragua. Even though President Rafael *Yglesias was offered the presidency of this new state, Costa Rica refused to join it.

AMERINDIANS. See: INDIANS.

AMIGHETTI RUIZ, Francisco (1907-). Painter, essayist, poet. Amighetti is one of the most important forces in Costa Rican art in this century. He studied in Costa Rica, North America, and Argentina. He has worked in oils, water color, and murals.

Many of his etchings appeared in Repertorio Americano. He maintained an Art Gallery for many years and was in the forefront of various artistic movements in the country. His literary works are also notable. Some of the most important are: Poesía (1936), Francisco en Harlem (1947), Francisco en Costa Rica (1963). See also: PAINTING, and consult the biographical essay by Stefan Baciu in Las Américas 21 (2): 10-15, February 1969.

AMIGO DE LA PATRIA. Periodical published in Guatemala October 1820 to 1822. Founded by José Cecilio del Valle with an españolista or anti-independence viewpoint. Later it became a voice of moderate republicanism.

AMISTAD. National Park covering vast area in Talamanca mountain range. International; Panama extends this wilderness beyond its borders. [G.K.]

AMORY AND SON, J. M. British-owned (but Delaware-registered) company in dispute with Costa Rica when *petroleum exploration concessions granted it by the government of Federico TINOCO GRANADOS (q.v.) were repudiated.

ANARCHISM. In vogue among some intellectuals in Costa Rica during the first quarter of the twentieth century including a Spaniard, Anselmo Lorenzo. They were also influenced greatly by Leo Tolstoi and the French philosopher, Hamon. An anarchist newspaper called El Sol was published in *Alajuela City.

ANCORA PRIZE. A series of prizes awarded yearly by the cultural section of the newspaper La República for outstanding works in literature and the arts.

ANDE. See: ASOCIACION NACIONAL DE EDUCADORES.

ANDERSON MORUA, Luis (1875-1941). Chairman of the Washington Conference 1907 and one of the principal founders of the Central American Court (*Corte de Justicia Centroamericana). He was also foreign minister and one of the leaders of the Central American Unionist movement. He served as *deputy 1914-16. He was considered an outstanding international jurist and helped mediate several boundary disputes such as the Colombian-Peruvian dispute over Leticia and a dispute between Honduras and Nicaragua. Anderson always tried to promote the doctrines of obligatory arbitration of international disputes and nonintervention.

ANDERSON-PORRAS TREATY. An agreement signed in 1910 in which Costa Rica and Panama agreed to put their claims to the Atlantic coast region before Chief Justice White of the United States Supreme Court. The *White decision favored Costa Rica, but was not accepted by Panama. See also: FRONTIER QUESTIONS (SOUTH).

ANDRADA, Antonio. Acting *governor, April 1564.

ANDRADE, Antonio de. Priest active in 18th century Talamanca, q.v.

ANFE. See: ASOCIACION NACIONAL DE FOMENTO ECONOMICO.

ANGUCIANA DE GAMBOA, Alonso (b. 1535). Considered one of the conquistadors, since he accompanied Padre *Estrada Rávago, *Cavallón, and Juan *Vázquez de Coronado on expeditions. He was first *alcalde ordinario of *Cartago and founded the short-lived colony of Villa de *Castillo de Austria on the Atlantic coast. Unfortunately he became embroiled in conflicts with the Franciscan fathers because of his autocratic nature.

ANIBEL. Chief of a band of *Zambo-Mosquito Indians who in the early 1700s constantly attacked the *cacao plantation in the *Matina Valley. See also: PIRATES; TALMANCA; ZAMBO-MOSQUITOS.

ANTILLON, Ana (1934-). Poet born in San José. Her most important works are: Antro fuego (1955) and Demonio en caos (1972).

APRISTA MOVEMENT. Eventually a Peruvian political party, but when founder of the American Popular Revolutionary Alliance (Alianza Revolucionaria Americana, APRA), Victor Raúl Haya de la Torre, visited Costa Rica briefly while exiled from Peru in the latter 1920s his mystical Pan-Latin Americanism, critical of United States hegemony, intrigued young intellectuals. [G.K.]

ARAGON QUESADA, Manuel (1844-1921). *Deputy (1888-92) and president of Congress (1889-90).

ARAYA CHAVARRIA, Carlomagno (1897-1979). Writer and poet. One of the group of *San Ramón poets. His most important works are: Cenit (1914), Primavera (1930), Medallones (1947), and Poemas (1960), in which his celebrated poem "El bastardo" appears. This deals with social problems of the lower classes. Araya also wrote a poem praising Juan Santamaría called: La epopeya del hombre-antorcha. His last work was Poemas octogenarios (1977).

ARAYA MONGE, Rolando (1947-). Nephew of President Luis Alberto *Monge Alvarez, and candidate for the PLN (*Partido Liberación Nacional) nomination for the 1990 presidential election, but defeated in the party primary, partly because of questions about *drug money laundering. [G.K.]

ARCE, Manuel José (1787-1847). First president of Central America Federation and one of the principal leaders of the Central American independence movement. He was a Salvadoran who in 1844

invaded his own country in an unsuccessful effort to reunify
Central America.

ARCO. See: ASOCIACION REVOLUCIONARIA DE CULTURA
OBRERA.

AREA. See: TERRITORIAL EXPANSION.

ARENAL. (1) Volcano in the Northwest whose 1968 eruption killed
78 people. It has remained active ever since.
(2) Hydro-electric plant completed ca. 1980 creating a
lake rich in fishing.
(3) Pre-historic village uncovered from volcanic ash in
the 1980s. [G.K.]

ARGUELLO, Emilio (1947-). Sculptor. He was part of the so-
called "Heredia generation of sculptors of 1980." His work was
inspired by "raigambre." He specializes in feminine figures
with a naturalistic-expressionist style. See: SCULPTURE.

ARGUELLO, José Toribio (d. ca. 1834). Nicaraguan lawyer and
politician. Argüello was professor of law at the University of
León and in 1820 was *deputy to Guatemala. He opposed the
*Acta de los Nublados and in 1828 had to leave Nicaragua because
of threats on his life resulting from personal and political problems. He was mayor of *Guanacaste and then taught law in
the *Casa de Enseñanza de Santo Tomás. In 1831 he proposed
reforms in the teaching of philosophy. Because of his violent
nature he was constantly embroiled in various legal and
personal problems.

ARGUELLO, Rosendo. Nicaragua. One of the signers of the
*Pacto del Caribe and one of José *Figueres' chief lieutenants
in the *civil war of 1948. After the war they had a falling-
out and Argüello became Figueres' enemy and wrote books attacking him.

ARGUELLO MORA, Manuel (1835-1902). Writer and politician. He
served as minister of public works, then turned more to writing
in his later years. His most important works are; La trinchera
(1899) and Un drama en el presidio de San Lucas (1900).

ARGUERO CHAVES, Arturo (1907-). Poet, writer, and grammarian.
He was a *costumbrista writer and wrote of the people in the
*canton of *Coronado. He has also done several works on lan-
guage and the proper use of grammar. Most important works
are: Romancero tico (1940), La lechuza (1950), Libro del idioma
(1966), Literatura y Gramática Castellana (1963), and Origen
y desarrollo de la lingüística (1977).

ARIAS BONILLA, Juan Rafael (1877-1963). *Deputy in several
congresses and president of Congress 1936-38.

ARIAS DE AVILA, Pedro. See: PEDRARIAS.

ARIAS DE MALDONADO, Andrés (d. 1661). *Governor of Costa
Rica (1659-61). His was one of the better colonial administrations. Arias' generally mild manner brought temporary peace
to the colony. He successfully led an expedition to *Talamanca
which pacified that region. When he died there was a great
public sorrow; the people felt that they had lost a father more
than a governor.

ARIAS DE MALDONADO, Rodrigo (1637-1716). Interim *governor
of Costa Rica (1662-64) after the death of his father. In 1662
he led an unsuccessful expedition to *Talamanca, and lost a
great deal of money in his venture. In order to give him some
compensation for these losses, the Crown named him Marquis
of Talamanca. He was also *alcalde mayor of *Nicoya. Later
he renounced politics and became a Catholic priest. He took
the name Fray Rodrigo de la Cruz, and went to Mexico to live
out his life. He was one of the most interesting personages of
the colonial period and is the subject of a Costa Rican zarzuela
(Spanish operetta) called El Marqués de Talamanca.

ARIAS PLAN. The "Guatemala Peace Plan" or "Esquipulas II"
agreed to by five Central American presidents on August 7,
1987. It was designed to end armed conflict gradually in several republics. [G.K.]

ARIAS SANCHEZ, Oscar (1941-   ). Politician, writer, and university professor. President of the Republic (1986-1990). A graduate student at the University of Essex (U.K.) 1967-69, he
served as Minister of Planificación in the governments of *Figueres
(1970-74) and Oduber (1974-78). He was elected *deputy from
*Heredia in 1978 and in the same year became Secretary General
of the National Liberation Party (*Partido Liberacion Nacional).
He has written several works on political parties and pressure
groups. Was awarded the 1987 Nobel Peace Prize. See: ARIAS
PLAN.

ARIEL, Pablo. See: ABATE, John de.

ARISTA, Padre. See: CASTRO RAMIREZ, Vicente.

ARMED FORCES. The Costa Rican army was officially disbanded
December 1, 1948. Policing duties are divided between several
agencies governed by political appointees; there are no professional officers. The Civil Guard, under the Ministry of Public
Security, has primary responsibility for cities and border; the
Rural Guard, under the Ministry of the Interior (Gobernación),
for small towns and the countryside. The Ministry of Justice
also has investigative officials. Public Security has several
light aircraft and helicopters; a few vintage military planes were
briefly operated by the government during tension with Nicaragua

in 1948-49 and 1955. The navy peaked around 1900, with several small armed steamers; briefly, during the Second World War, a single-ship patrol vessel existed, but there was no force by 1948. A couple of patrol boats were acquired in the 1980s. The army was never formidable, but after the single great campaign versus William *Walker, there were several generals who remained "strong men" until the liberal era began at the end of the 1880s. A century later, increases in the size and status of security forces due to regional problems is resisted by much of the populace. [G.K.]

ARROBA. Premetric weight equivalent to 10.59 kg.

ARROYO, Manuel (1930-). Painter born in *Naranjo in *Alajuela Province. Studied in Costa Rica and in Europe. His style is modern expressionist, but most of his works are still-lifes and landscapes.

ART MUSEUM. See: MUSEO DE ARTE COSTARRICENSE.

ARTE NUEVO. A school of painting dominated by abstract and expressionist work, and flourishing in Costa Rica in the 1960s. See: PAINTING.

ARTIEDA (City of). A short-lived settlement founded by Diego de Artieda in 1577. It was located on the Bay of Almirante, now in Panamanian territory.

ARTIEDA CHIRINOS, Diego de (d. 1590). *Governor of Costa Rica and Nicaragua, he founded the city of Espíritu Santo (current day *Esparza). During his administration the official boundaries of the province of Costa Rica were fixed. Unfortunately they were not stated with enough precision and frontier questions later arose. See: FRONTIER QUESTIONS (NICARAGUA); FRONTIER QUESTIONS (SOUTH).

ASAMBLEA LEGISLATIVA. See: LEGISLATIVE ASSEMBLY.

ASERRI. A *canton in *San José Province located on the northern slopes of the Cerro de Candelaria. It was chartered November 27, 1882, and has a current population of 30,588. Its *cabecera is the town of Aserrí and the canton produces *coffee, sugar, corn, and beans. Original identity is as an *Indian town organized in the 1570s.

ASOCIACION CULTURAL DE ESTUDIANTES DE LEYES. National Association of Law Students founded in 1937 by a group of law students who clustered around Carlos *Monge Alfaro and Isaac Felipe *Azofeifa. They discussed contemporary problems. This association is one of the precursors of the later *Centro para el Estudio de Problemas Nacionales (Center for the Study of National Problems).

ASOCIACION NACIONAL DE EDUCADORES (ANDE). Teachers
union founded in 1941. Influential pressure group with membership of over 20,000. More conservative than other teachers'
groups. [G.K.]

ASOCIACION NACIONAL DE FOMENTO ECONOMICO (ANFE). National Association for Economic Development. A conservative
business-oriented pressure group which favors as much non-
intervention by the government in the economy as it can con-
vince the country to accept. Ex-President José Joaquín *Trejos
Fernández is a former president of this organization.

ASOCIACION REVOLUCIONARIA DE CULTURA OBRERA (ARCO).
Revolutionary Association of Workers' Culture. A discussion
group founded by law students, especially Gonzalo Montero Berry
in 1929. This group was important because it was one of the
precursors of the Costa Rican Communist Party (*Partido Comunista). Its most important members were: Manuel *Mora Valverde, Jaime *Cerdas, and Ricardo Coto Conde.

ASTUA AGUILAR, José (1859-1938). Politician and lawyer. He
was a *deputy in various congresses, vice-president of the Republic, president of the Central American Court (*Corte de
Justicia Centroamericana) 1908-13, president of the Senate 1919,
and professor of law. He wrote Tratado del delito and Tratado
de pena (both 1909), both valuable treatises on the law.

ATENAS. *Canton located in the province of *Alajuela about 13
miles from *Alajuela city. The canton was chartered August 7,
1868, and produces fruits and cereals. Its *cabecera is the
city of Atenas and it has a population of 15,011.

ATLANTIC. Costa Rican usage favors "Atlantic" over "Caribbean"
to designate the country's eastern seaboard. [L.H.]

ATLANTIC RAILROAD. See: FERROCARRIL DEL NORTE.

AUDIENCIA DE GUATEMALA, Real. The colonial court district
that included Costa Rica, 1570-1821. See: AUDIENCIA REAL;
OIDOR.

AUDIENCIA REAL. A council which had powers to limit and supervise the activities of royal authorities and also with responsibility
to protect the *Indians from abuse. This council had the judicial
functions in both civil and criminal cases and was the highest
court in the colony. Costa Rica was originally under the Audiencia de Santo Domingo, when that body was founded in 1526.
In 1538 it was placed under the newly created Audiencia de
Panama and in 1543 was transferred to the Audiencia de los
Confines (with its seat in the town of Gracias a Dios, Honduras).
When that audiencia was dissolved in 1564, Costa Rica was returned to the jurisdiction of the Audiencia de Panama. Finally,

despite vehement protests from the colonists, Costa Rica was placed under the jurisdiction of the Audiencia de Guatemala. The official date was 1568, but the actual transfer seems to have been in 1570. The audiencia was abolished in 1821, with independence.

AUSTRIA, Castillo de. See: CASTILLO DE AUSTRIA.

AUSTRIA, Villa de. See: CASTILLO DE SAN CARLOS DE AUSTRIA.

AUTOMOBILE ACCIDENTS. See: HIGHWAY ACCIDENTS.

AUTOMOBILES. In 1928 Costa Rica possessed 1,100 passenger cars and 500 commercial vehicles. Thirty years later these figures had become 15,000 and 8,700, respectively. In 1984 there were 48,200 passenger cars and 27,143 commercial vehicles. [L.H.]

AVIATION. The first flight in Costa Rica took place on January 1, 1912, the pilot being an American, Jesse Seligman. Several other foreigners also performed exhibition flights. Tobías Bolaños was the first Costa Rican aviator, despite having lost a leg learning to fly in France. Today the airfield at Pavas is named for him. Pan American Airways began international mail and passenger service in 1930. The first nationally operated air line was *ENTA (Empresa Nacional de Transportes Aéreos) founded in 1932. Soon after, Ramón Macaya, a Costa Rican pilot, founded *Aerovías Nacionales. A mail subsidy helped both endure until 1940, when they were absorbed by Transportes Aéreos Centro-Americanos, then an international system originating in Honduras. Pan American opposed the TACA network and organized LACSA (Líneas Aéreas Costarricenses, S.A.) in 1945 to compete. Eventually LACSA absorbed TACA, ended the tie with Pan American, and became the national airline, showing the flag and *oxcart symbol in Miami and elsewhere. SANSA (Servicios Aéreos Nacionales, Sociedad Anónima) was organized in 1979 to provide internal air service. The several hundred small airstrips in the country permitted mobility in the 1930s, before highways, but fifty years later present a problem due to smuggling flights. Consult Carlos María Jiménez, Historia de la aviación en Costa Rica. [G.K.]

AVILA, Diana (1950-). Poet born in San José. Her most important work is El sueño ha terminado (1976).

AVILA, Marjorie (1950-). *Arte Nuevo artist who specializes in semi-abstract oil paintings.

AYALA (GUDINO MEDINA Y CALDERON), Juan de Dios (d. 1819). Born in Panama, he was *governor of Costa Rica (1810-19). He was one of the better governors of the province. During

his term of office Ayala led the struggle to lift the restriction
that the *audiencia had placed on Costa Rican trade with Panama.

AZOFEIFA, Isaac Felipe (1912-   ). Academician and writer. One
of the most influential intellectuals of this century. He was
associated with the *Asociación Cultural de Estudiantes de Leyes
and one of the chief members of the *Centro para el Estudio
de Problemas Nacionales (Center for the Study of National Problems) and was a regular contributor to its publication, *Surco.
He has been head of the Spanish department of the *Universidad
de Costa Rica, editor of the Revista de la Universidad de
Costa Rica. He is a member of the Academia de la Lengua and
has written many articles on language and public issues which
appear regularly in the local newspapers. Azofeifa's most important works are: Teoría y práctica de la reforma educativa de
Mauro Fernández (1955), Canción (1964), Estaciones (1967),
and Días y territorios (1969). In 1983 he was named ambassador to the USSR.

- B -

BCIE. See: CENTRAL AMERICAN COMMON MARKET.

BADAJOZ, Villa de. See: VILLA DE BADAJOZ.

BADILLA, Crisanto (b. 1941). One of the so-called "*Heredia
group of sculptors." He uses a combination of pre-Columbian
and Creole styles. Most of his works have been in wood, but
he has recently done bronzes with a natural-realist look. See:
SCULPTURE.

BAGACES. *Canton in *Guanacaste Province. Formed December 7,
1848. Its *cabecera is the city of Bagaces. It produces corn,
rice, beans, *sugar, *cattle and forest products. In addition
there are sulfur deposits. Its population is 10,103.

BALANCE OF PAYMENTS. Until the 1930s, Costa Rica tended to
enjoy an export surplus. In 1915-1919 exports each year were
worth double the cost of imports. *Foreign loans were incurred
to cover budget deficits and pay for infrastructure development.
The situation was changed by the fall in the cost of primary
products (such as coffee and bananas) in the Great Depression.
Since then Costa Rica has suffered a chronic trade deficit, which
has been met with foreign aid (beginning with assistance in
building the *Pan American Highway), foreign loans, and stop-
gap methods such as temporary restrictions on foreign remit-
tances. Servicing such foreign loans has compounded the balance of payments problems, and sometimes, as in 1949, there
have been net outflows of foreign investment.

YEAR	EXPORTS	IMPORTS	TRADE BALANCE
	(In thousands of Costa Rican *pesos)		
1855	800	700	+100
1860	1,300	1,100	+200
1865	1,600	1,500	+100
1870	3,600	1,700	+1,900
1875	4,600	2,900	+1,700
1880	3,500	2,400	+1,100
1885	5,000	8,000	-3,000
1890	14,000	14,000	0
1895	11,000	8,000	+3,000
	(In thousands of Costa Rican *colons)		
1900	14,000	14,000	0
1905	17,000	11,000	+6,000
1910	18,000	17,000	+1,000
1915	21,000	12,000	+9,000
1920	27,000	48,000	-2,100
	(In thousands of U.S. dollars)		
1923-27av.	16,000	13,000	+3,000
1928	16,160	17,893	-733
1929	15,753	20,164	-4,411
1930	14,247	10,847	+3,400
1931	12,156	8,681	+3,575
1932	7,452	5,453	+1,998
1933	9,081	6,346	+2,734
1934	8,696	8,720	-24
1935	7,712	7,162	-550
1936	8,309	8,397	-87
1937	11,512	11,879	-366
1938	10,146	12,621	-2,475
1939	9,086	16,885	-7,798
1940	7,000	16,800	-9,800
1941	9,800	17,800	-8,000
1942	10,200	12,300	-2,100
1943	12,200	20,400	-8,200
1944	10,400	21,500	-11,100
1945	11,500	26,900	-15,400
1946	14,337	33,041	-18,704
1947	23,023	48,079	-25,056
1948	31,840	42,344	-10,505
1949	31,439	43,352	-11,912
1950	55,600	46,000	+9,600
1951	63,414	55,740	+7,674
1952	73,366	67,874	+5,492
1953	80,100	73,700	+6,400
1954	84,700	80,000	+4,700
1955	80,900	87,500	-6,600
1956	67,400	91,200	+23,800
1957	83,400	103,000	-19,600
1958	91,900	99,000	-7,100

1959	76,700	103,900	-27,200
1960	85,800	110,000	-24,200
1961	84,000	107,000	-23,000
1962	93,000	113,000	-20,000
1963	95,000	124,000	-29,000
1964	113,000	139,000	-26,000
1965	111,824	178,226	-66,402
1966	135,509	173,453	-42,944
1967	143,780	190,698	-46,918
1968	170,821	213,942	-43,121
1969	189,707	245,137	-55,430
1970	231,163	316,687	-85,524
1971	255,363	349,742	-124,379
1972	280,877	372,775	-91,898
1973	344,464	355,325	-110,861
1974	440,344	719,663	-279,319
1975	493,305	693,969	-200,664
1976	592,941	770,412	-177,471
1977	828,164	1,021,430	-193,266
1978	934,391	1,165,730	-300,823
1979	934,391	1,396,812	-452,421
1980	1,001,742	1,540,445	-538,703
1981	1,029,700	1,245,300	-215,600
1982	883,900	855,600	+28,300
1983	860,700	994,300	-133,600
1984	1,006,390	1,093,389	-86,999
1985	939,000	1,141,600	-202,600
1986	1,026,000	1,130,000	-104,000

The foregoing figures are of trade only. They exclude foreign aid ($80 million in 1986), foreign investments, or, on the debit side, debt servicing and capital outflows. These together produced an overall balance of -186,100 thousand dollars in 1986. See also: FOREIGN TRADE.

Sources of these statistics include Tomás Soley Güell, Compendio de historia económica y hacendaria de Costa Rica (San José: 1975), the British Board of Trade's Overseas economic surveys, the *Banco Central de Costa Rica's Informe de estadística mensual, the I.M.F. and the Latin American economic report. [T.C., G.K., L.H.]

BALBOA, Vasco Núñez de. See: NUNEZ DE BALBOA, Vasco.

BANANA STRIKE. (1) In 1934, after failure to obtain reforms of substandard conditions, as many as 10,000 workers in the Atlantic Zone went on strike. The strike was led chiefly by Communist Party (*Partido Comunista) leaders Carlos Luis *Fallas and Jaime *Cerdas. After several weeks of sporadic violence in which the government had to send troops, the *United Fruit Company agreed to grant better wages and working conditions. The strike was important in that it consolidated the Communist

Party's following with the banana workers, and was the first
successful strike against a foreign monopoly. It inspired Carlos
Luis Fala's novel, Mamita Yunai.
 (2) In 1966 workers in the Pacific zone went on strike
demanding a full *aguinaldo. It was settled by the government
paying one-half and the United Fruit Company the rest. Consult
Manuel Rojas Bolaños, Lucha social y guerra civil en Costa Rica
(1940-1948) (1980).

BANANAS. Large commercial plantings of this fruit were begun by
Minor C. *Keith, builder of the Atlantic Railroad (*Ferrocarril
del Norte) and later a founder of the *United Fruit Company in
1899. Keith had been granted several thousand acres along the
right-of-way of the railroad and developed the banana plantings
to have some income from this property. The first export ship-
ment was one of 3,500 bunches to New York in 1881. Production
increased and bananas became the country's leading crop. In
1913 a peak of 11,170,812 stems were exported. In the 1930's a
combination of labor troubles and disease made the company
start shifting operations to the Pacific coast. New contracts
were signed with the government in 1930, 1934 and 1938. As a
result of these contracts, the new port of *Golfito was opened
in 1941, and until 1985 it was the leading banana zone. In
1955 the *Standard Fruit Company started plantings in the Estrella Valley of *Limón Province and exported its first crop in
1959. In the 1970s Del Monte (Bandeco) began Costa Rican
operations. High production costs have however led to curtail-
ment of output, with resultant loss of thousands of jobs and
millions of dollars in export earnings. In 1982 banana exports
were $238,714,000 or 995,791,000 kilos. They were $240,300,000
in 1983, $251,000,000 in 1984, $212,200,000 in 1985. Also see:
BANANA STRIKE; CAVENDISH; GROSMICHEL; KEITH, Minor C.;
PANAMA DISEASE; STANDARD FRUIT COMPANY; UNITED FRUIT
COMPANY.

BANCO ANGLO COSTARRICENSE. Founded in 1863, it issued money
for the first time in 1864, which was considered the legal tender
of the country after 1866. It was the bank of issue until superseded by *Banco Internacional in 1914. Nationalized in 1949.

BANCO CENTRAL DE COSTA RICA. Founded in 1950, it is the
money-issuing bank of the country. It also controls foreign
exchange and sets general policy for the state-run banking
system.

BANCO DE COSTA RICA. Originally founded as El Banco de la
Unión in 1877 by Gaspar Ortuño, its name changed to Banco
de Costa Rica in November 1890. It had the power to issue
banknotes between 1881 and 1884 after the demise of the second
Banco Nacional; a contract was signed with the government (1890)
permitting it to continue issuing banknotes.

BANCO DE CREDITO HIPOTECARIO. See: CREDITO HIPOTECARIO DE COSTA RICA.

BANCO DE EMISION. Founded in 1877 as the state bank, but it could not attract enough capital, therefore closed after a year and a half.

BANCO DE LA UNION. Founded in 1877 after the demise of the second Banco Nacional de Costa Rica. Its name was changed in 1890 to Banco de Costa Rica.

BANCO DE MEDINA. A bank that was to be founded by Crisanto Medina in 1858 and was to be the bank of issue. It was opposed by the country's capitalists because Juan Rafael *Mora, then president, was one of the partners; this venture was partially responsible for the ultimate overthrow of Mora's government.

BANCO INTERNACIONAL DE COSTA RICA. (1) Founded in 1914 as an emergency measure to ease exchange problems caused by World War I, it became the banknote-issuing agency. Name changed to Banco Nacional de Costa Rica in 1936 when some of its functions were changed. See also: CAJA DE CONVERSION.
    (2) A private bank which opened July 27, 1987.

BANCO LYON. See: LYON, Arthur P.

BANCO MERCANTIL DE COSTA RICA. See: BENNETT, James Gordon.

BANCO NACIONAL DE COSTA RICA. (1) Founded in 1936 by reorganizing the *Banco Internacional de Costa Rica into three distinct departments (mortgage, emission of money, and commercial). Until the founding of the *Banco Central it had exclusive right to issue money.
    (2) The first Banco Nacional existed from 1858 to 1859.
    (3) Another Banco Nacional opened in 1867 but could not charge enough interest to make a success and therefore entered into liquidation in 1877. (4) That same year a bank with the same name opened a branch in *Limón but after losing its right of emission in 1884 it also went out of business.

BANCO NACIONAL DE SEGUROS. See: INSTITUTO NACIONAL DE SEGUROS.

BANCO POPULAR Y DE DESARROLLO COMUNAL. A government entity created in 1969 to help workers accumulate some capital by obligatory contributions of workers and employers.

BANCO RURAL DE CREDITO HIPOTECARIO DE COSTA RICA. Created in 1872 with a capital of $4 million to lend money for agricultural needs. Because of a lack of further capital it had little success, and ceased functioning in 1873.

BANCOS, Pablo [Fray]. Priest and physician in charge of first Hospital *San Juan de Dios (then in *Cartago) in 1784. He managed to keep the hospital open despite opposition of Governor *Vásquez y Téllez. Left Costa Rica in 1794.

BANDAS. See: INSTITUCION DE LAS BANDAS, La.

BANKS AND BANKING. Costa Rica's first bank was the *Banco Anglo-Costarricense of 1863. Various attempts were made from the mid-19th century to form a national bank, but under the LEY DE BANCOS (q.v.) of 1900, private banks were allowed to issue their own banknotes. Following the *Civil War of 1948, the ruling junta had the government take over all banks (see: NATIONALIZED BANKING SYSTEM). Some private banking was allowed again in the 1970s, and in late 1988 the World Bank made any renegotiation of Costa Rica's *foreign debt conditional on comprehensive privatization. Under the new law, enacted October 1988, not only may private banks now accept accounts on deposit and contract foreign loans, but their representatives now form a majority on the board of the Central Bank, the *Banco Central de Costa Rica, which is now, inter alia, forbidden to make loans to agriculture. [L.H.]
See also names of individual banks.

BARAHONA, Macarena (1957-   ). Poet. His poetry is of the protest nature with the hope of the betterment of human conditions. His first work was published in 1980, Contraatacando.

BARAHONA JIMENEZ, Luis (b. 1908). Professor of philosophy at the *Universidad de Costa Rica and writer. A founder of the Costa Rican Christian Democratic Party (*Partido Demócrata Cristiano). Some of his works are El ser hispano-americano (1959), El gran incógnito (Visión interna del campesino costarricense) (1953), and Apuntes para una historia de las estéticas en Costa Rica (1982).

BARBERENA, Manuel. First president of the Supreme Court (1825).

BARBOZA, Carlos (b. 1943). Engraver. Educated in Costa Rica and Spain. His engravings explore the psychological makeup of the local people, especially those in the countryside. His works have been shown in Spain, Costa Rica, United States and Brazil.

BARING BROTHERS LOAN. A loan of £150,000 used to buy gold to mint the new gold *Colón coins used after 1896. See: GOLD STANDARD.

BARRA HONDA. National Park in *Guanacaste Province noted for its underground caverns. [G.K.]

BARRIO DE LOS PARDOS. See: VIRGIN OF THE ANGELS.

BARRIOS, Gerardo [General] (1813-1865). Ex-president of El
Salvador who was granted political asylum in Costa Rica in 1865.
The other Central American republics objected and demanded
his expulsion. The incident almost provoked a war, but established a strong tradition of political asylum in Costa Rica.

BARROETA BACA, Rafael (1813-1890). Politician and *cattle rancher.
He served as acting head of state December 2, 1873 to February
28, 1874, after Gen. Tomás *Guardia Gutiérrez dismissed Salvador
*González Ramírez whom he had previously installed in the same
post.

BARROETA CASTILLA, Rafael (d. 1826). Lieutenant *governor
(1811). *Alcalde of *Cartago and *San José. Legado Extra-
ordinario from San José in the *Junta de Legados de los Pueblos.
President of the first *Junta de Gobierno and one of the writers
of the *Pacto de Concordia. He also was president of the Provincial Congress in January 1822 and a supporter of the *Imperialists during the independence movements.

BARVA. *Canton in *Heredia Province, located two miles north
of Heredia City. Originated as a Huetar Indian pueblo in the
1570s, named for the local cacique (see: HUETARES). A recent
project was to restore the "colonial" hispanic atmosphere of the
past century. [G.K.]

BASEBALL. Baseball was first played in *Limón in 1897, using
equipment imported by the railroad and *banana companies.
But the sport has not flourished in Costa Rica as it has in Nicaragua, and elsewhere in the Hispanic Caribbean areas. [G.K.]
    See also: STAHL, Juan F.

BASTIDAS, Rodrigo de. Discovered the Isthmian region before
*Columbus. In 1500 he touched at what is now called Cape
Nombre de Dios in Honduras.

BATTLES. See: EMPALME, El; OCHOMOGO; PIRATES; RIVAS;
SANTA ROSA; WARS. [G.K.]

BAUDRIT GONZALEZ, Fabio (1875-1954). *Costumbrista writer.
Cifra anatológica (1956) is a posthumous collection of his works.

BEBOUT, Nina (b. 1947). *Arte Nuevo artist born in Nicaragua,
and a United States citizen, but a long time resident of Costa
Rica. She paints semi-abstract bowls of fruit and domestic scenes.

BEECHE AGUERO, Octavio (1866-1950). Financier and politician
with some progressive ideas for his time. He served for many

years as Costa Rican Consul in New York; president of the
Supreme Court (1934); candidate for the presidency (1936);
and member of the Electoral Tribunal (1946-48).

BEEF. See: CATTLE.

BELEN. *Canton in *Heredia Province, founded June 8, 1907.
Its *cabecera is San Antonio, which also has the popular aquatic
resort "Ojo de Agua." It has a mild climate, many poultry farms.
It produces grains, tomatoes and onions. Its population is 11,993.

BELLAVISTAZO. In February 1931, after a hotly contested electoral campaign, several men, including losing candidate Manuel
Castro Quesada, seized the Bellavista Army Barracks (now the
site of the *National Museum). The other barracks remained
loyal to the government. An exchange of heavy fire resulted
and lasted for several days, during which 15 people were said
to have been killed. The conspirators finally surrendered and
were given an amnesty the following year.

BELLY, Félix (1816-1876). Journalist born in Grenoble, France.
Defended the cause of Central America in the war against William
*Walker. Bélly first came to Costa Rica in 1858 hoping to promote
a Nicaraguan canal and later wrote several accounts of life in
Central America; the most important is L'Amerique centrale; Le
Nicaragua et le canal interocéanique (1867).

BENAVIDES, Enrique (1915-1986). Award-winning editorialist of
the conservative newspaper, La *Nación. Former member of
Communist party who became an enemy of the Left. "El crimen
de Colima" (1966) pioneered investigative journalism and led
to the release of three improperly convicted prisoners and to
reforms in the penal code. [G.K.]

BENEFICIO. A processing plant where *coffee is dried and made
ready for sale. Usually a beneficio buys coffee from small producers at prices fixed by the government. But in cases of
large farms a beneficio will only process its own coffee.

BENEMERITO. A special award of honor conferred from time to
time by the Legislative Assembly to outstanding citizens who
have made an extraordinary contribution to the country. Those
who have been so honored are listed here in the order that
they have been proclaimed Benemérito. Consult Guillermo Solera
Rodríguez, Beneméritos de la patria (2d ed., 1964).

Beneméritos de la Patria
1) Rafael Francisco *Osejo
2) José María *Peralta de la Vega
3) José María *Castro Madriz
4) Juan *Mora Fernández

5) José Rafael *Gallegos y Alvarado
6) Juan Rafael *Mora Porras
7) Tomás *Guardia Gutiérrez
8) Próspero *Fernández Oreamuno
9) Bernardo *Soto Alfaro
10) Jesús *Jiménez Zamora
11) Bernardo Augusto *Thiel
12) Francisco *Aguilar Barquero
13) Manuel María *Peralta y Alfaro
14) Ricardo *Jiménez Oreamuno
15) Rafael *Calerón Muñoz
16) Colodomiro *Picado Twight
17) Ricardo *Fernández Guardia
18) Alberto *Echandi Montero
19) Cleto *González Viquez
20) León *Cortés Castro
21) Carlos Luis *Valverde Vega
22) Ricardo *Moreno Cañas
23) Carlos Durán Cartin
24) Anselmo *Llorente y Lafuente
25) Julio *Acosta García
26) Alfredo *González Flores
27) Mauro *Fernández Acuña
28) Joaquín *García Monge
29) Miguel *Obregón Lizano
30) Victor *Sanabria Martínez
31) Alberto *Brenes Córdoba
32) Julián *Volio Llorente
33) Rodrigo *Facio Brenes
34) Juan *Flores Umaña
35) Leónidas *Pacheco Cabezas
36) Moisés *Vicenzi Pacheco
37) Omar *Dengo Guerrero
38) Braulio *Carrillo Colina
39) Gregorio José *Ramírez Castro
40) Florencio del *Castillo Solano
41) Emilie *Solórzano de Guardia
42) Roberto *Brenes Mesen
43) Julio Peña Morua
44) Rafael Angel *Calderón Guardia
45) Otilio *Ulate Blanco
46) José María *Orozco Casorla
47) Francisco José *Orlich Bolmarcich
48) Manuel María *Gutiérrez
49) José María *Zeledón Brenes
50) Carlos Luis *Fallas Sibaja
51) Abelardo *Bonilla Baldares
52) Solón Nuñez Frutos
53) Emma *Gamboa Alvarado
54) Dr. Carlos *Sáenz Herera
55) Armando Céspedes Marín

56) Alejandro *Aguilar Machado
57) Rafael *Yglesias Castro
58) Jorge *Volio Jiménez

Beneméritos de la Enseñanza
Valeriano *Fernández Ferraz
Luis Felipe *González Flores
Carlos *Monge Alfaro

Beneméritos de las Letras Patrias
Manuel *González Zeledón
Aquileo J. *Echeverría Zeledón

Benemérito de las Artes Patrias
Manuel *Salazar Zúñiga

Benemérito de las Ciencias Costarricenses
Alberto Manuel *Brenes Mora

Benemérito de la Cultura Nacional
Isabel Carvajal Quesada (Carmen *Lira)

BENNET, James Gordon (1858-1941). An American dentist, he was
born in San Francisco and came to Costa Rica in 1883. He in-
vested in land and with the help of an inheritance founded the
Banco Mercantil de Costa Rica in 1908. He was one of the chief
shareholders in the *Banco de Costa Rica and served as president of the *Banco Anglo Costarricense until his death. The
noted financier Jaime Solera Bennet is his descendant.

BENZONI, Girolamo (ca. 1519-ca. 1572). Wrote La historia del
Mondo Nuovo (1565), reputed to be one of the first accounts
of the exploration of Costa Rica. Sailed with Diego de *Gutiérrez in 1544.

BERROCAL, Alberto (b. 1937). Artist. He studied in Costa Rica,
Mexico, and Italy. His paintings are geometric with vivid colors.
Berrocal has had his works exhibited in Costa Rica, South Amer-
ica, and in Europe.

BERRY, James (d. 1892). A Scotch Presbyterian, he came to
Costa Rica in the 1840s. He was very important in improving
the *cattle and dairy industry. Berry imported Kerry cows
from Ireland as well as Jerseys, Guernseys, and Herefords to
improve the breed in Costa Rica. In addition he imported Irish
grass seed which helped improve nutrition. He founded the
Carnation Milk farm and developed new breeds of cattle. These
things greatly advanced the national dairy industry, and especially in developing the *Coronado area into the prime dairy
area that is is today.

BERTHEAU, Margarita (1913-1976). Artist. Born in *San José,
she studied in Cuba and Colombia. She was one of the most

important forces in recent Costa Rican art. She was one of
the original faculty of the Academia de Bellas Artes and one
of the leaders of the so-called Nationalist generation of Costa
Rican painters. Bertheau painted both oils and water colors
specializing in landscapes which show people from all walks of
life. In addition to her artistic talents she was one of the prime
forces in furthering the development of classical ballet in Costa
Rica. For a discussion of many of the terms mentioned, see:
PAINTING.

BETANZOS, Pedro de [Fray]. Born in La Coruña Province, Spain.
He came to Costa Rica around 1550 and is considered the first
Catholic missionary and first Franciscan to come to Costa Rica.
He also served in Guatemala, where he mastered several Indian
languages and wrote Arte y vocabulario, a treatise on Guatemalan
Indian languages.

BEYER, Karl. German citizen reputed to have been in charge of
Nazi subversive activity in Costa Rica.

BIENVENIDA, Lorenzo de [Fray]. A Franciscan who came to the
New World in 1542 and to Costa Rica in 1564. When he returned
to Spain to explain the spiritual needs of the colony, King Philip
II agreed to send additional priests and supposedly gave him the
statue of the Virgin of *Ujarrás to take back to Costa Rica.
See: UJARRAS.

BIERIG, Alexander (d. 1963). Illustrator and painter. Born in
Germany, he came to Costa Rica in 1938, working in the Section
of Entomology of the Ministry of Agriculture and later as professor in the Escuela de Bellas Artes. He did portraits and local
scenes using bright colors. His work has been exhibited at
the *National Museum of Costa Rica.

BIGOT, Aquiles (1809-1884). Painter. Born in Paris he later
migrated to Costa Rica, where he became active in the Free
Masons. He painted a series of official portraits for the government and the *Masons.

BI-METALISM. Both *gold and silver provided equal monetary
standards in colonial times. This bi-metalism continued after
independence and was legally confirmed by the monetary reforms
of 1863 and 1870. The unrealistic ratio adopted served however
to drive gold out of circulation and establish a de facto silver
standard until the formal adoption of the GOLD STANDARD (q.v.)
in 1896. [L.H.]

BIRTH AND DEATH RATES. Costa Rica's birthrate has traditionally
been very high, but it has begun to fall a little in the last
twenty years. This decrease has, however, been offset by
a decline in deaths and in particular of infant mortality, both

of which peaked around 1920. Since then improvement in health
services, nutrition and sanitation have helped effect significant
reductions, as the following figures (per 1,000 inhabitants)
show. (Data from 1927 is taken from Chester Zelaya's Costa
Rica Contemporánea and the Dirección General de Estadística y
Censos [National Census and Statistics Office]). [L.H.]

YEAR	BIRTHS	DEATHS	INFANT MORTALITY
1900	41.5	23.0	(not known)
1910	41.7	25.6	197
1920	38.5	28.6	248
1927	47.9	22.6	166.7
1930	47.4	22.5	160.2
1935	45.2	22.9	157.0
1940	45.3	18.1	132.4
1941	45.5	18.1	157.3
1942	43.7	17.7	116.8
1944	44.2	16.7	125.0
1945	46.8	15.5	110.1
1946	45.0	13.9	101.6
1947	45.6	14.9	84.4
1948	44.5	13.2	92.1
1949	44.2	12.7	97.4
1950	46.5	12.2	90.2
1951	47.6	11.7	87.2
1952	49.8	11.6	97.9
1953	47.9	11.9	96.7
1954	49.4	10.8	92.3
1955	48.9	10.7	89.5
1956	48.5	9.8	84.4
1957	47.9	10.4	86.0
1958	47.2	9.2	78.8
1959	48.3	9.3	78.2
1960	47.6	8.8	76.2
1961	46.7	8.2	73.9
1962	45.1	8.9	80.8
1963	45.0	9.0	83.3
1964	42.9	9.4	83.6
1965	41.9	8.6	75.3
1966	40.5	7.4	71.0
1967	38.5	7.1	66.7
1968	35.9	6.5	64.7
1969	34.4	6.9	68.6
1970	33.3	6.6	62.7
1971	31.5	5.9	58.8
1972	31.2	5.9	54.8
1973	28.5	5.2	43.0
1974	29.5	5.0	38.8
1975	29.5	4.9	37.9
1976	29.7	4.6	33.2
1977	31.0	4.3	27.8

1978	31.8	4.1	22.3
1979	31.6	4.2	23.4
1980	31.2	4.0	20.2
1981	31.3	3.9	19.1
1982	31.3	3.9	19.3
1983	30.0	3.9	18.6
1984	32.7	4.5	18.9
1985	30.5	4.2	16.5
1988			13.6

BISCHOFFSCHERN AND GOLDSCHMIDT. A London firm which headed a consortium that agreed to lend Costa Rica Ł1 million. Under the terms of the loan Costa Rica received only about Ł560,000 in cash and agreed to make payments of Ł84,999 for 25 years. The loan and the way it was negotiated is considered one of the most unfortunate chapters in Costa Rica financial history. See also: BRITISH LOANS, and consult Cleto González Víquez, Historia financiera de Costa Rica and Tomás Soley Güell, Historia económica y hacendaria de Costa Rica.

BIZCOCHO. A type of hardtack or biscuit made of wheat flour grown in the province of Costa Rica. It was exported to Cartagena, Colombia, after going to Portobelo over a mule trail from Cartago. During the seventeenth century this constituted Costa Rica's chief source of income.

BLACKS. Few slaves were imported into the poor and sparsely populated colony and when independent Costa Rica abolished slavery in 1824 there were less than 200: perhaps as few as 50. The "disappearance" of these few was studied in Lowell Gudmundson's Estratificación socio-racial y económica de Costa Rica, 1700-1850 (1978). West Indian Blacks, many from Jamaica, were brought in at the end of the 19th century to build the *Ferrocarril del Norte and work at *banana plantations. They numbered c. 1,200 in 1904 but are now about 30,000. Forbidden until 1948 to migrate westward from the *Limón area they suffered serious unemployment when banana cultivation was shifted to the Pacific coast to escape Panama disease. Protestants, and still speaking the Creole English of Jamaica, they are prominent in the national sports of baseball and *soccer. Their heritage is presented by the writer Quince *Duncan, in the oral history of Paula Palmer and in the general study of M. D. Olien (see bibliography). [G.K., L.H.]

BLANCO RODRIGUEZ, Máximo [General] (1822-1886). Soldier and politician. He participated in the Transit Campaign (*Campaña del Tránsito) during the war against William *Walker, and saw action at Fort *San Carlos and La *Trinidad. With General Lorenzo *Salazar he led the August 14, 1859 revolt which toppled Juan Rafael *Mora Porras. He and General Salazar became the leading political force in Costa Rica and were responsible for other coups d'etat. Blanco was finally forced to resign from the *army in 1869 by Tomás *Guardia Gutiérrez, thus ending his political domination of the country.

BLANCO ZAMORA, José Julián. Priest. *Deputy on various occasions. President of Congress March-September 1837 and president of the Consejo Representativo March-May 1835.

BLANCO ZAMORA, Luz (b. 1801). President of Corte Superior de Justicia (1837-1845) and senator (1846). He led a regiment of 200 men in the war against William *Walker 1856-57.

BLOQUE DE LA VICTORIA. Political party formed as a result of an agreement signed September 1943 between Manuel *Mora and Dr. Rafael Angel *Calderón Guardia. This party elected Teodoro *Picado for the presidency in the *election of 1944.

BLOQUE DE OBREROS Y CAMPESINOS. Name used by the Costa Rican Communist Party (*Partido Comunista) between 1932 and 1943.

BOLANDI, Dinora (1923-). Artist. She studied in Costa Rica and abroad and spent 15 years in New York. She paints and has also dedicated herself to graphic arts and teaching.

BOLANOS, Tobías. See: AVIATION.

BOLSA DE CAFE. Market in which *coffee for internal consumption is sold. See: OFICINA DE CAFE.

BONILLA, Hermenegildo. One of the Costa Rican representatives to the *Diputación Provincial in 1823. He inclined toward association with Mexico. Bonilla took an active part in the first *civil war on the *imperialist side, for which he was imprisoned for a short time.

BONILLA, Juan Francisco de. Acting military governor (1816) in the absence of Governor *Ayala.

BONILLA, Miguel de. Called Father "Tiricia." Enemy of the *imperialist forces, which were trying to ally Costa Rica with *Iturbide's Mexican Empire.

BONILLA, Policarpo (1858-1926). President of Honduras and promoter of Central American Union. See: AMAPALA, PACT OF; UNIONIST PARTY.

BONILLA, Ronald (1951-). A poet born in San José. His most important works are: Viento dentro (1969) and Las manos de amor (1951).

BONILLA BALDARES, Abelardo (1899-1969). Writer and philosophy professor. Member of the committee that wrote the Constitution of 1949. President of the Legislative Assembly 1952-53. Second vice-president of the country 1958-62, and in that capacity served as acting president July 13-23, 1961. He also wrote several works of history, philosophy, and literary criticism. The most important of these are: La crisis del humanismo (1934) and Historia y antología de la literatura costarricense (1957).

BONILLA CHAVARRI, Jesús. Born in *Guanacaste. Bonilla is best known for his popular songs, "Luna Liberiana," "He guardado," "Nocturnas," and "Pampa." However he has also written some novels and books used in musical education.

BONILLA NAVA, Juan Diego (1803-1837). *Deputy on various occasions and president of Congress May-July 1833 and May-July 1834.

BONILLA NAVA, Manuel Antonio (1806-1880). Second head of state 1841, and acting chief executive (April 5-12, 1841) in absence of Braulio *Carrillo Colina. President of Constituent Assembly 1871, and president of Congress 1872-74 and 1874-76.

BONILLA SALMON-PACHECO, Félix (ca. 1776-1834). Member of the Third Constituent Assembly, *deputy 1825-26, consejero (1831-34) and president of Congress on four occasions.

BOOK PUBLISHING. See: PUBLISHING.

BORRASE POVEDANO, Carmen (1959-). Artist noted for a series of paintings showing textiles in various twisted and hanging forms. Exhibitions since 1981 and during 1986-87 in the United States. [G.K.]

BOUNDARY DISPUTES. See: FRONTIER QUESTIONS.

BOURBONS. The reigning house in pre-revolutionary France, a branch of which became the ruling dynasty in Spain c. 1700, with the accession of Philip V. Many new methods, most of them French-inspired, were introduced into Spanish and Spanish-American administration during its rule. These are known as the Bourbon reforms (e.g. the system of intendancies--see: INTENDANTS). Most of the reforms were introduced during the reign of Charles III (1759-88). [L.H.]

BRANA, Adolfo. Born in Cuba. One of the more important activists in the early days of the Costa Rica Communist Party (*Partido Comunista). He was elected to the San José municipal government in 1932. He was later temporarily exiled for supposed agitation against government.

BRAULIO CARRILLO NATIONAL PARK. National park in a diverse
region only a few miles north of San José and accessible via a
new highway which passes through it to Guápiles. More than
500 species of birds are found in this park, named for nineteenth-
century President *Braulio Carrillo Colina. [G.K.]

BRAVO DE LAGUNA, Alonso (d. 1674). Bishop of Nicaragua and
Costa Rica from 1660 to 1670. During his term in office there
appeared for the first time the image of the Virgin of *Ujarrás.
This image was used to inspire the Costa Rican forces in repel-
ling a *pirate attack in 1666. Bravo de Laguna had the dubious
distinction of being the first bishop to die in Costa Rica and
was given a sumptuous funeral.

BREALEY, Richard [Doctor] (1812-1864). Physician born in Notting-
ham, England. Dr. Brealey was shipwrecked off Cuba and finally
found his way to Costa Rica in the mid 1830s. He settled in
*Cartago and also was physician of the mines of *Monte de Agua-
cate. Slowly, he acquired a large amount of land. He was
co-founder with Captain William *Le Lacheur of the first *Protestant church in Costa Rica. The Brealey family has distinguished
itself in farming, commerce, law, and government.

BRENES, Miguel Angel. See: SCULPTURE.

BRENES, Víctor. Staunch Catholic conservative and philosopher.
He defended traditional morality and wrote articles on the dangers
of pornography and divorce. Founder of the office of film cen-
sorship, existent in Costa Rica with little power.

BRENES CORDOBA, Alberto (1858-1942). Lawyer and judge. He
has written some of the few works in Costa Rica on jurisprudence.
His most important are: Historia del derecho (1913), Tratado de
las obligaciones y contratos (1923), and Tratado de las personas y
contratos (1933). Declared *Benemérito de la Patria (1961).

BRENES MESEN, Roberto (1874-1947). Poet, critic, politician, and
philosopher. Studied at *Liceo de Costa Rica and in Chile.
He helped lead an anti-clerical campaign in 1908. Named director
of a high school in *Heredia, he pioneered co-education, provoking
conservative religious opposition. Later he served as minister
of education and Costa Rican minister to Washington. One of
the leaders of the theosophy movement in Costa Rica. He lived
in the United States from 1919 to 1939, where he taught chiefly
at Northwestern University. On his return he influenced the
youth of his country to look for the solutions of the country's
problems with improvement of education and the formation of
ideological political parties. He had a decided influence in the
development of the *Centro para el Estudio de Problemas Nacionales (Center for the Study of National Problems). His principal works are: Gramática histórica y lógica de la lengua castellana

(1905), En el silencio (1905, a book of poems), Hacia nuevos umbrales (1913, a novel), El misticismo como instrumento de la investigación de la verdad (1921), and Lazarillo de Betania.

BRENES MORA, Alberto Manuel [Doctor] (b. 1876). Scientist and sportsman. He investigated and catalogued many of the local flora and fauna. Several plants bear his name. He was also important in promoting sports, helping finance teams and especially the trip to New York in 1906 of the "La Libertad" *soccer club, the first team from Costa Rica to play in the United States.

BRIBRI. (1) A dialect derived from *Huetar.
    (2) Name applied to a few hundred Indians living in the *Talamanca and *Buenos Aires regions. Consult Enrique Margery Peña, Diccionario Fraseológico bribrí-español/español-bribrí (1982).

BRICENO BALTODANO, Leonides (1875-1926). Journalist and politician. Born in *Nicoya, *Guanacaste. He wrote articles for local newspapers and served in Congress in 1924. In that year he pronounced his famous Oración Cívica (civic eulogy) which was a panegyric hailing the 100th anniversary of the annexation of his native *Guanacaste Province to Costa Rica.

BRIGADA CANTA RANA (Singing Frog Brigade). A group of young men who went throughout the streets in 1947, under the direction of Joaquín Garro, yelling violent anti-communist slogans. One of the pre-insurgent groups dedicated to creating a climate favorable to a revolution. "Singing frog" refers to the Maya notion of an impending event (rain).

BRITISH INVESTMENT. The most considerable United Kingdom investment in Costa Rica was the *Ferrocarril de Norte which amounted to Ł3,180,000 by 1895 and Ł3,356,000 by 1913. [L.H.]

BRITISH LOANS. The first loan raised at the London money market by newly independent Costa Rica was one of Ł13,608 in 1825: this was fully paid off in 1840. In 1871 two 6% loans of Ł467,700 at an issue price of only 72% and of 473,500 at only 74% (i.e., less than 3/4 of the normal amount on which interest calculated was actually loaned) were negotiated with *Bischoffschern and Goldschmidt, and in the following year Ł1,750,100 was borrowed at 7% (and an issue price of 82%) from Knowles and Foster. The government defaulted almost immediately in 1874. There was also a nominal Ł905,000 loan--producing only Ł488,100--from Emilio Erlanger & Co., on which payment was suspended in 1880. All the debt was renegotiated in 1886 as two consolidated loans from Glynn, Mills, Currie & Co. totalling Ł2,000,000 but Costa Rica defaulted again in 1895-1896. Further renegotiations took place in 1897 and another default in 1901. Minor C. *Keith

renegotiated the debt in 1910, at 5% through Dunn, Fisher &
Co., once more for Ł2,000,000. There were further small loans
in 1912 and 1933. In 1948 Ł1,650,000 was still outstanding and
had been in default since 1932. See also: FOREIGN DEBT.
[L.H.]

BROCHISMO. "Hypocrisy." Used in political circles; said to have
originated during the late 1930s.

BROCKMAN, Patricia. A Chilean singer and musician who also
served as director of the Escuela de Bellas Artes.

BRUNKAS. Indigenous tribes of Chibcha origin who lived along
the Térraba River, El General, Golfo Dulce, and Osa Península
regions. They spoke Brunka and are said to have numbered
about 1,000 at the time of discovery. They were a warlike people
who made slaves of their prisoners. The Brunkas had no organized clergy, but were polytheistic. They lived in round palm
leaf huts in a circular compound and cultivated corn, beans,
manioc, cotton, and ayote. They are well known for their gold
and copper work and made stone spheres ranging from six inches
up to six feet in diameter. The use of these stone spheres
is still unknown. Replicas are used today in the capital as
public lawn decorations. Some Brunka descendants still live
in the *Térraba region.

BRUSELAS (villa). See: VILLA DE BRUSELAS.

BRYAN-CHAMORRO TREATY. Treaty signed between the United
States and Nicaragua, August 5, 1914, in which the United States
was given the perpetual right to build an interoceanic canal within
Nicaragua, the right to a naval base on the Gulf of Fonseca,
and a 99-year lease on the Corn Islands. The United States
was to pay Nicaragua $3 million. Costa Rica objected because of
its claims to sovereignty over part of the San Juan River area.
This treaty indirectly led to the break-up of the Central American
Court. See also: CORTE DE JUSTICIA CENTROAMERICANA;
FRONTIER QUESTIONS (NICARAGUA).

BUENOS AIRES. *Canton in *Puntarenas Province located on the
Interamerican Highway between San Isidro del General and Palmar Norte. An extensive region which is partially mountainous
and sparsely populated. Some of it is an Indian reserve, created
July 17, 1915. Population 27,716.

BULA DE LA CRUZADA. Probably dated back to an 1166 Bull
of Pope Urban II. First read in Costa Rica, 1608. It imposed
a seven percent property tax in favor of the Church. It was
abolished in 1824. See: CHURCH-STATE RELATIONS.

BULLON Y FIGUERO, Isidro Marín de (d. 1748). Bishop of Nicaragua

and Costa Rica (1746-48). He adopted the policy of forcing
people to live near churches (so they could attend mass) by
burning houses in the outlying districts. It is said that he
caused 21 houses to be burned. In Nicaragua he started construction of the Cathedral in León, the largest in Central America. See also: POMAR Y BURGOS, Juan.

BULOW, Alejandro [Baron] (1856). A German who served as chief
of military operations in 1856. He was also an advisor on defense and general strategy in the *Guanacaste region.

BULWER-CLAYTON TREATY. See: CLAYTON-BULWER TREATY.

BUSES. See: PUBLIC TRANSPORTATION.

BUSTAMANTE Y VIVERO, Manuel [Governor] (1693-98). He re-
populated *Esparza after the *pirate raids, and in 1697 conducted
a census of the *Indian towns in the colony. He was accused of
malfeasance in office, but was acquitted of this charge and returned to *Cartago.

- C -

CABECAR. A group of *Talamanca Indians speaking a dialect
derived from *Huetar.

CABECERA. Literally means "head." It is used to designate the
principal town in a *canton, where the governmental offices
and courts are located. This term is somewhat analogous to
a county seat in the United States.

CABILDO. A form of municipal government or council, usually
but not necessarily consisting of the governor, a *corregidor,
or *alcalde mayor, two *alcaldes ordinarios, and a variable number of *regidores. In Costa Rica, after the practice of selling
the local position of *regidor had fallen into disrepute, the regidores were elected by the people, thus giving the cabildos a
certain popular quality. The first cabildo existed in Costa Rica
in *Garcimuñoz in 1561.

CABILDO ABIERTO. An extension of the *cabildo, except that it
was a type of town meeting in which any citizen could speak.
In practice it was limited to the leading citizens of the town.
In Costa Rica the cabildo abierto was more open than in the
other, more wealthy, provinces of Central America. The cabildo
abierto was the vehicle used by the Central American provinces
to declare themselves independent in 1821.

CABULLA. Spanish for Sisal; also spelled Cabuya in accord with
its Hispanic American pronunciation. See: FIBER.

CACAO. Native American fruit. Cacao was first exported about
1650 to Nicaragua. This caused the expansion of the plantations
of the *Matina Valley (today *Limón Province). There were
130,000 trees reported in 1678. The production of cacao was
the first source of wealth for this impoverished colony. The
production of cacao began to decline because of *pirates, devas-
tation by tribes of *Zambo-Mosquitos from Nicaragua, and orders
in 1690 that *Indians were to be treated in a more humane manner. This latter deprived many of the absentee owners of *Cartago of a source of labor. From 1709 until the mid-1800s cacao
beans were legal tender for small purchases because of the scarcity of currency. Because of market fluctuations and plant
diseases, cacao production has diminished. It was unable to
compete for labor with the banana industry, but did come to
be planted on land abandoned by the banana company because
of Panama disease and enjoyed a brief resurgence in the 1940s
and 1950s. Often the pods are harvested today only in years
of high prices. Since 1979 the groves have been devastated
by fungus disease. In 1982 an estimated 2,419,000 kilos were
exported, worth $2,011,000 but this fell to $1,000,000 in 1983,
$1,500,000 in 1984. [T.C., L.H.]

CACIQUE. (1) An Indian chief.
(2) Name given to a local political leader similar to a boss
in American politics. See also: GAMONAL.

CACOS. Group that favored independence in Guatemala. It consisted largely of *creoles led by José Matías Delgado and Dr.
Pedro *Molina.

CADIZ. Spanish port and mercantile center during colonial era.
See also: CORTES DE CADIZ. [G.K.]

CAHUITA. National park beyond the town of Cahuita on the Atlantic coast south of *Limón. Beaches and a coral reef are the
main attractions. [G.K.]

CAJA COSTARRICENSE DE SEGURO SOCIAL. The name of the
Costa Rican social security system. It was created October 22,
1943, as one of the principal acts of the *Calderón Guardia ad-
ministration. The Caja administers the social medical system.
Consult Mark B. Rosenberg, "Social Security Policymaking" in
"Costa Rica: A Research Report" in Latin American Research
Review, XIV, No. 1 (1979).

CAJA DE CONVERSION. Created in 1922 as a division of the
*Banco Internacional de Costa Rica in accord with the gold ex-
change recommendations adopted at a conference in Geneva that
same year. Acting as a foreign exchange agency, it kept the
*colón stable at about four to the dollar until it ceased function-
ing in 1931.

CALDERA. Chief Pacific port during colonial times. Founded by Juan de *Cavallón in 1561, it began to decline around 1814 with the opening of *Puntarenas. A major project has recently reconstructed Caldera and restored it as the country's major port.

CALDERON FOURNIER, Rafael Angel (b. 1949). Born in Nicaragua during the exile of his father Dr. Rafael Angel *Calderón Guardia after the 1948 *civil war. He is a lawyer and politician. He is the leader of the *Calderonista forces and of the Christian Social Unity Party (*Partido Unidad Social Cristiano). He served as *deputy 1974-78, and was foreign minister 1979-80 until he quit to run unsuccessfully for the presidency in 1982. He was again defeated in 1986. "Junior" Calderón remains the primary leader of the PUSC, and as such was finally elected President in 1990.

CALDERON GUARDIA, Francisco (1906-1980). Politician. A first designate, he substituted for his brother in power December 1-6, 1941. He was also president of the National Unification Party (*Partido Unificación Nacional) and important in the machinations of the *Calderonista movement.

CALDERON GUARDIA, Rafael Angel (1900-1970). Physician and politician. Educated in France and Belgium. President of the National Assembly 1938-40 and president of the Republic 1940-44. During his term of office the *Universidad de Costa Rica was reopened, a labor law was written, a social security system was started, and a program of government-assisted housing was institutionalized. In addition an agreement was reached over the disputed southern frontier with Panama. Calderón was defeated for the presidency in a violent election in 1948. The attempted nullification of that election resulted in a *civil war in which forces of José Figueres triumphed. Calderón went into exile in Mexico. He later returned to run unsuccessfully for the presidency in 1962. He was one of the principal forces in the founding of the National Unification Party (*Partido Liberación Nacional). Calderón can be called the father of social reform in Costa Rica and was one of the country's most important presidents. See also: CAJA COSTARRICENSE DE SEGURO SOCIAL; CIVIL WARS (1948); FRONTIER QUESTIONS (SOUTH); and consult Theodore S. Creedman, "The Political Development of Costa Rica: 1936-1944" (1971), Eugenio Rodríguez Vega, De Calderón a Figueres (1980), and J. M. Salazar, Calderón Guardia.

CALDERON MUNOZ, Rafael (1869-1943). Physician and politician. Catholic conservative during much of his political career. *Deputy and senator on various occasions. President of the Senate 1919 and of the Constituent Assembly 1931-32. Acting president of the Republic January 25 to February 4, 1943. Declared *Benemérito de la Patria in 1943.

CALDERON NAVARRO, Pedro (1864-1909). Musician and composer. His most famous composition is "Himno patriótico a Juan Santamaría." Other works include: "Desde el cielo," and "Viacrucis," a religious piece.

CALDERONISTA. Political follower of Rafael Angel *Calderón Guardia. See also: MARIACHI; PARTIDO REPUBLICANO NACIONAL.

CALENDAR. The Spanish empire adopted the Gregorian Calendar in October 1583, creating a discrepancy between Spanish and Anglo-American sources for colonial dates until the English-speaking world followed suit in September 1757. See also: HOLIDAYS. [L.H.]

CALERO, Alonso. Spanish explorer. Associate of Diego *Machuca, he participated in the first explorations of the San Juan River in 1539.

CALVO, Fernando (b. 1951). Sculptor born in *Heredia. His favorite subjects are figures of country workers of the central valleys of the country.

CALVO CASTILLO, Francisco [Father] (1819-1890). Founder of the Costa Rican Masonic lodges. He also used the name "Ganganelli," in honor of Pope Clement XIV (named Giovanni Vicenzo Ganganelli), who suppressed the Jesuits in 1767. Calvo was educated in León, Nicaragua, and taught at the *Universidad de Santo Tomás. After being slightly involved with Juan *Mora Fernández's attempt to regain power in 1860, Father Calvo went to Peru, where he became a member of the Masonic Order. He returned to Costa Rica in 1864 and founded the first Masonic Lodge in 1865. In 1871 this lodge became independent of its parent lodge in Colombia. Calvo was active in the Church and was candidate for the Bishopric after the death of Bishop *Llorente. Consult Rafael Obregón Loría, Presbítero Doctor Francisco Calvo (1963). See also: MASONS.

CALVO-HERRAN TREATY (1856). A treaty with New Granada (Colombia) that was never ratified; it would have given Costa Rica most of the land it claimed in the Almirante region. See: FRONTIER QUESTIONS (SOUTH).

CALVO MORA, Joaquín Bernardo (1852-1915). Historian and journalist. Son of Joaquín Bernardo *Calvo Rosales. Founded El *Diario de Costa Rica (1884). He wrote several historical works, the principal ones being The Republic of Costa Rica (1894), published in Washington, and Estudios sobre la campaña nacional contra los filibusteros en 1856-57 (1909).

CALVO ROSALES, Joaquín Bernardo (1799-1865). Politician and journalist. He is called the father of Costa Rican journalism because he founded El *Noticioso Universal (1833), one of the first newspapers. He served as member of the Constituent Assemblies of 1838, 1843-44, and 1846-47. In addition Calvo was *deputy to the Central American Federal Congress, a member of the Costa Rican Senate 1863-66, and president of that body 1864-65.

CALVO SANCHEZ, Virgilio (1920-1988). *Deputy (1962-66). Resigned the office of second-vice-president in 1969 to form a new political party, Frente Nacional (national front) to run unsuccessfully for the presidency.

CAMARA DE REPRESENTANTES (House of Representatives). The name of the lower house of the national legislature under the 1844, 1859, and 1869 constitutions. Under the 1848 constitution it was the name applied to the unicameral legislature.

CAMARA DE SENADORES (House of Senators). The upper house of the national legislature under the 1844, 1859, 1869, and 1917 constitutions.

CAMINO DE MULAS. A trail that extended from *Cartago via the port of *Caldera to Chiriquí in Panama. Opened in 1601 it was a great advantage in the export of mules, which was the chief product of Costa Rica at the time. The road also helped pacify the *Indians in the *Terraba region.

CAMINO REAL ("royal road" cf. English "the king's highway"). During Spanish colonial rule, a road maintained (in theory) at government expense, as opposed to a camino de tierra, a trail fit only for horsemen. The two principal "royal roads" in Costa Rica were the so-called CAMINO DE MULAS (q.v.) and the mule track from the meseta down to *Puntarenas. [L.H.]

CAMPABADAL, José. Musician and music editor. Born in Spain, he came to Costa Rica in 1876. He helped strengthen music education in the schools and co-authored an anthology of music for schools called Cantos Escolares (1888).

CAMPABADAL GORRO, Roberto (1881-1931). Musician and son of José Campabadal. He was director of the military bands in *Cartago and then in *San José. He wrote many popular songs and a "Misa de Réquiem."

CAMPANA DEL TRANSITO. (1) "Transit Campaign" is used in a general sense to refer to the war against William *Walker (1856-57).
        (2) Specifically, it refers to the actions along the San Juan River-Lake Nicaragua area, where Costa Rica and Central American forces seized control of the TRANSIT ROUTE, q.v. in

various military actions in 1856-57. See also: WALKER, William; and consult Rafael Obregón Loria, La campaña del tránsito, Jeffrey Roche, Historia de los filibusteros (1980), and William O. Scroggs, Filibusters and Financiers.

CAMPANA NACIONAL. One of the names for the war against William Walker, 1856-57. See also: CAMPANA DEL TRANSITO; WALKER, William.

CAMPO GUERRERO, José Gabriel del (1788-1862). Priest and politician. *Deputy 1831-33, and president of Congress 1832. Member of Constituent Assembly 1838 and member of *Cámara de Representantes 1844-45.

CAMPO PAGADO. A paid political advertisement in a newspaper. These are a feature of Costa Rican political life. Even when (as often in the 1950s) political passions lead newspapers to cease carrying any news whatever concerning their political opponents, campos pagados from the opposition continue to be accepted and published. [G.K., L.H.]

CANAL. See: FRONTIER QUESTIONS (NICARAGUA); TRANSIT ROUTE; TRATADO DEL CANAL INTEROCEANICO (1870).

CANAS, José María de [General] (d. 1860). Born in El Salvador, he was general of the Costa Rican armed forces during the 1856-57 war against William *Walker. Named inspector general of the allied (Central American) forces January 1857 and later commander in chief of all allied forces. Executed at *Puntarenas along with ex-President *Mora following a failed invasion of exiles. Considered one of the country's national heroes. See also: WEBSTER-MORA CONTRACTS.

CANAS DE TRUJILLO, Juan Manuel. Lieutenant governor for military affairs June 10 to December 3, 1819; interim *governor of the colony December 3, 1819 to November 12, 1821. As governor at the time of independence he gave his support to independence, even though (in 1811) he had led the Provincial Battalion from Costa Rica, which helped put down an independentist insurrection in Nicaragua. See also: INDEPENDENCE; JUNTA DE LEGADOS DE LOS PUEBLOS.

CANAS ESCALANTE, Alberto (b. 1920). Cañas falls into many categories, being a lawyer, novelist, playwright, critic, and politician. He started his political career by supporting *Calderón Gardia in 1939; later he became a member of the *Centro para el Estudio de Problemas Nacionales (Center for the Study of National Problems). He helped in the 1948 revolution and was one of the founders of the National Liberation Party (*Partido Liberación Nacional). He served as first Minister of Culture in the *Figueres Ferrer government (1970-74) and as a member of the Legislative

Assembly. Later he became dean of the Colegio de Bellas Artes in the *Universidad de Costa Rica. His most important novels are Aquí y ahora (1965), the prize-winning, Casa en el barrio del Carmen, Feliz año Cháves Cháves (1975). He has written two political works: Los 8 Años and Sangre, sudor y lágrimas, both of which give the Figueres view of the *civil war. Cañas is also one of the most important playwrights in Costa Rica. His most important plays are "El luto robado" (1963), "La *Segua" (1974), and "Ya ni mi casa es mi casa" (1982).

CANAS-JEREZ TREATY, 1858. Treaty with Nicaragua in which the *San Juan River was awarded to Nicaragua, but with Costa Rica having the right of free navigation. It also confirmed Costa Rica's annexation of Guanacaste. See: FRONTIER QUES-TIONS (NICARAGUA); GUANACASTE.

CANO, Pedro Alonso (d. 1564). He is considered one of the con-quistadors of the country, having arrived with *Cavallón. He served as *regidor and *alcalde ordinario in *Cartago. Cano died in a shipwreck while accompanying *Vázquez de Coronado back from Spain.

CANTON. Subdivision of a province, somewhat equivalent to a county in the United States. Costa Rica has 81 cantons divided into *distritos.

CANTONS OF COSTA RICA. By provinces, date of foundation and present population (based on the 1984 census):

*Alajuela Province
*Alajuela City and surrounds

(cantón central)	Dec. 7, 1848	127,472
*Alfaro Ruiz	June 21, 1915	7,005
*Atenas	Aug. 7, 1868	15,011
*Grecia	July 24, 1867	38,361
*Guatuso	Mar. 17, 1970	6,774
Los *Chiles	Mar. 17, 1979	11,404
*Naranjo	July 29, 1882	23,588
*Palmares	July 30, 1888	17,815
*Poás	Oct. 15, 1909	13,939
*Orotina	Aug. 1, 1908	10,494
*San Carlos	Sept. 26, 1911	75,576
*San Mateo	Aug. 7, 1969	3,783
*San Ramón	Aug. 21, 1856	39,963
*Upala	Mar. 17, 1970	26,061
*Valverde Vega	Oct. 26, 1949	10,716

*Cartago Province

*Alvarado	July 9, 1908	8,338
*Cartago City (cantón central)	Dec. 7, 1848	87,125
El *Guarco	July 26, 1939	20,807
*Jiménez	Aug. 19, 1903	11,861

*Oreamuno	Aug. 17, 1914	24,145
*Paraíso	Dec. 7, 1848	27,823
La *Unión	Dec. 7, 1848	41,005
*Turrialba	Aug. 19, 1903	50,567
*Guanacaste Province		
*Abangares	June 4, 1915	12,575
*Bagaces	Dec. 7, 1848	10,104
*Cañas	July 12, 1878	17,284
*Carrillo	June 16, 1877	18,475
La *Cruz	July 23, 1969	10,876
*Hojancha	Nov. 2, 1971	5,879
*Liberia (city)	Dec. 7, 1848	28,067
*Nandayure	May 9, 1962	9,604
*Nicoya	Dec. 7, 1848	36,626
*Santa Cruz	Dec. 7, 1848	31,133
*Tilarán	Aug. 21, 1923	14,586
*Heredia Province		
*Barva	Dec. 7, 1848	18,933
*Belén	June 8, 1907	11,993
*Flores	Aug. 12, 1915	9,015
*Heredia (cantón general)	Dec. 7, 1848	54,896
*San Isidro	July 13, 1905	8,528
*San Pablo	July 18, 1961	11,802
*San Rafael	May 28, 1885	22,871
*Santa Bárbara	Sept. 29, 1882	16,643
*Santo Domingo	Sept. 28, 1869	12,985
*Sarapiquí	Nov. 18, 1970	18,909
*Limón Province		
*Guácimo	May 8, 1969	16,472
*Limón (cantón central)	July 25, 1892	52,602
*Matina	June 27, 1969	14,723
*Pococí	Sept. 19, 1911	44,187
*Siquirres	Sept. 19, 1911	29,079
*Talamanca	May 20, 1969	11,013
*Puntarenas Province		
*Aguirre	Oct. 30, 1949	13,319
*Buenos Aires	July 29, 1940	27,716
*Corredores	Oct. 29, 1973	28,366
*Coto Brus	Dec. 10, 1954	31,650
*Esparza	Dec. 7, 1848	14,998
*Garabito	Sept. 25, 1980	3,144
*Golfito	July 10, 1949	29,043
*Montes de Oro	July 17, 1915	7,444
*Osa	July 23, 1923	26,294
*Parrita	July 15, 1971	9,774
*Puntarenas (cantón central) (city)	Dec. 7, 1848	74,135
*San José Province		
*Acosta	Oct. 27, 1910	14,853

*Alajuelita	July 4, 1909	31,390
*Aserrí	Nov. 27, 1882	30,588
*San José (cantón central)	Dec. 7, 1848	241,464
*Curridabat	Aug. 21, 1929	31,954
*Desamparados	Aug. 7, 1868	108,824
*Dota	July 23, 1915	4,934
*Escazú	Dec. 7, 1848	33,101
*Goicoechea	Aug. 6, 1891	79,931
*León Cortés	June 12, 1962	8,087
*Montes de Oca	Aug. 2, 1915	39,065
*Mora	May 25, 1883	12,584
*Moravia	Aug. 1, 1914	33,038
*Pérez Zeledón	Oct. 9, 1931	82,370
*Puriscal	Aug. 7, 1868	23,123
*Santa Ana	Aug. 31, 1907	19,605
*Tarrazú	Aug. 7, 1868	8,845
*Tibás	July 27, 1914	57,693
*Turrubares	July 31, 1920	4,471
*Vásquez de Coronado	Nov. 15, 1910	24,514

CAPITAL PUNISHMENT. See: DEATH PENALTY.

CAPITANIA GENERAL. The highest office below that of the
*Viceroy. Capitanías Generales were areas where the indigenous
population had not been completely pacified. The Capitanía
General de Guatemala extended roughly from Chiapas to Panama.
In 1543 it was given semi-independent status from the Viceroy
of Mexico and consisted of four intendencies: San Salvador
(El Salvador), Chiapas (Mexico), Comayagua (Honduras), León
(Nicaragua); and the gobernación de Costa Rica; eight *alcaldes
mayores; and two *corregimientos.

CAPITULACION DEL PARDO, 1573. Agreement signed between
Philip II of Spain and Captain Diego de *Artieda. It delineated
the frontiers of Costa Rica as roughly the *San Juan River and
the Ducado de *Veragua. Consult Imported Spices (1981).

CAPTAINCY GENERAL. See: CAPITANIA GENERAL.

CARANA. An aromatic liquor made of copal (resin extracted from
tropical tree of same name), somewhat like turpentine, though
it is not wood alcohol. Also used as an embalming fluid in pre-
Columbian times.

CARAZO, Claudio (b. 1916). Painter, illustrator and cartoonist.
He was a member of the *Grupo Taller. He is considered as
an expressionist painter, dealing with human emotion and its
problems in his work. He won a national prize for drawing
in 1978 and in 1982 a national prize for his paintings. His works
have been shown in Central America, Mexico, and the United
States.

CARAZO BONILLA, Manuel José (1808-1877). Politician. He was elected president of the Assembly 1848-49, president of the Senate 1860-61, and again 1862-63. In the category of vice-president he served as Acting President of the Republic March 13 to April 4, 1849.

CARAZO ODIO, Rodrigo (b. 1926). Accountant, politician, and president of Costa Rica (1978-1982). Carazo was also president of the Legislative Assembly. He was a member of the National Liberation Party (*Partido Liberación Nacional) and opposed José *Figueres in a party primary during the 1970 electoral campaign. Carazo lost and founded his own political party, *Partido Renovación Democrática. He ran unsuccessfully in 1974, but in 1978 as head of a coalition, *Partido Unidad (unity party) he won the presidency. He served in that post until 1982. During his administration the Sandinista revolution broke out in Nicaragua. Carazo supported this movement, allowing Costa Rica to be used as a rebel base. There was large scale arms smuggling during that time, and the opposition-dominated Congress condemned Carazo for supposed implication in this business. During Carazo's administration many roads were built and he founded the *University for Peace (Universidad de la Paz). Toward the end of his term the country suffered an acute financial crisis, which was at least brought on by years of deficit spending. There was a de facto devaluation of the country's money by more than 400%, and an inflation level of more than 100% a year. Consult Eduardo Oconitrillo: Un siglo de política costarricense (1981).

CARAZO PERALTA, Juan Manuel (1814-1892). *Deputy and president of Congress 1883-86.

CARAZO SOTO, Francisco (b. 1741). *Alcalde ordinario of *Cartago and lieutenant governor exercising political functions after the death of Juan *Fernández de Bobadilla January 29 to April 11, 1781.

CARDENAS, Juan de (b. 1536). *Conquistador. One of the founders of *Garcimuñoz. Served under Juan *Vázquez de Coronado and *Perafán de Ribera. He also founded the city of Nombre de Jesús.

CARDONA, Ismael (1877-1965). Composer and musician. He was director of the national symphony for several years and has written "Suites para orquesta de cuerdas" and some chamber music.

CARDONA, Jenaro (1863-1930). *Costumbrista novelist and poet. His most important poems are "La caída del árbol" and "La lavandera." Most important novel, El primo (1905), criticizes loss of rural values in frivolous *San José.

CARDONA, Rafael (1892-1973). Son of Jenaro *Cardona, he was a modernist poet, novelist and essayist. Most important work Poemas de las piedras preciosas (1914) and Oro de la Mañana (1916).

CARDONA PENA, Alfredo (1917). Poet, essayist and novelist. He has lived mostly in Mexico since 1938. Important works: Poemas numerales (1950), Pablo Neruda y otros ensayos (1955), Semblanzas mexicanas: Artistas y escritores del México actual (1955) and Fábulas contadas (1972).

CARDONA QUIROS, Edgar (1916). Politician and businessman. Cardona was one of the principal members of the *National Liberation movement: In 1946 he was an active participant in the *Almaticazo and one of the most important officers of the Figueres' forces during the 1948 *civil war. He was appointed minister of public security in the ruling *junta. However, as a result of strong differences of opinion with José *Figueres Ferrer, ostensibly over the nationalization of the country's banks, he led an abortive revolution popularly called the "Cardonazo." On April 2, 1949, Cardona and a small band seized the artillery barracks. In the brief fighting six people were killed and 29 hurt. Cardona was jailed briefly.

CARDONAZO. See: CARDONA QUIROS, Edgar.

CARIACAS. See: TARIACAS.

CARIARI. (1) Landfall of Christopher *Columbus near Puente *Limón. (See: UVITA, La).
    (2) A district of *Pococí Canton with a population of 11,576.

CARIBBEAN LEGION. Name bestowed by U.S. journalists on what began as a motley collection of Latin American liberal exiles, gathered in Cuba under President Grau's protection, with the intention of invading the Dominican Republic and ending the Trujillo dictatorship. United States pressure forced Grau to expel the exiles who accepted the offer of refuge in Guatemala, whose President Juan José Arévalo dreamed of using them to overthrow the dictatorships of *Picardo Michalski in Costa Rica and of Somoza in Nicaragua. This Arévalo saw as the necessary first step to restoring the *Central American Federation. His hope was formalized in the PACTO DEL CARIBE (q.v.). When, in March 1948, a revolt broke out in Costa Rica, Arévalo provided *Figueres Ferrer with what was now a small, but relatively well armed and trained, army. Its aid was vital to Figueres' success. It was especially active in the capture of Puerto *Limón, and it also served as a valuable cadre for training the rest of the insurgent forces. After his victory, Figueres delayed using the Legion against Somoza. Instead, in December 1948, pro-*Calderón Guardia forces invaded Costa Rica from Nicaragua, with Somoza's connivance. The *Organization of American States intervened to restore peace, and Figueres sent the now mainly Nicaraguan Caribbean Legion (and its weapons) back to Guatemala. [L.H.]

Consult: Piero Gleijeses, "Juan José Arévalo and the Caribbean Legion," Journal of Latin American Studies 21(1); 133-145 (February 1989).

CARIBBEAN BASIN INITIATIVE. Passed in Washington in 1982, providing twelve years of tariff-free entry to the U.S. market for various exports from small, poor and politically vulnerable nations, including Central America. Non-traditional exports have developed from Costa Rica despite various complications. See: COALICION COSTARRICENSE DE INICIATIVAS DE DESARROLLO. [G.K.]

CARNIVAL. The principal festive days do not preceed Lent, but occur in August, at the Caribbean port, *Limón. See: GUI-PI-PIA.

CARO DE MESA, Diego. *Alguacil mayor of the province of Costa Rica (1532-1538). On an expedition to *Talamanca in 1564 he discovered the Estrella River and successfully panned gold from that river. This gave rise to the legend of the "Lavados del Río Estrella" (Gold Panning of the Estrella River). As a reward for finding gold Caro de Mesa was made *alguacil for life of *Cartago by the King of Spain. See also: TALAMANCA.

CARO QUINTERO, Rafael. Major Mexican drug boss arrested in March 1985. Aroused controversy on getting easy access to Costa Rican refuge; it raised the question of cocaine-money corruption of officials. [G.K.]

CARRANDI Y MENAN, Francisco Antonio de. Interim governor of the province of Costa Rica 1736-1739. During his administration he obliged the clergy to pay certain taxes on importation of mules and the export of *cacao. The clergy brought charges against him and he was removed from office by the *Audiencia de Guatemala.

CARRANZA, Rafael. Dramatist and journalist. He is reputed to be the first person to have regularly written plays for the Costa Rican theatre, during the first part of the nineteenth century. His best known plays are: "Un desafío," "Un duelo a muerte," and "Un duelo a la moda."

CARRANZA RAMIREZ, Bruno (1822-1891). President of the Republic in 1870 and journalist by profession. He also served as rector of the *Universidad of Santo Tomás and *deputy. He was named president April 27, 1870 after the overthrow of Jesús de *Jiménez Zamora. But when he realized that General Tomás Guardia actually wielded the power he resigned his office (August 8, 1870). See also: GUARDIA GUTIERREZ, Tomás.

CARRASCO, Pancha (1816-1890). Heroine of the war against William *Walker (1856-57). Buried in 1890 with honor due a general.

CARRERA, Rafael. Guatemalan guerrilla fighter whose 1840 defeat of Francisco *Morazán effectively ended the first Central American Federation. See: REPUBLICA FEDERAL DE CENTRO-AMERICA.

CARRILLO. A *canton in *Guanacaste Province, chartered June 16, 1877, whose *cabecera is Filadelfia. It was named in honor of Braulio *Carrillo Colina and is largely a cattle-raising region. However, it has a famous resort (Playas de Coco) and in Santa Bárbara a cooperative is producing ceramics copied from *Chorotega styles. The population of the *canton is 18,475.

CARRILLO AGUIRRE, Nicolás (1764-1845). Priest, conservative politician. President of the *Junta de Legados del Pueblo 1821, *deputy in the Constituent Assembly (1825). Also implicated in the War of the League (1835).

CARRILLO COLINA, Braulio (1800-1845). Lawyer and politician. *Deputy (1827-28), president of the Congress (1828), president of the Republic (1835-37) and (1838-42). In his first term of office he abolished the *tithes (diezmos) and also some religious rites and holidays. He tried to establish a permanent capital at *Murciélago (now San Juan de Tibás). He kept the country unified through the War of the League and the invasion of *Quijano. In 1838 he deposed Manuel *Aguilar and declared Costa Rica a "free state," thus removing it from the *Central American Federation. He was declared president for life in 1841, dissolved Congress, and suspended personal freedoms. In the same year he was overthrown by Francisco *Morazán. He fled to El Salvador where he was brutally murdered, as a result of "a personal quarrel." See also: CIVIL WARS (1835); LEY DE BASES Y GARANTIAS; MORAZAN, Francisco; PACTO DEL JOCOTE; QUIJANO, Manuel; GUERRA DE LA LIGA; and consult Francisco María Iglesias, Braulio Carrillo.

CARRILLO COLINA, Joaquín (1792-1848). Ultra conservative priest of *Heredia City who helped foment discontent and strongly opposed joining the *Central American Federation, fearing that it would bring religious toleration for non-Roman Catholic religions. He insisted that Catholicism be the exclusive religion of the country. He also opposed the *Ley Fundamental and was arrested for his part of fomenting demonstrations against swearing allegiance to it. In 1826 he was implicated in the José *Zamora plot. He served as *deputy 1847-48.

CARTAGO (canton). Canton comprising the city of Cartago and some of the surrounding area; created December 7, 1848. Population is 87,125.

CARTAGO (city). City in central Costa Rica at 9°50'N, 83°52'W, 1,426 meters above sea level. Founded by the Spanish in 1563, situated in the *Guarco Valley and serving as capital of the colony and capital of the independent country until moved to *San José as a result of the first *civil war (1823). It contains the basilica of the *Virgin of the Angels, patron saint of Costa Rica. The city, destroyed almost totally by earthquake in 1910, has been rebuilt. Population was 3,491 in 1892, 4,536 in 1904, 7,143 in 1927, 18,083 in 1963, 22,500 in 1975, 23,884 in 1984.

CARTAGO (province). Located in the east central part of the country, largely in the central valleys. Produces *coffee, *cattle, *sugar, corn, beans, and vegetables. Population was 58,770 in 1910, 269,860 in 1984 and 271,671 (est.) in 1987. It has eight *cantons and 46 districts. It was created July 24, 1867.

CARVAJAL, Jorge. A self-taught artist born in *San Ramón. He specializes in landscapes and has had several shows. One of his paintings was selected for a postage stamp in 1980.

CARVAJAL, María Isabel. See: LIRA, Carmen.

CASA DE CONTRATACION DE LAS INDIAS. Established January 20, 1503, and existed until 1790. First functioned in Seville then moved to *Cádiz. It was in charge of supervising maritime commercial trade, taxation and emigration to the Spanish colonies. It registered ships, levied taxes, and even sponsored some expeditions. In certain criminal and commercial matters it served as a court of first instance. The Casa de Contratación was also an informal center for the exchange of information of the Indies. It gradually lost its power and became subordinate to the *Consejo de Indias (Council of the Indies).

CASA DE ENSENANZA DE SANTO TOMAS. As a result of efforts by Father Manuel de *Alvarado funds were collected by popular subscription and a school was opened in *San José in 1814 under the rectorship of Bachelor Rafael Francisco *Osejo. It taught writing, grammar, and moral philosophy. It had its own building by the end of 1817, the first building built for educational purposes in Costa Rica. Although similar institutions were attempted in *Heredia and *Cartago, this was the only successful effort in the colonial period. It was transformed into the *Universidad de Santo Tomás in 1843.

CASA DE ENSENANZA PUBLICA. Although it had several antecedents in the later colonial times, this particular school was created December 10, 1824 by the state and gave instruction at the

secondary level. Consult Felipe González F., Historia del desa-
rrolo de instrucción pública en Costa Rica (2 vols., 1945).

CASA DEL ARTISTA, La. Organized formally under the influence
of Olga Espinach in 1951. It gives art classes mostly to poor
people and offers facilities to those who probably otherwise could
not afford them. It has sponsored exhibitions from time to time
and has been a positive force in furthering the study of art
in the country.

CASAS BARATAS. See: LEY DE CASAS BARATAS.

CASEMENT, John S. [General]. An American civil engineer. Casement had worked on the United States transcontinental railroad.
(He was the man who actually drove in the golden spike in Ogden,
Utah.) In Costa Rica he helped build the Pacific Railroad as
far as Orotina. Work was temporarily stopped there in 1902
because of lack of funds. See also: FERROCARRIL ELECTRICO
DEL PACIFICO.

CASTANADA, Francisco de. Harsh acting lieutenant governor of
the province of Costa Rica (1531-1535). He absconded to newly-
conquered Peru with a large sum of money, for which he was
censured by a *residencia.

CASTANEDA, Juan de. Sent by *Pedrarias to accompany *Ponce de
León on an expedition in 1519 to the *Golfito region. Considered
a co-discoverer of the Golfo Dulce and the Gulf of *Nicoya.

CASTELLANO. A monetary unit of Castile, Spain. It had the
value of one half doubloon (*doblón) at the time of Ferdinand
and Isabella.

CASTILLO, Carlos Manuel (1928-   ). Economist; has held many
national (president of *Banco Central) and international positions.
University of Wisconsin Ph.D. Member of Legislative Assembly
1978-82; first vice-president and minister of the Presidency
1944-78. Pre-candidate for nomination of National Liberation
Party (*Partido Liberación Nacional) in 1982, 1986, and again
for 1990.

CASTILLO, Francisco. Musician and oboist. He was educated
at the Conservatorio de Castella and is a prolific composer.
Some of his more important compositions are: "Concierto para
oboe y orquesta," "Concierto para timbales y orquesta," and
the following overtures: "Homenaje a Salvador Allende," "Tiempo
grueso," and "Controversias para oboe y flauta."

CASTILLO, Oscar. See: COMPANIA NACIONAL DE TEATRO.

CASTILLO, Vicente del. Spanish soldier accompanying *Perafán de Ribera on his unsuccessful march through *Talamanca in 1570. Del Castillo was accused of leading a mutiny against Perafán at Arariba and despite his protestations of innocence, was hanged. Perafán denied him the right of appeal to the *Audiencia de Guatemala or the right of appeal directly to the king. Perafán was censured for this action.

CASTILLO DE AUSTRIA. (1) Settlement founded by Father *Estrada Rávago in 1561 near the present site of Bocas del Toro. It lasted for only a few months.

(2) Settlement founded by Alonso *Anguciana de Gamboa in 1576 near the mouth of the *Suerre River, which also lasted for only a few months.

CASTILLO DE GARCIMUNOZ. See: GARCIMUNOZ.

CASTILLO DE ORO. Name applied to Panama for a short period after 1513 because of the belief that the land had large gold deposits.

CASTILLO DE SAN CARLOS DE AUSTRIA (Villa). Constructed in 1666 on the San Juan River in an attempt to prevent pirate raids. It was itself destroyed by *pirates. The fort was rebuilt in 1670 and lasted for a short time.

CASTILLO SOLANO, Florencio del (1778-1834). Studied in León, Nicaragua, and entered the priesthood. Representative of Costa Rica at the *Cortes de Cádiz, which he served as president and secretary. He was notable for his defense of the rights of the *Indians and *Blacks and for his ideas on natural rights. Later he went on to Oaxaca, Mexico where he was appointed bishop. He was named consejero by Agustín de *Iturbide and also served as president of the Mexican Constituent Assembly. Considered one of the most outstanding men of the colonial period.

CASTILLO VIEJO. Strong point on the *Transit Route (Vía del Tránsito) on the San Juan River. It was the scene of heavy fighting in February 1857, and was captured by the Costa Rican forces.

CASTILLO Y GUZMAN, Alonso del. Spaniard. Served as *governor of the province (1619-1624). Called "Alonso of the Devil" because of his irascible nature. He led a punitive expedition to *Talamanca to avenge the killing of Father Rodrigo *Pérez from which he brought back many prisoners who were distributed via *repartimiento among the citizens of Cartago.

CASTRO BEECHE, Ricardo (1894-1968). *Deputy on various occasions. President of the Assembly 1935-36 and later publisher of La *Nación.

CASTRO CARAZO, José (1893-1976). Musician and composer who spent most of his life in the United States where he composed music for dance bands, wrote light classic music and was director of the Louisiana State University band. Some of his more well known compositions are: "Cada hombre un rey," "Fight for LSU," and "Obertura a una pieza imaginaria."

CASTRO CERVANTES, Fernando (1885-1967). Wealthy businessman and rancher. One of the organizers of the *Almaticazo (1946) and candidate for the presidency (1953) for the *Partido Demócrata. Credited with introducing the humped Brahman or Zebu into Costa Rica, thus improving the quality of beef.

CASTRO FERNANDEZ, Alfredo (1899-1966). Popularly known as MARIZANCE. He studied and lived in France for many years and wrote most of his plays in French. They were later translated into Spanish. The most important of them are: "El vitral," "Espíritu de rebeldía," "Fragata bar," "Juego limpio," and the last two which deal more directly with Costa Rica: "El punto muerto," and "Aguas Negras."

CASTRO MADRIZ, José María (1818-1892). Doctor of laws from León, Nicaragua. One of the founders of the *Universidad de Santo Tomás and for 16 years its rector. Founder of *Mentor Costarricense, an early attempt at a newspaper. President of the Supreme Court 1866, president of the *Cámara de Representantes 1845, and president of the Constituent Assembly 1859. In 1847, he was elected president of the Republic, scarcely 29 years old, the youngest person ever elected president. On August 31, 1848, he declared Costa Rica an independent republic, thus severing even a nominal connection with the *Central American Federation. As a result of strong political pressure he was obliged to resign from office in 1849, but he was reelected in 1866. During his second term of office he encouraged the betterment of elementary education, opened the Bay of *Limón for commerce and inaugurated the first telegraph in the country. He was overthrown by military coup November, 1868. The learned Dr. Castro was often a minister in governments of other presidents. Declared *Benemérito de la Patria.

CASTRO QUESADA, Angela (1884-1954). Painter born in San José. Considered one of the member of the so-called *academic generation. She served for a brief period as dean of the Academia de Bellas Artes. See: PAINTING.

CASTRO RAMIREZ, José Antonio [Father] (1791-1846). *Deputy (1826-29) and president of the Congress (1827). Member of the second and third Constituent Assemblies.

CASTRO RAMIREZ, Ramón (1795-1867). Senator from *Cartago and *San José. President, Cámara de Justicia (1843).

CASTRO RAMIREZ, Vicente [Father] (1790-1845). Called "Padre Arista" and one of the members of a group called "La Tertulia." *Deputy to the Constituent Assemblies of 1823 and 1838, *deputy on various occasions, and president of Congress (1828).

CASTRO-VALENZUELA TREATY (1864). Proposed treaty with Colombia which would have ceded most of the land Costa Rica claimed in the Bay of Almirante region. Never ratified. See also: FRONTIER QUESTIONS (SOUTH).

CATANIA RODRIGUEZ, Carlos (b. 1932). Dramatist, director, and writer. Born in Argentina, came to Costa Rica in 1966 at the behest of the *Trejos Fernández government to help develop better theatre in the country. Since then he has been an important force in the development of Costa Rican *theatre.

CATHOLIC CHURCH. See: CHURCH ADMINISTRATION; CHURCH-STATE RELATIONS.

CATHOLIC UNION PARTY. See: PARTIDO UNION CATOLICO.

CATIE. Agricultural research station. See: TURRIALBA.

CATTLE. First brought to Costa Rica in 1510 by Diego de *Nicuesa then reintroduced in 1561 by Juan de *Cavallón. The first cattle ranch was established by *Anguciana de Gamboa in 1574. By 1797 there were reportedly 30,135 head of cattle in the colony. After 1855 all cattle had to be branded. In 1920 the cattle were improved by the importation of named Brahman (or Zebu) bulls from India and excellent pasture developed, largely by sowing reclaimed forest areas with English grass seed. But development was hindered for many years by poor communications, lack of refrigeration facilities, and a shortage of labor. In 1948, some $825,260 was spent on imported canned and powdered milk, and meat was still largely absent from the average Costa Rican's diet. Most of the beef cattle are raised in *Guanacaste Province, but efforts are being made to encourage production in other provinces. Most of dairy cows are raised in the *cantons of *Moravia and *Coronado (*San José Province). After the Second World War *cattle production expanded, and exported beef is one of the leading producers of foreign exchange. In 1982 Costa Rica exported 24,267,000 kilos which earned $53,056,000. Exports in 1986 earned $62,900,000. There is also some export of live cattle: $1,600,000 worth in 1982, but only $200,000 in 1984. See also: LIVESTOCK; BERRY, James; CASTRO CERVANTES, Fernando.

CAUTY, George I. English sailor who helped the Costan Rican forces in the war against William *Walker. He helped organize finances and planned the attacks on the forts along the San Juan River. Cauty participated in some military actions and

negotiated the surrender of San Juan del Norte April 13,
1857.

CAVALLON, Juan de (1524-1565). Spanish explorer and one of
the principal conquistadors. Organized an expedition with Father
Juan de *Estrada Rávago, which arrived in 1561. Named *alcalde
mayor for the province of *Cartago and Costa Rica in May 1561.
He discovered the central valley, founded *Garcimuñoz and reintroduced *cattle into the colony. Left in 1562 to become oidor
of the *Audiencia in Guatemala.

CAVENDISH. *Banana supposed to produce 235 stems per acre,
replacing the *Panama disease-susceptible *Gros Michel.

CCTD. See: CONFEDERATION COSTARRICENSE DE TRABAJA-
DORES DEMOCRATICOS.

CEDULA DE TALAVERA, 1541. See: FRONTIER QUESTIONS
(NICARAGUA).

CENSUSES. Colonial censuses were taken in 1522, 1569, 1611,
1700, 1720, 1741, 1751, 1771-78 and 1801. After independence
there was an incomplete population count in 1824, and a supposed census in 1836. A population count of 1844 was apparently
based on parish registers. An Oficina Central de Estadística
was established in 1864 to carry out the census of that year,
vitiated by a widespread lack of cooperation by the citizenry.
Although this was supposed to be the first of a regular decen-
nial series, there was not another census until 1883. This excluded *Indians and underestimated the rest of the population
by 10%. The next census, in 1892, was at least as inaccurate,
and may have been even 12% below reality. Apart from a 1904
census limited to the city of *San José, the next census, by
the Oficina Nacional del Censo, was carried out in 1927, but
only published in 1960. Inadequately trained census takers
and the poor state of the nation's communications were blamed
for another large underestimation. A censo de personas sin
trabajo of 1932 enumerated the unemployed. The Dirección General
de Estadística y Censos carried out the May 22, 1950 census in
which the undercounting was down to 5%. The census of April 1,
1960 covered population, housing and agriculture, as did the
May 14, 1973 census. There had been previous agricultural
censuses in 1904 and 1905. In 1915 there was a censo comercial.
The most recent census was that of 1984. See also: OFICINA
DE ESTADISTICA Y CENSO; POPULATION. [L.H.]

CENTAVO. One hundredth of a *peso. See also: CENTIMOS.

CENTENO GUELL, Fernando (b. 1908). Modernist poet and essayist. Most important works are El ángel y las imágenes (1953)
and Carne y espíritu (1928).

CENTIMOS. With the introduction of the COLON (q.v.) to replace
the *peso, centavos became céntimos. Inflation since the decimalization of the *coinage had made the one centavo coin unneces-
sary, and a two-céntimo coin was the lowest denomination minted.
By the 1930s this too had been withdrawn, and the smallest
coin became the 5 céntimo. Currently both 5 and 10-céntimo
coins are being withdrawn, leaving the 25-céntimo piece the
smallest to remain circulating. [L.H.]

CENTRAL AMERICAN BUREAU. See: INTERNATIONAL CENTRAL
AMERICAN BUREAU.

CENTRAL AMERICAN COMMON MARKET (CACM). See: MERCOMUN.

CENTRAL AMERICAN COURT OF JUSTICE. See: CORTE DE
JUSTICIA CENTROAMERICANA.

CENTRAL AMERICAN FEDERATION. The successive attempts to
form a Central American union have been:
      (1) The PROVINCIAS UNIDAS DEL CENTRO DE AMERICA
(q.v.), 1823-1824, which became the REPUBLICA FEDERAL DE
CENTRO-AMERICA (q.v.), 1824-1840, although Costa Rica withdrew before the final dissolution;
      (2) The CONFEDERACION CENTROAMERICANA (q.v.) of
1842-1845, which Costa Rica never joined;
      (3) A REPUBLICA DE AMERICA CENTRAL (q.v.) was
attempted in 1852;
      (4) Another REPUBLICA DE AMERICA CENTRAL (q.v.)
was attempted in 1889;
      (5) The REPUBLICA MAYOR DE AMERICA CENTRAL (q.v.)
of 1896-1898, which became the ESTADOS UNIDOS DE CENTRO-
AMERICA (q.v.) for its last four months, August-November
1898;
      (6) The FEDERACION DE CENTRO-AMERICA (q.v.), 1921-
1922, which Costa Rica did not join;
      (7) The present, very shaky, tariff union, or "common
market," MERCOMUN (q.v.), in existence since 1963.
      See also: NACAOME MEETINGS.

CENTRAL AMERICAN PEDAGOGICAL INSTITUTE. Established in
*San José in 1907, and ratified at the *Washington Conference
of the same year. This institute sought to foster Central American unionism by promoting a common school system. It ceased
functioning in 1913.

CENTRAL BANK. See: BANCO CENTRAL DE COSTA RICA.

CENTRAL MESETA. See: MESETA CENTRAL.

CENTRO GERMINAL. Founded as a study group during the First
*World War period principally by Carmen *Lira and Joaquín

*García Monge. It became increasingly Marxist-oriented with
the success of the Russian Revolution and was disbanded by
the *Tinoco Granados dictatorship. This group is considered
one of the precursors of the present Costa Rican Communist
Party (*Partido Comunista). See also: GARCIA MONGE, Joaquín;
LIRA, Carmen; MORA VALVERDE, Manuel.

CENTRO PARA EL ESTUDIO DE PROBLEMAS SOCIALES. A study
group organized in March 1940 by law students and young professionals under the guidance of Roberto *Brenes Mesén. It
published a monthly magazine called *Surco. Although its membership never exceeded a few hundred, it had a great deal
of influence over the future course of Costa Rican politics. Its
most important recommendations were in the fields of increased
suffrage, ideological political parties, government efficiency,
organization of cooperatives, and public education. See also:
PARTIDO LIBERACION NACIONAL; ODUBER QUIROS, Daniel.

CERDA, Cayetano de (b. 1798). Nicaraguan republican who fled
his country after it was occupied by Mexican Imperialist forces.
He rendered valuable service to Gregorio *Ramírez Castro during the first *civil war, for which he was given the rank of
colonel by a grateful Constituent Assembly. Cerda had severe
differences with Ramírez and was forced to resign when the
government reduced the size of his army. He left the country
and later led a group of 800 men in the service of Francisco
*Morazán at a battle of Mixco, Guatemala, where he was severely
defeated.

CERDAS MORA, Jaime (1904-   ). One of the founders of the Costa
Rican Communist Party (*Partido Comunista). He was *deputy
in the National Legislature (1946-48) and one of the leaders
of the Atlantic zone *banana strike (1934).

CERSOSIMO, Emilia (b. 1944). An *Arte Nuevo artist, who specializes in *painting landscapes in oils. She has had several
exhibitions of her works both in Costa Rica and the United States.

CHACON, Edwin (b. 1943). Lawyer. He ran unsuccessfully for
the presidency in 1978 and 1982, on the Independent Party (*Partido Independiente) ticket. He received less than 1% of the
vote.

CHACON, Juan Rafael (b. 1894). Sculptor. Studied and lived in
Spain and Paris for much of his life. He won the National Prize
for Sculpture in 1964. Two of his most famous works are: "Ca-
beza de Antonio Zelaya" (stone, ca. 1946), and "El hijo pródigo"
(wood, 1963).

CHACON DE LUNA, Sebastián. Spanish soldier. Sent by *Governor
*Ocón y Trillo in 1610 to save the beleaguered *Sojo forces caught

in an uprising in *Talamanca. He also led an expeditionary force that established a presidio in the *Chirripó region called San Mateo de Chirripó. See also: TALAMANCA.

CHACON TREJOS, Gonzalo (1890-1969). Author. Most important work is Tradiciones costarricenses (1930).

CHALCHIHUITL. (1) A chin ornament set in gold used by pre-Columbian *Indians.
(2) An inferior quality emerald.

CHAMORRO, Fernando [General]. Nicaraguan who participated in the war against William *Walker, commanding a mixed Costa Rican-Nicaraguan force at *Rivas (April 1857).

CHAMORRO-WEITZEL TREATY (1913). See: FRONTIER QUESTIONS (NICARAGUA).

CHANG DIAZ, Franklin (1950-). Born in *San José. Naturalized U.S. citizen; Ph.D. from Massachusetts Institute of Technology (1977). NASA astronaut, COLUMBIA space shuttle (January 1986). [G.K.]

CHAPETON. Derisive name given to Spaniards during the later part of the colonial period.

CHAPUI DE TORRES, Manuel Antonio. Rich colonial priest and merchant of *San José who left lands which were later sold to construct the Asilo Chapuí (mental hospital), now the Chapuí National Psychiatric Hospital but moved from its original site where the children's hospital (*Hospital Nacional de Niños) now stands. The area in the western part of San José from Hospital *San Juan de Dios to La *Sabana was once owned by Padre Chapuí. [G.K.]

CHAQUIRAS. Short cylindrical beads made of oyster shells used by pre-Columbian *Indians for trade.

CHARPENTIER, Jorge (b. 1933). Poet and professor of philosophy and Spanish. His most important works are: Diferente al abismo (1955), Poemas para dormir a un niño blanco que dijo que no (1959), and his prize-winning Rítmico Salitre (1967).

CHARTER OF SAN SALVADOR. This document was signed at the Foreign Ministers Conference in San Salvador (1951). It created the Organization of Central American States (ODECA). See: ORGANIZATION OF CENTRAL AMERICAN STATES.

CHASE, Alfonso (b. 1945). Poet and novelist. He was one of the prime movers of the *Círculo de Poetas Costarricenses in the 1960s and he frequently writes on contemporary social problems. His most important works are: Poesía contemporánea de Costa Rica (1967), Juegos furtivos (1968), and Las puertas de la noche (1974), Mirar con inocencia (1975), Obras en marcha; Poesía 1965-1980 (1982), and Arbol del tiempo (1967).

CHATFIELD, Fredrick. Chatfield arrived in Central America in 1834 to negotiate a commercial treaty and stayed on as British consul general in Central America until 1852. During that time he was considered the most important foreigner in Central America. He intrigued with various governments to safeguard British claims to Belize and the Bay Island (of Honduras), and British interests on the Mosquito Coast (of Nicaragua). At one point he tried to make Costa Rica a British protectorate, and negotia- ted a trade treaty in 1848. He is frequently blamed, but possi- bly unfairly, for the breakup of the *Central American Federation. Consult Mario Rodríguez, A Palmerstonian Diplomat in Central America (1964). See also: MISKITO INDIANS.

CHAVARRIA, Lisimaco (1878-1913). Poet. He dealt with the every- day themes of life and the poverty of the people. He eventually died in poverty himself. Most important works: Desde los Andes (1907) and the posthumous Manojo de guarías.

CHAVERRI, Fructuoso. This man is credited with inventing what has become the typical geometric design of Costa Rica oxcart wheels. The colorful/circular emblem appears on LACSA's jets as a national symbol. He started in *Sarchí in the 1920s. Al- though *oxcarts are not too common today, they are still seen in country areas. Oxcart souvenirs are produced as tourist handi- crafts by the Chaverri family in Sarchí. [G.K.]

CHAVES, Cristóbal de [Alferez] (1533-1629). Born in Badajoz, Spain. He came to Costa Rica with *Cavallón, after having participated in Pedro de Alvarado's conquest of Guatemala. He was alcalde of *Cartago in 1600 and owned land in Pacaca (*can- ton of *Mora) and Mata Redonda. However, because of a per- sonal dispute with the governor he was deprived of much of his land and lost his social position.

CHAVES Y MENDOZA, Juan de. *Governor of the province of Costa Rica 1644-1650.

CHAVEZ TORRES, Rafael (1839-1907). Musician and composer. He was a member of several local bands and wrote several musi- cal scores. The most famous is "El duelo de la Patria," which he wrote in 1882 for the funeral of Tomás *Guardia Gutiérrez. This has come to be almost the official funeral march as it is played at all state funerals.

CHICHA. An intoxicating beverage usually made with corn and fermented with saliva. A sacred beverage to *Indians. In modern times it may be made with pineapple or other fruits, usually drunk around Christmas time or at the festival of the *Santo Cristo de Esquipulas in *Alajuelita (*San José Province) in January.

CHICHIMECAS. A small tribe of Mayan-descended *Indians mixed with *Huetar stock who lived in the Atlantic region. Discovered by Sánchez de Badajoz in 1540. Many of them perished with his unsuccessful expeditions and in the defense of Marbella. See: SANCHEZ DE BADAJOZ, Hernán; TALAMANCA.

CHILE, Relations with. Chile in 1832 became the first important foreign market for Costa Rica's *coffee exports. Nazario *Toledo Murga, who represented Costa Rica in Chile during the negotiation of the CHILEAN LOAN (q.v.), was one of Costa Rica's first diplomats abroad. His Chilean opposite number, chargé d'affaires Soto Astaburuaga helped in the war against the *filibusters. And for many years the two countries could claim to be the only genuine democracies on the Pacific coast of Hispanic America. [L.H.]

CHILEAN LOAN. Through the efforts of Gregorio *Escalante, Chile loaned Costa Rica $100,000 to help finance the war against William *Walker.

CHILES, Los. Isolated *canton on the Río Frío in *Alajuela Province. Its *cabecera is Los Chiles and it produces grains, *cattle, lumber, and extract of Ipecacuana. Its population is 11,404 and it was chartered March 17, 1970. It has been the site of various armed conflicts between anti- and pro-Sandinista forces.

CHINANDEGA, Pacto de. See: CONFEDERACION CENTROAMERICANA.

CHIRITE. Popular name for an illegally distilled alcoholic beverage made from sugarcane.

CHIRRIPO. (1) A dialect derived from *Huetar.
     (2) Highest mountain in Costa Rica at 12,533 feet in the *Talamanca Range.
     (3) National Park. Remote, high altitude backpacker area surrounding the mountain.

CHOLERA. There have been few epidemics, but the most serious occurred in 1856. It caused thousands of deaths and forced Costa Rica to withdraw temporarily from the war against William *Walker.

CHOMES. Coastal town (population 2686) north of *Puntaremas where Pan American Airways flying boats began international service in 1929. Named after a sixteenth century *Indian leader. [G.K.]

CHOROTEGAS. One of the most advanced of the aboriginal *Indian tribes, they inhabited the region between Soconusco and the Gulf of Nicoya (Costa Rica). They were of Otomí-Tepanec origin and were said to have migrated from Mexico in the 8th century A.D. They spoke Mangue or Chiapaneca, and lived in rectangular houses in large settlements. *Nicoya City (*Guanacaste Province) was a major Chorotega settlement. They generally practiced monogamy and lived in family units, although the chiefs were polygamous. The Chorotegas were excellent ceramists and their polychromes are highly prized today. In addition they worked in stone and wove cotton fabrics. The chief agricultural product was corn but they also raised cotton, *cacao and *tobacco. They believed in one supreme force and the immortality of the soul, but also worshiped natural forces such as the sun, moon, fire, and wind. They were governed by a chief and a council of elders; frequently they engaged in wars and made slaves of their prisoners. In addition they sometimes engaged in ritual cannibalism and other types of human sacrifice. In general their society was organized somewhat along the lines of European feudalism. Today very little except ceramics remain of their culture. One hundred farming families were provided a reservation at Matambu, *Guanacaste in 1977.

CHRISTIAN DEMOCRATIC PARTY. See: PARTIDO DEMOCRATA CRISTIANO; PARTIDO UNIDAD SOCIAL CRISTIANA; INSTITUTO DE ESTUDIOS POLITICOS.

CHURCH ADMINISTRATION. The relative unimportance of colonial Costa Rica is well attested by the fact that it was ecclesiastically part of the diocese of Nicaragua, which in turn lay within the archdiocese of Guatemala. Only in March 1850 did Costa Rica acquire the right to its own bishop. Anselmo *Llorente y Lafuente was consecrated the first bishop of *San José by the Archbishop of Guatemala in 1851. Later, *Cartago, *Heredia, *Puntarenas and *Guanacaste were separated from the diocese of San José and given their own bishops. Costa Rica finally became a separate ecclesiastical province by a papal bull of February 16, 1921, which also made *Alajuela a bishopric and *Limón an apostolic vicariate. Rafael Otón Castro was consecrated first archbishop of San José August 2, 1921. [L.H.]

CHURCH-STATE RELATIONS. In general, Church-State relations in Costa Rica have been less of a problem than in most Latin American countries. However there have been serious difficulties from time to time.

(1) In 1824 much of the clergy opposed Costa Rica's joining the *Central American Federation and favored associating the country with Iturbide's Mexican Empire under the "Three Guarantees." The clergy also opposed the *Junta Gubernativa's abolishing a 7 percent church tax on property (see: BULA DE LA CRUZADA). The clergy, especially Father Joaquín *Carrillo,

fomented disturbances so that the citizenry would not swear allegiance to the new government.

(2) In 1858 Bishop Anselmo *Llorente y Lafuente was expelled from Costa Rica because of a dispute with President Juan Rafael *Mora Porras over church taxes.

(3) A clerical plot against José María *Castro Madriz was nipped in the bud in 1867. Clerics supposedly tried to overthrow him because of his liberal ideas.

(4) The 1884 *Liberal Laws curtailed Church activities and led to the expulsion of the *Jesuits and Bishop *Thiel.

(5) The *Partido Unión Católica, formed to repeal these laws, appeared to be winning the 1894 elections when some irregularities prevented victory. An uprising in *Grecia was soon put down, and the idea of a purely religious party discredited.

(6) The 1949 Constitution reestablished the Roman Catholic Church.

See also: PATRONATO. [T.C., L.H.]

CINDE. See: COALICION COSTARRICENSE DE INICIATIVAS DE DESARROLLO.

CIRCULO DE POETAS COSTARRICENCES. A group of young poets in the 1960s. They were the first group to do protest poetry with social implications. Most important members were Jorge *Debravo, Laureano *Albán, Julieta *Dobles Yzaguirre, Alfonso *Chase, and Germán Salas. They published a bimonthly magazine called Poesía para todos.

CITIES. See: ALAJUELA; CARTAGO; GOLFITO; HEREDIA; LIMON; PUNTARENAS; SAN JOSE; SUBURBANIZATION.

CIUDAD DE LODO (City of Mud). Site of the original city of *Cartago situated at the confluence of the Puires and Taras Rivers, in the valley of *Guarco River. Original city founded by Juan *Vázquez de Coronado in 1564. It was called the city of mud because of the construction of adobe houses. It was moved to the present site of Cartago. See also: CARTAGO.

CIUDAD NEILY. *Cabecera of *Corredores canton. Formerlly Villa Neily, it was organized by the immigrant Lebanese merchant Ricardo Neily in the 1950s.

CIVIL MARRIAGE. See: LIBERAL LAWS.

CIVIL WAR OF 1823. Imperialist forces of *Cartago allied with forces from the city of *Heredia fought a combined army of a few hundred men recruited from *San José and *Alajuela. The issue was whether Costa Rica should join the *Provincias Unidas de Centro-America, or be part of the Mexican Empire of Agustín de *Iturbide. On April 5, 1823, in a three-and-a-half-hour

battle, on the heights of *Ochomogo, forces from Alajuela and
San José, led by Gregorio *Ramírez Castro, defeated the imperialist forces. As a result, Costa Rica was able to join the *Central
American Federation. One of the underlying causes of this
war was the emergence of San José as the commercial center of
the country. Therefore, another result of the war was the
removal of the capital to San José.

CIVIL WAR OF 1835. See: GUERRA DE LA LIGA.

CIVIL WAR OF 1848. The Civil War of 1848, also known as the
*War of National Liberation (Guerra de Liberación Nacional),
had its roots in the discontent that arose during the administration of Dr. Rafael *Calderón Guardia. Dr. Calderón, in a
tacit alliance with the Catholic Church and Communist Party,
had enacted an extensive program of social reforms. Conservative forces tried to combat these reforms. A climate of violence
and questionable elections emerged. In 1946 groups of conservative forces, Social Democrats, and ex-members of the *Centro
para el Estudio de Problemas Nacionales coalesced in opposition
to the government. After the annulling of the election of February 1948, in which their candidate, Otilio *Ulate appeared to
have won, an insurrection began in the southern part of *San
José Province (April 1948). The anti-government forces were
led by José Figueres Ferrer, a *hacienda owner, who during
his exile in Mexico had planned this. In addition Figueres had
brought some foreign mercenaries to help him in his project.
All these forces aided by the general unpopularity of the government ultimately overthrew the Teodoro Picado government. This
civil war established José Figueres as the dominant political
figure in Costa Rican politics. See also: CALDERON GUARDIA,
Rafael Angel; CENTRO PARA EL ESTUDIO DE PROBLEMAS NA-
CIONALES; FIGUERES FERRER, José; PACTO DEL CARIBE;
PARTIDO COMUNISTA; PARTIDO LIBERACION NACIONAL; PICADO
MICHALSKI, Teodoro.

CLAYTON-BULWER TREATY, 1850. Treaty between U.S. and United
Kingdom to resolve differences in Central America, after U.S.
efforts to effect restoration of the *Central American Federation
(as an anti-British move) had failed and when France was en-
deavoring to persuade the Costa Rican and Guatemala governments
to accept French protection (see: GENIE, Le). The United
Kingdom renounced its protectorate over the Mosquito Coast
of Nicaragua (see: MISKITO INDIANS), the boundaries of British
Honduras (Belize) were defined and agreed, and both countries
accepted the neutrality of the isthmus of Panama (then Colombian
territory), undertaking not to maintain exclusive control of any
transoceanic canal built across it. John Middleton Clayton (1796-
1856) was Secretary of State to U.S. President Zachary Taylor.
Sir Henry Bulwer, later Baron Dalling (1801-1872) was appointed
U.S. ambassador in Washington, D.C. in 1849.

CLEVELAND DECISION, 1988. See: FRONTIER QUESTIONS (NICARAGUA).

CLUB UNION. Opened in 1925 as the elite social club of downtown *San José. Destroyed by fire on March 9, 1983. Rebuilt and reopened in 1987 with its first female members. [G.K.]

COALICION COSTARRICENSE DE INICIATIVAS DE DESARROLLO (CINDE). Established in 1984 as a means to expand exports and attract foreign investment. USAID funds from Washington have helped "The Costa Rican Coalition of Development Initiatives" to take advantage of the *Caribbean Basin Initiative. See: COFISA. [G.K.]

COCOA. The powder obtained from the seed of the CACAO, q.v.

COCOS ISLAND (Isla del Coco). An uninhabited island at 5°33'N, 87°W, c. 290 km southwest of the *Osa Peninsula. Well-watered and isolated, it was frequented by *pirates, and later by whaling ships. Treasure supposedly buried there includes $100,000,000 worth of gold evacuated from Lima by the colonial authorities in the 1820s to prevent its falling into the hands of San Martín's army of liberation. Such legends inspired Robert Louis Stevenson's Treasure island, and some 500 expeditions by treasure seekers, but nothing has ever been found. The island fauna includes some unique species, and the wild descendants of swine introduced by the whalers as a permanent meat supply. The pigs now number 2,000 and are causing an erosion problem. Cocos was claimed by Costa Rica in 1948. Since 1979 it has been one of the country's *national parks, but its permanent three-man garrison has been unable to prevent illegal inshore fishing, particularly of lobsters and sharks (for shark-fin soup). [L.H.]

CODESA. See: CORPORACION COSTARRICENSE DE DESARROLLO.

CODO DEL DIABLO. (1) A sharp curve along the Atlantic Coast Railroad bordering on the Reventazón River in *Limón Province.
        (2) During the period of a Calderonista counterrevolution (December 1948) this area was the scheme of an incident which became a symbol for the anti-Figueres Ferrer forces. Several persons of opposition parties who were supposedly being taken as prisoners to *San José, were taken out of a railway car and shot for reasons still unclear, but probably as a warning to communists and *Calderonistas to stop counterrevolutionary activities.

COFFEE. Coffee from Java was introduced into the French Indies in 1723, and reached Central America, by way of Cuba, at the end of the century. The precise circumstances of its arrival in Costa Rica are shrouded in legend. The *Academia de

Geografia e Historia says that the first clear mention of coffee
growing was by Father Félix Valverde in 1816. But its introduction has also been attributed to Cuban-born Tomás de *Acosta
during his 1797-1810 governorship, and to Father Juan Francisco
Carazo in 1790. Another version is that 15 coffee plants appeared
in a list of articles imported in 1787. The first recorded export
is one of a single *quintal (46 kg) bag to Perico in Panama in
October 1820. By 1829 it had become the country's chief export
crop. But the actual amounts involved were not significant
until German-born merchant Jorge Stiepel began a trade with
Valparaíso, Chile, in 1832. During the 1830s output rose from
500 to 9,000 quintales, and by 1840 a number of coffee exporting
firms were in existence. But the real boom began with exports
to England by William *Le Lacheur (who had heard about the
trade to Chile) in 1844. By 1861 exports were 100,000 quintales:
4.6 million metric tons.

Costa Rican coffee has traditionally been high-grade arabica,
almost all of it grown on the high central *meseta: altitude
tends to improve quality, at the expense of total yield. It was
therefore particularly suited to the British market, where coffee
until recently was primarily the after-dinner drink of the well-
to-do, who have been willing to pay more for a better-class
mild coffee. Until the First World War a half of Costa Rica's
coffee went to the U.K., where it supplied two-thirds of the
market (over 80% in the 1880s). Britain remained a major cus-
tomer until the Second World War, but the dollar-shortage of
the immediate postwar years forced British importers to turn
to sterling area producers, notably Jamaica and Kenya, exclusively.

Costa Rica's first large coffee plantations were owned
by Mariano *Montealegre who can be considered its first coffee
baron. The export boom transformed the country, bringing
it into active contact with the outside world for the first time.
As the chief money-crop it dominated the socio-economic structure of Costa Rica until it was rivaled by *bananas at the end
of the 19th century. Its cultivation was actively encouraged
by the state, and most improvements in communications were
carried out to help its development. The mule trail down to
*Puntarenas was replaced by a road for oxcarts in 1846. Fif-
teen years later the Atlantic railroad (*Ferrocarril del Norte)
was built to connect the meseta with *Limón on the Caribbean,
and so circumvent the long sea route to Europe around Cape
Horn (and the alternative, high-priced, rail route across Panama).

After climbing steadily, coffee production reached a plateau
in the mid-1880s which endured for forty years: 19 thousand
metric tons were exported in 1884, 15,000 in 1890, 17,000 in
1900, 13,000 in 1910 and again in 1920. Exports had climbed
to 23,000 by 1930, but then stagnated at the new level for twenty
years more: 22,000 in 1940, 24,000 in 1950. With the collapse
of the British market, Costa Rica's chief coffee customers became West Germany, and the United States (where Costa Rica's

superior coffee was mostly used for blending with other varieties).
Earnings have always fluctuated owing to the vagaries of world
supply and demand. Prices fell markedly in the depressions
of the 1890s and early 1930s, and in such glut periods as the
early years of this century. Income in 1954, for instance, was
29 million dollars, compared with only 7.5 million in 1945, even
though the latter year's was the much larger crop. More recently, the world price in U.S. cents per pound fell from 220.1
in 1986 to 123.5 in 1987. In 1940 Costa Rica established the
*Oficina de Café to control national production, and in 1963
she entered the "International Coffee agreement."

In 1960 a USAID report advised that Costa Rica should
change to cultivating the higher yielding inferior varieties in
order to take full advantage of the increasing world demand
for soluble (i.e. instant) coffee, and, to some extent, this has
been done. Exports grew to 54,000 tonnes in 1960, 73,000 in
1970, 82,000 in 1975, and 93,768 valued at $236,714,000 in 1982.
Exports in 1984 totalled $267,300,000 and in 1986 totalled
$354,400,000. The coffee harvest of November 1987-February
1988 employed 200,000 persons to produce over 3,000,000 quintal
sacks: 138 million tonnes. With the decline of El Salvador,
Costa Rica is the most efficient producer of its 2.5% of the
world supply. Consult Anales (1977-1978), pp. 181-183; Ciro
Cardoso, "La formación de la hacienda cafetelera" (1977); Carolyn
Hall, El café y el desarrollo histórico geográfico de Costa Rica
(1976); and Samuel Stone, La dinastía de los conquistadores
(1975). [L.H.]

COFISA. See: CORPORACION COSTRARRICENSE DE FINANCIA-
MIENTO INDUSTRIAL, S.A.

COFRADIAS. Religious clubs dedicated to the care and devotion of
a saint or church. During the colonial period they were well
organized and some of them were wealthy, owning land. The
most important cofradías during the colonial period were San
Nicolás de Tolentino, Las Animas, Los Angeles, and La Soledad.
In 1777 a decree prohibited some celebrations, and in 1805 pro-
cessions were further limited. During the administration of
Braulio *Carrillo other activities were curtailed. Today the
cofradías are only in evidence during Holy Week celebrations.

COINAGE. In pre-Columbian Costa Rica *cacao beans did duty as
money: they in fact remained as legal tender for small amounts
in 1850. Otherwise, insofar as the colonial Costa Rican economy
was monetarized at all, it used coins minted in Spain exclusively,
until a mint was established in Guatemala City in 1733. A Casa
de Rescate to produce a Costa Rican coinage was decreed in
1824--a bone of contention with the Central American federal
authorities--and inaugurated in 1828. The Spanish system of
coins continued however until decimalization in 1863 which introduced silver coins for two, five, ten, twenty-five and fifty

centavos, i.e., hundredths, of a *peso. It also introduced
the country's first nickel coin, one centavo. Nevertheless many
types of foreign currency also continued to circulate until the
silver peso was replaced by the gold *colon following the 1896
decision to go onto the *gold standard. See also: CASTELLANO;
CENTAVO; CENTIMO; DOBLON; DURO; ESCUDO; EXCHANGE
RATE; MARAVEDI; PESO; PLATA QUINTADA; REAL; REAL
CUNO.... [L.H.]

COLEGIO DE PERIODISTAS (Guild of Journalists). An official
association of professionally qualified journalists, created by
law 4420 of 1969 to enhance their standing and competence,
and to conform to the Costa Rican practice of licencing all the
liberal professions. All domestic reporters must hold approved
professional qualifications, and all future training must be done
at the (allegedly marxist-dominated) school of journalism of the
*Universidad de Costa Rica. The law was welcomed for its fav-
orable impact on journalists' salaries, but it has been criticized
as creating a vested interest and as abridging press freedom.
After José Phillips, editor of the weekly San José News had
been convicted of practising unlicensed, and thereby barred
from further work as a newspaperman, Stephen B. SCHMIDT
(q.v.) of the *Tico Times invited prosecution, declaring the
law an infringement of basic human rights. Although his three-
month suspended sentence was upheld on appeal to the *Organization of American States' *Inter-American Commission on Human
Rights, Horacio Aguirre (president of the Inter American Press
Association) persuaded President *Arias to seek an advisory
opinion from the *Inter-American Court of Human Rights on
the compatibility of Costa Rican law 4420 with article 13 of the
American Convention on Human Rights. The Court's November
13, 1985 ruling declared the law incompatible with the Convention. This came as a surprise to the Costa Rican authorities,
who pointed out that an advisory opinion, as such, was not
binding. [L.H.]

COLEGIO SAN LUIS GONZAGA. Founded in 1842 in *Cartago by
decree of Francisco *Morazán, but it did not start functioning
until Valeriano *Fernández Ferraz came to the country to be
its director in 1869. It was the first secondary educational
institution in *Cartago. It became a *Jesuit institution from
1876 to 1884, then came under state control. It was the most
important educational institution outside of *San José. The
most noted graduate is President Ricardo *Jiménez Oreamuno.

COLOMBIA. See: FRONTIER QUESTIONS (SOUTH).

COLON. (1) Costa Rica monetary unit, named for Christopher
Columbus ("Colón" in Spanish), due to its introduction soon
after the fourth centenary of the discovery, in 1892. The laws
of October 24, 1896 decreed a gold coin of 0.778 grams of 90%

pure gold, which gave it a value of 1 shilling 11 pence English money, or the same as the silver *peso it replaced. From April 17, 1900 it became the country's exclusive currency and maintained its value until 1914. The monetary symbol is ¢, and is divided into *céntimos. See: EXCHANGE RATE, GOLD STANDARD. [L.H.]

COLUMBUS, Bartholomew. Brother of Christopher *Columbus: in Spanish, Bartolomé Colón.

COLUMBUS, Christopher (d. 1506). Landed at what is now Costa Rica on his fourth voyage, at a place called *Cariarí, now Puerto *Limón (September 18, 1502) where he stayed for 17 days. He left to search for the legendary golden city, Zorabaro. Chroniclers of this voyage refer to the "Rich Coast" (Costa Rica), but the name of the country does not seem to have come from this time. See: COSTA RICA.

COMAL. A flat stone used to cook tortillas.

COMBRARIAZA, Guillermo. A Colombian artist who resided in Costa Rica. He was affiliated with the *Grupo Ocho.

COMISION DE LEGACION DE LOS PUEBLOS. See: JUNTA DE LEGADOS DE LOS PUEBLOS.

COMITE DE UNIFICACION DE LAS ASOCIACIONES ANTITOTALITARIAS. A pro-Allied committee which organized the July 4, 1942 rally that protested the torpedoing of a ship in *Limón harbor. This rally was notable in that it degenerated into a major riot with much looting, mostly Italian and German-owned shops.

COMITE PRO-FRANCO. A pro-fascist antisemitic group that operated in the country in the late 1930s.

COMMON MARKET. See: MERCOMUN.

COMMUNIST PARTY. See: PARTIDO COMUNISTA.

COMPANIA NACIONAL DE TEATRO. Founded in 1971 by the new Ministry of Culture. This new company was formed from the "Teatro Universitario," "Teatro Arlequín," and the "Grupo Israelita de Teatro." It was reorganized by Oscar Castillo into five sections: community, schools, puppetry, industries, and a dramatic workshop. Carlos *Catania Rodríguez was first artistic director, followed by Ebe Lemoine Grandoso (1977), and the current director, Mimi Prado Castro. They have gone on tours including a successful trip to Mexico. The repertoire is varied; they have presented works of Lope de Vega, Cervantes, Bertolt Brecht, Ibsen, Shakespeare and local writers. Since 1975, the group has received thirty percent of a six percent entertainment tax.

CON WONG, Isidro (b. 1931). Born in *Puntarenas of Chinese ancestry he is one of the most important primitive painters in the country. Considered one of the *Arte Nuevo painters he specializes in semi-abstract country scenes painted in vivid acrylic colors. He has had his works exhibited in Japan, Europe, and Latin America.

CONCHO. The Costa Rican peasant. The colorful dialect and customs were a part of *costumbrista novels, particularly by Aquiles J. *Echeverría Zeledón. [G.K.]

CONCORDIA. See: PACTO DE CONCORDIA.

CONFEDERACION CENTROAMERICANA. A loose confederation proposed in a conference in Chinandega, Nicaragua (March 1842). It went into effect July 29, 1842, with only Nicaragua, El Salvador, and Honduras joining it. Costa Rica agreed to join if certain modifications were made. This attempt at Central American unification lasted until 1845 when it was disbanded. Known as the Pacto de Chinandega.

CONFEDERACION COSTARRICENSE DE TRABAJADORES DEMOCRA-TICOS. An anti-communist labor union organized in 1966. It evolved out of the *Confederación Costarricense de Trabajadores "Rerum Novarum" and several smaller unions.

CONFEDERACION COSTARRICENSE DE TRABAJADORES "RERUM NOVARUM." A labor union organized August 1943 by Father Benjamín *Núñez Vargas at the behest of Msgr. *Sanabria who felt it was incumbent on the Church to organize a non-communist labor movement. In 1966 it merged into the *Confederación Costarricense de Trabajadores Democráticos.

CONFEDERACION DE TRABAJADORES COSTARRICENSES. Organized in 1920, it became Costa Rica's first major labor union. By strike in 1921, it was successful in securing the 40-hour week. It was said to have come under communist domination and therefore was disbanded by the governing junta in 1948. It was also known as the Confederación General de Trabajadores.

CONGRESO CONSTITUCIONAL. Official name for the unicameral national legislature which operated under the Constitution of 1871.

CONGRESO DE DIPUTADOS. Official name for the unicameral national legislature which operated under the Constitutions of 1825 and 1847.

CONGRESO PROVINCIAL DE COSTA RICA. Governing body of
Costa Rica March 3-19, 1823. It was composed of 25 members,
met in *Cartago, and was dominated by republican elements
who followed Rafael *Osejo. On March 8, 1823, it declared Costa
Rica independent, and later by a 19-5 vote declared for union
with Colombia, presumably to forestall the entrance of troops
from *Iturbide's Mexican Empire. It finally created a three-
man tribunal to rule the country. See also: INDEPENDENCE;
OSEJO, Rafael; TRIBUNAL SUPERIOR DE JUSTICIA.

CONQUISTADOR. A leading participant in the sixteenth century
Spanish conquista (conquest) of the New World. [L.H.]

CONSEJO DE INDIAS. Established 1519 as an outgrowth of the
*Junta de Indias and basically had the same functions. Ceased
functioning 1524 when Charles V (Charles I) founded the Consejo
Real Supremo de las Indias. The Council of the Indies (the
normal English name for both bodies) remained the prime colonial
bureau for Spain until it became subordinate to the new Secretariat of the Indies in 1714. It was abolished in 1834.

CONSEJO NACIONAL DE PRODUCCION. Autonomous government
institution established September 10, 1948 to stimulate production and eliminate speculation in basic commodities. It operates
granaries, buys directly from the producer, and operates a
chain of retail stores which compete with the traditional *pul-
perías.

CONSEJO SUPERIOR DE EDUCACION. A governmental panel established under Article 81 of the Constitution of 1949 and the 1953
"Ley Constitutiva del Consejo Superior de Educación." It is
presided over by the Minister of Education and has representatives from the *ANDE, retired teachers, representatives from
all levels of education and a representative of the President
of the Republic. It is charged with coordinating all levels of
national education including the universities. Sometimes it is
politically manipulated and by its sensitive nature has at times
generated controversy. Especially during the 1960s when it
approved educational reforms. See also: EDUCATIONAL RE-
FORMS, 1962; LEY FUNDAMENTAL DE EDUCACION.

CONSERVATIVES. See: SERVILES.

CONSERVATORIO DE CASTELLA. Founded in 1953 by Arnoldo
*Herrera who served as Director. It started as a music school
for children but has expanded over the years into a baccalaureate
granting institution. It has new modern facilities which include a
large theatre. It is one of the principal training grounds for
musicians and composers in the country.

CONSPIRACY OF LA SOLEDAD, April 18, 1860. A group of men

disguised as musicians were supposed to enter a military barracks located in front of the La Soledad church. They were then going to start a revolt to bring Juan Rafael *Mora Porras back to power. The plot was discovered and failed.

CONSTITUTIONS OF COSTA RICA. Listed by name and year adopted.

Pacto Social Interino de Costa Rica (*Pacto de Concordia) (December 1, 1821; amended January 10, 1822).
*Primer Estatuto Político de la Provincia de Costa Rica (March 17, 1823)
*Segundo Estatuto Político de la Provincia de Costa Rica (May 16, 1823) See: CENTRAL AMERICAN FEDERATION
Constitución de la República de Centro América (December 22, 1824)
*Ley Fundamental del Estado Libre de Costa Rica (January 25, 1825) (drastically amended in 1825 and 1830)
Constitución Federal de Centro América con las Reformas Decretadas en 1835 (in reality a new constitution; February 13, 1835)
*Ley de Bases y Garantías (March 8, 1841). See also: CARRILLO COLINA, Braulio.
Constitución Política de 1847 (February 10, 1847)
Constitución Política de 1859 (December 27, 1859)
Constitución Política de 1869 (April 15, 1869)
Constitución Política de 1871 (December 7, 1871; major amendments 1882, 1913, and 1943). This constitution was suspended during the Tinoco dictatorship, 1917-1919.
Constitución Política de 1917 (June 8, 1917)
Constitución Política de 1949 (November 7, 1949)

Consult Hernán G. Peralta, Las constituciones de Costa Rica (Madrid, 1962).

CONTADORA. A meeting in January 1983 on the Panamanian island of this name by Colombia, Mexico, Panama and Venezuela. Eventually a "support group" of additional countries on the basis of Contadora's concepts. The 21 points of the so-called Contadora Group were supplanted in August 1987 by the ARIAS PLAN (q.v.). [G.K.]

CONTINUISMO. A method of keeping a president in office beyond his legally expired term of office. This practice has been used only minimally in Costa Rica, but there have been notable exceptions. See: CARRILLO COLINA, Braulio; GUARDIA GUTIERREZ, Tomás; and YGLESIAS, Rafael for examples.

CONTRALOR GENERAL (Comptroller General). An important nonpartisan fiscal inspector serving an eight-year term. See: LEY ORGANICA DE LA CONTRALORIA GENERAL DE LA REPUBLICA. [G.K.]

CONTRERAS, Rodrigo de (d. 1558). *Governor of the province of Nicaragua and Costa Rica (1535-1541). In 1536 he explored the *San Juan River and was the first to follow it to the Caribbean Sea. In 1540 he had Hernán *Sánchez de Badajoz arrested because Sánchez's expeditions had encroached on his territory. Contreras was noted for his harsh rule and had to go to Madrid twice to defend his actions. His harsh treatment of the settlers engendered so much resentment that he and his family were forced to leave for Peru, where he died in 1558.

CONVERGENCIA. An art movement started in the early 1980s. It is according to its adherents: "Coincidence of styles ... and more of an attitude toward life." The paintings range from abstract to neo-cubism to realism. Leaders of this movement are: Oscar Atmella, Rolando *Cubero Murillo, Miguel Hernández, Marco Tulio Arias Vargas and Hernán *Pérez. They held expositions in *San José (September 1983) and again in late 1984.

COOPER, Henry. Born in York, England. He came to Costa Rica in 1826 and is considered the first permanent English settler. He worked for Richard *Trevithick in the *Montes de Aguacate gold mines and later bought land in *Cartago. He cooperated with road and port surveys. Ex-President Rodrigo *Carazo Odio is one of his descendants.

COOPERATIVES. Frequently organized in Costa Rica and currently numbering about 600. Two of the more successful are the "Dos Pinos" milk cooperative, important in maintaining nutritional levels despite urbanization, and "Coopesa," an aircraft maintenance facility doing substantial international business. Smaller *coffee growers also have organized co-ops (see: Cazanga Solar thesis, in bibliography). [G.K.]

COQUIBI. See: COQUIVI.

COQUIVI. An *Indian chief who opposed Juan de *Cavallón in the Ciudad *Colón (*San José Province) area.

CORCOVADO. National Park in southwesternmost part of the country in the Osa Peninsula. Lowland jungle area. Problems of independent *gold prospectors affecting ecology. [G.K.]

CORDERO, José Abdulio (1927-   ). Writer. His most important work is El ser de la nacionalidad costarricense, which was his licentiature thesis and was published in Spain in 1964.

CORINTO, Pacto de. See: TRIBUNAL OF CENTRAL AMERICAN ARBITRATION.

CORN, Fight for. See: LUCHA POR EL MAIZ.

CORO DE LA ORQUESTA NACIONAL. Organized April 25, 1974 under the Italian Marco *Dusi, who served as its first director. It has about 95 members and has performed in Europe and South America. Most of its repertory is international with about 20% of its music by Costa Rican composers.

COROBICES. The original *Indians living in the *Tempisque-Gulf of *Nicoya area. They were conquered by the *Chorotegas and numbered only about 900 at the time of the conquest. Their language was Corobicí.

CORONADO. *Canton on the western slopes of the volcano *Irazú. Its *cabecera is San Isidro and it was created November 15, 1910. It produces *coffee, vegetables, but is most important for dairy farming. Its population is 24,514. Its name was changed to Vázquez de Coronado in 1981.

CORPORACION COSTARRICENSE DE DESARROLLO (CODESA). Established in 1973 to foment development via governmental investment. By the 1980s, slated for dissolution due to heavy financial losses by most of its businesses. The International Monetary Fund provided credit to the government on the basis of fiscal restraint, such as eliminating this agency. [G.K.]

CORPORACION COSTARRICENSE DE FINANCIAMIENTO INDUSTRIAL S.A. (COFISA). Founded in 1963 as a vehicle for foreign aid funds during the Alliance for Progress. COFISA became especially active after the passage of the *Caribbean Basin Initiative in 1982. See: CINDE. [G.K.]

CORREDORES. The tenth *canton of *Puntarenas Province, created October 19, 1973, with its *cabecera *Ciudad Neily. It was formed from parts of the neighboring cantons of *Golfito and *Coto Brus. It lies along the border with Panama and contained a large portion of the *United Fruit Company banana plantations.

CORREGIDOR. Generally the same as an *alcalde mayor, except it usually designated someone governing a territory in a more remote, less populous area. This term was sometimes used interchangeably with alcalde mayor, except that the alcalde mayor was named by the *Audiencia.

CORREGIMIENTO. Territory ruled over by a *corregidor.

CORREQUE. *Huetar chief who removed his people from the *Ujarrás region to excape the conquest. He was finally baptized and became known as don Fernando Correque.

CORROHORE. One of the principal rulers of the *Brunkas. He was chief of the Quepos regions and warmly welcomed Juan *Vazquez de Coronado in 1563.

CORSO, Pablo. A Spanish soldier with the Hernán Sánchez de
Badajoz expedition. He was supposedly killed personally by
Governor Contreras because he refused to tell him where some
gold was hidden. See also: CONTRERAS, Rodrigo de; SAN-
CHEZ DE BADAJOZ, Hernán.

CORTE DE JUSTICIA CENTROAMERICANA. Central American Justice Court established at the *Washington Conference of 1907
for an extendable period of ten years. It consisted of five
judges (one for each Central American country) and had wide
judicial powers to settle international disputes. The court started
functioning in *Cartago, Costa Rica, in 1908, but moved to *San
José after the 1910 *earthquake. The court had an early success
settling a dispute between El Salvador and Honduras, and probably avoiding a war. However, the court was weakened in 1912
when after a revolution in Nicaragua one faction refused to accept the court's jurisdiction. After the signing of the *Bryan-
Chamorro Treaty (1912), Costa Rica and El Salvador objected
that their rights had been violated. The court ruled that although it had not jurisdiction over the United States, the Bryan-
Chamorro Treaty had violated earlier agreements (1858 and 1888)
between Costa Rica and Nicaragua. As a result Nicaragua withdrew from the court. Having lost prestige, the court was allowed to expire at the end of the treaty's statutory life. Consult Thomas Karnes, The Failure of Union, (Chapter IV).

CORTES CARVAJAL, Beltrán. A crazed mental patient who shot
and killed several people in August 1938. Among them was Dr.
*Moreno Cañas, who was a strong candidate for the 1940 presi-
dential election.

CORTES CASTRO, León (1882-1946). Politician. He held various
municipal posts, *deputy on various occasions, president of
the Assembly 1925-26, minister of education 1929-30, public
works 1930 and 1932-36, and president of the Republic 1936-
40. He conducted a rather strong-armed administration but
also constructed many public buildings and roads. In addition
the Banco Nacional de Costa Rica was founded (1936) and a
government assisted low cost housing program initiated. He
was an unsuccessful candidate for reelection in 1944. See also:
BANCO NACIONAL DE COSTA RICA; LEY DE CASAS BARATAS.
Consult Carlos Calvo Gamboa, León Cortés y su época (1982),
and León Cortés y su tiempo (1969).

CORTES DE CADIZ. During the French captivity of Ferdinand VII
and Napoleon's 1808 intervention the Spanish resistance convoked
a junta of government that sent out a call for elections to a
parliament to establish a constitutional system. The colonies
sent 63 of the 303 members of the first Cortes. Costa Rica
was ably represented by Florencio del *Castillo Solano. The
liberal legislation of the Cortes had a great effect on Costa Rica.

Among other things the *Cortes abolished the *encomienda, *tributos of the *Indians (forced labor), liberalized trade, and opened the port of *Matina for foreign commerce with tax exemptions for ten years. In 1813 it granted *Cartago the title of "Ciudad muy noble y leal," declared *San José a city, and declared *Heredia, *Ujarrás, and *Alajuela to be towns. This was all done in gratitude for Costa Rica's help in putting down a revolution in Nicaragua. These reforms were largely abrogated after the return to power of Ferdinand VII in 1814.

CORTES FERNANDEZ, Otto (1908-1973). Lawyer and son of President León *Cortés Castro. *Deputy 1938-48; 1953-58. President of the Congreso Constitucional 1940-41, and of the Asamblea Legislativa 1956-58.

COSTA RICA. The "rich coast." Although it is mentioned as such in chronicles of *Columbus' discovery on his fourth voyage, the name was not used until 1539 when it was designated Costa Rica by the *Audiencia de Panama, probably because of rumors of great gold deposits.

COSTUMBRISMO. A literary movement that began in the 1890s with the publication of such works as Hojarasca (1891) by Ricardo *Fernández Guardia; La propia (1901) by Manuel *González Zeledón, Chamarasca (1898) by Carlos *Gagini, and El moto (1900) by Joaquín *García Monge. This style incorporated themes from everyday life, mostly in rural areas and uses the everyday speech of the people. Costumbrista style has dominated Costa Rican literature in the twentieth century.

COSTUMBRISTA. In the style of COSTUMBRISMO, q.v.

COTA, Ignacio (b. 1530). Conquistador. He came with *Cavallón in the capacity of *alferez. He was part of the expedition that discovered the central valleys, and the valleys of the *Guarco, Ujarrás, and Orosí rivers. In 1563 he went on an expedition to the Coto and Quepos regions. He also served as *alferez under *Rávago Estrada and Juan Vázquez de Coronado. He had a rebellious nature and was implicated in an uprising in Garcimuñoz. He left the colony and finally settled in San Salvador.

COTO. A Brunka Indian chief.

COTO BRUS. *Canton in the extreme southern part of the country in the highlands bordering on Panama. Originally an Italian settlement, it produces coffee. Its *cabecera is San Vito de Java, founded after Second World War and named after the fourth century Italian saint. The canton was created December 10, 1965, and has a population of 31,650.

COTO WAR, 1921. The disputed region of the Coto Valley (near

*Golfito in *Puntarenas Province) had been awarded to Costa
Rica in arbitration by the president of France (1900). This
was reconfirmed by the *Anderson-Porras Treaty of 1910. But
Costa Rica resented Panamanian officials exercising authority
in what it considered its national territory. As a result it sent
an expeditionary force in February 1921, which was defeated
by Panama in actions in the Coto region of the Pacific coast.
On the Atlantic side Costa Rican forces captured the port of
Almirante. United States intervention halted hostilities. About
three dozen soldiers were killed in the battles. See also: FRON-
TIER QUESTIONS*(SOUTH); LOUBET DECISION; PADILLA CAS-
TRO, Guillermo.

COUNCIL OF THE INDIES. See: CONSEJO DE INDIAS.

COUP D'ETAT (GOLPE DE ESTADO). See: REVOLUTIONS.

COURT OF IMMEDIATE SANCTIONS. A special court created by
the revolutionary *junta to try persons accused of crimes before
and during the 1948 *civil war. Because this court was not part
of the established legal system there was no appeal of its decision.

COXELE. *An Indian chief who befriended Hernán Sánchez de
Badajoz. He was taken prisoner by the vengeful *Governor
Rodrigo de *Contreras and led around on a chain. He managed
to escape and led an uprising against Contreras.

COYOL. A wine made from the sap of a palm tree. Usually made
during the dry season and most typical of *Guanacaste Province.

CREDITO HIPOTECARIO DE COSTA RICA. Government mortgage
bank, created January 20, 1927, with a loan of $100,000 from
the state; it could make loans of up to 50 percent of the value
of property. It had modest success in filling a need for small
loans. Eventually its functions were absorbed by the *Banco
Nacional, Department of Mortgages. See also: BANCO NACIONAL
DE COSTA RICA.

CREOLE (Spanish criollo). Anything or anyone born, bred or
created in the Americas that is not wholly indigenous in origin.
Hence creole cattle (local descendants of the longhorns introduced by the first settlers, as opposed to breeds imported from
England and India in the last 150 years), creole coffee (traditional local varieties) and creole languages (especially Africanized
dialects of European languages, such as the Jamaican *English
spoken by *Blacks in *Limón). Creole whites (or just "Creoles")
were the native-born descendants of Spanish settlers, as opposed
to the peninsulares: European-born immigrants and officials.
[L.H.]

CRUZ, La (canton). Canton in the extreme northwest *Guanacaste

Province along the Nicaraguan border. Created July 23, 1969. Its *cabecera is Ciudad La Cruz and its major product is *cattle. It has 10,876 inhabitants.

CRUZ, Rodrigo de la [Fray]. See: ARIAS MALDONANDO, Rodrigo.

CRUZ GONZALEZ, Manuel de la (b. 1909). *Arte Nuevo painter. Born in *San José and self-educated, although he has also widely traveled in the Americas. He was important in new art movements, being associated with the *vanguardista or abstract school of painting. He was also part of the *Grupo Ocho and directed the *Grupo Taller. De la Cruz has won many awards and has had several shows of his work. He had a great influence in Costa Rican painting. In addition to his painting, De la Cruz has worked in radio theatre and has written short stories, most of which are still unpublished.

CRUZ ZUMBADO, Juan de la. Priest of *Barva who was imprisoned by *Governor *Valderrama and brought before the *Inquisition for trial in 1734. His imprisonment caused the governor to be temporarily excommunicated.

CUBERO MURILLO, Rolando (b. 1957). Artist born in *Barva de Heredia. His paintings are mostly of suffering people with exaggerated movements done mainly in pastel colors. His work seems to have been inspired by Salvador Dalí. One of his paintings was selected for a postage stamp in 1980.

CUBILLO, Diego de. Spanish captain sent by *Governor *Ocón y Trillo to aid the besieged colonists of the *Indian uprising of 1610.

CUBUJUQI. Original name for *Heredia. Founded in 1706 with the construction of a small church in the area now called Lagunilla. See also: HEREDIA.

CUEVA, Fernando de la (1569-1599). *Governor of the province of Costa Rica from 1595 until his death in 1599. This governor was involved in several amorous and financial problems during his stormy administration. De la Cueva was accused of thievery for illegally embargoing a ship. Because of his influence in the *Audiencia de Guatemala, he was allowed to retain his post as governor of Costa Rica.

CUNO COLONIAL. The Royal Mint established 1733 in Guatemala City. See: REAL CUNO DE GUATEMALA.

CURANDERO. A type of homeopath whose homemade cures range from those bordering on a witch doctor's to some knowledge of modern medicine. Most prevalent in the rural areas and among the lower classes of the urban centers.

CURRENCY. See: CACAO; CASTELLANO; CENTAVO; CENTIMO; COLON; DOBLON; DURO; ESCUDO; EXCHANGE RATE; MONETARY REFORM; MARAVEDI; PESO; PESO DURO; PETACA; PLATA QUINTADA; REAL; and also BANKS AND BANKING; BIMETALLISM; COINAGE; GOLD, GOLD STANDARD.

CURRIDABAT. *Canton created August 21, 1929, located about five miles from *San José. Its *cabecera is Curridabat and it produces *coffee. It is developing more and more into a bedroom community for the capital. Present population is 31,954. Original identity as an *Indian pueblo established in the 1570s.

CURTI, Esteban (c. 1751-1825). Italian physician brought to Costa Rica in 1790 by *Governor Vázquez Téllez, as his personal physician. Dr. Curti became the center of a controversy. He was used by Governor Vázquez Téllez as an instrument in his fight to close the Hospital *San Juan de Dios. Curti was accused before the *Inquisition of superchería (mystification). As he was being taken to Havana, Cuba, to serve a prison term, he escaped and found his way to Philadelphia where he lived out his life.

- D -

DAEL, Luis (b. 1927). Artist born in *Heredia. He was a member of the *Grupo Ocho and in 1970 received first prize in a contest to pick a design to be used for a postage stamp. His style ranges from realism to abstraction. He has had several exhibitions of his work.

DAIRY FARMING. See: CATTLE; MONTEVERDE.

DAVILA, Pedrarias (Pedro Arias de Avila). See: PEDRARIAS.

DAVILA SOLERA, Luis (1872-1948). Lawyer and president of the Supreme Court, 1935.

DAVIS, Charles Henry [Captain]. Commander of the U.S.S. Santa María. He offered his services as mediator after the surrender of William *Walker in 1857. He actually escorted Walker from *San Juan del Sur, Nicaragua to Panama.

DEATH PENALTY. Abolished for all crimes except treason in 1871, and completely abolished in 1882. See also: SOLORZANO DE GUARDIA, Emilia.

DEATH RATE. See: BIRTH AND DEATH RATES.

DEBRAVO, Jorge (1938-1967). Poet born in *Turrialba. When he was killed in a tragic motorcycle accident, Debravo was beginning

to be acknowledged as a leading young poet. His protest style
of poetry fit in with the *Círculo de Poetas Costarricenses,
of which he was a prime mover. Debravo shared a national
poetry prize in 1966 for his Nosotros los hombres. Other works
are: Milagro abierto (1951), Consejo para Cristo al comenzar el
año (1960), and Devocionario de amor sexual (1963).

DEBT. See: FOREIGN DEBT.

DECIMALIZATION. See: COINAGE.

DEMOCRATIC PARTY. See: PARTIDO DEMOCRATA.

DENGO, Juan. Captain in the Spanish army. Lieutenant *governor
of the province of Costa Rica in military matters January–February
1819. He supported *independence and Costa Rica's joining
*Iturbide's Mexican Empire. During the first *civil war he fought
on the side of *Cartago. It was he who actually gave the order
that started the fighting at *Ochomogo. After the war Dengo
was imprisoned a few months, then exiled. He was pardoned
in 1827 because of his age and the poverty of his family.

DENGO GUERRERO, Omar (1888-1928). Educator and essayist.
Director of the *Liceo de Costa Rica, and the *Escuela Normal
Nacional 1919-1928. Exercised a great influence in his efforts
to elevate the general level of pedagogy in the country. Among
his disciples are Joaquín *García Monge, Roberto *Brenes Mesén,
and Elias *Jiménez Rojas. A collection of his works was published
under the title Escritos y discursos (1961).

DENT, John (d. 1842). He was born in Newcastle, England and
came to Costa Rica in the 1820s. Initially he was involved with
the mining industry and eventually he established a cloth weaving
mill near *Cartago City. He is the founder of the Dent Family.
Barrio Dent is a *San José neighborhood on former family land.

DEPUTY (diputado). Name generally given to the members of the
national legislature. See: LEGISLATIVE ASSEMBLY (Asamblea
Legislativa).

DESAGUADERO. Original name for the San Juan River.

DESAMPARADOS. *Canton about three miles from *San José known
for its *coffee, *sugar, grains, and porcine products. Its
*cabecera is Desamparados. It was created August 7, 1868,
and has a population of 108,824.

DIARIO DE COSTA RICA. (1) Morning newspaper originally founded
in 1885.
        (2) Reestablished in 1920. During the 1940s it was the
instrument of Otilio *Ulate and the forces opposed to President

*Calderón Guardia. It ceased publication for financial reasons in 1965.

(3) For a short period it resumed publication in 1970, under totally different ownership and editorial policy.

DIEZ NAVARRO, Luis (1699-1780). Interim governor of the province 1748-50. During his term of office the government cooperated with Bishop *Bullon y Figuero to force people to concentrate in towns by burning people's houses in the country.

DIEZMO. See: TITHES.

DIOCESE OF NICARAGUA AND COSTA RICA. A diocese was created in León, Nicaragua, by Clement VIII on February 26, 1531. At that time Costa Rica was dependent on the Diocese of Panama. By a royal decree (1545), Costa Rica was incorporated into the Diocese of Nicaragua, which became known as the Diocese of Nicaragua and Costa Rica. There were 39 bishops of which only 11 actually visited Costa Rica, the first being Bishop Pedro *Villarreal, in 1608. After independence there was pressure that a separate diocese be created for Costa Rica; this was ultimately done in 1850.

DIPUTACION DE COSTA RICA. Also called the *Triumvirate. It was a three-man council that replaced the *Junta Superior Gubernativa on March 20, 1823. It was headed by Rafael Osejo, but encountered strong opposition from the *imperialists, and ceased to function with the outbreak of the first *civil war (March 29, 1823). See also: CIVIL WARS; JUNTA SUPERIOR GUBERNATIVA; OSEJO, Rafael Francisco; RAMIREZ CASTRO, Gregorio José.

DIPUTACION PROVINCIAL. A form of government established by the *Cortes de Cádiz in which Costa Rica and Nicaragua were combined into one province. It consisted of a council of seven people and three substitutes, presided over by the chief officer of the province. Councilors were elected for four-year terms at staggered intervals. Their function was to supervise finances and disbursement of public funds, further education, report abuses of the public treasury to the governor, gather statistical information on the province, and report any infractions of the 1812 Constitution to the Cortes. This reform never took effect before independence a few years after.

DIPUTADO. A *deputy, or member of the national legislature. See: LEGISLATIVE ASSEMBLY (Asamblea Legislativa).

DIQUIS. Synonym of the BRUNKAS, q.v. and the Rio TERRABA, q.v.

DIRIANGEN. Nicaraguan *Indian chief. In 1513 he plotted to kill

Gil *González de Avila and his party of explorers by feigning that he would present his people for baptism, but at the same time planning to ambush the Spaniards.

DISTRITO. Subdivision of a *canton, headed by a jefe político, appointed by the president of the Republic. There are over 400 organized districts in Costa Rica.

DOBLES, Fabián (b. 1918). Poet and novelist who specializes in writing about social problems. Most important works are: Ese que llaman pueblo (1941), Los leños vivientes (1962), Verdad de agua y del viento (1947), El sitio de las abras (1950), Historia de tata mundo (1955), Yerbamar (1961/in collaboration with Mario Picado), and En el San Juan hay tiburón (1967).

DOBLES, Gonzalo (b. 1904). Lawyer and judge. He served as a judge of the Supreme Court of the Republic and wrote various novels and poems, most of which deal with his native *Heredia Province. Most important published works are: La voz de la campaña (1927), Jardines olvidados (1929), Estampas del camino (1933), and the prize winning La raíz profunda (1956).

DOBLES SEGREDA, Luis (1891-1956). Investigator, diplomat, novelist. Director of several colegios, secretary of education, and minister to France. Among his more important novels is Caña brava (1926). His most important historical work is the nine-volume Indice bibliográfico de Costa Rica (1927-36).

DOBLES YZAGUIRRE, Julieta (b. 1943). Poet born in *San José. She was one of the leaders in the *Círculo de Poetas Costarricenses. Her most important works are: Reloj de siempre (1965), El peso vivo (1968), Hora de lejanza (1982), and Los pasos terrestres (1976).

DOBLON. A colonial unit of currency. Originally worth two castellanos, hence the name. It had various values which changed over the course of time. It was generally a name used for multiple escudos and was adapted by Philip II in 1537 as a unit of currency. There were many varieties of doubloons after that date. Doubloons were also called macacos (or pieces of eight) because of their value (eight reales) and irregular shape. The coin continued in circulation until the 1863 decimalization of the coinage. Anthony *Trollope gives its 1858 value as Ь3 8s (circa $16).

DOMINICAL. Tiny Pacific Coast port at 9°16'N, 83°52'W. See: PLAN SUNDAY.

DOTA. *Canton in the extreme eastern part of *San José Province. Its *cabecera is Santa María and it produces *coffee, wood, grains, and some wine. It was created July 23, 1925, and its present population is 4,934. During the 1948 *civil war, some of the most important fighting took place within this canton.

DOUBLOON. See: DOBLON.

DRUGS. Smuggling of cocaine by air to the United States from South America became a crisis in the 1980s. Marijuana use is a long-standing problem. See: CARO QUINTERO, Rafael; and consult William E. Carter, ed., Cannabis in Costa Rica; A Study of Chronic Marihuana Use. [G.K.]

DUI Y MEXICANOS. See: DUY Y MEXICANOS (Province of).

DUNCAN, Quince (b. 1940). A black writer and intellectual from *Limón. One of the few of his race to achieve prominence in Costa Rican letters. His most important works are: El pozo y una carta (1969), Bronce (1970), Una canción el la madrugada (1970) and with Carlos Meléndez, El Negro en Costa Rica (1972), Hombres curtidos (1971), El Negro en la literatura costarricense (1975), La paz del pueblo (1978), and Final de calle (1978).

DUNLOP, Robert Glasgow (1815-1847). Scottish Presbyterian merchant who visited Central America 1844. In 1847 he published his Travels in Central America, an important source of information on the period.

DURAN AYANEGUI, Fernando (b. 1939). Educator, scientist, and novelist. He has a doctorate in sciences and began service as rector of the *Universidad de Costa Rica in 1980. His most important novels are: Dos reales y otros cuentos (1961) and El último que duermo (1976), which deals with parapsychological themes.

DURAN CARTIN, Carlos (1852-1924). Physician and politician. Studied medicine in England. Founder of the Asilo Chapuí and the tuberculosis sanitarium called "Dr. Durán." He was also rector of the *Universidad de Santa Tomás and president of Congress. He assumed the presidency of the Republic (November 7, 1889) after a demonstration against electoral fraud provoked the resignation of Bernardo *Soto Alfaro. He served until the end of Soto's term (May 8, 1890) and used his office to ensure a free election 1889. He was declared *Benemérito de la Patria in 1949.

DURO (or peso duro). A monetary unit of the colonial period, worth ten reales.

DUSI, Marco (b. 1927). Born and educated in Milano, Italy. He migrated to Chile where he was professor of choral music. He was brought to Costa Rica in 1972 to help formulate the chorus of the National Symphony Orchestra. He remained in Costa

Rica until 1979. See also: CORO DE LA ORQUESTA
NACIONAL.

DUVERRAN, Carlos Rafael (b. 1935). Poet and professor of literature. His most important works are: Paraíso en la tierra
(1953), Lujosa lejanía (1958), Poemas del corazón hecho verano
y tiempo delirante (1963), and the prize winning Redención del
día (1971). He also edited an anthology of poetry: Poesía
contemporánea de Costa Rica (1973). His latest work is Estaciones de los sueños (1981).

DUY Y MEXICANOS (Province of). A province created in Talamanca
by the *Audiencia de Guatemala with the specific purpose of
appointing Gonzalo Vazquez de Coronado as its governor to compensate him for his father's financial losses on earlier expeditions.
But because of the rivalry between Vázquez de Coronado and
*Governor Ocón y Trillo, Costa Rica claimed that it had built
the fortress of Santiago and therefore had prior rights to the
area in 1610 under Diego Sojo but because of Sojo's cruel treatment of the *Indians they revolted and Sojo's forces had to
be rescued by another expedition. Talamanca and the fortress
of Santiago were abandoned and the province of Duy y Mexicanos
ceased to exist. See also: OCON Y TRILLO, Juan de; SOJO,
Diego de; SANTIAGO DE TALAMANCA; TALAMANCA; VAZQUEZ
DE CORONADO, Juan.

- E -

EARTHQUAKES. Central America is particularly prone to earthquakes because several major fault lines criss-cross the area.
In Costa Rica frequent seismic movements are caused by the
movement of two plates off the Pacific Coast. They are called
the "Caribbean Plate" and the "Cocos Plate." Each one moving
in a different direction has caused Costa Rica to suffer many
earthquakes throughout the centuries. The worst ones occurred
in 1841 and 1910, each of which destroyed the city of *Cartago.
Dates and data of major seismic movements are as follows: (Earthquakes were originally named after the saint's day on which
they occurred.)

DATE	PARTICULARS
July 14, 1756	Tremor of San Buenaventura.
February 22, 1798	Tremor in *Matina.
May 7, 1822	Earthquake in San Estanislao.
September 2, 1841	Severe earthquake which destroyed the city of *Cartago.
April 13, 1910	A strong shock which shook the city of *San José.
May 4, 1910	Second destruction of the city of *Cartago.
March 4, 1924	Earthquake felt in the central part of the

	country, and in the *San Ramón and *Orotina area. Reported to be 7.0 on the Richter scale.
December 21, 1939	Earthquake felt in the *Golfito area. No damage was reported due to the sparse population at that time. It was reported 7.3 on the Richter scale.
October 5, 1950	Earthquake in the *Guanacaste and Los *Chiles zone. Recorded as 7.7 on the Richter scale.
April 2, 1983	Earthquake felt principally in the *Osa region, but also in other parts of the country. Reported as 7.2 on the the Richter scale.
July 3, 1983	A strong tremor in the *Pérez Zeledón zone. Recorded as 5.7 on the Richter scale.

ECHANDI, Enrique (1866-1959). Painter. He founded a school of fine arts in *San José. Echandi studied in Germany (1887-1897) and is considered the first Costa Rican painter to have seriously studied *painting in Europe. He greated influenced art in Costa Rica during the first half of the twentieth century.

ECHANDI JIMENEZ, Mario (b. 1915). Lawyer and politician. Ambassador to the United States 1950-51, foreign minister 1951-53, *deputy 1953-58. During his term in the Assembly he became an outstanding leader of the anti-*Figueres Ferrer forces. He was elected president of the Republic for the term 1958-62. During his term of office he tried to conduct a conciliatory government, despite the opposition of the Legislative Assembly. The most important accomplishments of his administration were the "Plan Vial," for improvement of the antiquated road system, and the "Ley de Desarrollo y Fomento Industrial," which encouraged foreign investments. Echandi helped organize the National Unification Party (*Partido Unificación Nacional) and ran unsuccessfully for reelection to the presidency in 1970 and 1982. He is the son of Alberto *Echandi Montero.

ECHANDI MONTERO, Alberto (1870-1944). Lawyer and politician. Active in directing the *San Juan de Dios Hospital. Minister of treasury, commerce and public works 1909 and 1914-15; treasury and commerce in the government of Julio *Acosta García, and foreign relations under *Calderón Guardia. In 1920 his mediation averted a war between Nicaragua and Honduras and he negotiated the treaty with Panama in 1941 which settled the long-smoldering boundary question. See: ECHANDI MONTERO-FERNANDEZ JAEN TREATY; FRONTIER QUESTIONS (SOUTH). Candidate for the presidency for the Partido Agrícola, and seemed to have the advantage in a disputed election (1923). When faced with possible violence he withdrew his candidacy saying: "The

presidency is not worth a drop of blood of even one Costa Rican."
Declared *Benemérito de la Patria 1944.

ECHANDI MONTERO-FERNANDEZ JAEN TREATY (1941). The treaty
that formally settled the disputed border questions between
Panama and Costa Rica. It granted Panama most of the area
it claimed in the Atlantic side and Costa Rica was given most
of the area it claimed in the Pacific zone. See also: COTO
WAR; FRONTIER QUESTIONS (SOUTH).

ECHAUZ, Juan de. *Governor 1624-30. During his incumbency he
undertook the conquest of the *Voto and *Brunka Indians.

ECHEVERRIA ALVARADO, Francisco (1885-1966). President of the
House of Representatives 1869-70 and member of the Constituent
Assembly in 1880.

ECHEVERRIA LORIA, Arturo (1909-1966). Poet and essayist. He
resided for many years in Mexico and the United States. He
founded the review Brecha. His most important works are:
Poesías (1937), Fuego y tierra (1963), Himno a la esperanza
(1965) and De artes y letras; opiniones y comentarios (1972).

ECHEVERRIA ZELEDON, Aquileo J. (1866-1909). Poet. He was
called "The national poet of Costa Rica" by Rubén Darío. The
yearly national prize for poetry is named for him. He wrote
largely of the common people (*conchos) using their language
and customs. His most important works are: Concherías (1905)
and Romances (1903).

ECO CATOLICO. Weekly newspaper published by the Costa Rican
Catholic Church.

ECONOMY, The. Costa Rica was easily the poorest of Spain's
Central American colonies: at the nadir of its prosperity in
the mid 18th century the inhabitants were said to make their
clothes from tree-bark. In a mainly subsistence economy, the
first cash-crop was *cacao, of which a little was exported to
Nicaragua, and much more traded illegally with foreign ships
(who sold it in England). The next export crop was *tobacco,
mainly for a decade or so from 1787 when Costa Rica was given
the monopoly of supply for the estanco (government retail tobacco
monopoly) throughout the *Audiencia of Guatemala. The product
for which the country is most famous, *coffee, became important
from the 1820s. When the *Ferrocarril de Norte was built to
facilitate the steadily increasing coffee exports, its builder,
Minor C. *Keith introduced *bananas as a crop to plant on land
near the railway that was unsuited for coffee. From the 1930s
the bananas were hit by Panama disease and production was
transferred to the Pacific coast. For some years the old banana
plantations were simply abandoned, but in the Second World War

they were planted with Manila hemp to satisfy the demand for
*fiber created by the Japanese occupation of the Philippines.
Later, other new crops were introduced on such lands, notably
the African oil palm (see: AFRICAN PALM OIL). The creation
of the Central American Common Market (MERCOMUN, q.v.)
in the post-war years encouraged the growth of light industry
(processed foods, cement, fuel oil, textiles, tires, fertilizers,
paints, pharmaceuticals, furniture), made possible by the government investment in hydroelectric plants. The need to decrease dependence on imports now that Costa Rica was developing a chronic adverse trade balance (see: BALANCE OF PAY-
MENTS) led to increased beef production from the 1960s (see:
CATTLE), and the development of dairy farming and the *fishing industry. The growth of manufacturing and the tendency
to less labor intensive forms of agriculture (such as ranching)
reduced the percentage of the labor force employed in agriculture from 51% in 1960 to 38% in 1985 (with 12% in manufacturing,
21% in services and 18.2% in commerce). Mining has had an
intermittent success. It is hoped to develop bauxite as more
hydroelectric power becomes available. A number of other
metallic ores have been found, but only *gold and small quantities of silver are currently being mined. The Mexican state
petroleum concern, PEMEX, has done some prospecting for oil,
but without success. Costa Rica's recent economic history has
been dominated by financial problems. The adverse trade balance is exacerbated by the need to service the very large *foreign debt. The government's budget deficit has been reduced,
but only by the temporary expedient of privatization. The year
1982 was a particularly bad one with 81.7% inflation, 9.9% urban
employment and a negative 7.3% growth in the gross domestic
product (in a country still noted for its very high rate of population growth). There has been some improvement since. Inflation in 1987 was down to 16.4%, and urban unemployment down
to 5.6%; GDP grew, but only by 3%. [L.H.]
See also: EXPORTS; FOREIGN TRADE; IMPORTS.

EDITOR CONSTITUCIONAL, El. A pro-independence colonial newspaper published in Guatemala by Pedro *Molina. Consult Richard
E. Moore, Historical Dictionary of Guatemala (1967), p. 95.

EDITORIAL. See: PUBLISHING for various printing outlets for
books.

EDUCATION. Colonial Costa Rica had only a few elementary schools.
Until the late 18th century, when some small individual classes
came into existence, secondary education had to be sought in
Nicaragua or Guatemala. In 1812 the *Casa de Enseñanza de
Santo Tomás was formed, followed in 1824 by the *Casa de Enseñanza Pública. The first public education law, May 4, 1832,
declared education obligatory from ages 8 to 14, and the 1869
constitution included a commitment to free, state supported,

compulsory education, but effective implementation came only in the 1880s (see: EDUCATION LAWS). In 1888 Costa Rica had some 20,000 pupils attending 300 primary schools. In 1915 there were 34,703 primary school pupils, and in 1920 teachers received life tenure. A decree of November 16, 1869 had given munici- palities the right to create secondary schools, but as late as 1902 it was being seriously argued that education at the secondary level was no business of the state, and its provision was not definitively accepted until 1914. By 1950 there were 108,000 pupils in school, 105,635 of them in primary schools. By 1979 these totals had grown to 546,073 and 347,649, respectively. The best summary is Chapter 8 in Biesanz, Los costarricenses. [L.H.] See also:

COLEGIO SAN LUIS GONZAGA
CONSEJO SUPERIOR DE EDUCATION
CONSERVATORIO DE CASTELLA
DENGO G., Omar
ESCUELA DE ARTE Y DECORACION
ESCUELA DE CRISTO
ESCUELA NORMAL
FACIO, Justo
FERNANDEZ ACUNA, Mauro
FERNANDEZ FERRAZ, Juan
FERNANDEZ FERRAZ, Valeriano
GONZALEZ FLORES, Luis Felipe
JIMENEZ ZAMORA, Jesús de
KRAUSISM
LICEO DE COSTA RICA
LICEO DE NINAS
LIENDO Y GOICOCHECA, José A.
LIRA, Carmen
LITERACY
MACAYA LAHMAN, Enrique
MONGE ALFARO, Carlos
NATIONAL LIBRARY
NATIONAL UNIVERSITY
OROZCO CASORLA, José Maria
PLAN NACIONAL DE DESARROLLO EDUCATIVO
QUESADA SALAZAR, Napoleón
SEGREDA ZAMORA, Vicente
UNIVERSIDAD AUTONOMA DE CENTRO AMERICA (UACA)
UNIVERSIDAD DE COSTA RICA
UNIVERSIDAD DE SANTO TOMAS
UNIVERSIDAD NACIONAL DE COSTA RICA
UNIVERSITY FOR PEACE
VOLIO JIMENEZ, Jorge

EDUCATION LAWS. (1) LEY FUNDAMENTAL DE INSTRUCCION PUBLICA (August 12, 1885). One of the *liberal laws promoted by Minister of Education Mauro *Fernández Acuña. It established a basis for secular education and laid the groundwork for the

more comprehensive Ley General de Educación Común (1886).
(2) LEY GENERAL DE EDUCACION COMUN (February 26,
1886). Probably the most important of the *liberal laws enacted
under the aegis of Minister of Education Mauro *Fernández Acuña.
This law implanted free, primary education for children between
seven and fourteen years of age, and set up the first *escuela
normal. It established scholastic zones, in which at least one
school for both sexes had to be established. It also established
local "Juntas de Educación" to supervise the schools as well as
other administrative offices. Under this law various subsequent
decrees were issued which among other things: established
regulation for public instruction, a scholastic treasury (to administer funds), and finally the closing of the moribund "Universidad de Santo Tomás (June 1, 1886). This law has been
called the cornerstone of Costa Rican democracy and probably
accounts for much of the high literacy in the country. As a
result education was declared free, secular, and compulsory.
(3) LEY FUNDAMENTAL DE EDUCATION (September 1957).
This law sought to make educational programs, such as voca-
tional training and modernizing the basic educational approach.
It also sought to bring textbooks more in line with the realities
of Costa Rican culture. These reforms had their inception with
the ideas of the *Centro para Estudios de Problemas Nacionales
in the 1940s, the basic philosophy of the National Liberation
Party (*Partido Liberación Nacional) and the then Minister of
Education Uladislao Gómez Pittman (1952), the reforms of the
Liceo Renovado in Chile, and an educational seminar in Santiago
de Chile in 1954. Consult Carlos Monge Alfaro, Educación para
la democracia en el mundo convulso (1963).

EFFINGER, Max (1893-1955). Engineer. A German citizen who
during the 1930s was the director general in the Ministry of
Public Works. He was given the task of determining if prospective immigrants were or were not Jewish. He was finally interned
during Second World War when Costa Rica declared war on the
Axis powers. Important as an example of pro-German sentiment
during that era. After the war he returned to Costa Rica and
died in *San José in 1955.

EISENACH. A German ship scuttled by its crew in *Puntarenas
harbor, 1941, along with an Italian freighter, the Fella. It
blocked *Puntarenas harbor for a few months and helped foment
the anti-Axis sentiment in the country.

ELECTIONS. Although Costa Rica has had the form of free elections for many years, they have frequently been questionable
and the institution of free elections with alternability of government was not really established until after the 1948 civil war.
Until 1913 voters selected an electoral college. Frequently no
candidate received a plurality and the president had to be selected by the National Congress. This process frequently led

to various abuses and violence. The following list includes
the candidates, political parties, and approximate results of
the elections since 1913. In the following tabulation these ab-
breviations are used to indicate political affiliation: BOC is
*Bloque de Obreros y Campesinos, *BV is Bloque de la Victoria,
FN is Frente Nacional, MN is Movimiento Nacional, OST is Organización Socialista de Trabajadores, PA is Partido Agrícola,
PASO is Partido Acción Demócrata, PCG *Partido Confraternidad
Guanacasteco, PCo is *Partido Constitucional, PD is *Partido
Demócrata, PDC is *Partido Demócrata Cristiano, PI is *Partido
Independiente, PLN is *Partido Liberación Nacional, PN is *Par-
tido Nacional, PNa is Partido Nacionalista, PNI is *Partido Na-
cional Independiente, PP is Partido "Peliquista," PPCoa is Par-
tido Pueblo Coalición, PR is *Partido Republicano, PRN is Par-
tido Republicano Nacional, PRf is *Partido Reformista, PRnD
is Partido Renovación Democrática, PSC is Partido Socialista
Costarricense, PU is *Partido Unidad, PUC is *Partido Unión
Católica, PUfN is *Partido Unificación Nacional, PUN is Partido
Unión Nacional, PUSC is *Partido Unidad Social Cristiana, UCoa
is Unidad Coalición.

1913:	Máximo *Fernández Alvarado	PR	27,000
	Carlos *Durán Cartin	PUN	22,000
	Rafael *Yglesias Castro	PUC	18,000
1917:	Federico *Tinoco Granado	PP	58,000
1919:	Julio *Acosta García	PCo	45,000
	José María Soto	PD	5,000
1923:	Ricardo *Jiménez Oreamuno	PR	29,000
	Alberto *Echandi Montero	PA	25,000
	Jorge *Volio Jiménez	PRf	14,000
1928:	Cleto *González Víquez	PUN	42,000
	Carlos María Jiménez Ortiz	PUN	30,000
1932:	Ricardo *Jiménez Oreamuno	PRN	35,000
	Manuel Castro Quesada	PUN	22,000
	Carlos María Jiménez Ortiz	PR	17,000
	Maximiliano *Koberg Bolandi	PNa	3,000
1936:	León *Cortés Castro	PRN	91,000
	Octavio *Beeche Agüero	PN	30,200
	Carlos Luis Sáenz	BOC	4,500
1940:	Rafael Angel *Calderón Guardia	PRN	91,000
	Manuel *Mora Valverde	BOC	10,700
	Virgilio *Salazar Leiva	PCG	6,300
1944:	Teodoro *Picado Michalski	BV	90,400
	León *Cortés Castro	PD	46,443
1948:	Otilio *Ulate Blanco	PUN	54,931
	Rafael Angel *Calderón Guardia	PRN	46,443

1953:	José María *Figueres Ferrer	PLN	123,444
	Fernando *Castro Cervantes	PD	67,324
1958:	Mario *Echandi Jiménez	PUN	102,851
	Francisco *Orlich Bolmarcich	PLN	94,788
	Jorge *Rossi Chavarría	PI	23,910
1966:	José Joaquín *Trejos Fernández	PUfN	222,810
	Daniel *Oduber Quirós	PLN	218,590
1970:	José María *Figueres Ferrer	PLN	295,883
	Mario *Echandi Jiménez	PUfN	222,372
	Virgilio *Calvo Sánchez	FN	9,554
	Lisimaco *Leiva Cubillo	PASO	7,221
	Jorge Arturo *Monge Zamora	PDC	5,015
1974:	Daniel *Oduber Quirós	PLN	294,609
	Fernando Trejos Escalante	PUfN	206,149
	Jorge González Martén	PNI	77,788
	Rodrigo *Carazo Odio	PRnD	61,820
	Gerardo Wesceslao Villalobos	PD	18,832
	Manuel *Mora Valverde	PASO	16,081
	Jorge Arturo *Monge Zamora	PDC	3,461
	José Francisco *Aguilar Bulgarelli	PSC	3,417
1978:	Rodrigo *Carazo Odio	PU	419,824
	Luis Alberto *Monge Alvarez	PLN	364,285
	Rodrigo Gutiérrez Sáenz	PUnido	22,740
	Guillermo Villalobos Arce	PUfN	13,666
	Jorge González Martén	PNI	3,323
	Carlos Coronado Vargas	OST	1,868
	Rodrigo Cordero Víquez	PD	1,512
1982:	Luis Alberto *Monge Alvarez	PLN	568,374
	Rafael Angel *Calderón Guardia	UCoa	325,187
	Mario *Echandi Jiménez	MN	37,127
	Rodrigo Gutiérrez	PPCoa	32,186
	Edwin *Chacón	PI	1,955
	Edwin Retana	PD	1,744
1986:	Oscar *Arias Sánchez	PLN	620,314
	Rafael Angel *Calderón Fournier	PUSC	542,434
	Other parties:		
	Alianza Popular		9,099
	Pueblo Unido		6,599
	P. Alianza Nacional Cristiana		5,647
	*Partido Independiente		1,129

ELECTRIC POWER. Turned on August 9, 1884 in *San José. See:
INSTITUTO COSTARRICENSE DE ELECTRICIDAD.

ELIZONDO ARCE, Hernán (b. 1921). Novelist and one of the first
poets from his native *Guanacaste Province to achieve national
prominence. He writes about the lives, customs, and problems

of the poor people of his province. His most important works
are: Memoria de un pobre diablo, which won a national prize
in 1964. Other works are: La ciudad y la sombra (1971) and
La calle, Jinete y yo (1975), El Santo, el niño y el mar (1980),
and Muerte de amanecer (1982).

EMPALME, Battle of El (March 14-15, 1948). A point located south
of *Cartago City on the Inter-American highway at the turnoff
to La *Lucha Sin Fin, farm of José *Figueres. A battle took
place at this point when government forces tried to advance
on La Lucha. The government lost troops and material while
the insurgents' victory gave them control of the mountainous
area of the *cantons of *Dota and *Pérez Zeledón. This provided them with a solid base for operations against *Cartago
City.

EMPRESITO FRANCES (1911). A loan of 35 million French francs at
5 percent interest which was to be used to pay the country's
internal debt. It was renegotiated in 1925. In 1948 Fcs. 5,826,500
was still outstanding, and in default.

ENCISO HITA, Bartolomé (1600-1639). Lieutenant *governor for a
few months in 1634 after the death of Governor *Villalta. Also
*corregidor of *Tierra Adentro (*Talamanca).

ENCOMIENDA. A system in the colonial era in which a number of
*Indians were distributed (see: REPARTIMIENTO) to work in
the land of a conquistador and be taught the Christian faith.
In practice it was a system of slavery which lent itself to some
of the worst abuses of the Spanish colonial system. The government tried to eliminate it by royal decree in 1720, but the system
endured in one form or another until the end of the colonial
period. In Costa Rica it was not entrenched as in other colonies
because of the scarcity of Indians. However, it contributed
to the decimation of the Indians. See: INDIANS and consult
Rafael A. Bolaños (Thesis, 1981).

ENGLISH. The West Indians brought in to work on the *banana
plantations (see: BLACKS) brought with them their *creole
English. This still survives to some extent in the *Limón area,
mostly among the older generation--an estimated 50,000 speakers
in 1977--; it is heavily hispanicized. [L.H.]

ENGLISH LOANS. See: BRITISH LOANS.

ENTA (Empresa Nacional de Transportes Aéreos). Pioneer airline
founded by Bill Schoenfeldt, March 2, 1932, and absorbed in
1940 by Compañía de *Taca de Costa Rica. See: AVIATION.
[L.H.]

ENTERTAINMENT TAX. Since 1975, Costa Rica has had a 6%

entertainment tax, used for cultural purposes. Thirty percent of it goes to the *Compañía Nacional de Teatro, six percent to the *Museo de Arte Costarricense, and fifty percent to the *Teatro Nacional itself. [L.H.]

ESCALANTE, Gregorio. Special representative in Chile (1856) who negotiated the loans to finance the war against William *Walker. See also: CHILEAN LOAN.

ESCALANTE, Manuel (d. 1847). Director of postal services and vice-president of the Constituent Assembly of 1823. He also served as president of the Representative Council in September, 1831.

ESCALANTE, Manuela [Srta.] (1816-1849). During the nineteenth century she was respected as one of Costa Rica's leading intellectuals. This was unusual in those times when women did not participate in public life. She has been called the first feminist in Costa Rica.

ESCALANTE NAVAS, Juan Vicente (b. 1804). *Deputy 1833-37. Consejero 1835-37 and involved in a conspiracy against Manuel *Aguilar Chacón. Commander of the Costa Rican troops in the federal army. He was exiled in 1840 because of his implication in a plot against Braulio *Carrillo Colina. He returned to the country and became active in politics. He served as acting president of the Republic April 17 to June 30, 1858 and April 13 to May 4, 1859.

ESCALANTE NAVAS, Napoleón. President of the House of Representatives (August 1863), and member of the Constituent Assemblies of 1869 and 1870.

ESCALANTE NAVAS, Rafael (1801-1862). Politician. Ranking officer of the Costa Rican contingent in the Central American Army. Later he was a member of Braulio *Carrillo Colina's cabinet, but was exiled in 1840 because of his complicity in a plot against the government. Escalante also occupied such posts as representative to the Central American Diet in Sonsonate (El Salvador), vice-president of the Republic, and acting president of the Congress (1857-59).

ESCAZU. *Canton in *San José Province, a picturesque and wealthy suburb of the capital. It is known in local folklore for witchcraft. Its *cabecera is Escazú. The canton was created December 7, 1848. Its population is 33,101.

ESCOCESES (Scotsmen). A group of people or "party" who supposedly favored the election of Manuel *Aguilar Chacón in the 1833 election. The term supposedly originated out of an internal conflict within the Masonic lodges. There is now some doubt that this term was actually used at that time. See: YORKINOS.

ESCUDO DE ORO. A colonial coin that received its name from the shield of the royal coat of arms. Its value varied, but in Spain it was worth one-half doubloon or four reales.

ESCUELA DE ARTE Y DECORACION (ESEMPI). An art school founded in 1955 under the leadership of the painter José Francisco *Alvarado Abella. It gives classes in both theoretical and practical aspects of various art forms.

ESCUELA DE ARTES MUSICALES. After the closing of the National Conservatory of Music, the University of Costa Rica established it (1941) as its music school.

ESCUELA DE CRISTO. A school opened in 1782 as a result of the efforts of Bishop *Tristán. It taught Latin, grammar, morality, philosophy. It was established primarily to provide preliminary training for the priesthood. The school became engaged in a conflict as to where it would hold its classes since the same building was needed for a hospital.

ESCUELA DE MUSICA SANTA CECILIA. A school of music which functioned in *San José from 1894-1956. It was tantamount to a national conservatory of music, but with limited facilities.

ESCUELA NACIONAL DE BELLAS ARTES. Founded (March 14, 1897) under the leadership of the Spaniard Tomás Povedano. It was incorporated into the *Universidad de Costa Rica in 1940. See also: ECHANDI, Enrique.

ESCUELA NORMAL. Training college for school teachers. The first such was established in the Ley General de Educación Común of 1885 (see: EDUCATION LAWS).
    See also: DENGO GUERRERO, Oscar; GARCIA MONGE, Joaquín; GONZALEZ FLORES, Alfredo.

ESPARTA. See: ESPARZA.

ESPARZA (city). Located in the province of *Puntarenas, with a current population of 9,649. It was founded by *Anguciana de Gamboa in 1574 with the name of Espíritu Santo de Esparza. It began to be an important center in the colonial period and was a prosperous *cattle region until the invasion of English *pirates. The invasion of 1685 and 1686 forced the population to seek the relative security of the highlands and Esparza began to decline.

ESPARZA (canton). *Canton in *Puntarenas Province whose *cabecera is Esparza City. Originally created a canton December 7, 1848, as Esparza. Name changed to Esparta September 3, 1879; changed back to original Esparza in 1974. It is in a zone of about 900 feet above sea level and produces *cattle, grain, and fruit. The present population is 14,998 (including the city of Esparza).

ESPINACH, Olga. See: CASA DEL ARTISTA.

ESPINACH ESCALANTE, Carlos (1918-   ). Engineer. *Deputy 1962-66, president of the Legislative Assembly 1962. He was also first minister of transportation.

ESPINOSA, Gaspar (1484-1537). Conquistador and lawyer. He formed part of *Pedrarias expedition to Darién (1514) and was a cofounder of the city of Panamá (1519). He explored the Gulf of *Nicoya region and later became oidor in Santo Domingo. Later he tried to reconcile differences between Pizarro and Almagro in Peru.

ESPINOSA, Rudy (b. 1953). Engraver. His works have won several national prizes. His style is symbolic of everyday things. Some of his works are: "A.M.," "Rutina," and "Ciclo."

ESPIRITUALISTAS. A conservative faction within the Costa Rican Catholic Church which during the 1930s favored concentrating on spiritual rather than social problems. Consult James Backer, La iglesia y el sindicalismo en Costa Rica (1978).

ESQUIPULAS. See: ARIAS PLAN; SANTO CRISTO DE ESQUIPULAS.

ESQUIVEL AZOFEIFA, José María (1770-1835). Priest. He was president of Congress May-July 1830.

ESQUIVEL IBARRA, Ascención (1847-1923). Lawyer and politician. Born in Rivas, Nicaragua. President of the Supreme Court 1917-20. Unsuccessful presidential candidate for the 1902-06 term of office, he tried to conduct a conciliatory government despite a crisis caused by a sharp drop of *coffee prices.

ESQUIVEL SAENZ, Aniceto (1824-1898). Lawyer and politician. Served in various ministries, the Consejo de Estado 1870. Elected to the presidency for the term 1876-80, he incurred the enmity of the military by his conciliatory efforts to avoid war with Nicaragua over *frontier questions. He was overthrown by a group headed by General Tomás *Guardia Gutiérrez (November 1876). He later served as President of Congress 1886-89 and May-June 1891.

ESTADO LIBRE DE COSTA RICA. Official name of the country (1825-1844), the years that it was affiliated with the *Central American Federation.

ESTADOS UNIDOS DE CENTRO AMERICA. An attempt by Honduras, Nicaragua, and El Salvador to strengthen the *Republica Mayor de América Central. The treaty signed August 27, 1898 was particularly opposed by General Regalado, who took over the Salvadorean government after a revolution and claimed it was never ratified by the people. This abortive attempt at Central American union was officially terminated in November 1898.

ESTANCO. A government monopoly. See: AGUARDIENTE; INSURRECTION OF 1811; JIMENEZ ZAMORA, Jesú; TOBACCO. [L.H.]

ESTETE, Martín. Spanish explorer sent by *Pedrarias to explore the San Juan River area in 1529. His expedition got as far as the Tortuguero area, where they were forced to turn back because of strong opposition of the *Indians. Estete is recognized as the discoverer of the *Reventazón (*Suerre) River.

ESTRADA, Rafael (1901-1934). Modernist poet. His most important works are: Huellas (1923), Viajes sentimentales (1924) and Canciones y ensayos (1929).

ESTRADA RAVAGO, Juan de. Priest and one of the most important of the conquistadors. He came to the New World in 1550 and was given the post of *corregidor in Guadalajara, Mexico, He was selected to be bishop of Honduras in 1552 and in 1556 was transferred to Guatemala. He agreed to finance Juan de *Cavallón and in 1560 even helped lead a successful expedition down the Atlantic coast to Bocas del Toro. When Cavallón was named to a post in Guatemala, Estrada Rávago served as *governor of the province of Costa Rica (January-November 1562). He was later appointed vice-general of *Cartago and was always well-received by the *Indians, learning some of their languages. Unfortunately Estrada Rávago became embroiled in a personal dispute with Governor Juan *Vázquez de Coronado and returned to Mexico.

EVANGELICALS. Whereas the traditional *Protestant churches have either had little impact (the case of the Methodists), or are largely confined to specific immigrant groups and their descendants (the Quakers or the *Jamaican Anglicans and Seventh Day Adventists), United States evangelical Christians have been relatively successful at proselytizing. Evangelical missionaries arrived at the end of last century. They had some 1,000 converts by 1920, 4,000 by 1940, and over 20,000 by the mid-1950s. By the late 1970s they had perhaps 80,000 members in 38 different organizations. [L.H.]

EXCELSIOR. Short-lived (1974-1978) *San José daily paper, introduced to represent the viewpoint of José *Figueres Ferrer's National Liberation Party (*Partido Liberación Nacional) when La *República ceased to be available, and with U.S. fugitive financier Robert *Vesco as one of its backers. Costa Rica's

only non-tabloid Spanish-language paper, it lost heavily and
was obliged to close within four years. [L.H.]

EXCHANGE RATE. Following the adoption of the *gold standard
and introduction of the *colon to replace the *peso at the end
of the 19th century, Costa Rica's currency maintained a stable
rate of exchange of ¢2.15 to the U.S. dollar until the difficulties
of the First *World War, which drove it at one point as low
as ¢4.50. After the war a new parity of ¢4.00 was maintained
by the *Caja de Conversión until the great worldwide depression
that followed the Wall Street crash of October 1929. It then
fell to ¢4.50 in 1931, and to ¢6.80 by December 1935. In late
1936 it had recovered to ¢5.61 which remained the official rate
until the troubles of 1947-1948, although the "free" rate *colon
was usually slightly cheaper (¢5.70 to the dollar in 1940). In
1948-49 the official rate was ¢6.20 while the free rate fell to
¢8.74. In 1950 there was an improvement to ¢5.92 although
the free rate reached ¢9.10. From 1951 to 1960 the official rate
was held at ¢5.64 (with the free rate hovering around ¢6.70).
In 1961 there was a devaluation to ¢6.64 (official rate) and a
further devaluation to ¢8.57 in 1974 following the world oil crisis.
This lasted until 1981 when the *colon began to fall precipitously.
Although the "official" rate was held in theory at ¢20.00 from
January 1982, a number of rates were employed by the authorities. The real rate for non-official transactions was approximately as follows:

December 1980	¢ 8.57	
December 1981	¢36.09	
December 1982	¢40.25	
December 1983	¢43.40	
December 1984	¢47.75	
December 1985	¢53.70	
December 1986	¢58.88	
December 1987	¢68.30	
December 1988	¢78.00	– free rate
December 1989	¢85.60	" "
September 1990	¢97.50	" "

[L.H.]

EXPORTS. In the very early days of Spanish settlement in Costa
Rica, the only thing found worth exporting was SARSAPARILLA
(q.v.), which could be gathered wild in the forests. By the
late 16th century Costa Rica had developed trading relations
with the great colonial entrepôt of Portobello on the Caribbean
coast of Panamá, paying for its (very limited) purchases of
European goods with corn and *wheat (both mainly in the form
of BIZCOCHO, q.v.), and mules, which were in constant demand
to transport goods across the Isthmus of Panamá; see: CAMINO
DE MULAS. By the end of the 17th century, CACAO (q.v.)
exports had become significant, and for a brief while a century
later, TOBACCO (q.v.) also. The export of COFFEE (q.v.)

began in 1820, and that of BANANAS (q.v.) in 1872. The short-
ages of *World War Two led to the cultivation of Manila hemp
(abaca) for export, but this is no longer significant (see: FIBER).
SUGAR (q.v.) has been exported in quantity since the mid-
19th century, and for a while was third in value after coffee
and bananas. Since World War Two, however, beef has pushed
it into fourth place--see: CATTLE. Currently the fifth-ranking
export is artificial FERTILIZER (q.v.). Exports of live cattle
are also economically significant. The country's economic difficulties of the 1980s have greatly stimulated non-traditional agricultural and fishery exports. In 1984 these included $11,800,000
worth of seeds, $8,900,000 worth of prawns and shrimps,
$7,300,000 of melons, pineapples and other fresh *fruit, $4,500,000
of cut flowers, $4,000,000 of cassava (yucca) and other root
crops, and $2,100,000 of other vegetables.

Costa Rica's manufacturing sector is now making an important contribution to exports: fertilizer apart, some $99,500,000
in 1984. Clothing, yarn and textiles contributed the most:
$18,300,000. Electrical goods--batteries, cables, switches, etc.--
came next with $10,700,000 worth, closely followed by pharma-
ceuticals ($9,300,000). In addition, some $26,100,000 worth
of foreign manufactures were assembled, finished or otherwise
processed in Costa Rica, mainly as a way for countries such
as Brazil to take advantage of Costa Rica's easier access to
the United States and Central American markets through tariff
concessions, making a grand total (still excluding fertilizers)
of $125,600,000 worth of industrial exports in 1984. [L.H.]

See also: BALANCE OF TRADE; FOREIGN TRADE;
MERCOMUN.

- F -

FACIO, Justo (1859-1931). Educator and lyric poet. Born in
Santiago, Panama. Minister of education, founder of the Ateneo
de Costa Rica. He was active in founding the circle of poets
in *San Ramón (*Alajuela Province). He specialized in philology
and classical Castilian. Most important works are Mis versos
(1894) and Origen y desenvolvimiento del romance castellano
(1931).

FACIO BRENES, Rodrigo (1914-1961). Lawyer, economist and political philosopher. One of the organizers of the *Centro para el
Estudio de Problemas Nacionales in which he influenced their
belief that Costa Rica had to organize permanent ideological
political parties. For this reason he is remembered as one of
the ideologists of the present National Liberation Party (*Partido
Liberación Nacional). Facio was the principal theoretician of
the 1949 Constitution. He was also rector of the *Universidad
de Costa Rica (1953-58) during which time he supervised the
building of a new university city, which bears his name. His

98 / FACIO SEGREDA

most important works are: <u>Trayectoria y crisis de la Federación</u>
<u>Centroamericana</u> (1949) and <u>La moneda y la banca central en</u>
<u>Costa Rica</u> (1947). Declared *Benemérito de la Patria 1961.

FACIO SEGREDA, Gonzalo (b. 1918). Lawyer and politician. One
of the founders of the *Centro para el Estudio de Problemas
Nacionales. Major in the *National Liberation Army (1948), member of the revolutionary government (*Junta Fundadora de la
Segunda República) (1948-49). One of the founders of the National Liberation Party (*Partido Liberación Nacional). Served
as president of the Legislative Assembly 1953-58, Ambassador
to the United States, delegate to various international conferences, and foreign minister 1970-1974.

FAERRON SUAREZ, Francisco (1873-1961). *Deputy 1900-04 and
1912-17. President of the Cámara de Diputados 1918-1919.

FAIGEZICHT DE ICKOWCZ, Vilma. An *Arte Nuevo painter. Her
works have a surrealistic magical quality to them with exaggerated
human forms. She has had her works exhibited in Costa Rica.

FALLAS SIBAJA, Carlos Luis (1912-1966). Novelist, labor leader,
and one of the founders of the Costa Rican Communist Party
(*Partido Comunista). "Calufa," after working in the *banana
fields, helped to organize and direct the *banana strike of 1934.
Military leader of the government forces in the 1948 *civil war.
His most important novels are <u>Mamita Yunai</u> (1940), one of the
most well-known of all Costa Rican novels, inspired by the *banana strike of 1934; <u>Marcos Ramírez</u>, and <u>Gentes y gentecillas</u>,
all of which deal with social problems. He was a *deputy 1944-48.

FANEGA. An amount of grain (1.6 bushels or 400 litres), or a
weight of *coffee (271.2 lbs.) or an area of land judged sufficient to produce this much (1.59 acres). [L.H.]

FECOSA (Ferrocarriles de Costa Rica). See: RAILROADS.

FEDERACION DE CENTRO-AMERICA. At a conference in *San
José in December 1920, an attempt was made at a confederation
under a type of federal assembly. Its organization was formalized
in the Pacto de la Unión, El Salvador, January 19, 1921. Costa
Rica refused to join, and Guatemala withdrew, January 1922.

FEDERAL REPUBLIC OF CENTRAL AMERICA. See: REPUBLICA
FEDERAL DE CENTRO-AMERICA.

<u>FELLA</u>. Italian merchant ship scuttled by its crew along with the
German ship *Eisenach in *Puntarenas harbor in 1941. Its block-
ing of *Puntarenas harbor helped increase anti-Axis sentiment
in the country.

FELONIA DEL TENIENTE DE MATINA. In 1756 two Dutch and
one English ships were allowed to sell merchandise in the port
of *Matina after paying a bribe to the Governor of the Port.
However, the populace of the area attacked the sailors, killed
about 60 of them, and expropriated the merchandise. The authors
of these acts were later rewarded by the Spanish government.

FEMALE SUFFRAGE. See: WOMEN'S SUFFRAGE.

FERIAS DE MATINA. Because of the high price on goods brought
from Spain, and the absolute prohibition of trade with other
countries, illegal merchandise was brought to *Matina twice a
year to coincide roughly with the *cacao harvests. This illegal
trade was generally overlooked by the authorities. However,
Governor *Serrano de Reyna was convicted of illegally trading
in this market. On the other hand, Governor José *Perié Barros
encountered strong opposition from the people of *Cartago when
he tried to stop this practice. See also: FELONIA DEL TENIENTE
DE MATINA.

FERNANDEZ, Cívido (1934-   ). Journalist. Editor of La *Nación
(1968-80), into which he introduced many modern ideas. As
a result of a disagreement with his employers over coverage
of the Sandinista revolution in Nicaragua he resigned and went
into television news. [L.H.]

FERNANDEZ, Lola (b. 1926). An artist born in Colombia. Came
to Costa Rica when she was three years old and was important
in the *Vanguardista school of painting, and as a member of
the "*Grupo Ocho." Her works have won many awards, and she
has had several exhibits of her works. In 1980 one of her paintings was put on a postage stamp.

FERNANDEZ, Rafael (b. 1935). A prolific *Arte Nuevo painter who
specializes in surrealism, trying to create deformed and monstrous
subjects as an exaggeration of the problems of the human condition of life. His latest paintings are less extreme.

FERNANDEZ ACUNA, Mauro (1843-1905). Educator and statesman.
He received a bachelor's degree from the *Universidad de Santo
Tomás in law and then went on to study in Europe where he
learned English and French. He served as a judge of the Supreme Court and then in 1880 as Secretary of the Constituent
Assembly. Fernández also served as ambassador to El Salvador
and then minister of finance. He did his most valuable work
as minister of education (1885-1889); he redesigned the public
education system and earned the title "Organizer of Public Education." Among his most important accomplishments were publishing a journal for educators, inspiring the "Ley Fundamental de
Instrucción Pública" (1855) which established a system of public

education along liberal lines (see: EDUCATION LAWS). In 1886 he decreed the closing of the *Universidad de Santo Tomás. He felt that the country's meager resources should be used to educate as many people as possible and that the funds were not well utilized on a university which had a small enrollment. He also founded the "Instituto de Alajuela" in 1887 to provide for teacher training, and founded two important high schools, the *Liceo de Costa Rica for men in 1887 and the Colegio Superior de Señoritas in 1888. He also established the National Museum in 1887 and the *National Library in 1888. He was one of the most important men in the development of Costa Rica, declared *Benemérito de la Patria in 1955.

FERNANDEZ ALVARADO, Máximo (1858-1933). Lawyer, writer and politician. As a writer Fernández published La Lira Costarricense in 1890 which was an anthology of Costa Rican poetry and the first of such things published in the country. In politics Fernández was one of the founders of the Republican Party (*Partido Republicano) (1897) and later was its president for many years. He served in Congress 1866-1888, 1912-14, 1916-20 and was minister of the interior in 1888. He ran for the presidency in 1901, 1905, and 1913. He was exiled for political reasons three times, and helped renegotiate the *foreign debt in New York in 1901 during one of his exiles. In 1917 he supported the *Tinoco Granados dictatorship. After the fall of Tinoco, Fernández withdrew from public life. Consult Orlando Salazar, Máximo Fernández (1974).

FERNANDEZ BONILLA, León (1840-1887). Historian and essayist. He studied in Belgium and Guatemala. He was the founder of the National Archives and can be considered the country's first scientific historian. His most important work is Colección de documentos para la historia de Costa Rica bajo la dominación española 1502-1821. He was murdered in revenge for a duel in which he killed Eusebio *Figueroa Oreamuno.

FERNANDEZ CHACON, Manuel (1786-1840). Vice-jefe de estado under President *Gallegos and acting president (March 17 to May 5, 1835). *Deputy 1832-34 and president of the Consejo de Gobierno 1833-37.

FERNANDEZ DE BOBADILLA, Juan (d. 1781). *Governor of the province of Costa Rica (1773-78) and (1780-81). He had served earlier as governor and commander of Darién (Panama). While in Costa Rica he tried to improve the condition of the *Indians.

FERNANDEZ DE BONILLA, Juna (b. 1745). Lieutenant governor, acting *governor 1796-97 after Governor *Vázquez y Téllez left for Venezuela.

FERNANDEZ DE CORDOBA, Francisco (d. 1526). *Conquistador.

Founded *Villa de Bruselas in 1524. Also founded the cities of León and Granada in Nicaragua. Unfortunately he became involved in a controversy over who had the right to colonize, fell into *Pedrarias's hands, and was executed.

FERNANDEZ DE HEREDIA, Alonso (d. 1772). *Governor of Costa Rica (1746-53), and commander general of arms of Costa Rica and Nicaragua. He spent most of his time in Nicaragua and left Costa Rica in the hands of temporary governors. He conferred on *Cubujuquí the title of villa. Later he was appointed president of the *Audiencia de Guatemala and in his honor the city of *Heredia took its name. See also: CUBUJUQUI; HEREDIA.

FERNANDEZ DE LA PASTORA, Francisco (1712-1756). Lieutenant governor in political matters 1746 and November 1747- January 1748, and interim *governor December 11, 1754 to July 2, 1756. During his incumbency he made efforts to get residents of the *Aserrí and *Escazú valleys to move to what is now *San José. He was killed in an expedition against *Zambo-Mosquitos July 2, 1756.

FERNANDEZ DE OVIEDO, Gonzalo (1478-1557). Spanish historian. He wrote Historia general y natural de las Indias, which relates the experiences of the Gil *González Dávila expedition in Costa Rica and Nicaragua.

FERNANDEZ DE SALINAS Y DE LA CERDA, Juan. *Governor of Costa Rica (1650-59) and fourth *adelantado (1675), a title which he acquired by marrying a descendant of Juan *Vázquez de Coronado. In his term of office he established segregation in *Cartago so that mulattoes and *Blacks could not mix with the white community. He also built the *Castillo de San Carlos de Austria, a fort on the San Juan River. He attempted to conquer *Talamanca in 1662 and establish a settlement on the *Suerre river in the Atlantic region. Later he served as governor of Nicaragua.

FERNANDEZ FERRAZ, Juan (1849-1904). Born in the Canary Islands and studied in Madrid. He came to Costa Rica in 1871 and had various government posts such as director of the Imprenta Nacional (government printing office), inspector of schools. He founded La Prensa Libre (1889) and an educational magazine called La Enseñanza (1884-86). He was particularly important as one of the leaders of the liberal movement of the period. His most important published work is Teoría de lo bello.

FERNANDEZ FERRAZ, Valeriano (1831-1925). Philosopher and educator. Born in Santa Cruz de Palma, Canary Islands. Received doctorate in classical philosophy from the University of Madrid. He was one of the leading proponents of *Krausism. He organized and served as director of the new *Colegio San

Luis Gonzaga (1870-74), was professor of philosophy of the
*Universidad de Santo Tomás. He went to Cuba in 1882 because
of political problems. However, the government invited him back
and he returned with 30 Spanish teachers to improve educational
quality in the country. He was declared *Benemérito de la Enseñanza in 1923.

FERNANDEZ GUARDIA, Ricardo (1867-1950). Historian and novelist.
He was perhaps the most important historian Costa Rica has
produced. He studied in Paris for six years and tried to apply
the new scientific methods to Costa Rican history, which had
been largely panegyric biographies and recapitulations of myths.
He also served as minister of foreign relations and was intru-
mental in the introduction of the *costumbrista novel. His most
important works are: Hojarasca (1894) and Cuentos ticos, both
in the costumbrista style. His historical works include: El
descubrimiento y la conquista (1905), Cartilla histórica de Costa
Rica (first published 1909), Documentos posteriores a la independencia (1918), Crónicas coloniales (1921), and La independencia: la historia de Costa Rica (1941). He was declared
*Benemérito de la Patria in 1944. He also wrote plays, the most
important being, "Magdalena."

FERNANDEZ GUELL, Rogelio (1868-1918). Principal exponent of
the idea of "esoteric philosophy," which became theosophy. He
founded the periodical El Imparcial and was one of the leaders
of the frustrated revolution of 1918 against the *Tinoco Granados
dictatorship. He was executed by the Tinoco forces when they
overtook him as he was trying to flee the country. His most
important works include Psiquis sin velo and Tratado de filosofía
esotérica (1912). He is considered one of the martyrs of the
anti-Tinoco fight.

FERNANDEZ OREAMUNO, Próspero [General] (1834-1885). President
of the Republic 1882-85. He studied in Guatemala, and distinguished himself in the war against William *Walker. He helped
General Tomás *Guardia Gutiérrez overthrow Jesús *Jiménez in
1870 and was later elected to his own term of office. During
his administration the *liberal laws of 1884 were enacted, the
*metric system was legally enacted (although still not used com-
pletely in practice), electric lights were installed in *San José,
and civil marriage was legalized. Because of a problem with
the Guatemalan dictator Rufino Barrios, Costa Rica actually declared war. Fernández led an expedition, but when the news
of Barrios' death reached Costa Rica, the war was called off.
On the way back Fernández died suddenly in *Atenas (*Alajuela
Province). He was declared *Benemérito de la Patria in 1883.

FERNANDEZ TENORIO, Félix (1754-1830). Lieutenant governor in
military matters March-May 1819, lieutenant colonel of the militia
of the province of Costa Rica. He was proclaimed military chief

of the province of Costa Rica, by the *governor of León, Nicaragua, but this was not accepted by the *Junta Superior Gubernativa. In 1822 he was finally granted the title of commander of arms by the *junta but retired from public life the next year.

FERRO ACOSTA, Luis (b. 1930). Artist and writer. His most important works are: Andrés Bello en Costa Rica (1962), Arbol de recuerdo (1968), Ensayistas costarricenses (1971), Costa Rica precolombina (1977), La Escultura en Costa Rica (1973), Grabados en madera (1973), and Literatura infantil costarricense (1958).

FERROCARRIL DEL NORTE. The so-called Northern or Atlantic Railroad was British-built between 1871 and 1890 to connect *San José with the Caribbean port of *Limón, a distance of 165 km. The line's total mileage of 335 (522 km) makes it the country's longest. Difficult terrain necessitated steep grades, sharp curves and low speed--five hours from *San José-*Limón. The heavy rainfall makes upkeep costly while declining *banana production has reduced income. But the climb along the mountainsides overlooking the *Reventazón River gives magnificent views: since 1980 the line has sought tourist revenue by promoting its "Jungle Train." See also: RAILROADS. [L.H.]

FERROCARRIL ELECTRICO DEL PACIFICO. The first contract for the Pacific Railroad to connect *San José with *Puntarenas was signed with Cyril Smith in 1890, but in 1897 this was replaced by a contract with American John S. Clement who undertook to build it for $2,898,971. Financial difficulties delayed the work which was incomplete when it passed into government ownership in 1903: the first train to reach *Puntarenas from the capital did not run till July 23, 1910. Electrification of the 162 km line was financed by a $1,800,000 American loan, and completed by the German A.E.G. firm in 1934. Built over less difficult terrain than the *Ferrocarril del Norte it still provided a very slow service (4 1/2 hours for the 116 km between the capital and the coast) and was suffering serious road competition by the 1940s. In 1974 its operation was entrusted to the INSTITUTO COSTARRICENSE DEL PUERTO DEL PACIFICO, q.v. [L.H.]

FERTILIZERS. This is a relatively new industry. Its chief producer is FERTICA, a semi government corporation. In 1982 Costa Rica exported 48,635,000 kilograms of artificial fertilizers, valued at $7,840,000 but this fell to $5,500,000 in 1983, $5,800,000 in 1984, recovering to $7,700,000 in 1985. Most of the fertilizers were exported to Central America, but they also exported this product to Canada, Colombia, Chile, and Peru.

FIBER. Cabulla or cabuya (sisal, henequén) also known as Mauritius hemp has long been grown in small quantities for the domestic

market. When the 1942 Japanese occupation of the Philippines
cut the United States off from its normal source of Manila hemp
(abacá), Costa Rica was encouraged to cultivate it. By 1947
this new crop was the country's fourth most important export
(after *coffee, *bananas and *cacao), worth $1,330,100. But
cultivation without fertilizer, and too rapid and drastic cutting
produced a yield that could not be sustained, and caused a
rapid depletion of the soil. There was also contraction of the
market as wartime demand ceased, synthetic fibers became widespread, and supplies from the East became available again. The
plant retained some importance into the early 1960s, but is now
no longer grown to any extent. [L.H.]

FIEL EJECUTOR. Office of the colonial ayuntamiento. An inspector
who supervised the honesty of merchants, and also some aspects
of public health. He had the power to punish those who violated
regulations.

FIGUERES FERRER, José María Hipólito (1906-). Head of the
ruling governmental *junta May 8, 1948 to November 1949. Elected
president of the Republic for the terms 1953-58 and 1970-74.
Born in *San Ramón (*Alajuela Province) in 1906. As a youth
he spent several years in the United States where he attended
some public lectures at the Massachusetts Institute of Technology
and did extensive reading at the Boston Public Library (the
latter he claims as his alma mater). On returning to his country he bought a ranch in *Perez Zeledón *canton (*San José
Province) and engaged in experimental farming of hemp. He
came to national attention in July 1942 when he made a strong
speech criticizing the government of Dr. *Calderón Guardia,
for which he was exiled to Mexico. While in Mexico he came
in contact with other Caribbean emigres and started planning
the 1948 revolution, signing the Caribbean Pact (*Pacto del
Caribe). After winning the 1948 war he served as president
of the *Junta Fundadora de la Segunda República (May 8, 1948
to November 8, 1949). This Junta instituted some changes in
the structure of the government, the most important being the
nationalization of the banks. In addition, it conducted trials
against some of the former government officials. Figueres was
one of the principal founders of the National Liberation Party
(*Partido Liberación Nacional), which was formed in 1952 to
give him a party for his electoral campaign of 1953. He con-
siders himself a social democrat. In general his chief works
were in expanding the social reforms of the early 1940s and
in ensuring free and honest elections, the latter perhaps being
his most important contribution to the country. See also: CIVIL
WARS (1948); JUNTA FUNDADORA DE LA SEGUNDA REPUBLICA;
PARTIDO LIBERACION NACIONAL; SOCIAL DEMOCRATIC PARTY.
Consult José Albertazzi, La tragedia de Costa Rica; Alberto
Baeza, La lucha sin fin; Patrick Bell, Crisis in Costa Rica; Arturo
Castro, José Figueres; El hombre y su obra; and Hugo Navarro,
José Figueres en la evolución de Costa Rica.

FIGUEROA OREAMUNO, Eusebio (1827-1883). Lawyer and politician. President of the Supreme Court (1876), *deputy, founder and first president of the Colegio de Abogados, and rector of the *Universidad de Santo Tomás. He was instrumental in forcing the resignation of General *Blanco Rodríguez and thus ending the power of the military. He was acting president for two days in May 1869 in the absence of President Jesús *Jiménez Zamora. Later he helped in the reorganization of public instruction while serving in the cabinet of President *Fernández Oreamuno. He was considered one of the most important men of his time. He was killed in a duel with the historian León *Fernández Bonilla over some supposed criticism of the government written by Fernández.

FILIBUSTER. A corruption of the Dutch Frijbuiter, "free-booter," probably via the French flibustier or the Spanish filibustero. Originally meaning a West Indian pirate, it came to mean a soldier of fortune in the same geographical region, and in particular those recruited by the Venezuelan Narciso López to invade Cuba in the 1840s and 1850s, and by William *Walker for his Central American adventures in the late 1850s. See also: LOCKRIDGE, Col. S. A.; HENNINGSEN, Charles F.; JAMISON, James Carson; SANDERS, Edward J.; SCHLESINGER, Louis; WALKER, William. [L.H., G.K.]

FINCA. A farm or *hacienda, but on a smaller scale, especially coffee land.

FIREFIGHTERS. The first organized firefighter group was in *San José in 1865. In 1866 they acquired their first firetruck. There are organized fire departments in all the major cities and some of the larger towns.

FIRST CONSTITUTIONAL GOVERNMENT. A name given to the government of Costa Rica (January 13, 1822 to December 31, 1822). See also: JUNTA SUPERIOR GUBERNATIVA DE COSTA RICA.

FISCAL. (1) A poll watcher at elections. (2) A member of a board of directors.

FISHING. The Hispanic world was exempted from the traditional obligation to eat fish on Fridays following the 1571 Battle of Lepanto. Domestic consumption of fish was in consequence always very small in Costa Rica. In 1949 the bulk of the demand was being met by one boat based at *Puntarenas. At the same time some 30 U.S. boats were visiting the port, where the Van Camp firm had a processing plant which canned or froze their catches for re-export to California. A Costa Rican fishing industry has however developed since then: 2,900 tons were landed in 1964, mostly TUNA (q.v.), shrimps and sardines; by 1982 this had increased to 10,900 tons, of which 200 tons were caught in the Caribbean, 500 in rivers and lakes and 10,200 in the Pacific. [L.H.]

FLAG. See: NATIONAL FLAG.

FLORES. *Canton in *Heredia Province. Its *cabecera is San Joaquín and it was created August 12, 1915. It produces *coffee, *sugar, oranges, and grains. Present population is 9,015.

FLORES, Bernal (b. 1937). Musician. Studied in Costa Rica and then received a Ph.D. from the Eastman School of Music in Rochester, N.Y. (1961). From 1966-69 he was professor of music theory in the Eastman school. In 1971 he became director of the Music Section of the new Ministry of Culture. He has written two biographies of musicians: Julio Fonseca (1973) and José Daniel Zúñiga (1976). He also wrote La música en Costa Rica and has a valuable article "La Música" in Chester Zelaya et al., Costa Rica Contemporánea Tomo II (1979). Among his musical compositions are: "Concierto para clarinete y orquesta," "Siete tocatas para piano," (which is the first music written by a Costa Rican on the 12 tone scale), "Ciclo de canciones para contralto y orquesta," (1962) and an opera based on a story by William Butler Yeats called "The Land of Heart's Desire," (1964).

FLORES PEREZ, Joaquín (1795-1866). Priest and politician. President of Congress and member of the Constituent Assemblies of (1825), (1838), and (1847). He also served as vicar general and president of the Consejo Representativo.

FLORES SANCHEZ, Juan. Interim governor (1781-85). During his term of office he constructed a road to *Esparza, put cobblestones in some of the streets of *Cartago and constructed the thermal baths at Agua Calienta (*Cartago Province). It was also during his administration that the city of *Alajuela was founded.

FLORES UMANA, Juan J. (1843-1903). Physician and politician. He studied medicine at New York University, the first Costa Rican to have studied medicine in the United States. He organized the first medical clinic in *Heredia and was a presidential candidate in 1893 and 1897. Flores was exiled from the country as a result of his anti-*Yglesias Castro campaign in 1897. He later returned and was selected as minister of the interior in the conciliatory government of Ascención *Esquivel Ibarra. He was declared *Benemérito de la Patria in 1963.

FONSECA, Harold. Painter. Member of the GRUPO OCHO, q.v.

FONSECA, José Nereo (d. 1833). Priest and politician. He was a member of the *Junta de Legados December 13, 1821 to January 13, 1822 and head of the Church in *Heredia Province (1827-33). He was president of Congress May-July 1831.

FONSECA, Juan Rodriguez de (d. 1524). Bishop of Burgos, Spain. As a member of the Consejo de Castilla he was in charge of colonial affairs from 1493 until the creation of the *Casa de Contratación January 20, 1503.

FONSECA CHAMIER, Francisco (b. 1901). *Deputy 1942-48 and president of the Congress (1946-48).

FOOTBALL, Association. See: SOCCER.

FOREIGN DEBT. Costa Rica inherited a debt of Ł13,608 as its one twelfth share of the debt of the *Central American Federation. This was liquidated in 1840. A series of loans raised on the London money market (see: BRITISH LOANS) resulted in a total government foreign debt at the eve of First World War of Ł2,000,000 sterling and 35,000,000 French francs (see: EM-PRESITO FRANCES).
    Since the Second World War, and partially since the world oil crisis of 1974, Costa Rica has borrowed very heavily abroad and now has perhaps the largest per capita debt in the free world. The total outstanding in February 1988 was $4,400 million. [L.H.]

FOREIGN INVESTMENT. See: BRITISH INVESTMENT; UNITED STATES INVESTMENT.

FOREIGN LOANS. See: BARING BROTHERS LOAN; BISCHOFF-SCHERN AND GOLDSCHMIDT; BRITISH LOANS; CHILEAN LOANS; EMPRESITO FRANCES; FOREIGN DEBT.

FOREIGN RELATIONS. In general, see: FOREIGN DEBT; LEAGUE OF NATIONS; NEUTRALIDAD, Estatuto de; ORGANIZATION OF AMERICAN STATES; UNITED NATIONS;
    With Brazil, see: EXPORTS;
    With Central America, see: ARIAS PLAN; CARIBBEAN LEGION; CENTRAL AMERICAN FEDERATION; CONTRADORA; CORTE DE JUSTICIA CENTROAMERICANA; INTERNATIONAL CENTRAL AMERICAN BUREAU; MERCOMUN; ORGANIZACION DE ESTADOS CENTROAMERICANOS;
    With Chile, see: CHILE, Relations with;
    With Colombia, see: FRONTIER QUESTIONS (SOUTH);
    With France, see: EMPRESITO FRANCES; GENIE, Le;
    With Germany, see: EISENACH; WORLD WARS;
    With Italy, see: FELLA; ITALIANS; WORLD WARS;
    With Japan, see: WORLD WARS;
    With Nicaragua, see: FRONTIER QUESTIONS (NICARAGUA); PASTORA GOMEZ, Edén;
    With Panama, see: FRONTIER QUESTIONS (SOUTH);
    With the United Kingdom, see: BRITISH INVESTMENT; BRITISH LOANS; CHATFIELD, Frederick; CLAYTON-BULWER TREATY; LE LACHEUR, William; PIRATES; TAFT DECISION; ZAMBO-MOSQUITOS;

With the United States, see: BRYAN-CHAMORRO TREATT; CLAYTON-BULWER TREATY; COTO WAR; HULL, John; QUIROS SEGURA, Juan Bautista; UNITED FRUIT COMPANY; UNITED STATES INVESTMENT; WALKER, William; WASHINGTON CONFERENCE.

FOREIGN TRADE. Costa Rica's leading trading partners are: Central America, the German Federal Republic, United States, Italy, Mexico, Japan, and Venezuela. Leading exports for 1981 and 1982 were:

Product	(1) 1981		(2) 1982	
	Dollars	Kilos	Dollars	Kilos
Coffee	240,057,000	96,293,000	236,714,000	93,768,000
Bananas	224,775,000	1,002,340,000	238,713,000	995,791,000
Sugar	42,007,000	72,086,000	14,654,000	54,766,000
Meat	73,948,000	33,056,000	53,056,000	24,276,000
Cacao	2,712,000	2,019,000	2,011,000	2,419,000
Fertilizer	15,626,000	86,001,000	7,898,000	48,635,000

COUNTRY	1982 EXPORTS	IMPORTS
Guatemala	64,727,787	54,842,374
El Salvador	33,740,878	33,107,830
Honduras	22,059,048	11,876,353
Nicaragua	44,253,787	21,353,573
Panama	36,425,945	9,777,368
United States	270,077,882	314,129,875
Canada	7,125,442	14,106,765
Mexico	17,115,806	178,604,243
Switzerland	2,027,492	5,685,849
Curaçao	6,359,939	17,067,341
Puerto Rico	27,265,814	1,097,671
Colombia	3,405,821	4,268,614
Venezuela	5,638,982	107,226,083
Brazil	19,000	12,080,479
China (Taiwan)	859,144	5,799,375
W. Germany	122,591,239	33,121,475
Belgium-Lux.	10,442,465	5,205,893
USSR	1,263,436	522,104
Finland	19,280,549	1,257,229
Spain	5,366,140	14,635,050
France	11,520,504	11,863,130
U.K.	20,211,296	11,462,755
Italy	33,394,929	12,762,374
Netherlands	24,727,245	4,073,571
Sweden	9,084,898	9,440,875
Japan	6,170,403	36,633,548

(3)
1981

COUNTRY	EXPORTS	IMPORTS
Guatemala	75,804,000	64,193,000
El Salvador	43,619,000	36,375,000
Honduras	34,863,000	16,287,000
Nicaragua	84,141,000	33,936,000
Panama	48,027,000	31,642,000
United States	275,895,000	398,282,000
Canada	5,189,000	27,022,000
Mexico	22,233,000	110,396,000
Switzerland	3,852,000	9,079,000
Curaçao	11,406,000	25,909,000
Puerto Rico	23,877,000	1,423,000
Colombia	5,357,000	4,037,000
Venezuela	3,131,000	84,518,000
Brazil	31,000	17,535,000
China (Taiwan)	508,000	7,780,000
W. Germany	111,561,000	54,425,000
Belgium-Lux.	20,954,000	7,505,000
USSR	1,251,000	1,380,000
Finland	17,475,000	494,000
Spain	5,124,000	25,009,000
France	9,597,000	19,214,000
U.K.	12,299,000	19,007,000
Italy	23,720,000	25,354,000
Netherlands	25,284,000	6,972,000
Sweden	12,299,000	8,630,000
Japan	5,403,000	115,406,000

(4)
1980

COUNTRY	EXPORTS	IMPORTS
Guatemala	65,469,002	100,551,118
El Salvador	52,487,801	67,648,248
Honduras	28,256,427	18,767,272
Nicaragua	125,115,249	32,802,448
Panama	41,363,530	30,150,817
United States	327,487,171	502,101,193
Canada	3,652,176	34,524,593
Mexico	1,964,332	96,874,207
Switzerland	2,391,425	10,472,295
Curaçao	5,661,834	53,408,067
Puerto Rico	19,202,237	1,623,626
Colombia	3,585,185	5,670,896
Venezuela	2,179,492	108,155,909
Brazil	2,911,470	21,696,370
China (Taiwan)	58,926	12,078,547
W. Germany	116,293,632	70,891,547
Belgium-Lux.	22,397,637	7,007,527
USSR	0	1,749,844

Finland	25,551,243	391,273
Spain	4,894,849	33,247,534
France	17,503,613	17,587,257
U.K.	2,654,192	25,800,682
Italy	42,395,211	23,394,385
Netherlands	29,155,392	11,093,713
Sweden	9,186,430	12,196,226
Japan	8,049,144	171,264,856

TOTALS (5)	Exports	Imports
1978	$ 864,900,000	$1,165,700,000
1979	934,300,000	1,396,800,000
1980	1,001,742,000	1,540,400,000
1981	962,334,000	1,211,224,000
1982	883,946,000	855,593,000
1983	860,900,000	989,700,000
1984	985,900,000	1,093,700,000
1985	939,000,000	1,005,000,000
1986	1,212,900,000	1,136,600,000
1987	1,200,000,000	1,250,000,000
1988	1,250,000,000	1,320,000,000

One factor inhibiting the development of foreign trade is the poverty of the other Central American countries, with whom Costa Rica traditionally has a favorable trade balance: at the end of 1985 the other members of the MERCOMUN (q.v.) owed her 369 million dollars (Nicaragua $221 million, Guatemala $22 million, Honduras $18 million).

See also: EXPORTS; IMPORTS.

NOTES

1. Departmento de Transacciones Internacionales, Banco Internacional de Costa Rica. The figures for 1981 are definitive, those of 1982 are preliminary and should be used with caution, since they may change when made final.
2. These statistics are preliminary and should be used with great caution since the definitive figures when available could vary a great deal.
3. Banco Central de Costa Rica, Departamento de Transaccions Internacionales, cifras preliminares para 1980-81. Those are preliminary figures and should also be used cautiously.
4. Costa Rica, Ministerio de Economía y Comercio, Dirección General de Estadística y Censos. "Balanza Comercial, acumulado al año 1980." (16 de octubre de 1981). These figures are definitive.
5. Comercio Exterior de Costa Rica, Compendio 1978-1979-1980-1981 (Banco Central de Costa Rica, Departamento de transacciones, 1983).

FORESTS AND FORESTRY. Lack of transport for anything as cumbersome as logs meant that timber felled in land clearance was almost entirely wasted until the end of last century. The ecological dangers of excessive deforestation, at least on steeply sloping land was recognized and legal measures taken in an attempt to restrict it by the 1880s. Outside the central *meseta, however (where forest removal was almost complete by the 1930s), Costa Rica was still largely wooded at mid-century (an estimated 78% of the country was still under virgin forest in 1942). Since then deforestation has been much more rapid: in 1977 forest covering was estimated at 39% of the total land area. By 1989 Costa Rica had, outside national parks, the highest deforestation in the Western Hemisphere. Causes have included the timber industry, the growth of livestock rearing, and encroachment on woodland by squatters, desperate for land to farm. Particularly affected has been the dry tropical, deciduous forest along the Pacific seaboard, of which only 2% of the original forest area remains. Unlike the rainforest of the Atlantic coast, the dry tropical forest creates good soils, eminently suited to farming and ranching. The Ley forestal (forest law) of 1969 was set up to limit deforestation by legal and administrative means. It also created a series of *National Parks, including the 10,500 hectare Guanacaste National Park (to be expanded eventually to 70,000 hectares) to preserve some of the few remaining areas of dry tropical forest.

FORT SAN CARLOS. See: SAN CARLOS (Fort).

FORT SAN FERNANDO. See: FUERTE DE SAN FERNANDO.

FOURNIER, Cristina (b. 1937). *Arte Nuevo painter who studied in Costa Rica, Italy, and California. She specialized in flower scenes done in water colors. In addition to having had her works exhibited in Central America and the United States, she won the *Ancora Prize for plastic arts in 1970.

FRANKFORT. See: GOLPE DE FRANKFORT.

FREE MASONS. See: MASONS.

FREEDOM OF THE PRESS. See: COLEGIO DE PERIODISTAS; NEWSPAPERS.

FREMONT, John C. American explorer and presidential candidate. He and a group of New York businessmen arranged a contract with the Costa Rican government in 1867 to build an interoceanic railroad between *Caldera and Puerto *Limón, but nothing came of this project.

FRENCH LOAN. See: EMPRESITO FRANCES.

FRESES DE NECO, Juan. A leading figure in the *Cartago revolt of 1823 and one of the important commanders of the *imperialist

forces at *Ochomogo. Permanently expelled from the country
as a result of his actions, the rationale being that he was Spanish
and not Costa Rican. See: CIVIL WARS (1823).

FRONTIER QUESTIONS (NICARAGUA). The original limits with
Nicaragua were fixed November 29, 1540 as the land between
the Ducado de *Veragua (Panama today) and the Río Grande
(San Juan) River. Later a dispute arose and the San Juan
River was divided between the two provinces in 1541 in the
*Cédula de Talavera, with both Nicaragua and Costa Rica having
the right to navigation. In 1561 Juan *Cavallón was granted
the title of *alcalde mayor of Costa Rica with jurisdiction over
the San Juan River region, and in 1573 the limits between the
two provinces were reconfirmed as extending to the "mouth of
the *Desaguadero." In 1813 an additional problem was created.
In that year the *Cortes de Cádiz in order to give Costa Rica
the required minimum population to send a representative, combined the area around *Nicoya Peninsula (see: NICOYA, Partido
de) with the rest of the province. This helped bring the *Guanacaste area closer to Costa Rica. Finally as a result of constant
civil wars in Nicaragua this area voted to join Costa Rica. The
date of this vote (July 25, 1824) is still celebrated as Annexation
Day and is a *national holiday. The annexation of *Guanacaste
was approved by the Central American Congress (December 9,
1825), but Nicaragua did not accept it and the Guanacaste question lingered for a long time.
    Nicaragua made an attempt to reannex this area at the
time of the breakup of the *Republica Federal de Centro-America,
but Guanacaste again voted to remain with Costa Rica. In 1840
another problem arose with the English asserting the *Zambo-
Mosquito Indians' claim to the San Juan River area, in exchange
for an agreement with those *Indians that English interests would
be granted a concession to build an interoceanic canal. Throughout the William *Walker episode Nicaragua still claimed Guanacaste.
Finally through the mediation of El Salvador the *Cañas-Jeréz
Treaty (April 15, 1858) confirmed Costa Rica's right to Guanacaste but awarded all of the San Juan River to Nicaragua, although guaranteeing Costa Rica free navigation of that waterway.
In 1876 diplomatic relations between the two countries were broken
after Nicaragua signed a treaty with France that would have
excluded Costa Rican participation in a proposed interoceanic
canal (see: CLAYTON-BULWER TREATY). Arbitration by Grover
Cleveland (1888) reconfirmed Costa Rica's rights to navigate
the San Juan River area under the 1858 treaty, but excluded
Costa Rican warships.
    Problems cropped up again in 1901 with the signing of
the *Hay-Pauncefote Treaty between Nicaragua and the United
States because the latter was granted the rights to build an
interoceanic canal. Later the *Chamorro-Weitzel Treaty (1913)
and the *Bryan-Chamorro Treaty (1918) reiterated the United
States concession to build a canal in the region without Costa

Rica having any say in the matter. The problem was taken
to the Central American Court (*Corte de Justicia Centroamericana) which ruled in favor of Costa Rica, but the decision was
not accepted by the United States and Nicaragua withdrew from
the court. The matter was finally settled in a treaty in 1940
in which Costa Rica was granted free navigation of any canal
that would be built. In the late 1970s, new problems arose
from the disturbances caused by the Sandinista Revolution.
In 1979 the region became a staging area for the anti-Somoza
forces. Nicaragua forces stopped and searched Costa Rican
vessels on the San Juan River, seemingly in violation of existing treaties. Later, part of the border area became a staging
area for anti-Sandinista (contra) forces. In September 1983
those forces attacked the Nicaraguan frontier post of Peñas
Blancas. The Nicaraguan security forces fired on the Costa
Rican frontier post, which they occupied for several hours.
There have been other sporadic incidents and relations have
been very tense. Costa Rica also has a problem with the large
influx of REFUGEES, q.v.

FRONTIER QUESTIONS (SOUTH). In 1560 the limits of Costa Rica
were fixed at Río de Culebra and Costa Rica was given the right
to the Bay of Almirante region. However, in 1803 a royal order
temporarily put the whole Atlantic Coast region as far north
as Cape Gracias a Dios (Honduras) under the *Audiencia de
Santa Fé (Colombia). This action was the basis for later territorial claims of Colombia (and Panama after its independence
in 1903) to the Almirante area. Proposed treaties in 1856, 1864,
1873 (see: CALVO-HERRAN TREATY; CASTRO-VALENZUELA
TREATY; MONTUFAR-CORREOSO TREATY) which would have
given Almirante to Costa Rica were not ratified. Conventions
were signed in 1880 and 1886 in which the matter was to be
arbitrated by Spain, but nothing came of them. An arbitration
agreement emerged in 1896 in which the president of France,
Emille Loubet, was to adjudicate the matter. In 1900 when *Loubet's
decison was announced (in which the Colombian claims were
favored), Costa Rica refused to accept the decision. A proposed
treaty in 1905 (see: PACHECO DE LA GUARDIA CONVENTION)
generally accepted *Loubet's decision, but was not ratified by
the Costa Rican Congress because of the announced opposition
of President *González Víquez.
    In 1910 the *Anderson-Porras Treaty accepted the *Loubet
decision in the Pacific but left the dispute in the Atlantic region
to be arbitrated by U.S. Chief Justice E. Douglas White. The
*White decision awarded some territory to Costa Rica, but Panama
refused to accept it. In 1921 a short war broke out over the
Coto region in which the Costa Rican forces were badly defeated
on the Pacific side, but captured the Panamanian port of Almirante on the Atlantic. United States intervention forced a truce
(see: COTO WAR). In 1929 and 1938 (see: ZUNIGA-ESPRIELLA
TREATY) attempts were made to settle the matter, but their

efforts were frustrated by strong opposition of the Costa Rican people. During 1939 negotiations continued and at a dramatic meeting on a railroad bridge over the *Sixaola River, presidents *Calderón Guardia of Costa Rica and Arnulfo Arias of Panama announced the settlement of the long-standing dispute. This agreement was incorporated in the *Echandi Montero-Fernández Jaén Treaty (May 1, 1941) in which Costa Rica was awarded most of its claims in the Pacific, some territory in the mountains, but ceded most of the Atlantic territory to Panama. For more information consult Ernesto Castillero Pimentel, Panamá y los Estados Unidos (1953), Chapter V on the Coto War; various works by Pedro Pérez Zeledón and Manuel Peralta cited in the bibliography; José Pozuelo, Por la patria y por el amigo (1943); and Marco Tulio Zeledón, Fronteras de Costa Rica (1946).

FRUIT. Although BANANAS (q.v.) have been a major export crop since the late 19th century, cultivation of other tropical fruits for export has only become important in the 1980s. They include pineapples, melons and mangoes. The last come mainly from *Orotina canton; their export is exclusively to Europe. Mangoes are not admitted to the United States for fear of infestation with the Mediterranean fruit fly. [L.H.]
See also: EXPORTS.

FUEROS. Special legal privileges and tax exemptions pertaining to social classes such as the clergy and the military. Liberal reforms ended such colonial leftovers at the time of independence. See: LEY FUNDAMENTAL DEL ESTADO LIBRE DE COSTA RICA. [G.K.]

FUERTE DE SAN CARLOS. See: SAN CARLOS (Fort).

FUERTE DE SAN FERNANDO. As a result of the invasion of 1666, forts were ordered built by a cédula real (July 4, 1677). However, nothing was done until *Governor *Gemmir in 1741 decided to build a fort in the *Matina Valley. This fort cost 39,900 pesos and had four bronze and two iron cannons. On August 13, 1747, the fort, poorly defended by 50 men, was easily captured and burned by a force of *Zambo-Mosquito Indians transported by English ships and led by Thomas Owens.

FUSCALDO, Margarita (b. 1942). Painter. Born and educated in *San José. Professor in the Conservatorio de *Castella. She does mostly abstracts of human forms. Her work has been shown locally and also in Mexico.

- G -

GACHUPIN. A name of derision given to Spaniards during the colonial era. Derived from the type of boot they wore.

GAGINI, Carlos (1895-1925). Novelist and philologist. Director of
various educational institutions, he wrote several studies dealing
with the Costa Rica form of expression and with regional literature. His most important works are Chamarasca (1898) and
Cuentos grises (1918), both *costumbrista works. His novels,
La caída del aquila (1920) and El árbol enfermo (1918), deal with
nationalistic and anti-imperialist themes. The latter has been
translated by E. Bradford Burns as Redemptions (1985). He
also wrote several works on grammar and philology; the most
notable being the zarzuela (Spanish operetta), El Marqués de
Talamanca (1900) and Don Concepción.

GALLARDO, Jorge (b. 1924). Painter born in *San José studied
art in Spain. His paintings are sometimes realist. His favorite
themes are women done in an expressionist style but with a
strong indigenous flavor. Some of his works were used on the
postage stamps in 1975.

GALLEGO, Juan. A *conquistador. He arrived with *Cavallón
and served as one of his chief lieutenants. Juan Gallego was
the first to enter the valleys of Garabito and La Cruz. He
was also a *regidor of *Garcimuñoz.

GALLEGOS, Daniel (b. 1930). Playwright and director. One of the
most important figures in contemporary Costa Rican *theatre.
He studied in the Actor's Studio in New York and was influenced
by the contemporary English theatre during his stay in that
country. Among his works are: "Los Profanos," (1959), "Ese
algo de Dávalos," (1967), "Punto de referencia uno," (1971)
and "El séptimo círculo" (1982). He won national prizes for
the theatre in 1960, 1967, and 1982.

GALLEGOS, Mía (b. 1953). Poet born in *San José. She wrote
Golpe de almas (1977).

GALLEGOS, Nicolás (1818-1882). Philosopher and educator. Rector
of the *Universidad de Santo Tomás 1846, 1864, and 1875-76.
He wrote the first philology books published in the country
and was the only one to receive the doctorate in philosophy
from the *Universidad de Santo Tomás. This degree was given
in partial recognition of his work in writing these books. Gallegos was also a publisher of several newspapers, including La
*Tertulia and *Mentor Costarricense.

GALLEGOS Y ALVARADO, José Rafael (1784-1850). Chief of State
1835-36 and 1845-46. He was a member and president of the
*Junta Gubernativa and during the independence period advo-
cated association with Guatemala. After the first *civil war
Gallegos, in order to reconciliate the country, urged the par-
doning of the rebels, especially his half-brother José Santos
*Lombardo Alvarado. In the first election for head of state he

was defeated by Juan *Mora Fernández by 16 to 13 electoral
votes. However, Gallegos was chosen as vice-chief of state
1825-29 and 1828-33. In a stormy and questionable election
in 1833 he was elected chief of state. However, he remained
in office against his will. Because of the nature of his election
he never had much popular support. Chiefly for these reasons
he resigned on March 4, 1835. During his term of office the
*Ley de Ambulancia was passed. Gallegos returned to public
life and served as senator in 1844, and then was reelected chief
of state in 1845 and served in that office until overthrown in a
military revolt in 1846. During his second term of office he
founded the *Junta de Caridad de San José, which ultimately
became the *San Juan de Dios Hospital in *San José. He was
declared *Benemérito de la Patria in 1849.

GALLO PINTO. Literally means a painted rooster. It is the traditional national dish. It consists of rice mixed with black beans
and may have onions and/or meat. It is usually eaten for break-
fast, thus utilizing leftovers from the day before.

GAMBOA ALVARADO, Emma (1901-). Educator. Received doctorate in education from Ohio State University; dean of the Faculty
of Education at the *Universidad de Costa Rica, and president
of the (Costa Rican) National Association of Educators (*ANDE).
She favored education integrated with the culture of the country
and was one of the leaders in introducing John Dewey's philosophy
to the educational system. Declared *Benemérita de la Patria.

GAMERO MEDINA, Luis (1841-1928). Jesuit and educator. Born in
Honduras, he came to Costa Rica after his order was expelled
from Guatemala. He fostered musical education at the end of
the nineteenth century and was influential in the *Colegio San
Luis Gonzaga in *Cartago.

GAMONAL. A political boss. A term used in connection with rural
area or smaller towns. Typically a successful farmer; the term
does not have a negative connotation, as in Peru.

GARABITO. (1) *Chorotega Indian *cacique who organized a 119-
strong resistance to Juan de *Cavallón and almost annihilated
the conquistadors' forces several times. He was finally won
over to Christianity by Father Juan de *Estrada Rávago.
     (2) A new *canton in *Puntarenas Province chartered
September 25, 1980. Its *cabecera is Jacó. The *canton consists mostly of Playas de Jacó, a growing beach resort complex.
Total population is 3,144.

GARABITO, Andrés. Lieutenant governor of the province left in
charge of *Villa de Bruselas in 1524 when *Fernández de Córdoba went on an expedition to the *Huetar area.

GARAVITO. See: GARABITO.

GARCIA, Rafael A. Painter. Member of the GRUPO OCHO, q.v.

GARCIA ESCALANTE, Manuel. See: ESCALANTE, Manuel García.

GARCIA-ESCALANTE NAVAS, Rafael. See: ESCALANTE NAVAS, Rafael García.

GARCIA FLAMENCO, Marcelino (1888-1919). Salvadorean school-teacher in Buenos Aires (*Puntarenas Province) where he witnessed the execution of Rogelio *Fernández Güel and other revolutionaries following the frustrated 1918 uprising against Tinoco. He wrote a manifesto detailing the crime and then escaped to Panama. His disclosure of the events helped to turn public opinion against the Tinoco regime. García Flamenco was later killed in fighting in the Sapoá River region. See: SAPOA, Revolution of; TINOCO GRANADOS, Federico; and consult Rafael Obregón, Conflictos militares y políticos de Costa Rica (1951).

GARCIA JEREZ, Nicolás (d. 1825). Last bishop of Nicaragua and Costa Rica named by the crown (1810-25). Under his patronage the *Casa de Enseñanza de Santo Tomás opened its doors in 1814 and he also helped to reopen the *San Juan de Dios Hospital. García Jerez was somewhat reluctant to accept *independence, but finally pledged allegiance to the Constituent Assembly in Guatemala City; however, his loyalty was suspect and he was recalled to Guatemala City where he died.

GARCIA MONGE, Joaquin (1881-1958). Writer and journalist. García Monge studied in Chile and was one of the chief exponents of the *costumbrista novel in Costa Rica. He was one-time director of the *Escuela Normal and minister of education. Between 1919 and 1958 he published 1181 issues of the internationally renowned review Repertorio Americano. He was influenced by Tolstoy, Emile Zola, and Marxist philosophy, and participated in various radical groups (see: CENTRO GERMINAL). In 1958 he was proposed for the presidency but his party was ruled illegal because of its Communist ties. Nevertheless he was declared *Benemérito de la Patria (October 25, 1958). His house in *Desamparados was made a museum in 1988. His most important works are: El moto, Hijas del campo, Abnegación (1900), and La mala sombra (1918).

GARCIA MONGE AWARD. See: NATIONAL LITERATURE AWARDS.

GARCIA PICADO, Rafael Angel (1928-). Painter and architect. He studied in London where he helped found a group called "New Vision." He served for a time as director of "Arts and Letters," and founded others with the *Grupo Ocho, an art collective. His style is abstract with bright colors, which is sometimes called "action painting." He has also done some impressionist urban scenes. Since 1971 his style has become more conventional.

GARCIMUNOZ. The first permanent Spanish settlement in Costa Rica. It was founded by Juan de *Cavallón in March, 1561, and lasted until March, 1564 when its population was moved to *Cartago. Although the exact location is still disputed it is generally believed to have been located on the plains of Turrucares near the Ciruelas River and the present city of *Santa Ana.

GARITA, Disfredo (b. 1943). A self-taught painter. Born in *Alajuela. His works have their inspiration in the ways of the country people and the indigenous population. He uses bright colors and *Indian themes. His works have been exhibited in Costa Rica, El Salvador, and Mexico.

GARITA, Juan (1859-1914). Priest and writer. He was considered one of the precursors of the *costumbrista school. As a priest in a small town in *Cartago Province he wrote several articles and stories in newspapers dealing with the daily life of people.

GARNIER, Albert H. (d. 1981). Publicist. He founded the first public relations agency in Costa Rica and has written several books on the subject. Two important ones are: A través del humo (1968) and El triunfo del Agente Vendedor (1966).

GARNIER, Leonor (b. 1945). Poet and writer born in *San José. Her most important works are: Líneas hacia la soledad (1970), De las ocultas memorias (1974), Antología Femenina de ensayo costarricense (1976), Otra noción de la verdad (1979).

GARNIER U., Eduardo (1889-1956). Professor of physical education in the *Liceo de Costa Rica and also in the *Instituto de Alajuela for over thirty years. One of the founders of the National Football (*Soccer) league in 1921 and promoter of *sports in general.

GARRET Y ARLOVI, Benito (d. 1716). Bishop of Nicaragua and Costa Rica (1710-16). While Bishop he became involved in several disputes with the civil authorities. At first he accused the *governor (see: LACAYO DE BRIONES, José Antonio) of illegal trading. The governor was absolved, and this weakened the prestige of Bishop Garret. Later the Bishop was involved in several amorous problems and became embroiled in a jurisdictional conflict with the *Audiencia de Guatemala. These controversies finally caused his expulsion from the colony. He died in San Pedro Sula (Honduras) as he was returning to Spain. Consult Historia eclesiástica de Costa Rica (1967).

GARRON, Francisco (1843-1939). Born in Lyon, France, he settled in Costa Rica in 1872. He was the founder of the Garrón family. Francisco started a soap factory and later grew *coffee in *Puriscal. In 1910 he opened another soap factory in *Limón and also started to expand family interests in that region. Consult Victoria Garrón de Doryán, François Garrón Lafond (Francisco Garrón) (1981).

GARRON DE DORYAN, Victoria (b. 1920). Writer, biographer, and poet. Born in *San José, her most important works include: El aire, el agua y el árbol (1962) and Para que existe la llama (1972). She has also written a few biographies for the Ministry of Culture. First female vice-president (1986).

GARRON SALAZAR, Hernán (b. 1927). Businessman and politician who has spent most of his life expanding the family business in *Limón Province. He served as president of the Puerto *Limón city council 1953-58; *deputy in the national Congress 1958-62, 1966-70, 1982-86; and president of that body in the 1982-83 term. In addition he was minister of industries 1962-64, minister of agriculture 1974-76, and minister of public security 1986. He was director of *RECOPE for six months in 1971, and president of the *Banco Central of Costa Rica, and from 1972-74 was director of *JAPDEVA. He unsuccessfully tried to win a presidential primary in 1978, but was defeated by Luis Alberto *Monge Alvarez. Hernán Garrón was editor of La República (a newspaper) 1962-64.

GARROND LAFOND, François. See: GARRON, Francisco.

GASOLINE MONOPOLY. From 1931 to 1942 all gasoline was sold only in state-owned stations. A gasoline tax was substituted with the state seemingly making more of a profit. In 1975 gasoline stations were again put under state control. See also: RECOPE.

GEMMIR Y LLEONART, Juan (d. 1747). *Governor 1740 until his death in 1747. Built San Fernando Fortress (see: FUERTE DE SAN FERNANDO) at the mouth of the *Matina River which was destroyed by pirates.

GENERACION ACADEMICA, La. See: PAINTING.

GENERACION NACIONALISTA, La. See: PAINTING.

GENERATION OF 1889. A nebulous term used for the liberals that emerged from the electoral struggle of that year and also the last class to have graduated from the *Universidad de Santo Tomás. This group included *Bernardo Soto Alfaro, Ascención *Esquivel Ibarra, Cleto *González Víquez, and Ricardo *Jiménez Oreamuno. See also: OLIMPICOS.

GENERATION OF 1940. A so-called generation of writers who sought for the first time to talk about social problems. Among the most important of this group were: Carlos Luis *Fallas Sibaja, Yolanda *Oreamuno, and Joaquín *Gutiérrez Mangel.

GENERATION OF 1948. A nebulous term to designate the group of young men who came from the *Centro para el Estudio de Problemas Nacionales and the Social Democratic Party. They were the ones who won the 1948 *civil war, and have tended to control the country ever since. They generally belong to the National Liberation Party (*Partido Liberación Nacional). Among them are: José *Figueres Ferrer, Luis Alberto *Monge Alvarez, Rodrigo *Facio Brenes, Alberto *Canas Escalante, José Francisco *Orlich Bolamacich, Daniel *Oduber Quirós.

GENIE, Le. Brig of the French navy, sent to *Puntarenas in 1847-48 to back up the demand by Charles Thierriat for $10,000 damages supposedly caused by a road the government had built across property which he claimed belonged to him, but also as part of an effort to persuade the Central American republics to seek French protection against the United States and the United Kingdom (both active in the region, and quarrelling over British involvement with the *Miskito Indians). Shortly afterwards the July Revolution (1848) overthrew the government of King Louis Philippe, so diverting the attention of the French authorities to their own internal affairs. [T.C., L.H.]

GOBERNACION DE COSTA RICA. The colonial political status of Costa Rica, within the *capitanía general of Guatemala, 1543-1795, and then, after 1795, under the intendancy of Nicaragua.

GOBERNACION DE OJEDA. A territory in the early colonial period which roughly comprised half of the Gulf of Darien region (up to the Vela Cape). Its name was in honor of Alonso de *Ojeda, navigator and companion of Amerigo Vespucci.

GOBIERNO DE LA ASAMBLEA. Government of Costa Rica from April 16 to May 10, 1823. It was formed by José Gregorio *Ramírez Castro after he successfully subdued *Cartago in the first *civil war. Its president was Manuel *Alvarado Hidalgo. This body changed the capital from *Cartago to *San José, decreed the first Costa Rican flag, coat of arms, system of *coinage, and set the conditions by which Costa Rica would join the *Central American Federation. It turned over the government to the Tercera (third) *Junta Superior Gubernativa.

GODOS (GOTHS). A pejorative term used for Spaniards during the colonial era.

GODOY, Juan Vicente. Lieutenant governor who served as acting *governor in the absence of Governor *Granada y Balbin (April-May 1708).

GOICOCHEA. *Canton about two miles from *San José. Its
*cabecera is the city of Guadalupe. In addition to being pri-
marily a suburban community, the canton is noted for *coffee
and truck farming. Originally called Barrio de los Santos in
1848. It was chartered (August 6, 1891). The present population is 79,931. The name Guadalupe was given to the cabecera
by Father Raimundo Mora.

GOLD. Gold was mined by the pre-Columbian *Indians and worked
into beautiful jewelry especially by the *Brunkas. The Banco
Central houses the Gold Museum of pre-Columbian artifacts.
There were mines in colonial times in *Monte de Aguacate and
*Abangeres. However the meager supply soon ran out. Of
late gold has been panned from streams, mostly in the Osa area.
There was some minting of gold coins from time to time. There
are still one or two small gold mines operating in Costa Rica.
Recently the Banco Central has decreed that all gold mined must
be sold to them at current prices (but in *colons). Gold production has been calculated at 17,000 ounces in 1982, 20,000 in
1983 and a projection of 25,000 in 1985. See: PATRON DE ORO,
and consult La Nación Internacional, (9 al 15 de febrero de
1984).

GOLD STANDARD. When Costa Rican currency was decimalized in
1863, the colonial bimetallic tradition was continued, but with
so unrealistic a ratio between gold and silver as to drive the
former out of circulation and establish a de facto silver standard.
By the last decade of the century, however, world monetary
fashion was forcing monetary authorities everywhere to go on
to the *gold standard (patrón de oro).
A law of October 24, 1896 introduced a new gold coin,
the *colon, with the same value (¢2.20 to the U.S. dollar) as
the silver *peso which it replaced on April 17, 1900. In order
to effect a monetary stabilization, backing the currency with
75% gold, the government borrowed Ⱡ150,000. The gold standard and consequent stable currency exchange rate was maintained until the First World War forced its abandonment. See
also: COINAGE; COLON; EXCHANGE RATE. [L.H.]

GOLFITO. (1) City and principal port in the southwest Pacific
region at 8°41'N, 83°10'W.
(2) *Canton in *Puntarenas Province, created July 10,
1949. It was the center of United Brands Company's *banana
operation and a major seaport. Its present population is 29,043.
The company began a shift to growing African palm in the Palmares area and decided in 1985 to abandon their banana plantations.

GOLFO DE SAN VICENTE. One of the old names for the Pacific
port of *Caldera.

GOLPE DE FRANKFORT. The decree issued in January 1852 in

which President Juan Rafael *Mora Porras closed Congress and
assumed dictatorial powers. This action derived its name from
the place where the decree was issued (Frankfort), Mora's farm,
located near Pavas (*San José Province).

GOMEZ, Matute. Nephew of Venezuela dictator Juan Vicente Gómez,
lived as wealthy exile in *San José from 1935 until expelled by
President *Figueres in 1953. His mansion is a landmark; "100
meters from [the house] Matute Gómez" is a standard form of
direction. [G.K.]

GOMEZ DE LARA, Miguel (b. 1632). *Governor of the province of
Costa Rica 1681-1693. During his administration *pirates attacked
*Nicoya and *Esparza. Therefore in 1691 he secured permission
to raise a provincial militia. Another achievement of his administration was the building of a church in Ujarrás to thank the
Virgin of Ujarrás for saving the country from the pirates. This
governor was later accused by the *cabildo of *Cartago of trading with the English pirates.

GONZALEZ, Gerardo (b. 1946). Painter born and educated in *San
José. His paintings are characterized by bright and highly
contrasting colors. He was associated with the *Grupo Totem.

GONZALEZ, Hernán (1922-1987). Artist and sculptor and one of
the leaders of the so-called *Generation of 1960. He was also
associated with the *Grupo Ocho. Many of his works are abstract or symbolic with animals as his subject. Some of his
most important sculptures are entitled: "Sapo cazador o gallinas,"
"La totalización," "Simbólico de la humanidad," and "Agonía."
Trained as a lawyer and active in the *National Liberation Party;
minister of culture in Monge Alvarez's administration (1982-86).

GONZALEZ, José. Organist and musician. Studied in the *Conservatorio de Castella. He specializes in organic and electronic
music. He won a prize in Colombia in 1977 for his organic work
"Extasis en el oasis." In that same year he won an award in
Japan for an electronic musical piece called "El diario de una
computadora."

GONZALEZ, Juan Federico (1841-1910). Born in *Heredia, he was
a *deputy in 1870. He signed the act protesting Tomás *Guardia
Gutiérrez's closing of the Assembly. He returned to serve as
*deputy in the administrations of *Soto Alfaro and Asención
*Esquivel Ibarra. González was a signer of the Grito de Yara,
which was a protest against the *continuismo of Rafael *Yglesias
Castro. He became a member of the Club Patriótico (1897).
He is credited with having picked the name for the Republican
Party (*Partido Republicano) which grew out of this club. In
1940 he was appointed to the Supreme Court.

GONZALEZ DE AVILA, Gil (d. 1526). Name also spelled González Davila. Spanish explorer and conquistador. He accompanied Andrés *Niño in an expedition to the Gulf of *Nicoya region in 1522-23 and it is claimed that he discovered the *San Juan River on this expedition. On this trip Gil González made contact and maintained peaceful relations with several *Chorotega tribes and the Nicaraguan Chief Nicaro. He also explored sections of Nicaragua and Honduras. Unfortunately González became involved in a jurisdictional conflict with *Pedrarias Dávila. He was captured by Pedrarias's agent, Hernando de Soto, and sent to Spain for trial as a rebel, but died at Avila before he could be judged.

GONZALEZ FEO DE SAENZ, Luisa (1889-1982). A realist painter and book illustrator. She painted local scenes and religious subjects.

GONZALEZ FLORES, Alfredo (1877-1962). Lawyer and politician. President of the Republic (1914-17), after being elected by Congress as a result of an impasse between the declared candidates. He tried to conduct a progressive administration, founding an *escuela normal in *Heredia, and instituting a progressive *income tax. However, the economic strains of the First World War period, pressures by foreign oil companies, and his questionable election turned public opinion against him. He was overthrown by his minister of war, General Federico *Tinoco Granados on January 27, 1917. González later represented Costa Rica in international litigation, and served as the first president of the *Banco Nacional de Costa Rica (1936-40). He was declared *Benemérito de la Patria in 1954.

GONZALEZ FLORES, Luis Felipe (1884-1973). Educator and historian. He studied in Argentina, was secretary of education in his brother's cabinet (1914-17). He was part of the group opposed to some of the ideas of John Dewey. He favored a philosophy called pedagogical socialism, or the use of national images. He wrote the Law of Public Education (1920), and is the founder of the Patronato Nacional de la Infancia. Among his most important works are: Historia de la influencia extranjera en el desenvolvimiento educacional y científico de Costa Rica (1921), Historia de la instrucción pública en Costa Rica (1945), and La Casa de Enseñanza de Santo Tomás (1941).

GONZALEZ MARTEN, Jorge. See: PARTIDO NACIONAL INDEPENDIENTE.

GONZALEZ RAMIREZ, Salvador (1831-1881). Acting president of the Republic, November 21 to December 1, 1873. When General *Guardia Gutiérrez decided to give up the reins of government he chose González, who was first vice-president, to succeed him.

But when González, began to form a conciliatory government
with members of the opposition General Guardia dismissed him
and called the second vice-president to form a government.
See: BARROETA BACA, Rafael; GUARDIA, Tomás.

GONZALEZ RANCANO, José. *Governor of Nicaragua (1749) and
interim governor of Costa Rica (1757-58). He had serious problems with the populace of *Cartago and had to flee disguised as
a woman.

GONZALEZ REYES, Juan (1808-1871). President of the municipality
of *Heredia and second *governor of that province. He signed
an act of non-recognition of the presidency of Francisco *Morazán,
which gave support to José María *Alfaro Zamora. He was *deputy
in 1857 and 1859 and was one of the leaders in the fight for
abolition of imprisonment for debts.

GONZALEZ RUCAVADO, Claudio (1878-1928). Lawyer, newsman
and politician. He served as *deputy in 1916 and wrote novels
dealing with regionalism and the struggle between the city and
the country. The most important works are: El hijo de un
gamonal (1901) and Escenas costarricenses (1906).

GONZALEZ VIQUEZ, Cleto (1858-1937). Lawyer, historian and
president of the Republic (1906-10) and (1928-32). One of the
chief examples of Costa Rican liberalism of his period. "Don
Cleto" also served as foreign minister and minister of finance.
His most important historical works are: Apuntes sobre geografía
de Costa Rica, El sufragio de Costa Rica ante la historia y la
legislación and Historia financiera de Costa Rica. He was declared *Benemérito de la Patria in 1944. See also: GENERATION
of 1889; OLIMPICOS.

GONZALEZ ZELEDON, Manuel (Magón) (1864-1936). Writer and
co-founder of the *costumbrista school of literature. His best
work is La propia (1901), which is an outstanding example of
costumbrista literature. He worked on several newspapers and
used his own newspaper, El País, as a voice of opposition to the
dictatorship of Rafael *Yglesias Castro. In addition to serving
as *deputy, he was also Costa Rican minister to Washington
(1932-36). He lived the last third of his life outside of Costa
Rica. A major literary prize is given each year in his honor.

GOOD SHEPHERD CHURCH. See: PROTESTANTS.

GORDIENKO, Xenia (b. 1933). Considered one of the more important
*Arte Nuevo painters. Her style could be characterized as use
of light in a somewhat mysterious way combined with an abstract
sensuality. Typical of this is her "Series de las piñas." Most
of her works are in oils.

GOVERNMENT MINISTRIES. In 1848 there were just two departments of state, termed "ministries" (ministerios): one for foreign affairs, the interior, justice, and church affairs (relaciones exteriores, gobernación, justica y negocios eclesiásticos), and the other for finance, education, the army and the navy, and shipping (hacienda pública, educación, guerra y marina). In 1866 the ministers (ministros) became secretaries of state (secretarios de estado) and their responsibilities were renamed portfolios (carteras). The term secretary of state persisted until the 1948 revolution, but portfolio was usually replaced by secretariat (secretaría). As the country developed the number of government departments naturally increased. By the early twentieth century they were: public instruction (instrucción pública), war and public safety (guerra y seguridad pública), trade and industry (fomento)--which included responsibility for the state railroads--, finance (hacienda), the interior (gobernación)-- which included control of local government authorities--, foreign affairs (relaciones exteriores), and justice, culture and welfare (justicia, cultura y beneficencia). A department of public health (salubridad pública) was added in 1927, and one of labor and social security (trabajo y prevención social) in 1928. As elsewhere in the world, department titles have been subject to political fashions: instrucción pública gave way to educación in 1940; salubridad pública became simply salud in 1948; prevención social is now bienestar social, and so on. The 1948 revolution restored the old terms ministro and ministerio in place of secretario and secretaría; its new constitution also specified that the health minister must be a qualified medical practitioner. Notable among subsequent changes has been the 1966 creation of a ministry of the presidency (ministerio de la presidencia). In 1983 there were seventeen ministries: agriculture and livestock (agricultura y ganadería); culture; economy and commerce; energy and mines; exports and investments; finance; foreign relations; health; industry; the interior and police (gobernación y policía)--whose responsibilities include the post office and civil aviation--, justice, labor and social welfare; national planning and economic policy; the presidency; public education; public safety (seguridad pública) and public works and transport (obras públicas y transportes). Since then economy, industry and commerce (economía, industria y comercio) has become a single ministry and the ministry of energy and mines became the ministry of natural resources, energy and mines in 1987. [L.H.]

GOVERNMENTS OF COSTA RICA. Costa Rica has changed governments many times since its independence from Spain. Here is a list of the forms of governments and their effective dates (some overlapping). These items are listed in greater details under separate headings.

*Junta de Legados de los Pueblos (Nov. 12 to Dec. 1, 1821)
Pacto Social Interino de Costa Rica (*Pacto de Concordia)
   (Dec. 1, 1821)

Comisión de la Legación de Costa Rica (Dec. 1 to Jan. 13, 1822)
*Junta Superior Gubernativa de Costa Rica (Jan. 13, 1822 to Dec. 31, 1822)
Second *Junta Superior Gubernativa de Costa Rica (Jan. 1 to March 20, 1823)
*Congreso Provincial de Costa Rica (Third Constituent Assembly) (March 3 to October 10, 1823, not in continuous session)
Primer Estatuto Político de la Provincia de Costa Rica (March 17, 1823)
*Diputación de Costa Rica (Triumvirate) (March 20-29, 1823)
Dictatorship of Gregorio José *Ramírez Castro (as commanding General) (April 5-16, 1823)
*Gobierno de la Asamblea (April 16 to May 10, 1823)
Segundo Estatuto Político de la Provincia de Costa Rica (May 16, 1823)
Third *Junta Superior Gubernativa de Costa Rica (May 10, 1823 to Sept. 6, 1824)
Congreso Constituyente (Sept. 6, 1824 to April 14, 1825)
Constitución de la Republica Federal de Centro América (Nov. 22, 1824)
*Ley Fundamental de Estado Libre de Costa Rica (Jan. 25, 1825)
Constitución Federal de Centro-América (with the reforms decreed) (Feb. 13, 1835)
Dictatorship of Braulio *Carrillo Colina (Nov. 1, 1838)
*Estado Libre de Costa Rica (Nov. 14, 1838--declared independence from the Federal Republic of Central America)
*Ley de Bases y Garantías (March 8, 1841--declared null June 6, 1842)
Asamblea Constituyente de 1842 (July 10 to Sept. 2, 1842)
Dictatorship of Francisco *Morazán (June 15, 1842, named "Jefe Supremo del Estado" with title "Liberator of Costa Rica." He declared Costa Rica part of the Republic of Central America July 20, 1842; overthrown Sept. 1842)
Provisional Government of José María *Alfaro Zamora (Sept. 1842 to June 1843)
Asamblea Constituyente de 1843-44 (June 1, 1843 to July 3, 1844)
Constitución Política del Estado de Costa Rica (April 9, 1844)
Dictatorship of José María Alfaro (June 7 to Sept. 15, 1846)
Asamblea Constituyente de 1846-47 (Sept. 15, 1846 to May 1, 1847)
Constitución Política de 1847 (Feb. 10, 1847)
Constitución Política Reformada (Nov. 30, 1848)
Dictatorship of José María *Montealegre Fernández (Aug. 16 to October 16, 1859)
Asamblea Constituyente (Oct. 16 to Dec. 26, 1859)
Constitución Política de 1859 (Dec. 27, 1859)
Dictatorship of Jesús *Jiménez Zamora (Nov. 1868 to Jan. 1, 1869)
Asamblea Constituyente de 1869 (Jan. 1 to Feb. 18, 1869)
Constitución Política de 1869 (April 15, 1869)
Dictatorships of Eusebio *Figueroa Oreamuno (April 26-27, 1869)

and Bruno *Carranza Ramirez (April 27 to August 8, 1870)
Asamblea Constituyente de 1870 (August 8 to Oct. 10, 1870)
Dictatorship of General Tomás *Guardia Gutiérrez (October 10, 1870 to October 15, 1871)
Asamblea Constituyente (October 15 to Dec. 7, 1871)
Constitución Política de 1871 (Dec. 7, 1871)
Dictatorship of Vicente *Herrera Zeledón (figurehead for Tomás Guardia) (July 30, 1876 to Sept. 11, 1877)
Asamblea Constituyente de 1880 (Aug. 29 to Sept. 23, 1880-- suspended by General Tomás Guardia)
Dictatorship of General Tomás Guardia (Sept. 23, 1880 to April 26, 1882)
Restoration of the Constitution of 1871 (with modifications) (April 26, 1882)
Dictatorship of Federico *Tinoco Granados (Jan. 27, 1917 to April 11, 1917)
Asamblea Constituyente de 1917 (April 11 to June 8, 1917)
Constitución Política de 1917 (June 8, 1917)
Transitional Government of Juan Bautista *Quirós Segure (Aug. 12 to Sept. 2, 1919)
*Junta Fundadora de la Segunda República (dictatorship of José Figueres) (May 8, 1948 to Jan. 15, 1949)
Asamblea Constituyente de 1949 (Jan. 15 to Nov. 7, 1949)
Constitución Política de 1949 (Nov. 7, 1949)

(Note: The term "dictatorship" is used when no Congress or Constituent Assembly functioned and the government came to power by irregular, non-electoral means). For a further discussion and interpretation of the various governmental changes, consult Cleto González Víquez, El sufragio en Costa Rica antes de la historia y la legislación (1858 ed.); Facultad de Ciencias y Letras, Universidad de Costa Rica, Antología de historia de la instituciones de Costa Rica (1969); Mario Alberto Jiménez, Desarrollo constitucional de Costa Rica (1962 ed.); Rafael Obregón Loria, De nuestra historia patria (8 vols.), and his Hechos militares y políticos (1981); Hernan Peralta, Las constituciones de Costa Rica (1961); Marco Tulio Zeledón, Digesto constitucional de Costa Rica (1946).

GOVERNORS. Governors are listed by name and year that they held office. More detailed information may be found under separate listings. It should be noted that before 1541 some of the governors exercised little or no authority over Costa Rica except on paper, but they are listed for the record; some dates and jurisdictions overlap.

Governors of *Veragua (which also included Costa Rica):
Diego de *Nicuesa, 1508-11
Vasco *Núñez de Balboa, 1511-14 (de facto)
*Pedrarias Dávila, 1523-31
Felipe *Gutiérrez, 1534-36
Hernán *Sánchez de Badajoz, 1539-41

Governors of Nicaragua and Costa Rica:
Gil *González Dávila, 1521-23 (head of expedition)
Pedro de los Ríos, 1526-27
Diego *López de Salcedo, 1527-28 (de facto)
Francisco de *Castañeda, 1531-36
Diego Alvarez de Osorio, Jan.-Nov. 1535
Rodrigo de *Contreras, 1535-41

Governors of the province of Costa Rica:
Diego de *Gutiérrez, 1541-44
Juan de *Cavallón, c. 1560-62
Juan de *Estrada Rávago, Jan.-Nov. 1562
Juan *Vázquez de Coronado, 1562-1565
Antonio *Andrada, April 1564 (acting)
Miguel *Sánchez de Guido, 1564-66 (acting 1564-65)
Pedro *Venegas de los Ríos, 1566-68 (interim)
*Perafán de Ribera, 1568-73
Antonio Alvarez Pereira, 1570-72; 1577-78, part of 1591 (acting)
Juan *Solano 1573-74, 1578-79 (acting), 1587 (acting)
Alonso *Anguciana de Gamboa, 1574-77 (interim), 1587 (acting)
Diego de *Artieda Chirinos, 1577-90
Juan de *Peñaranda, 1589-90 (acting)
Juan *Velázquez Ramiro, 1590-91 (interim)
Bartolomé de *Lences, 1591-92
Gonzalo de *Palma, 1591-95 (interim)
Fernando de la *Cueva, 1595-99
Gonzalo *Vazquez de Coronado, 1600-04 (interim)
Francisco de *Ocampo y Golfín, 1601 (acting)
Juan de *Ocón y Trillo, 1604-13
Juan de *Mendoza y Medrano, 1613-19
Alonso del *Castillo y Guzmán, 1619-24
Juan de *Echaúz, 1624-30
Juan de *Villalta, 1630-34
Bartolomé de *Enciso Hita, 1634 (acting)
Juan de *Agüero, 1634-36 (interim)
Gregorio *Sandoval, 1636-44
Juan *Chávez de Mendoza, 1644-1650
Juan *Fernández de Salinas y de la Cerda, 1650-59
Andrés *Arias de Maldonado, 1662-64 (interim)
Fernando de *Salazar, 1662-63 (acting)
Juan de Obregón, 1664 (interim)
Juan *López de la Flor, 1665-74
Juan Francisco *Saénz Vázquez, 1674-81
Francisco Antonio de *Rivas y Contreras, 1678 (interim)
Miguel *Gómez de Lara, 1681-93
Manuel de *Bustamante y Vivero, 1693-98
Francisco *Serrano de Reyna, 1698-1704
Diego de Herrera Campuzano, 1704-07 (interim)
Lorenzo Antonio de *Granda y Balbín, 1707-12
Juan Vicente *Godoy, 1708 (acting for a few months)
José de *Mier Ceballos, 1710 (acting)

José de Casasola y Córdoba, June-Nov. 1711, and Oct. 1712 to
   May 1713 (acting)
Francisco *López Conejo, May 1713 (acting)
José Antonio *Lacayo de Briones, 1713-17 (interim)
Pedro *Ruiz de Bustamante, 1717-18 (interim)
Diego de la *Haya Fernández, 1718-27
Baltazar Francisco de *Valderrama, 1727-36
Antonio *Vázquez de la Quadra, April-July 1736
Juan Francisco de *Ibarra y Calvo, July-Aug. 1736 (acting)
Dionisio Salmón-Pacheco, Aug.-Dec. 1736
Juan Rodríguez de Robrero, July-Dec. 1736 (acting in military
   matters)
Francisco Antonio de *Carrandi y Menán, 1736-39
Francisco de *Olaecha, 1739-40 (interim)
Juan *Gemmir y Lleonart, 1740-47
Esteban *Ruiz de Mendoza, 1745 (acting)
Alfonso *Fernández de Heredia, 1746-53
Francisco *Fernández de Heredia, 1746-53
Francisco *Fernández de la Pastora, 1746 (acting), 1747-48,
   1754-56
Francisco Javier de *Oriamuno Vásquez, Nov.-Dec. 1747 (acting),
   1760-62
Luis *Diez Navarro, 1748-50 (interim)
Cristóbal Ignacio de *Soria, 1750-54
José *González Rancano, 1757-58 (interim)
Manuel *Soler, 1758-60
José Antonio de *Oriamuno Vásquez, 1756-57, 1762-64 (interim)
José Joaquín de *Nava, 1764-73
Juan *Fernández de Bobadilla, 1773-78, 1780-81 (interim)
José *Perié Barros, 1778-89
Francisco *Carazo Soto-Barahona, Jan.-April 1781 (acting in
   political matters)
Rafael *Gutiérrez de Cárdenas, Jan.-April 1781 (acting in military
   matters)
Juan *Flores Sánchez, 1781-85 (interim)
José Antonio de *Oriamuno García, 1788-89 (acting)
Juan Esteban *Martínez de Pinillos, 1789-90 (interim)
José *Vásquez y Téllez, 1790-96
Juan *Fernández de Bonilla, 1796-97 (interim)
Gregorio *Oriamuno Alvarado, 1797 (acting)
Tomás Benito *Hidalgo Bonilla, 1797 (acting)
Tomás de *Acosta, 1797-1810
Joaquín de *Oriamuno, 1809, Nov. 1817 (acting)
Juan de Dios *Ayala Alvarado, 1810-19
Rafael *Barroeta Castilla, 1811 (acting)
José Santos *Lombardo Alvarado, 1816 (acting in political matters)
Juan Francisco de *Bonilla, 1816 (acting in military matters)
Juan *Dengo, 1819 (acting in military matters)
Félix *Fernández Tenorio, 1819 (acting in political matters)
Ramón *Jiménez Rodríguez, 1819 (acting in political matters)
Juan Manuel *Cañas de Trujillo, 1819-21

GRADO, Baltasar de. First native-born Costa Rican to complete ecclesiastical studies (1608-09). Parish priest of *Cartago at the time of the appearance of the *Virgin of the Angels (patron saint of Costa Rica), August 2, 1635.

GRANADA, Treaty of (1823). See: MONTEALEGRE, Mariano.

GRANDA Y BALBIN, Lorenzo Antonio de (d. 1712). *Governor (1707-12). The great revolt of *Talamanca Indians (1710) occurred during his administration. As a result 500 *Indians were distributed via *repartimiento in *Cartago. Granda y Balbín was accused of cruelty and removed by the *Cabildo of Cartago as being "inept." Although he died in the middle of the appeal process, the *Audiencia de Guatemala punished those who were involved in expelling the governor.

GRANJA NACIONAL DE AGRICULTURA. Created in 1900 to better agriculture by experimenting and supplying better information of agriculture to the farmers. It also published a review called El Agricultor Costarricense. Chronic lack of funds curtailed its effectiveness although at times it did manage to distribute better seed to some farmers.

GREATER REPUBLIC OF CENTRAL AMERICA. See: REPUBLICA MAYOR DE AMERICA CENTRAL.

GRECIA. *Canton in *Alajuela Province, chartered July 24, 1867. It produces *sugar and has an abundance of *trapiches (small sugar mills). Its present population is 39,314 and its *cabecera is Grecia, site of a unique iron church erected by a Belgian firm in the 1890s.

GREYTOWN. See: SAN JUAN DEL NORTE; TROLLOPE, Anthony.

GRILLO OCAMPO, Rafael Angel (1901-1947). *Deputy (1942-44), president of the Congress (1945-47) and noted surgeon.

GRITO DE YARA. Protest against the *continuismo of Rafael *Yglesias Castro.

GROS MICHEL. A thick-skinned *banana, whose cultivation by the *United Fruit Company is being curtailed because of its susceptibility to disease.

GRUPO OCHO, El. A group of eight artists who in 1961 called for a new emphasis on art. They advocated leaving classic Old World form and called for concentration on Costa Rican themes. Their first show (which caused a stir) was in December, 1961. The group held together about three years holding exhibitions, festivals and in general generating much new creative energy. The members of this group were: Luis *Daell, Harold Fonseca,

Rafael A. García, Hernán *González, Manuel de la *Cruz González,
Nestor *Zeledón Guzmán, Guillermo *Jiménez Sáenz, Cesar *Valverde. There were some other people who were also affiliated
with the group. Consult Guillermo Jiménez Sáenz, "Grupo Ocho"
in Tertulia (Revista Nacional de Cultura), Número 7, (Enero
1982), pp. 35-41.

GRUPO TALLER, El. An artistic movement which evolved out of
the *Grupo Ocho. It clustered around Manuel de la *Cruz González and existed from 1961 until 1970. Its purpose was to encourage artistic dialogue and promote all types of plastic arts
through public lectures and art shows.

GRUPO TOTEM, El. A group of artists which during the late 1960s
sought to promote art in the provinces by trying to make more
direct contact with the people.

GRUTTER, Virginia (b. 1929). Poet born in *Puntarenas. Her
most important works are: Dame la mano (1954), Poesía de este
mundo (1973), and Los amigos y el viento (1979), Desaparecido
(1980).

GUACIMO. A *canton in *Limón Province created May 8, 1971.
Its *cabecera is Guácimo and it has a population of 16,472. It
is mostly agricultural producing *cacao, *bananas and yucca.

GUADALUPE. *Cabecera of *Goicochea *canton.

GUANACASTE. (1) Province of Costa Rica in the warm, dry Northwest with a population of 32,989 in 1910, 193,024 in 1984, and
195,208 (est.) in 1987. Its capital is *Liberia, and it produces
most of the country's beef *cattle; in addition, it also produces
various fruits, grains, cotton, and some *coffee. Originally
called the Partido de *Nicoya (after its chief town of the time).
It was part of the province of Nicaragua, but included with
Costa Rica by the *Cortes de Cádiz in 1814 to supplement the
Costa Rican population to give them enough to elect a representative. As a result of *civil wars in Nicaragua the people in a
*cabildo abierto in Nicoya on July 25, 1824, voted to join Costa
Rica. This was accepted by the Federal Congress of Central
America (December 1825) but Nicaragua did not formally renounce
its claims to the area until the *Cañas-Jerez Treaty in 1858.
The province was also known as *Moracia (1854-60) in honor
of Juan *Mora Fernández. The southern tip of the Nicoya Peninsula was transferred to the province of *Puntarenas in 1915.
Guanacaste Province is known today for its folklore, and the
25th of July, the day of its annexation to the Republic, has
been celebrated as a national holiday. See also: FRONTIER
QUESTIONS (NICARAGUA); INSURRECTION OF 1811; MORACIA;
NICOYA, Partido de.
    (2) A large umbrella tree (enterolobium cyclocarpum) which

grows on the pampas of this province and is officially designated "National Tree."

GUANACASTE, El. Newspaper published by the Casa de Guanacaste and the *Partido Confraternidad Guanacasteco from c. 1938-42.

GUANACASTE NATIONAL PARK. Effort with international financial support to save the dry forest ecology of northwestern Costa Rica. Consult David H. Janzen, Guanacaste National Park: Tropical Ecological and Cultural Restoration, 1986; and Smithsonian, December 1986. [G.K.]

GUARCO. (1) *Canton in *Cartago Province, about two miles from *Cartago City. Its *cabecera is El *Tejar. It was founded as a canton July 26, 1939. It produces *coffee, corn, potatoes, beans and truck farm crops. The population is 20,807. During the 1948 civil war it was the site of possibly the most bloody battle in Costa Rica's history. See: EL TEJAR.
    (2) Valley of the river in which the city of Cartago is located, named for a chief of the *Huetar tribe.
    (3) Famous Huetar Indian chief, father of *Correque.

GUARDIA CARAZO, Jorge (1883-1956). Jurist. Minister of foreign relations in the government of *González Flores and president of the Supreme Court (1949-55).

GUARDIA DE ASISTENCIA RURAL. A type of rural constabulary created in 1970 to replace the *Guardia Fiscal, but with more general police powers. Until 1987 they were recognized by their yellow uniforms.

GUARDIA FISCAL. A rural constabulary empowered to enforce fiscal laws. It was used principally in detecting illegal *liquor operations and smuggling. Known as the Resguardo. Replaced in 1970 by the *Guardia de Asistencia Rural.

GUARDIA GUTIERREZ, Tomás [General] (1831-1882). President of the Republic 1870-72, 1872-76, 1877-82; during much of that time he exercised dictatorial powers. He had distinguished himself in the war against William *Walker and first came to power in April 1870 after engineering a plot to overthrow Jesús Jiménez Zamora. He was then the dominant force in Costa Rica politics until his death in April 1882, selecting and disposing of presidents virtually as he saw fit. During this period the unfortunate loans with England were negotiated, the *railroad to the Atlantic (*Ferrocarril del Norte) was started, and at the behest of his wife, Emilia *Solórzano de Guardia, the death penalty was abolished. He was declared *Benemérito de la Patria in 1876. See also: BRITISH LOANS; JIMENEZ ZAMORA, Jesús; RAILROADS.

GUARDIA GUTIERREZ, Victor (1830-1912). Actively participated in the war against William *Walker, occupied several ministries (1873-81), and served as vice-president of the Republic. He was a delegate to the Constituent Assemblies of 1870, 1871, and 1880, and president of Congress in 1882-83.

GUARDIA QUIROS, Víctor (1873-1959). Jurist. Member of the 1916 Constituent Assembly, president of the Supreme Court (1938-45). He wrote many legal commentaries. Some of his collected works appear in Escarceos literarios (1935).

GUARDIA Y AYALA, Victor de la (1772-1827). Born in Panama and a leading spokesman for the liberal position during the independence period. He served as intendant of the province of Costa Rica and later *deputy. In tracts like Apuntaciones (1824) he expounded the ideas of Montesquieu and Rousseau. Founder of the Guardia family in Costa Rica. He wrote "La Política del Mundo," which may be the first dramatic piece written in Costa Rica.

GUARIA MORADA (Cattleya Skinneri). A violet-colored orchid that usually blooms January to March. It is the "National Flower" of Costa Rica.

GUARO. A type of low quality aguardiente made from sugarcane for popular consumption, having the smell and taste of rubbing alcohol.

GUATEMALA. See: ACTA DE GUATEMALA (1821 independence); AUDIENCIA; CAPTAINCY GENERAL; KINGDOM OF GUATEMALA.

GUATUSO. (1) A dialect of Corobicí and a small tribe of *Indians living in the northeast part of the country.
(2) An isolated *canton in *Alajuela Province established March 17, 1970, with a population of 6,774. Its *cabecera is San Rafael. There are still some *Indians living there. Main products are *cacao, lumber and grains. Its development is hampered by poor roads.

GUAYABO DE TURRIALBA. An archaeological site 20 km north of *Turrialba City, containing mounds, stone house foundations, aqueducts, plazas and paved paths, from 1000-1500 A.D. Systematic excavation has been under way since 1968. The site was declared a *national park in 1973. Consult: Oscar Fonseca Zamora and Luis Hurtado de Mendoza, Algunos resultados de las investigaciones en la región de Turrialba (1982). [T.C., G.K., L.H.]

GUERRA DE LA LIGA, 1835 (War of the League). Costa Rica's second civil war, begun September 26, 1835. The cities of *Cartago, *Alajuela and *Heredia formed a league and elected Nicolás ULLOA (q.v.) as its president. This secessionist movement was motivated by resentment at their loss of importance to emerging San José. They were particularly resentful at the election of Braulio *Carrillo Colina, made possible by the votes of the San José area, over the strong opposition of the other cities. In October some 1,300 men from Cartago and 3,000 from Alajuela and Heredia besieged San José, but the forces of the latter were successful in battles at the Cuesta de Moras (present site of the Legislative Assembly Building), *Curridabat and *Ochomomgo. The war was ended by the Treaty of VIRILLA (q.v.). The outcome was to assure the dominance of San José as both the political and commercial capital of Costa Rica.

Consult: Rodolfo Cerdas, La formación del estado de Costa Rica (1947) and Ricardo Fernández Guardia, La Guerra de la Liga y la invasión de Quijano (1950).

GUERRERO DE ARCOS, Juan Simeón. He was brought to Costa Rica from his native Nicaragua by the Junta Gubernativa in 1824 to be judge and auditor de guerra. Named judge of the Corte Suprema de Justicia in 1825, 1831, and 1833.

GUI-PI-PIA. Exuberant expression of enthusiasm. This and other aspects of national charm were portrayed in the 1947 Hollywood movie "Carnival in Costa Rica." The *costumbrista poet Aquileo *Echeverría Zeledón wrote of this happy *concho cry. See also: CARNIVAL. [G.K.]

GUIER, George [Doctor]. He came to Costa Rica from Philadelphia in the 1850s. He was shortly joined by his brother, the pharmacist Henry Guier. They operated a pharmacy in *Cartago where they were the first to dispense medicines in glass bottles in the country. Henry returned to the United States, whereas George bought land in the Ujarrás Valley. He converted to Catholicism so he could marry, and established the Guier family line.

GUIER, Henry. See: GUIER, George [Doctor].

GUIER SAENZ, Enrique (1899-1970). Jurist. Law professor and president of the Supreme Court (1945-48).

GUTIERREZ, Adilio (1913-1942). Poet from *Heredia whose works appeared from time to time in newspapers and literary magazines. Most important work is A propósito del centenario de Garcilaso de la Vega (1936).

GUTIERREZ, Benjamin (b. 1937). Composer, musician and conductor. He was educated in Costa Rica and in the New England Convervatory of Music. He has done operas, concerti, and other types of music. His most noteworthy contributions are: "Marianela" (1957, an opera in three acts), "Música para siete instrumentos," "Preludio Sinfónico," (1962), "Homenaje a Juan Santamaría" (1976), and finally "El pájaro de Crepúsculo" (1982), and a semi-operatic work with ballet and choral music. He has won the Aquileo *Echeverría Zeledón award for music several times.

GUTIERREZ, Diego de (d. 1544). Conquistador. *Governor and captain general of *Cartago (1541-44). He led expeditions in the Atlantic region and in the San Juan River area and founded the short-lived city of *Santiago de Talamanca. While Gutiérrez was leading an expedition against the *Indian chiefs Cocorí and Camaquiurí, his expedition was ambushed near Mount *Chirripó and he was killed.

GUTIERREZ, Felipe. Spanish explorer. He led an unsuccessful expedition to the Atlantic region in 1534-35. He served as *governor of *Veragua 1534-35. During his term of office the first limits between Castilla de Oro and Costa Rica were established.

GUTIERREZ, Hernán (b. ca. 1532). A carpenter who accompanied *Cavallón and later *Perafán de Ribera in his unsuccessful expedition to the Estrella River. A founder of the short-lived settlement of Nombre de Jesús.

GUTIERREZ, José María (1812-1856). Army commander killed in the battle of *Santa Rosa. Just before dying supposedly said: "The Costa Ricans of my generation know how to die like the best men when liberty is imperiled." This phrase became an inspiration in the war effort.

GUTIERREZ, Manuel María (1829-1887). Musician. Writer of dance and patriotic music. He wrote the music for the *National Anthem of Costa Rica.

GUTIERREZ DE CARDENAS, Rafael. Lieutenant of the Spanish infantry. He served as acting governor in military matters (January-April 1781) in the absence of *Governor Fernández de Bobadilla.

GUTIERREZ DE MORALES, Esmeralda (1835-1921). She helped finance a hospital in *Heredia by selling some land and was also important in the local *Junta de Caridad. For many years she was considered the "dean of Heredian morality."

GUTIERREZ IGLESIAS, Ezequiel (1840-1920). *Deputy 1910-14, president of Congress (1910-13), and president of the Supreme Court (1916-17). He was important in the development of educational activities. He served in various ministries and was an unsuccessful candidate for the presidency in 1906.

GUTIERREZ LIZAURZABAL, Agustín (1762-1837). Guatemalan by birth, he was president of the Constituent Assembly (1824-25) and a member of the *Diputación Provincial de León y Costa

Rica. In 1834 he wrote the first book dealing with law published in Costa Rica called Prontuario de derecho práctico por orden alfabético. He was also president of the Consejo Representativo in 1833-34, and acting president of the Republic (June 27 to August 18, 1834).

GUTIERREZ MANGEL, Joaquín (b. 1918). Poet and novelist born in *Limón Province. He lived in Chile for many years and only returned to Costa Rica in 1973. His most important works are: Poesías (1937), Jicaral (1938), Cocorí, an internationally famous children's story, (1948), Puerto Limón (1950), Hoja del aire (1968), and Murámonos Federico (1973). The latter was later converted into a play, Te conozco, Mascarita (1981).

GUTIERREZ SAENZ, Rodrigo (b. 1931). Physician and politician. At one time he was Secretary General of the National Liberation Party (*Partido Liberación Nacional), but had a falling out with them. He ran unsuccessfully for the presidency of a coalition of leftist parties in 1978 and 1982. Professionally he founded the School of Physiology at the *Universidad de Costa Rica.

GUZMAN QUIROS, Gerardo (1874-1959). Lawyer. He was chosen president of the Supreme Court in 1948 during a difficult time of transition. He also served as magistrate of the *Tribunal Superior de Elecciones, and as minister of the interior in the cabinet of Otilio *Ulate.

- H -

HACIENDA. A large almost self-contained economic unit dedicated to agricultural production. Somewhat like an antebellum Southern (U.S.) plantation. In Costa Rica because of the limited use of the *encomienda and relative scarcity of labor, the hacienda system was not very extensive. A hacienda in Costa Rica usually consisted of an adobe house or ranchito de pajizo (thatch-roofed house) where the owner, his family and few if any workers lived and farmed their own land. This scarcity of labor and availability of land may be one of the reasons for the peculiar development of this country. The hacienda in Costa Rica is also called a *finca.

HALE, John. An Englishman who in 1826 tried to establish a colony of about 100 Englishmen in a place still called Montaña del Inglés (*Heredia Province). Although this venture failed, he wrote a pamphlet called Six Month's Residence and Travels in Central America, which is valuable for data on the country at the time of independence.

HAY-PAUNCEFOTE TREATY (1901). A treaty signed between the United States and Nicaragua giving the former rights to build an interoceanic canal along the San Juan River. Costa Rica objected, feeling that she had equal rights of navigation on that river and should have an equal say in the matter. See: FRONTIER QUESTIONS (NICARAGUA).

HAYA FERNANDEZ, Diego de la (1675-1734). *Governor of the province of Costa Rica (1718-27) and considered one of the most important governors. He wrote a description of the eruption of the volcano *Irazú in 1723, fought the incursion of the *Zambo-Mosquitos, and improved the port of *Caldera. His administration was characterized by a constant battle with the *Audiencia de Guatemala for more help for this underdeveloped province. Consult Luz Alba Umaña, Diego de la Haya.

HEADS OF STATE. See: GOVERNORS (to 1821); PRESIDENTS AND CHIEFS OF STATE.

HENNINGSEN, Charles F. Swedish-born soldier of fortune (*filibuster) who was one of William *Walker's chief lieutenants. Under orders of Walker, he supervised the burning of Granada on November 19, 1856. He later fought at San Jorge and other places along the *transit route. After Walker's surrender Henningsen went to Mexico where he was active in their civil wars.

HERALDO DE COSTA RICA, El. Newspaper founded by Pío *Víquez (1890) which disseminated the ideas of the *Generation of 1889.

HEREDIA (canton). A *canton created December 7, 1848, which comprises the city of *Heredia and some of the surrounding territory. Present population is 54,896. It produces *coffee, *sugar, and some fruit and *cattle.

HEREDIA (city). City of Central Costa Rica at 10°N, 84°04'W, 1,150 meters above sea level. Originally started as a small church in a place named Barreal or Lagunilla and called Mermita de Alvarilla. In 1706, through the efforts of the church and the government, people began to move into the area. In 1714, the settlement was transferred to a place called *Cubujuquí (its present site). It was declared a town as Villa de Cubujuquí by the *Audiencia de Guatemala (June 1, 1763) and adopted its present name in 1773 in honor of Alonso Fernández de Heredia, president of the audiencia. Throughout the independence period Heredia favored association with the Mexican Empire, and from December 1821 until the first civil war in 1823, it was not technically part of Costa Rica. Heredia also fought in the *Guerra de la Liga against *San José. It is considered one of the most conservative cities in the country. Its population has grown from 6,047 in 1892 to 7,151 in 1904, 7,631 in 1927, 19,249 in 1963, and 23,600 in 1975 but had fallen to 20,867 at the 1984 census. Since 1973 it has been the seat of the *Universidad Nacional de Costa Rica.

HEREDIA (province). One of the central provinces of the country
with a population of 41,957 in 1910, 195,389 in 1984, and 197,575
(est.) in 1987. Its capital and center of distribution is *Heredia
City. This province is one of the chief *coffee-growing areas,
but also produces *sugar, fruit, grains, and some *cattle. Its
limits with *Alajuela were set September 19, 1865.

HEREDIA MOVEMENT. See: SCULPTURE.

HERNANDEZ, Rafael (b. 1935). Painter born and educated in *San
José. He was affiliated with the *Grupo Taller. His early works
had their inspiration in local themes, but with people in mysterious and fantastic shapes. His style has moderated somewhat
and lately he has done murals, one of which is in the Social
Security building in *Desamparados.

HERNANDEZ DE GUIDO, Alonso (b. 1539). Spanish *conquistador
who accompanied Juan de *Cavallón. Served as procurador
general of *Cartago.

HERRERA, Arnoldo (b. 1923). Composer and musician. He founded
the National Opera Company. See also: CONSERVATORIO DE
CASTELLA.

HERRERA, Luis Diego (b. 1952). Composer and musician. Studied
in the *Conservatorio de Castella and the *Universidad de Costa
Rica. He is director of the Orquesta Sinfónica Juvenil and has
been guest conductor of the *Orquesta Nacional. Herrera has
written incidental music for plays and some chamber music. Some
of his most important compositions are: "Cuadros para Orquesta,"
"Retrato Momentáneo," "De la piedra," and "Trío y percusión."
In 1981 he was given an award from the Music Conservatory
of Strasbourg, France.

HERRERA CAMPUZANO, Diego de. As interim *governor of the
colony (1704-07), he helped to build the first church in *Cartago
and aided in the establishment of the new parish of *Cubujuquí.
See also: HEREDIA (City).

HERRERA GARCIA, Adolfo (d. 1975). Novelist. Wrote the novel
Vida y dolores de Juan Valera (1936), which deals with social
problems of a peasant who lost his land. It was a movement
toward writing novels of social significance, and directly inspired Carlos Luis *Fallas Sibaja.

HERRERA ZELEDON, Vicente (1821-1888). Lawyer. He received a
doctorate in laws in Guatemala and served as rector of the *Universidad de Santo Tomás, foreign minister (1874), and president
of the Supreme Court (1856). He was selected by Tomás *Guardia
Gutiérrez to be president of the Republic after the overthrow of
Aniceto *Esquivel Sáenz. He remained in office for 14 months.

HIDALGO BONILLA, Tomás Benito (b. 1747). Acting *governor in political matters (1797). Also served as *alcalde of *Cartago for various years.

HIGHWAY ACCIDENTS. In common with other tropical Third World countries, Costa Rica has a reputation for a high rate of traffic accidents. There were 419 highway deaths in 1980, a rate of 18.7 per thousand population, against 8.5 in Great Britain, 9.9 in Japan, 12.4 in West Germany, 16.4 in Brazil, 20.4 in France and 22.8 in the United States. A fairer comparison might be the rate per thousand vehicles (1.00 compared with 0.22 in Great Britain, 0.33 in the U.S.A., 0.37 in Japan, 1.79 in Brazil), or per 1,000 km of road (14.69, against 8.15 in the U.S.A., 10.38 in Japan, 12.64 in Great Britain, 14.17 in Brazil). Since 1980 there has been a considerable improvement: deaths fell to 292 in 1981, 285 in 1982 and 200 in 1983. [L.H.]

HIGHWAYS. The colonial south-north *camino real, leading from Panama along the Pacific coast to *Cartago, and roughly following the present *Inter-American Highway route through *San José to the western edge of Lake Nicaragua, was a mere mule track: in fact its main use was in exporting mules to Panama. When *coffee exporting began in the 1820s the beans were transported down from the central *meseta to the Pacific port of *Puntarenas on mule-back. The 1844-1846 construction by the *Sociedad Económica Itineraria of a dirt road for oxcarts between Cartago and Puntarenas revolutionalized communications with the outside world. Access to the Caribbean port of *San Juan del Norte still involved a hair-raising canoe trip down the *Sarapiquí until the *Ferrocarril del Norte was built in the 1870s. This was followed by the Pacific Railroad (later the *Ferrocarril Eléctrico del Pacífico), and roads declined in importance. The coming of the *automobile in the early 20th century had little impact before the 1930s. Costa Rica had only 150 km of all-weather highways in the mid-1920s. Even in 1918 the 30-mile route between San José, Cartago, Heredia and *Alajuela was described as a "cart road." In 1950 there were still only 560 km (350 miles) of all-weather roads, most of them, including the short completed section of the *Pan American Highway, in the meseta. Within two years this total had been almost trebled, to 1,498 km, but the preferential treatment of the meseta continued, with 408 km of all-weather roads, and 8,199 km of all types. In 1983 there were nearly 30,000 km of roads, although barely half of these were all-weather, and under 3,000 km were paved. Road traffic was carrying 70% of the nation's freight and 80% of its passengers by 1968 (see: PUBLIC TRANSPORT), even though the all-weather road between San Juan and Limón was still to be completed. [L.H.]

HINE, Marquis Lafayette [Doctor] (b. 1823). Born in Cairo, New York, he was the first consular representative of the United

States in Costa Rica. He stayed and prospered. Many of his
descendants distinguished themselves in the fields of *coffee
growing, archeology, and politics.

HINE SABORIO, Jorge (b. 1878). Banker. As first vice-president
he became acting president March 14-15, 1943. He was also
deputy director of the *Banco de Costa Rica, and one of the
most important politicians in the 1930s and 1940s. He was frequently mentioned as a prospective presidential candidate.

HOGAN, James (d. 1864). Physician born in Philadelphia. He
arrived in Costa Rica in the 1850s and served with the Costa
Rican forces in the war against William *Walker. Later he was
superintendent of the *San Juan de Dios Hospital from 1858
until his death.

HOJANCHA. *Canton in *Guanacaste Province created November 2,
1971. Its *cabecera is Hojancha City. It produces *cattle and
has a population of 5,879.

HOLIDAYS. Days officially feriados are:
Jan. 1   New Year's (Año Nuevo)
March 19   St. Joseph's Day (Fiesta de San José)
April 11   Anniversary of the Battle of *Rivas (Día de Juan
             *Santamaría)
May 1   International Labor Day (Día del Trabajo)
May 29   Corpus Christi
June 29   Saints Peter and Paul (Fiesta de San Pedro y San
             Pablo)
July 25   Anniversary of the Annexation of *Guanacaste
             Province
Aug. 2   Our Lady of the Angels (Virgen de los Angeles)
Aug. 15   *Independence Day
Oct. 12   Columbus Day (Día de la Raza)
Dec. 8   Immaculate Conception (Inmaculada Concepción)
Dec. 24   Christmas Eve (Nochebuena)
Dec. 25   Christmas Day (Navidad)--although the country
             virtually shuts down for the whole period from the
             day before Christmas Eve through Twelfth Night
             (Epifanía), December 23-January 6
Easter (Pascuas) is officially Maundy Thursday to Easter Day,
but in practice, the whole of Holy Week (Semana Santa).
     There are also local or less established holidays such as
August 24 (National Parks Day since 1986) or the December 1
anniversary of the abolition of the army (see: ARMED FORCES)
in 1948. See also: CARNIVAL. [G.K., L.H.]

HOSPITAL. See: SAN JUAN DE DIOS.

HOSPITAL NACIONAL DE NINOS. The children's hospital. A
landmark just west of downtown *San José, since opening in

1964 it symbolized the attention to public health particularly for children that characterizes the country. [G.K.]

HOUSE OF REPRESENTATIVES. See: CAMARA DE REPRESEN-TANTES.

HOUSING. See: INSTITUTO NACIONAL DE VIVIENDA Y URBAN-ISMO.

HUACA. An Indian tomb. Usually connected with ceremonial burials. It contains urns and other artifacts.

HUAQUERO. One who devotes himself to excavating relics from Indian tombs (*huacas) for a profit.

HUELGA DE BRAZOS CAIDOS. Merchants and anti-government people were concerned that the 1948 elections would not be honest. Therefore in 1946 as a protest against the government's policies, merchants closed their establishments and called for a general strike. After a few days the government agreed to appoint an imperial electoral commission with ample funds, and otherwise guaranteed free elections.

HUELGAS. See: STRIKES.

HUERTA CASO, José Antonio de la (d. 1803). Bishop of Nicaragua and Costa Rica 1798-1803. He was interested in furthering education and helped establish a school in *Cartago (*Casa de Enseñanza). He died tragically when a cat he was trying to punish attacked him and split his jugular vein.

HUETARES. Aboriginal *Indians of Chibcha (South American) origin numbering about 3,500 at the time of the conquest. They lived in the Atlantic region and in part of the central valleys, having their chief settlement at *Ujarrás. They spoke Huetar and had a supreme chief with a council of notables to assist him. Although they believed in one Supreme Will and the inmortality of the soul, they also worshiped the sun, moon, and other phenomena of nature. They were skilled hunters, making strong bows and arrows, and frequently engaged in wars to enslave prisoners who were occasionally sacrificed. They preferred a diet of roots rather than corn, but also cultivated beans, and palm nuts (*pehibaye). They were known for their work in stone, making distinctive circular *metates and human figures.

HUIPIL. Long cotton shirt worn by Indian women.

HUITZILOPOCHTLI. Mexican war god. Also worshipped by the *Nahuas in Costa Rica.

HULL, John (1921?-). Rancher of United States nationality

resident in Costa Rica whose extensive landholdings include airstrips located close to the Nicaraguan border. An Associated Press report in the late 1985 reported allegations of a "U.S. federal drug investigator" implicating him in the attempted murder of Edén *Pastora Gómez at La *Penca and in the trafficking of Colombian cocaine. In July 1987 two British mercenaries employed by the "contras" and captured by the Costa Rican authorities alleged that Hull was their main liaison with the United States C.I.A. In January 1989 Hull was arrested on a charge of espionage, and gun- and drug-smuggling. [G.K., L.H.]

HUMAN RIGHTS. Costa Rica's preeminence in respect for human rights was a reason that the Central American Court of Justice (*Corte de Justicia Centroamericana) was established in Costa Rica in 1908. More recently, the *Interamerican Court of Human Rights, autonomous branch of the Organization of American States, has been established in *San José since 1979. The court is slowly establishing legal grounds against human rights abuses in those countries of Latin America which have ratified the American Convention on Human Rights. The internal human rights commission (CODEHU), organized in 1985, at times criticizes forcible tactics by Costa Rican police groups versus landless squatters and other dissidents. See also: SCHMIDT, Stephen B.; VOLIO JIMENEZ, Fernando. [G.K.]

HURTADO, Francisco. Leader of an insurrection in *Guanacaste in 1811 over the government's *tobacco and aguardiente liquor monopoly. See: ESTANCO; INSURRECTION OF 1811.

HURTADO, Gerardo César (b. 1949). Novelist born in *Limón Province. His most important works are: Irazú (1971), which won the Bachiller Osejo Prize, and Así en la vida como en la muerte (1973), Los parques (1975), Los Vecinos (1977), and Como el primer día sobre la tierra (1981).

HUSCAR BLANCO. See: VARGAS COTO, Joaquín.

- I -

IBARRA Y CLAVO, Juan Francisco de (1680-1736). Interim *governor in political matters July-August 1736.

ICE. See: INSTITUTO COSTARRICENSE DE ELECTRICIDAD.

IDA. See: INSTITUTO DE TIERRA Y COLONIZACION.

IDEARIO COSTARRICENSE. A book whose full title is Ideario costarricense resultado de una encuesta nacional. It was published by a group from the *Centro para el estudio de Problemas

Nacionales in 1943. In addition to giving the Centro's views
of national problems it also contained letters by most of Costa
Rica's political leaders of that day. It foreshadowed the social
position that many of those of the *Generation of 1948 would
later take. See also: PARTIDO LIBERACION NACIONAL.

IGLESIAS, Joaquín de (1794-1840). During the independence era
he was considered one of the (minority) liberals from *Cartago.
Iglesias was an author of the *Pacto de Concordia, member of
the *Junta de Legados de los Pueblos, member and secretary
of the *Junta Superior Gubernativa. In 1835 he was one of
the leading figures on the side of the insurgents. See: GUERRA
DE LA LIGA.

IGLESIAS CASTRO, Rafael. See: YGLESIAS CASTRO, Rafael.

IGLESIAS LLORENTE, Francisco María (1825-1903). Educated in
Costa Rica as well as in Europe, he was one of the leaders of
the Central American *Unionist Party. He published three volumes called Pro Patria (1898-1900), which contain biographies
of Joaquín de *Iglesias and a plea for Central America unity.
In addition to this he was *deputy on various occasions; president of the Senate 1868; president of the Congress 1890-92,
1900-03; and acting president of the Republic November 1898 to
June 1899 and again January 8 to March 15, 1902. He also served
as director of the National Library and finally he wrote a series
of volumes, Documentos relativos a la independencia (1892-1902),
which are a valuable source for research in this area.

IICA. See: INSTITUTO INTERAMERICANO DE CIENCIAS
AGRICOLAS.

ILLANES DE CASTRO, Juan (b. 1518). He accompanied *Cavallón
and served as lieutenant for Juan *Vázquez de Coronado. Acting
*governor (July 1563 to April 1564). First alcalde of *Garcimuñoz,
and alférez real of the province. He supervised the removal of
the settlers from Garcimuñoz to the newly established city of
*Cartago.

IMMIGRATION LAWS. Costa Rica until the beginning of the twentieth century had no immigration laws to speak of, and immigration
permits were issued on an individual or contractual basis. In
1904 an immigration law prohibited entrance of "Arabs, Turks,
Syrians, Armenians, and Gypsies." In 1906 laws were passed
to encourage immigration of those of the "white race," and government funds were appropriated to encourage this. In the
1930s and early 1940s immigration was once again restricted,
especially for European Jews. Since the Second World War there
have been immigrations of North Americans (see: PENSIONADOS),
and Central Americans either in the form of workers in the *banana zones or, recently, political *refugees. All racial restrictions were finally removed in 1973.

IMPERIALISTS. A political group centered in *Cartago which advocated joining Agustín de Iturbide's Mexican Empire. They led
an insurrection (March 29, 1823) in Cartago which ultimately
led to the first *civil war. It was put down and Costa Rica
joined the Central American Federal Republic. See: CIVIL
WARS (1823); LOMBARDO ALVARADO, José Santos; OCHOMOGO.

IMPORTS. The limitations of industrial production in a small country leave the Costa Rican economy necessarily dependent on
imports of manufactured goods. In 1984 transportation machinery
and material imports (e.g. automobiles) came to $219,600,000;
chemical products cost $250,500,000, and other manufactures,
$259,000,000. The almost total failure of exploration for *petro-
leum accounts for the $166,700,000 spent on imported fuel and
lubricants. A preference in *agriculture for export crops over
self-sufficiency, even for staples (e.g. RICE and WHEAT, qq.v.)
means that $96,700,000 were spent on importing food, drink
and *tobacco. Government pricing policies have been blamed
for the low level of AFRICAN PALM OIL (q.v.) production,
and the consequent $7,500,000 spent on foreign animal and vege-
table oils and fats. Livestock imports in 1984 came to $7,500,000.
[L.H.]
See also: BALANCE OF TRADE; FOREIGN TRADE.

INCOME TAX. First enacted in 1916 by the Alfredo *González
Flores government, but very unpopular and abolished by the
*Tinoco Granados government. It was reestablished for a short
period of time in 1922, and finally enacted by the *Picado Michalski government in 1946. It has become an important part of the
Costa Rican tax structure. The "Tributación Directa" is calculated and filed each November (on past October-through-September
income), and paid by calendar's year end.

INCOP. See: INSTITUTO COSTARRICENSE DEL PUERTO DEL
PACIFICO.

INDEP. See: INSTITUTO DE ESTUDIOS POLITICOS.

INDEPENDENCE. September 15 is celebrated as Independence Day;
that day in 1821 a *cabildo abierto in Guatemala City declared
the *Kingdom of Guatemala independent from Spain: the so-
called ACTA DE GUATEMALA, q.v. However, the process in
Costa Rica was more complicated. The people in *Cartago did
not know that they were independent until the mail arrived from
Guatemala on October 13, 1821, with a copy of that act and
the "*Acta de los Nublados." A *cabildo abierto was held in
Cartago the next day and it was agreed to adhere to the provincial deputation's act, thus ratifying the provisional independence. Absolute independence was declared by the people of
Cartago November 1 of the same year. Major differences soon
developed between *Heredia and Cartago, cities which favored

joining Iturbide's Mexican Empire, and *Alajuela and *San José,
which favored association with the republican *Provincias Unidas
del Centro de América. There was even considerable sentiment
for joining Colombia. The matter developed into a *civil war
in which San José-Alajuela defeated Cartago-Heredia and declared
for the *Central American federation, now called the *Republica
Federal de Centro-América. Costa Rica withdrew from the Federation in 1838 and declared itself a republic in 1848. Spain ratified Costa Rican independence in 1850. Consult Ricardo Fernández Guardia, Historia de Costa Rica: La independencia, (1941).

INDIAN TOWNS. Towns created in the early colonial era in which
the *Indians had their own government with their own chief
named as mayor. There was also a priest in charge of indoc-
trinating them in Christian ways. These towns were created
largely to prevent the Indians from escaping to the mountains.

INDIANS. According to a study by Bishop Thiel there were about
27,200 American Indians in Costa Rica in 1522. By 1611 this
number had been reduced by 54.8% to about 14,908 and by 1801
to 8,281. The main Indian groups in the country were *Chorotegas, *Brunkas, *Nahuas, and *Corobices. Numbers were
down to 2,000 by the beginning of the 20th century. There
are now about 5,000 Indians living in Costa Rica, mostly in
*Talamanca, Brunka (*Puntarenas Province), and in *Guatuso
in the North. A Council for the Protection of the Nation's Native
Races was set up in 1945 and the first reservations created in
1956. See also: Individual listings for the various Indian tribes.
Consult Rafael A. Bolaños V., "Contribución al estudio del decimiento de la población nativa de Costa Rica en el período colonial
(1502-1821)" (1981 Thesis); M. Fernández, et al., La población
de Costa Rica (1976); Luis Ferrero, Costa Rica precolombina
(1977); Bernardo Augusto Thiel, Monografía de la población de
Costa Rica en el siglo XIX; and Elías Zamora Acosta, "Etnografía
histórica de Costa Rica."

INFANT MORTALITY. See: BIRTH AND DEATH RATES.

INQUISITION. The Holy Office was firmly established in Spain
under Ferdinand and Isabella to root out heresies. In Costa
Rica the Inquisition was not very harsh and never held an auto
de fé nor executed anyone. Most of the time it just gathered
information for the tribunals in Mexico or Guatemala. They
did, though, occasionally imprison people for short periods of
time. Two of the most important cases in Costa Rica involved
Comisario Manuel González Coronel in 1774 and Dr. Esteban *Curti
in 1794. The Inquisition was abolished by the *Cortes de Cádiz
in 1812.

INSTITUCION DE LAS BANDAS, La. A group of seven semi-
military bands, one for each provincial capital. The local bands

were administered from *San José by the Director General of
Bands. These bands played at local retretas and recreos, gave
concerts and participated in military, religious, and scholastic
parades. This was the only classical music many people ever
heard. In addition these bands served as a training ground
for many of Costa Rica's most important composers. These bands
still exist but in modified form.

INSTITUTO COSTARRICENSE DE ELECTRICIDAD (ICE). A public
agency created April 8, 1949, to administer the electric supply
of the country. In 1968 it bought 97 percent of the stock of
the Electric Bond and Share Company, thus nationalizing the
electric system. Increasing population along with greater electrical use from modernization have necessitated ICE's landmark
office building on the north edge of La *Sabana park. The
sudden increase in the cost of thermal generation of electricity
has led to several large hydro-electric dams. In 1986, surplus
power from a new Honduran project was purchased via the grid
linking with that country and with Panama and Nicaragua. Geothermal power may soon utilize the country's *volcanoes. A
subsidized 40% of usage is residential: an index of Costa Rica's
relatively egalitarian society. [G.K.]

INSTITUTO COSTARRICENSE DEL PUERTO DEL PACIFICO (INCOP).
A government commission established in 1974 to run the *railroad
to *Puntarenas.

INSTITUTO DE DEFENSA DEL CAFE. See: OFICINA DE CAFE.

INSTITUTO DE DESARROLLO AGROPECUARIO (IDA). See:
INSTITUTO DE TIERRA Y COLONIZACION.

INSTITUTO DE ESTUDIOS POLITICOS (INDEP). Organized by the
Christian Democratic leaders Drs. Rafael Alberto Grillo Rivera
and Andre Jenkins Dobles in July, 1978. It is run by the
Asociación de Estudios Ideológicos (ASEI) and largely financed
by the Konrad Adenauer Foundation of Germany. Although
the Institute is affiliated with the Unity Party (*Partido Unidad),
it is practically an organ of the Christian Democratic Party (*Partido Demócrata Cristiano) of Costa Rica. It conducts investiga-
tions, publishes books and serves as a meeting place for party
members. But its most important function is to improve the
party leadership and give courses in ideological capacitation.
Among the courses it offers are: "Elements of Social Christianity," "Political activism," "An introduction to contemporary political thought," and "public administration." See: INSTITUTO
DE FORMACION Y EDUCACION POLITICA.

INSTITUTO DE FORMACION Y EDUCACION POLITICA (INFED). A
school organized by the Christian Democratic party (*Partido
Demócrata Cristiano) of Costa Rica under the directorship of

Jaime González. It functioned from 1968 until 1978 when it was merged into the *Instituto de Estudios Políticos (INDEP). Its purpose was to train leaders and members in the Christian Democratic ideology and further the party.

INSTITUTO DE TIERRA Y COLONIZACION (ITCO). An autonomous government agency created in 1965. It is supposed to direct redistribution of the land, finance new agricultural colonies, and manage seacoast and state land. Reorganized in 1983 as the Instituto de Desarrollo Agropecuario (IDA).

INSTITUTO INTERAMERICANO DE CIENCIAS AGROPECUARIAS (IICA). (Interamerican Institute of Agricultural Sciences). Established October 7, 1942, at *Turrialba (*Cartago Province) on land confiscated from Axis nationals. The idea for the institute had been approved at the Inter American Conference of 1940. It conducts research, and has given some degree of training to over 20,000 people. The Tropical Agricultural Center for Investigation and Training (CATIE, Centro Agronómico Tropical de Investigación y Enseñanza) was established within IICA in 1973, focused on new productive plants for Central America.

INSTITUTO NACIONAL. Established in the 1870s to help solve problems of secondary education. Its director was Valeriano *Fernández Ferraz from 1879 to 1882, when it was reintegrated within the *Universidad de Santo Tomás.

INSTITUTO NACIONAL DE APRENDIZAJE. An autonomous government agency created January 1965 to help train artisans and mechanics in trades that are deemed necessary for the country.

INSTITUTO NACIONAL DE SEGUROS (INS). Established in 1924 as a government agency under the name Banco Nacional de Seguros as the only institution legally allowed to sell insurance in Costa Rica. Name changed to Instituto Nacional de Seguros in 1948. By 1980 INS was lodged in one of the modern tall office buildings in *San José. The branches of INS are where citizens pay various fees and fines.

INSTITUTO NACIONAL DE VIVIENDA Y URBANISMO (INVU). An autonomous government agency, founded August 24, 1954, which is in charge of constructing public housing. It had its antecedent in the *Ley de Casas Baratas. The major domestic campaign promise of President Oscar *Arias Sánchez (1986-   ) was to construct 80,000 houses during his term of office. The 1984 census found 500,788 houses in the country. Activist groups have urged an expanded program. [G.K.]

INSTITUTO TECNOLOGICO (ITCR or "TEC"). Begun after 1970 to produce technical and engineering professionals. Located near *Cartago. One of the country's public universities. [G.K.]

INSURRECTION OF 1811. A series of events in which some groups
   led by Francisco Hurtado in *Guanacaste, *Alajuela, *Cartago,
   and *San José mutinied against the authorities because of the
   suspension of government monopolies on aguardiente and *tobacco.
   However, because the people in Guanacaste were so far removed
   it took the government four years to take action there. Another
   cause was the prohibition of commerce with Panama. Consult
   Rafael Obregón Loria, Movimientos antiespañolistas en Centro
   América (1970).

INTENDANTS. Part of a system of reforms introduced by the
   *Bourbons of the eighteenth century (see: LEY DE ORDE-
   NANZAS DE 1786). These officials performed most of the functions of the former governor, but with more emphasis in safe-
   guarding public finances. In Central America after 1795 four
   intendancies were established: San Salvador (El Salvador),
   Chiapas (Mexico), Camayagua (Honduras), and Nicaragua (which
   also included Costa Rica). The Spanish terms are intendente,
   intendencía.

INTER-AMERICAN COMMISSION ON HUMAN RIGHTS (Comisión
   Interamericana de Derechos Humanos). A seven-member appointed
   body based in Washington DC, created in 1960 to promote obser-
   vance of the American Convention on Human Rights, and to
   act as the *Organization of American States' consultative organ
   in matters affecting human rights. [L.H.]

INTER-AMERICAN COURT OF HUMAN RIGHTS (Corte Interamericana
   de Derechos Humanos). An autonomous judicial institution established in 1979 in San José CR to decide cases referred to it by
   the *Inter-American Commission on Human Rights, and to issue
   advisory opinions on matters of human rights upon the request
   of an organ or member state of the *Organization of Human Rights.
   [L.H.]

INTERAMERICAN HIGHWAY. The 3,142 mile northern section of
   the PAN AMERICAN HIGHWAY (q.v.) between Laredo, Texas
   and Panama City.

INTERAMERICAN INSTITUTE OF AGRICULTURAL SCIENCES. See:
   INSTITUTO INTERAMERICANO DE CIENCIAS AGROPECUARIAS
   (IICA).

INTERNATIONAL CENTRAL AMERICAN BUREAU (Oficina Central
   Centroamericana). Established in Guatemala City, it started
   functioning September 15, 1907. Reestablished at the *Washington Conference November 1907. Its functions were to improve
   education, develop and expand commerce, establish uniform
   weights, customs, and legal codes for all the Central American
   republics. It served as a pro-unionist agency and was looked
   on with suspicion by anti-confederation forces in Costa Rica

and met with strong opposition in El Salvador. Its functions were curtailed in 1920 and it ceased functioning September 15, 1923.

INTERNATIONAL CENTRAL AMERICAN TRIBUNAL. Created at the second Washington Conference (1922-23), as an ad hoc court with more limited authority than the Central American Court of Justice (*Corte de Justicia Centroamericana). It could not rule on cases involving sovereignty or independence. This tribunal did little and was allowed to lapse in 1934.

INVU. See: INSTITUTO NACIONAL DE VIVIENDA Y URBANISMO.

IRAZU. One of the principal volcanoes in the central part of the country. A National Park. It erupted in 1723 with such force that it almost destroyed the city of *Cartago. Other notable eruptions (mostly ash) were in 1821, 1847, 1917, 1918, 1933, and 1963-5. This latter persistent eruption was featured by National Geographic in its July 1965 issue.

ISOGRO. A chanter in *Indian burial ceremonies.

ISTARU, Ana (b. 1960). Poet born in *San José. Her first Poemas para un día cualquiera (1974) won a prize for young writers. Her second volume, Poemas abiertos y otros amaneceres (1980), contains many poems of a feminist nature.

ISTARU, León (pen name of Enrique Soto Borbón). Writer and poet. Most important works are: La función de la planificación (1963), Introducción a la planificación del transporte (1980).

ITALIANS. See: COTO BRUS; FELLA; SOCIEDAD ITALIANA DE COLONIZACION AGRICOLA; STRIKE OF THE ITALIANS.

ITURBIDE, Agustín de (1783-1824). Liberator and emperor of Mexico who sent General Vicente Filísola to enforce his authority in Central America. This created a conflict between the cities of *Cartago and *Heredia which wanted to join with Iturbide, and *San José and *Alajuela which wanted to associate with the Central American Federal Republic. Iturbide was forced to abdicate March 19, 1823. See also: CIVIL WARS (1823); IMPERIALISTS; OCHOMOGO.

- J -

JAMAICAN IMMIGRATION. See: BLACKS.

JAMISON, James Carson. Lieutenant in William *Walker's army and historian. He wrote With Walker in Nicaragua and an account of the Battle of *Rivas.

JAPDEVA. See: JUNTA DE ADMINISTRACION PORTUARIA Y
DESARROLLO ECONOMICO DE LA VERTIENTE ATLANTICA.

JEFE POLITICO. A type of mayor-cum-justice of the peace; the
chief official of a town. Appointed and subject to removal by
the president of the Republic.

JENKINS DOBLES, Eduardo (b. 1926). Engineer, poet and writer.
Born in *Atenas (*Alajuela Province). His most important works
are: Riberas de la brisa, Otro sol de faenas (1955), Tierra
doliente (1951), Sonetos a las virtudes (1970), and Los Maros
de Dior y otros cuentos (1979).

JEREZ, Máximo (1818-1881). Philosopher and statesman. Born in
León, Nicaragua where he received the twin doctorates in canon
law (1837) and philosophy (1838). He fought against William
*Walker and was later exiled for his pro-Central American unifi-
cation activities, which included founding a *unionist party.
He became acquainted with the French positivists and is credited
with introducing *positivism into Costa Rica. He taught at the
*Universidad de Santo Tomás and founded the *Liceo de Costa
Rica. He negotiated the *Cañas-Jerez Treaty for Nicaragua
and also served in the cabinet of President Trinidad Cabañas
in Honduras.

JESUITS. Allowed to enter the country in 1872, as Guatemalan
liberals expelled them, they excelled in the field of education
and ran the *Colegio San Luis Gonzaga in *Cartago. They were
expelled by President Próspero *Fernández Oreamuno (1884)
but allowed to reenter the country in the administration of Rafael
*Calderón Guardia (1942).

JEWS. Much of the small but economically important Jewish popula-
tion is descended from a migration of the 1920s from Poland.
Consult Lowell Gudmundson, "Costa Rican Jewry: A Political
and Economic Outline" in the Jewish Presence in Latin America,
Judith Laiken and Gilbert Merkx, eds. [G.K.] See also:
IMMIGRATION LAWS.

JIMENEZ. *Canton in *Cartago Province located roughly between
*Turrialba and *Cartago City. It was created August 9, 1903,
and its *cabecera is Juan Viñas. Its chief product is *sugar
but it also produces some *coffee and livestock. The present
population is 11,861.

JIMENEZ, Aquiles (b. 1953). One of the so-called Heredia sculptors
of the *Generation of 1980. He is essentially a humanist using
anthropomorphic themes to give meaning to his bronze statues.

JIMENEZ, Domingo (1536-1600). Born in Spain, Jiménez is considered the first poet of Costa Rica. He fell into the bad graces

of *Governor *Anguciana de Gamboa because of a tract criticizing
his administration. As a result he had to go into hiding in
a convent. While there he wrote couplets (coplas) considered
the first poetry written in the colony (ca. 1574).

JIMENEZ, Jorge. See: SCULPTURE.

JIMENEZ, Mario Alberto (1912-1961). Lawyer and writer. He was
a traditionalist and defended what he saw were the country's
disappearing social values. His most important works are: Costa
Rica se viste la toga viril, Los Ticos y la máscara. His complete
works were published in 1962, by Editorial Costa Rica.

JIMENEZ, Max (1900-1947). Painter, poet, novelist and sculptor.
A wealthy bohemian type of person who lived most of the time
in Europe or South America. He was a sharp critic of Costa
Rican life. His most important work is El Jual (1937); it de-
scribes life in a small mountain town. It is illustrated with
his woodcuts. Other works include: Ensayos (1926), Ouijongo
(1933), and El domador de pulgas (1938). In addition he was
precursor of the *Arte Nuevo, which developed after his death.
His sculptures shocked Costa Rican sensibilities. He was one
of the most talented people Costa Rica has produced and was
so far ahead of his time that he was not really appreciated.
See also: PAINTING; SCULPTURE.

JIMENEZ, Mayra (b. 1938). Poet born in *San José. His works
include: Los trabajo del sol (1966), Puerto Limón (1962), Tierra
Adentro (1967), Abril (1972), A propósito del Padre (1975),
and Cuadro Poeta (1979).

JIMENEZ, Salvador (1835-1885). Studied law in Guatemala and was
considered one of the first writers of treatises on law. He wrote
Elementos de derecho civil y penal en Costa Rica (2 vols. 1874,
and 1876). One of the leaders of the Krausist School of Positivist
Thinking. See: KRAUSISM.

JIMENEZ CANOSSA, Salvador (b. 1922). Poet writer and ichthyologist.
He was director of the library of the *Legislative Assembly for
many years and is considered expert on ichthyology. His most
important works are: Tierra de cielo (1951), Cantarcillos de
un marinero ciego (1952), Balada del amor que nace (1959),
and Oda del regreso (1975).

JIMENEZ OREAMUNO, Ricardo (1859-1945). Lawyer and statesman.
President of the Republic 1910-14, 1924-28, and 1932-36. *Deputy
1902-10, and president of Congress 1903-04. President of the
Supreme Court 1890. "Don Ricardo" was one of the most important figures in Costa Rica in the twentieth century. His administrations were typified by liberalism in which he would engage
in long polemics in the newspapers and in so doing he helped

establish a tradition of free criticism of public officials. In his first administration he consolidated the public debt. During his second presidency he created the government insurance monopoly, the *Crédito Hipotecario de Costa Rica bank, and started electrification of the *Ferrocarril Eléctrico del Pacífico. During his third administration he had to deal with the depression and a rising tide of social unrest. He was a candidate for the presidency for a short period in 1940, but withdrew because of governmental pressure. He was declared *Benemérito de la Patria in 1942.

JIMENEZ ORTIZ, Carlos María. See: PARTIDO REPUBLICANO.

JIMENEZ QUIROS, Otto (b. 1918). Novelist. His most important work is El árbol criollo, which deals humourously with his family's history.

JIMENEZ RODRIGUEZ, Ramón (ca. 1779-1848). Acting *governor in political matters June 10 to December 3, 1819. Also occupied post of *alcalde ordinario of *Cartago for several years.

JIMENEZ ROJAS. Elías (1869-1945). Pharmacist, writer, and intellectual anarchist. He studied in Paris and was director of the *Liceo de Costa Rica 1905, and director of the School of Pharmacy 1899-1902. He published such periodicals as Apuntes, Renovación, and Eos. He constantly wrote in the daily press and was considered a type of public censor. His commentaries cover more than 1,500 pages.

JIMENEZ SAENZ, Guillermo (b. 1922). Painter, who studied in the Academia de Bellas Artes and was co-founder of the "*Grupo Ocho." His work is expressionist with abstract tendencies. He works in water colors, pen, and ink drawing, oils, and engravings. He has had several shows of his art works. In addition he has been active in developing Costa Rican theatre.

JIMENEZ ZAMORA, Jesús de (1823-1893). Physician and politician. President of the Republic 1863-66, 1868-70. After studying medicine in Guatemala, Jiménez Zamora started his political career serving in such posts as *deputy and governor of *Cartago. After three months in the presidency, he closed Congress and ordered new congressional elections. His first administration was characterized by a blend of harsh rule and strong laws coupled with progressive legislation. The harsh legislation involved establishing a women's jail, persecution of the Masonic lodges, and a vagrancy law. On the other side of the coin, he signed a law (1869) making primary education free and obligatory, and tried to improve the quality of education by bringing foreign teachers to the country. He was also instrumental in the foundation of the *Colegio San Luis Gonzaga in *Cartago. He abolished the state *tobacco monopoly. In the realm of foreign

policy, President Jiménez established the Costa Rican tradition
of political asylum, granting refuge to the Salvadorean Dictator,
General Gerardo *Barrios. In so doing he almost provoked a
war with the other Central American republics. He returned to
office in 1868 after a revolution toppled Dr. *Castro Madriz.
However, he was more or less a puppet for General Tomás *Guardia Gutiérrez, who deposed him in a military coup d'etat April 27,
1870. He was declared *Benemérito de la Patria in 1886.

JOCOTE. See: PACTO DEL JOCOTE.

JUNTA DE ADMINISTRACION PORTUARIA Y DESARROLLO
ECONOMICO DE LA VERTIENTE ATLANTICA (JAPDEVA). Autonomous government agency established February 1963 to administer
canalization of the Atlantic swamps and to manage the land.
It has also taken over administration of the port of *Limón,
and in 1972 became the administrator of the nationalized Atlantic
Coast *Railroad (*Ferrocarril del Norte).

JUNTA DE CARIDAD. See: JUNTAS DE PROTECCION SOCIAL.

JUNTA DE CARIDAD DE SAN JOSE. Beneficent society created in
the administration of José *Gallegos y Alvarado. It later evolved
into the *San Juan de Dios Hospital, the municipal hospital for
*San José.

JUNTA DE COOPERACION AGRICOLA. Created in 1937 to attempt
to solve some of the basic agricultural problems with emphasis on
developing and encouraging cultivation of corn, rice, and beans.
It was an antecedent of the later Ministry of Agriculture.

JUNTA DE CUSTODIA DE LA PROPIEDAD ENEMIGA. Created in
1942 with the power to confiscate, sell and manage property
of enemy aliens. It was dissolved July 1945. Its actions provoked several long law suits over abuse of its power. See:
NIEHAUS FAMILY.

JUNTA DE LEGADOS DE LOS PUEBLOS. (1) While Costa Rica was
deciding on what form of government it would have, the
ayuntamiento of *Cartago called for the election of a provisional
government of representatives from the principal towns. The
first junta met October 25 to December 1, 1821. It drafted
the *Pacto de Concordia. Factions developed between groups
favoring joining Mexico, led by José Santos *Lombardo and those
wanting a Central American Federation, clustering around Rafael
*Osejo.
    (2) The second junta held power December 1, 1821 to
January 13, 1822 under the name Comisión de la Legación de
los Pueblos. Consult Ricardo Fernández Guardia, Historia de
Costa Rica: la independencia (1941).

JUNTA DE PROTECCION SOCIAL DE SAN JOSE. See: JUNTAS
DE PROTECCION SOCIAL.

JUNTA FUNDADORA DE LA SEGUNDA REPUBLICA. The name
assumed by José Figueres Ferrer's ruling junta after the 1948
civil war. It governed the country May 8, 1948 to November 8,
1949 when it turned power over to Otilio *Ulate. It issued over
800 decrees, many of which were of an administrative nature.
Its most important accomplishments were the nationalization of
the country's banking system and the creation of the *Instituto
Costarricense de Electricidad (ICE), which in effect nationalized
the country's electrical system. It also completely changed the
government personnel and conducted ad hoc trials of former
government officials. See also: CIVIL WAR (1948); COURT
OF IMMEDIATE SANCTIONS; FIGUERES FERRER, José; NA-
TIONALIZED BANKING SYSTEM.

JUNTA PROTECTORA DE LAS COLONIAS. Founded (August 17,
1850) by Juan Rafael *Mora Porras. It was supposed to see
that immigrants were well treated in accord to the government's
policy of the time to encourage European *immigration to establish new agricultural colonies and produce more *coffee. Consult Carolyn Hall, El Café y el desarrollo histórico-geográfico
de Costa Rica.

JUNTA SUPERIOR GUBERNATIVA DE COSTA RICA. Three distinct
juntas, the first two January 13 to December 31, 1822 and January 1, 1823 to March 20, 1823 operated under the *Pacto de
Concordia, and the third May 10, 1823 to September 6, 1824
operated under the *Segundo Estatuo Político de la Provincia
de Costa Rica. The junta consisted of seven members and three
substitutes and theoretically held meetings for alternate three-
month periods in the four cities of the central highlands. Its
first president was Rafael *Barroeta Castilla. The junta became
a battle ground between *Imperialist and Republican forces and
was replaced by the *Estado Libre de Costa Rica as a constituent
state in the Central American Federal Republic (*República Federal
de Centro-América).

JUNTAS DE PROTECCION SOCIAL. These were originally founded
in 1845 under the name *Junta de Caridad. These are the local
committees of private citizens in the principal towns and cities
which administer hospitals and watch over public health in general. These juntas have virtually all disappeared during the
1970s as the locally administered hospitals were taken over by
the national Social Security system. The *Junta de Protección
de San José is a particularly active group, administering local
hospitals, which include *San Juan de Dios and the mental hospital *Chapuí. In addition it still runs a weekly drawing which
is tantamount to the national lottery.

JUSTICIA SOCIAL. A periodical founded by Jorge *Volio Jiménez
in 1901, published Sept. 16, 1902 to April 29, 1904. It was the
first publication with a social Christian orientation and detailed
much of the Volio program which was later incorporated into
his *Partido Reformista. Consult Marina Volio Brenes, General
Volio y el partido reformista (1972).

- K -

KANTOR, Harry (1911-1985). U.S. professor of political science
who pioneered the study of reformist Latin American political
parties, beginning with work on the *Apristas of Peru, and
continuing in the 1950s with Costa Rica. [G.K.]

KEITH, Minor Cooper (1838-1929). Builder of the Atlantic Coast
*Railroad (*Ferrocarril del Norte) and founder of the *United
Fruit Company. Keith came to Costa Rica in 1871 to supervise
construction of the Atlantic Coast Railroad at the behest of his
uncle, Henry C. *Meiggs, the railroad builder. Keith decided
to plant *bananas along the railroad right-of-way to have an
income from the considerable property he had acquired. In
1872 he exported his first 230 stems of bananas to New Orleans.
He expanded his plantation and organized the Tropical Trading
Company. In 1889 it merged with the Boston Fruit Company
to form the United Fruit Company. Keith was also involved
in renegotiating the *British loans and was one of the most pow-
erful men in Costa Rica where Minor became a fairly common
name. See: BRITISH LOANS; UNITED FRUIT COMPANY; and
consult Cleto González Víquez, Historia financiera de Costa Rica
(1965 ed.), p. 85ff., and Stewart Watt, Keith and Costa Rica
(1964).

KINGDOM OF GUATEMALA. A political subdivision of the Viceroyalty
of New Spain (Mexico). It comprised eight parts: Guatemala,
Chiapas, Honduras, Verapaz, Soconusco, San Salvador, Nicaragua,
and Costa Rica. It extended roughly from the Mexican territory
of Quintana Roo to Panama. At the time of the independence
Chiapas voted to join Mexico, and later Belize was absorbed by
England. Costa Rica by then had a *governor, but was subject
to the jurisdiction of the *Audiencia in Guatemala City.

KINGS OF SPAIN. Just before the discovery of the Americas,
Spain had been politically united through the marriage of the
Reyes Católicos (Catholic monarchs) Isabel I of Castile and Fer-
dinand II of Aragon. Isabel died in 1504, but their daughter
Joan the Mad (Juana la Loca) lost her reason following the pre-
mature death of her husband Philip I, the Fair, in 1506, and
Ferdinand ruled all Spain and the Indies (as Fernando V) until
his death in 1516. He was succeeded by Joan's son Charles I,

who in 1519 was elected Holy Roman Emperor as Charles V.
He abdicated in 1556. Subsequent kings of Spain and the Indies
during the colonial period were:
  Philip (Felipe) II, reigned 1556-1598, first of the Spanish
Habsburgs;
  Philip III, reigned 1598-1612;
  Philip IV, reigned 1621-1665;
  Charles (Carlos) II, reigned 1665-1700;
  Philip V, reigned 1700-1746, first of the Spanish *Bourbons;
  Ferdinand VI, reigned 1746-1759;
  Charles III, reigned 1769-1788;
  Charles IV, reigned 1788-1808, abdicating in favor of:
  Joseph Bonaparte, Napoleon I's brother, and his puppet
king of Spain as José I, until the French were driven out of
Spain in 1814;
  Ferdinand VII, regarded by most patriots as having suc-
ceeded his father Charles IV in 1808, but in fact a prisoner
of Napoleon until 1814. He reigned 1814-1833, but by then
all the Indies, except Cuba and Puerto Rico, had secured their
independence from Spanish rule. [L.H.]
  See also: INDEPENDENCE. '

KIRKLAND, William P. See: COMPANIA DE TRANSITO DE COSTA
RICA.

KNOWLES AND FOSTER. See: BRITISH LOANS.

KOBERG BOLANDI, Maximiliano (1894-1971). Merchant, politician,
and cattle rancher. Candidate for the presidency in 1932. In
1948 he was a member of the electoral commission that had to
rule on the validity of that *election. He was the only member
of the commission who did not certify *Ulate's victory, feeling
that the results were still incomplete. This gave a pretext for
annulling the electoral results and set the stage for the 1948
*civil war. He was considered a conservative and wrote El ver-
dadero orden social in 1944 to express his philosophy.

KOREA, Jorge (b. 1956). An *Arte Nuevo artist who specializes
in oil painting but also does some sculpture. He has had his
works exhibited in several Central American countries.

KRAUS, Karl (1781-1832). German philosopher, originated Krausist
philosophy, which was brought to Costa Rica by his Spanish
disciple, Julián *Sánz del Río.

KRAUSISM. This philosophy was disseminated into the educational
system by Valeriano *Fernández Ferraz in the late 1860s. Krausism places emphasis on classical learning and seeks to impose
self-responsibility on the student. Consult Constantino Láscaris,
Desarrollo de las ideas filosóficas en Costa Rica (1964), pp. 204-
246. See: KRAUS, Karl.

KREYSA DE GONZALEZ, Tanya (b. 1928). Artist studied in Costa Rica, Venezuela, and Cuba. She is a member of the *Grupo Taller and has participated in exhibitions of her works in various countries.

- L -

LABOR UNIONS. See: CONFEDERACION COSTARRICENSE DE TRABAJADORES DEMOCRATICOS; CONFEDERACION COSTA-RRICENSE DE TRABAJO "RERUM NOVARUM"; CONFEDERACION DE TRABAJADORES COSTARRICENSES; MONGE ALVAREZ, Luis Alberto; NUNEZ VARGAS, Benjamín; SANABRIA MARTINEZ, Victor; SOCIAL GUARANTEES; SOCIEDAD DE ARTESANOS; SOLIDARISTA MOVEMENT.

LACAYO DE BRIONES, José Antonio (b. 1679). Interim *governor of Costa Rica (1713-17). He was more important in Nicaragua where he occuped such posts as *alcalde, regidor, and governor of the province (1720-40). While *governor of Costa Rica, he was accused by Bishop *Garret y Arlovi of illicit trading with the English, but was absolved of this charge.

LACSA (Lineas Aéreas Costarricenses S.A.). Formed as a joint venture between the Costa Rican government and Pan American Airways, it began operation July 1, 1946. Pan American sold out in 1970. Current ownership is approximately 77% private, 14% government, 9% employees. LACSA possesses 3 Boeing-707s, 2 Boeing-757s, a DC-8, and a BAC One-eleven. It flies to Colombia, Guatemala, Honduras, Mexico and Venezuela, and to Los Angeles, New Orleans and Miami in the U.S. [L.H.]
    See also: AVIATION.

LAGUNA, La. See: OCHOMOGO.

LAJUELA, La. Oratory founded in 1782 which was the first settle-ment of what became *Alajuela City. See: ALAJUELA.

LARA ARIAS, Juan José. After the resignation of José Rafael *Gallegos y Alvarado he was called by Congress to be acting chief of state March 4-17, 1835. He was also *deputy from *Ala-juela on various occasions and was involved in several plots against his political enemy, Braulio *Carrillo Colina. He was unsuccessful candidate for the presidency in 1835.

LARA BUSTAMANTE, Fernando (1911-?). Lawyer and politician. *Deputy 1942-48, 1949-53, and 1958-62. President of the Legis-lative Assembly 1960-61, and foreign minister in the administra-tions of Olitio *Ulate and José Joaquín *Trejos Fernández.

LARA ESQUIVEL, Apolonio (1796-1837). *Deputy on various

occasions and president of the Congress October 1834 to February 1835.

LARA ZAMORA, Salvador (1839-1912). Politician. Acting president of the Republic June 10, 1881 to January 23, 1882, while General *Guardia Gutiérrez was in Europe.

LE CAPELLAIN, Ida. Born in Guernsey, in the Channel Islands. She came to Costa Rica in 1872 and married Mauro *Fernández in 1875. Her influence probably was responsible for establishing the Colegio Superior de Señoritas, the first secondary school for women in the country. Consult Anita G. Murcie, Imported Spices.

LE LACHEUR, William (1803-1863). Guernsey-born sailor. In 1844 he found himself on the Pacific coast without a return cargo. Hearing of the coffee trade between Costa Rica and Valparaíso, Chile, he sailed his clipper Monarch to *Puntarenas, climbed the trail to the meseta and bargained directly with the growers. The next year he returned with $36,700 in English coin to pay the people who had trusted him. This virtually began Costa Rica's coffee boom, and also established a direct link between Costa Rica and England. By the 1850s Le Lacheur was running a fleet of ten clippers between Puntarenas and Liverpool by way of Cape Horn. Captain Le Lacheur with Dr. *Brealey established the first *Protestant church in the country (the Church of the *Good Shepherd) after having secured permission from the government in 1848 to conduct public worship services. He imported many bibles. Le Lacheur left Costa Rica in 1857, but his descendants established the Banco Lyon, S.A., the one private bank allowed to survive the 1948 nationalization, on condition it not receive deposits. [T.C., L.H.]

LEAGUE OF NATIONS. Costa Rica joined in 1920 and sent Manuel María de *Peralta y Alfaro as their permanent representative. However, in 1924 President Ricardo *Jiménez Oreamuno withdrew Costa Rica from the League feeling that it did not give enough weight to the opinions of smaller nations.

LEGISLATIVE ASSEMBLY (Asamblea Legislativa). The Asamblea Legislativa provided in the 1949 Constitution has 57 *deputies elected each four years, during the presidential election, by proportional representation within provinces. No immediate re-election is allowed, thus limiting the legislature's political power. [G.K.]

LEGISLATURES. See: CAMARA DE REPRESENTANTES; CAMARA DE SENADORES; CONGRESO CONSTITUCIONAL; CONGRESO DE DIPUTADOS; CONGRESO PROVINCIAL DE COSTA RICA; DIPUTACION PROVINCIAL; LEGISLATIVE ASSEMBLY PRESIDENTS: Presidents of the Legislative Branch.

LEIVA CUBILLO, Lisímaco (1926). Physician. Was active in the
*Partido Confraternidad Guanacasteco. Assistant director of
the Tuberculosis Hospital and candidate for the presidency in
1970.

LEIVA QUIROS, Mario (1913). Lawyer and politician. President
of the *Cartago Municipal Council 1946-48. *Deputy to the Constituent Assembly of 1949, *deputy 1950-54; 1958-62, and president of the Legislative Assembly in 1970.

LENCES, Bartolomé de. Interim *governor of Costa Rica (1591-92).

LEON, Treaty of (1823). See: MONTEALEGRE, Mariano.

LEON CORTES. *Canton in the eastern part of *San José Province.
Its *cabecera is San Pablo and it was created June 12, 1962.
The chief products are *coffee, *sugar, and timber. The pres-
ent population is 8,087.

LEON HERRERA, Santos (1874-1950). Engineer and politician. As
third vice-president he was chosen to serve out Teodoro *Picado
Michalski's term of office after the latter surrendered to the
insurgent forces of José *Figueres Ferrer. He was in power
April 14 to May 8, 1948.

LEON PAEZ BROWN, Pedro María (1835-1903). Lawyer and educator,
born in Cartagena, Colombia. He came to Costa Rica in 1880
and founded a secondary school in *Cartago, taught in the *Universidad de Santo Tomás, served as a judge of the Supreme
Court, and as *deputy on various occasions. In addition he
held various ministries in the government of José Joaquín *Rodríguez Zeledón and was president of Congress 1894-1900.

LEY DE AMBULANCIA. In an effort to calm the rivalry between
the four principal cities of the highlands, President *Gallegos
y Alvarado had a law passed (April 1825) in which the government would rotate every four years between the cities of *San
José, *Alajuela, *Cartago, and *Heredia. To ensure its compli-
ance the chief executive was prohibited from leaving the capital
without the express permission of Congress. Unfortunately
this law caused more problems than it solved, and was repealed
as unworkable in August 1835. See also: CIVIL WARS; GALLE-
GOS Y ALVARADO, José Rafael; and consult Rodolfo Cerdas
Cruz, La formación del estado de Costa Rica (1967).

LEY DE BANCOS OF 1900 (Bank Law of 1900). In effect this law
adopted a system of plural emissions of money. Under provi-
sions of this act various banks were permitted to print money,
backed by gold, if they had capital over $500,000.

LEY DE BASES Y GARANTIAS. After Costa Rica withdrew from

the *Central American Federation it was technically without a
constitution. To rectify this situation and to justify his regime,
Braulio *Carrillo Colina decreed the Ley de Bases y Garantías,
May 27, 1838. It established Carrillo as lifetime "first chief
of the supreme power of the state" (primer jefe del poder supremo
del estado). It also declared Costa Rica an independent sovereign
state, thus restating its withdrawal from the *Central American
Federation. This constitution was declared null and void in
decrees signed June 6 and August 27, 1842.

LEY DE CASAS BARATAS. A law passed in the administration of
León *Cortés, which started a program of government-built houses
which was the forerunner of the present *Instituto Nacional
de Vivienda y Urbanismo (INVU).

LEY DE NOGUERA, María (b. 1892). Teacher and writer of children's books. She was born in Lagunilla de Santa Cruz (*Guanacaste Province) and taught in elementary schools in Santa Cruz.
Many of her experiences and local folklore were incoporated in
her books. In 1956 she was named "Woman of the year." Her
most important works are: Cuentos viejos (1923) and De la
vida en la costa (1955).

LEY DE NULIDAD. This law was passed in 1919 in spite of a veto
by President *Acosta. It declared null and void all agreements
and payments considered excessive that were contracted by
the preceding Tinoco government. Acosta's veto was based
on his belief that this law was a reprisal against the Tinoco
faction. See: ACOSTA GARCIA, Julio; LEY DE RECOMPENSA;
TINOCO GRANADOS, Federico.

LEY DE ORDENANZAS DE 1786 (Ordinance Law of 1786). It changed
much of the existent colonial pattern of administration. It declared Costa Rica part of the "Intendencia de León," with the
rank of gobierno político y militar (military and political government).

LEY DE RECOMPENSA (Compensation Law). A law which allowed
people to collect reparations for damages suffered in the uprisings against the *Tinoco Granados government. It allocated
$205,000 for foreign military personnel involved in the war,
$144,000 for Costa Ricans who fought in the war, and $60,000
for families of people who fought against the government of
Tinoco. It was paid by a tax of 25 cents on each bottle of
liquor produced by the government *liquor factory and passed
over the vehement veto of President *Acosta. See also: ACOSTA
GARCIA, Julio.

LEY FUNDAMENTAL DEL ESTADO LIBRE DE COSTA RICA. The
Constitution of Costa Rica under the *República Federal de Centro
America. Decreed January 25, 1825, and amended 1827 and 1830.

It was patterned after the Central American constitution and
gave extensive power to a unicameral congress, whose membership ranged between 11 and 22 members. This document established equality of all Costa Ricans before the law, which was
opposed by the clergy and the military because of the loss of
certain rights (*fueros). Catholicism was declared the religion
of the state but private practice of other religions was tolerated.
This constitution remained in force until the overthrow of the
Manuel *Aguilar Chacón government in 1838.

LEY GENERAL DE FERROCARRILES (General Railroad Law) (1909).
Declared the principle of state ownership of the railroads and
limited to 99 years the concessions granted to foreign *railroad
companies. It was more a statement of policy than a reality
until 1972 when the English-owned Northern Railway Company
(*Ferrocarril de Norte) to the Atlantic coast was nationalized.
There are still some railroads owned by the *United Fruit Company in the Pacific and Atlantic banana zones, but they are
disappearing.

LEY ORGANICA DE LA CONTRALORIA GENERAL DE LA REPUBLICA
(Organic Law of the Comptroller's Office of the Republic). Passed
in 1954, it made the comptroller's office an autonomous agency
with the right to formulate its own budget. Supposedly this
law gave the comptroller's office more power to make impartial
audits without worrying about their budget being cut in reprisal.

LEYES DE LAS INDIAS. These were various laws decreed in Spain
pertaining to the colonies ("the Indies"). They were collected
and published in 1681 and then revived and revised again in
1805. These laws are better known as "Recopilación de las Leyes
de las Indias." In general these laws governed every part of
life in the colonies and show Spain's mercantile philosophy and
desire to protect both colonists and Indians from abuses. Unfortunately these laws were not always followed.

LIBERAL. (1) In Costa Rica and Central America this term has
been applied to someone who is generally opposed to the extension by the church of its powers in such things as cemeteries,
education, and government. Commonly such persons are in
favor of public education, freedom of the press, and religious
toleration. However, a liberal does not necessarily favor advanced social legislation; such persons are referred to as pro-
gressives.
    (2) The so-called liberal period in Costa Rica encompassed
roughly 1880-1940. See: GENERATION OF 1889; GONZALEZ
VIQUEZ, Cleto; JIMENEZ OREAMUNO, Ricardo; LIBERAL LAWS.

LIBERAL LAWS. A series of laws passed in the mid-1880s under
the governments of Próspero *Fernández Oreamuno and Bernardo
*Soto Alfaro, in which religious orders were expelled from the

country, cemeteries were secularized, civil marriage introduced, education was made free and secular under the state, and all types of religious communities were prohibited. See also: EDU-CATION LAWS; FERNANDEZ OREAMUNO, Próspero; THIEL, Bernardo Augusto.

LIBERALES ILUSTRADOS. Usually refers to the presidents of the liberal period (1880-1940), but more specifically to Cleto *González Víquez and Ricardo *Jiménez Oreamuno.

LIBERIA. City, *canton and capital of the province of *Guanacaste. It was founded September 4, 1769, as a small church (hermitage). It was officially given the title of v̲i̲l̲l̲a̲ (town) in July 1831, but had been known unofficially as La Villa de Guanacaste since 1776. The name Guanacaste came from a kind of fan-shaped tree growing in that area. In 1836 President Braulio *Carrillo Colina conferred the title of c̲i̲u̲d̲a̲d̲ (city) and in 1842 designated it capital of the department. In the civil reorganization of 1848, the city of Guanacaste was named as capital of the province of the same name. On May 29, 1854 the name of the city was changed from *Moracia to Liberia, its present name. Liberia is also called La Ciudad Blanca (the white city) because of the predominant color of the buildings. It is a distribution center for this part of the country and center for livestock sales and exhibitions. The city population has grown from 2,226 in 1892 to 2,831 in 1904, 3,161 in 1927, 6,087 in 1963, 14,093 in 1984. The canton population in 1980 was 28,067. It is also the site of *Llano Grande international airport.

LIBRA. Premetric pound of 0.46 kg. [L.H.]

LICEO DE COSTA RICA. (1) A glorified primary school founded by Máximo Jerez in *San José in 1864.
        (2) A secondary school, originally created in 1884 as a secondary level department of the *Universidad de Santo Tomás, which was given its new title when it was permitted to continue after the abolition of the University itself in 1887. As one of the country's oldest and most prestigious schools, the Liceo was at the centre of a 1988 controversy over an education ministry attempt to extend the standard national school uniform (introduced in 1978) to all secondary schools, replacing the Liceo's traditional gray. [L.H., G.K.]

LICEO DE NINAS. Established May 19, 1847 by President *Castro Madriz as the first secondary school for girls in the country.

LIENDO Y GOICOECHEA, José Antonio (1735-1814). Father Liendo y Goicoechea was awarded the doctorate in canon laws from the University of San Carlos in Guatemala. After spending two years in Spain he returned to his alma mater and started his long academic career. He was important in bringing the ideas

of the enlightment to Central America by fostering new methods
of teaching geometry, physics, and mathematics. He introduced
scientific experimentation into the curriculum and wrote several
volumes on science and theology. Although most of his intellectual activity took place out of the country, he is considered
one of the outstanding Costa Ricans of the colonial period.

LIFE EXPECTANCY. In general Costa Ricans have the best life
expectancy in Central America. According to the Dirección
General de Estadística y Censos, the life expectancy for people
born in 1983 is 70.8 years for those in the central valleys and
64.7 for people living in rural areas. This has improved from
previous years. In 1950 the life expectancy for people born
in that year was 54.6 for males and 57.1 for females; in 1963
61.9 and 64.9; and in 1973 it was 66.3 years for males and 70.5
for females.

LIGA, Guerra de la. See: CIVIL WARS: GUERRA DE LA LIGA.

LIMON (canton). Includes the city of Puerto *Limón and some of
the surrounding territory. This *canton was chartered July 25,
1892, and has a present population of 52,602. It is a distribution center and chief port of the Atlantic region. In the *Moín
area the government (*RECOPE) has the country's only oil refinery. Some *cacao is produced in the outlying areas of the
canton, while *bananas remain significant.

LIMON (city). Port on the Atlantic coast at 10°N, 83°01'W. Limón
was discovered by *Columbus on his fourth voyage in 1502.
Through most of the colonial period Puerto Limón was not important since the chief port was *Matina. However, geographic
conditions changed and a new Atlantic port was needed. Puerto
Limón was declared a port in 1865 and officially opened September 20, 1867. The completion of the Atlantic *Railroad (*Ferrocarril del Norte) stimulated its growth and today it is also being
developed as a tourist area. One of its most distinctive charac-
teristics is the large number of *Blacks, most of whom came
from Jamaica to help build the railroad in the 1870s. The population of 1,500 in 1865 grew to 2,144 in 1892, 3,171 in 1904,
15,642 in 1927, 19,432 in 1963, 42,600 in 1975, and 43,158 in
1984. See: CARNIVAL. For more details consult Quince Duncan and Carlos Meléndez, El negro en Costa Rica (1973), and
Jaime Granados Chacón and Ligia Estrada Molina, Reseña histórica
de Limón (1967).

LIMON (province). The province consists of all the Atlantic Coast
region. It was organized as a comarca (June 6, 1870), and
incorporated as a province in 1907. Its present population is
168,076 which includes a relatively high percentage of *blacks
and *Indians, making its population different from the rest of
the country. The chief products are *bananas, *cacao, *cattle,
and timber. See also: TALAMANCA.

LINDO, Cecil Vernor (1870-?). The Lindos were originally a
Sephardic Jewish family who emigrated from France to Jamaica
via the Channel Islands. Lindo came to Costa Rica c. 1898 and
with his brother gradually acquired land and opened several
general stories in *Limón. Around 1907 the Lindos purchased
land in the Juan Viñas area (*Cartago) and established one
of the largest *coffee and *sugar businesses in the country.
Cecil Lindo owned land in Cachí and is the founder of the Lindo
family in Costa Rica.

LINEA VIEJA (Old Line). Refers to that area of *Limón Province
in the *canton of *Pococí where the first *railroad ran before
the route was changed. It is a *banana and *cacao producing
area. See also: RAILROADS.

LINEAS AEREAS COSTARRICENCES, S.A. See: AVIATION.

LIQUOR. A governmental monopoly (Fábrica Nacional de Licores)
was established in 1853 to raise income and reduce alcoholism.
It failed in the latter goal, but the aromatic landmark, once
adjacent to the presidential residence, contributed substantial
funds to the treasury. See: AGUARDIENTE; CHICHA; CHIRITE;
COYOL; GUARO. [G.K.]

LIRA, Carmen (pen name of María Isabel Carvajal) (1888-1949).
Teacher, women's political leader, and novelist. She was involved
in progressive politics, intellectual movements and educational
activities most of her life, and is one of the most important
women Costa Rica has produced. She studied in Europe and
was one of the principal members of the *Centro Germinal. Later
she joined the Costa Rican *Aprista movement and later the
Communist Party (*Communist Party). Carmen Lira was one
of the group that pushed the development of the *National Library, and she opened the first kindergarten in the country.
In addition she published a magazine called El Maestro which
devoted itself to discussions of educational and social problems.
As a novelist she wrote Las fantasías de Juan Silvestre (1918),
En una silla de ruedas (1918), and Cuentos de mi tía Panchita
(1922). Her most famous work is a collection of children's stories. She died in exile in Mexico City, having fled the country
after the 1948 *civil war. She was later declared *Benemérita
de la Patria.

LIRA COSTARRICENSE. A two-volume anthology of poems by various Costa Rican poets compiled by Máximo *Fernández Alvarado
in 1890. This work is important as a "coming of age" of Costa
Rican poetry.

LITERACY. Before the educational reforms of Mauro *Fernández
Acuña, Costa Rica had a very low rate of literacy: 11% in 1860,
12% in 1883. Since then the nation's commitment to education

has produced the most literate country in Central America, and one of the most highly literate in all Latin America. The official figures were 66% in 1927, 82% in 1943, 89% in 1973. The *census, however, records anyone as literate who has received schooling. The high school drop-out rate means that many continue to leave school before becoming functionally literate. Poverty severe enough to limit newspaper purchasing means that many more relapse into illiteracy as adults. Perhaps the rate of functional literacy is no higher than 70%. This is still high by Latin American or Third World standards. [L.H.]

LIVESTOCK. Costa Rica's principal livestock has always been CATTLE (q.v.). Herds have increased from 262,596 head in 1888 to 333,000 in 1910, 339,000 in 1929, 641,000 in 1949, 1,496,000 in 1970, and 1,700,000 in 1985.

Swine have increased from 70,000 in 1910 to 83,000 in 1929, 215,790 in 1945, 112,000 in 1949, and 1,496,000 in 1970.

There were 50,738 horses in 1888, 85,000 in 1929, 77,000 in 1949, 112,000 in 1975, and 113,000 in 1983. In the early colonial period, mules had been Costa Rica's main export, whence the *Camino de Mulas. Poultry numbered a million in 1929, five million in 1975, and six million in 1983. Sheep have never been widely kept: there were 2,125 of them in 1888. [L.H.]

LIZANO GUTIERREZ, Joaquín (1829-1901). *Governor of *Heredia and *Puntarenas provinces. Held various ministries in several governments. Candidate for the presidency in 1970. As first designate he filled in for President *Guardia Gutiérrez (May 21 to November 5, 1875) as acting president.

LIZANO GUTIERREZ, Saturnino (1826-1905). *Governor of *Puntarenas Province, he also held various ministries. President of the Republic after the death of General Tomás Guardia Gutiérrez (July 6 to July 20, 1882).

LLANO GRANDE DE CARTAGO. Small village north of *Cartago City on the slopes of *Irazú Volcano. In February 1944 it was the scene of electoral disturbances in which several people were killed. It has become a symbol for the *Partido Liberación Nacional (National Liberation Party) of the violence that they fought against in the 1948 *civil war.

LLANO GRANDE DE SAN MIGUEL DE LIBERIA. A meadow a few miles from *Liberia which is now the site of a big alternative international airport. In 1937 it was the site of an open-air convention attended by a few thousand people who named Dr. Francisco *Vargas Vargas as legislative candidate for the *Partido Confraternidad Guanacasteco. Because of the repression of the León *Cortés Castro government it became a symbol of the province's struggle for recognition.

LLANURA DE GUANACASTE. The flatlands or pampas extending roughly from the *Nicoya peninsula to the north of the River *Tempisque, and encompassing the city of *Liberia. It was the center of a rich *cattle-growing area. In addition it has been a fount of much of the country's folklore traditions. See: GUANACASTE; PUNTO GUANACASTECO; and consult Jorge Luis Acevedo, La música en Guanacaste.

LLANURAS DEL ATLANTICO (Atlantic coastal plains). The level part of the Atlantic coast province of *Limón, roughly extending from the *Talamanca mountain range up to the San Juan River. Much of this area is low-lying swampy terrain, which is in the process of being drained. It is an area which produces *bananas, *cacao, and *livestock.

LLORENTE Y LAFUENTE, Anselmo (1800-1871). First bishop of Costa Rica from the consecration of the bishopric in 1851 until his death. Born in *Cartago, he received his university education in Guatemala. He was considered a conservative churchman. In 1858 as the culmination of a church-state controversy involving payment of church *tithes, President Juan Rafael *Mora Porras decreed Llorente's expulsion from the country. He was permitted to return after the fall of Mora's government. Throughout his career he tried to strengthen the church's position in the country, strongly fighting against the *Masons and supporting the Tridentian Seminary he founded in 1854.

LOCKRIDGE, S. A. [Col.]. American military man who commanded a ship for the *filibusters and unsuccessfully tried to open the San Juan River for William *Walker's forces.

LOMBARDO ALVARADO, José Santos (ca. 1775-1831). A conservative politician who during the independence era favored association with Mexico. During the colonial era Lombardo served as acting *governor for short periods in 1816 and 1819, *alcalde of *Cartago, and as a teacher in a primary school in *San José in 1797. After independence he was one of the most prominent members of the *Junta de Legados and he served as president of the Second *Junta Gubernativa. In this latter post he became the focal point of opposition to the liberal, pro-Central American Federation faction of Rafael *Osejo. During the 1823 *civil war Lombardo served as commander of arms for the forces of *Cartago and was imprisoned for a few months for his part in that rebellion. He had his citizenship restored and served as a member of the 1824 Constituent Assembly.

LOOTS DEBLAES, Juan (b. 1875-?). A Belgian flutist who came to Costa Rica to become the Director General of the Military Bands. In 1926 he organized the short-lived *Orquesta Sinfónica de Costa Rica.

LOPEZ, José Luis (b. 1941). Painter born and partially educated in Spain. He was a member of *Grupo Taller. His works are generally a combination of abstract-geometric shapes with a strong trace of primitive or indigenous influence.

LOPEZ CONEJO, Francisco (b. 1662). A *sargento mayor in the Spanish army, he was named acting governor of the province in May 1713.

LOPEZ DE CORRAL, Tomás. As *alcalde ordinario of *Cartago, he took severe measures to force settlers living in the country to move closer to populated areas, so they could be controlled and could also attend mass more frequently. Thusly, he was instrumental in the settlement of *Alajuela Province.

LOPEZ DE LA FLOR, Juan. *Governor of the province of Costa Rica (1665-1674). He successfully led an improvised army which repulsed the pirate invasion of 1666. See: PIRATES.

LOPEZ DE SALCEDO, Diego (d. 1530). As *governor of Honduras he also claimed Nicaragua and forced Pedro de los *Ríos out of that territory. López served as governor of Nicaragua and Costa Rica 1527-28 and became involved in a territorial conflict with *Pedrarias Dávila over who had the right to govern *Villa de Bruselas. He fell into Pedrarias' hands and was imprisoned for seven months. López was particularly known for his harsh treatment of *Indians.

LOTTERY. See: JUNTAS DE PROTECCION SOCIAL.

LOUBET DECISION, 1900. Arbitral decision by the president of France, Emile Loubet, which awarded most of the disputed territory in the Almirante region to Costa Rica. Costa Rica did not accept it. See: FRONTIER QUESTIONS (SOUTH).

LUCHA POR EL MAIZ, La (The Fight for Corn). The struggle between the *Indians and Spaniards for food. The Indians planted enough corn for their own needs. The Spaniards after the arrival of Juan de *Cavallón instead of cultivating land went to search for gold and therefore had to take the Indians' corn. This resulted in interminable conflicts.

LUCHA SIN FIN, La. Name of José *Figueres Ferrer's plantation in the southern part of *San José Province. It was the site of the planning, training, and first battle of the 1948 *civil war. The name means "endless struggle."

LUJAN, Fernando (1912-1967). Poet and writer. His most important works are: Tierra marinera (1938), Poesía infantil (1941), Himno al mediodía (1964) and Anochecer de otoño (1964).

LUMBER INDUSTRY. See: FORESTS AND FORESTRY.

LYON, Arthur P. Founder of Banco Lyon. Son-in-law of William
LE LACHEUR, q.v.

- M -

MACAYA DE LA ESQUINA, Miguel [Doctor] (d. 1885). Jurist.
Born in Colombia. He emigrated to Costa Rica where he joined
Costa Rican Bar Association in 1856. He was *deputy, the first
professor of political economy in the *Universidad de Santo Tomás,
and president of the Supreme Court in 1878.

MACAYA LAHMAN, Enrique (1905-1982). Educator, writer, and
lawyer. He studied in Paris and received a Ph.D. from Cornell.
He was professor of musicology and a key figure in the University reform of 1956. He always tried to stress the teaching
of the humanities.

MACAYA LAHMAN, Ramón (1903-   ). Aviator and airline executive.
See: AVIATION.

MACEO GRAJALES, Antonio. A black Cuban revolutionary against
Spain who tried to establish a colony of Cubans near La Mansión
(*Guanacaste Province) in May 1890. This was before the war
for Cuba's independence was renewed in 1895. By 1899 the
colony was finally given up, with much of the land reverting
to the government of Costa Rica.

MACHUCA DE SUAZO, Diego [Captain]. Explored the San Juan
River region as it flowed out of Lake Nicaragua with Alonso
*Calero in 1539.

MADRIGAL, Gerardo (b. 1951). An *Arte Nuevo painter who specializes in pastel still lifes.

MADRIGAL NIETO, Rodrigo (b. 1924-   ). Lawyer and public administration specialist. *Legislative Assembly president (1978-79)
as member of Social Christian party, having left for a time the
National Liberation Party. Founded Universidad weekly newspaper as a *Universidad de Costa Rica law student in 1947.
Minister of foreign affairs in the *Arias administration (1986-   ),
and active in diplomacy to bring peace to the region. [G.K.]

MADRIZ, Juan de los Santos (1785-1852). Politician and principal
author of the *Pacto de Concordia. He received his doctorate
in canon law from the University of León, Nicaragua. He was
chosen as a representative to the *Cortes de Cádiz, but did
not take his seat. After independence he was a member of the
*Junta de Legados, where he participated most actively in writing

the Pacto de Concordia. He was representative to the Constituent
Assembly of Central America and one of the signers of the Central
American Constitution of 1824. Dr. Madriz was also representative
in various congresses, helped negotiate peace after the War
of the League (*Guerra de la Liga), was a philosophy teacher
(1818-21) in the *Casa de Enseñanza of Santo Tomás, and first
rector of the newly established *Universidad de Santo Tomás
in 1844. When he died he left about $30,000 to help finance
the *San Juan de Dios Hospital.

MADRIZ, Juan José de la. Priest of *Cartago who during the 1760s
tried to take harsh measures against abuses of the *cofradías.
His cause was later taken up by Monsignor Lorenzo de *Tristán.

MAGON. See: NATIONAL LITERARY AWARDS.

MANDAMIENTO. The practice in the early part of the colonial
period by which the chief authority of each town selected a
certain number of *Indians to work for a time on public works;
or loaned them out for private labor. This service was obligatory
and lent itself to serious abuse.

MANIFIESTO DE SAPOA. Pronouncement issued by a revolutionary
committee in May 1919 announcing their invasion of Costa Rica
from Nicaragua with the purpose of overthrowing the *Tinoco
Granados dictatorship.

MANILA HEMP. See: FIBER.

MANPOWER. See: WORKFORCE.

MANUEL ANTONIO NATIONAL PARK. Sandy beaches and jungle
vegetation on the Pacific Coast, south of Quepos. More accessible than most such "paradises." [G.K.]

MANZANA. A measure of area, equivalent of 1.727 acres, a block.
[L.H.]

MARBLEHEAD (U.S.S.). At the behest of President Theodore
Roosevelt a conference was held on board this ship (July 20,
1906) in the Bay of Fonseca. Representatives of Honduras,
El Salvador, and Nicaragua discussed problems relating to this
international waterway. This led to a further conference held
in *San José which tried to reestablish the Central American
Tribunal of Arbitration.

MARCHENA, Julián (1897-). Modernist poet who also served as
director of the *National Library. His most important work
is Alas en fuga (1941).

MARIA AGUILAR. One of the two principal rivers flowing through

*San José, on the south. The name comes from colonial times.

MARIA CECILIA, La. The first locomotive to make the trip on the *railroad from *San José to *Puntarenas. The locomotive was named for María Cecilia Lynn Yglesias, daughter of the chief construction engineer.

MARIACHI. A term invented during the *Huelga de Brazos Caídos and which has come to signify a follower of Dr. Rafael Angel *Calderón Guardia. It came from a cartoon appearing in one of the newspapers portraying a group of the Doctor's followers who were sent from the lowlands to the cold climate of *San José to keep order during this period of commotion. For protection from the cold they wrapped themselves in blankets, and were thus linked humorously to the Mexican mariachi singers. The name took hold and is still used especially during electoral campaigns.

MARIANI, Hugo (b. 1899). Violinist and musical director. He was born in Mesina, Italy; migrated to Uruguay in 1912. In 1940 he was brought to Costa Rica to be director of the *Orquesta Sinfónica Nacional. He was director of this orchestra until his death in the 1970s.

MARIN CANAS, Jose (1904-1980). Novelist. His most important works are El infierno verde (1938), treating the Chaco War in South America, and Pedro Arnáez (1942). He is the only Costa Rican included in the vast 3-volume anthology Latin American Writers (Scribner's, 1989).

MARIZANCHE. See: CASTRO FERNANDEZ, Alfredo.

MARR, Wilhem (1819-1904). Born in Magdeburg, Germany. A journalist who first came to Central America in 1852 and unsuccessfully tried to start a colony for Germans in 1853, he lived in *Puntarenas for a while and eventually went back to Germany and wrote a two-volume work, Travels to Central America (1860-61).

MARSHALL JIMENEZ, Francisco José (Frank) (1925-). Businessman, soldier, and politician. Educated in Germany and served as one of José *Figueres Ferrer's chief generals during the 1948 *civil war. He later served as minister of public security. An extreme conservative, he founded the *Partido Unión Cívico Revolucionario (UCR) and served as *deputy in 1958-62 and 1966-70. During his second legislative term he was arrested and jailed for a short time for smuggling liquor. His party joined the National Unification Party (*Partido Unificación Nacional in 1970).

MARTEN, Alberto (1909-   ). Economist. Head of *Acción Demócrata
and served in Figueres' junta as minister of finance. Later he
originated the *Solidarista movement in Costa Rica. He wrote
Teoría metafísica del dinero, El movimiento solidarista (1947),
and Principios de economía política (1944). See also: SOLIDAR-
ISTA MOVEMENT.

MARTINEZ DE PINILLOS, Juan Esteban. Interim *governor of
Costa Rica 1789-90.

MASONS. See: CALVO CASTILLO, Francisco; ESCOCESES;
YORKINOS; and consult Rafael Obregón Loria and George F. A.
Bowden, La masonería en Costa Rica (1938).

MATA, Julio (1899-1969). Musician. He was educated in the
United States. Among his most important works are: "Rosas
de Norgaria" (1933), an opera; "Toyupan" (1938), a zarzuela
(Spanish operetta); "Suite Abstracción" (1941); "Suite piedras
preciosas" (1945). In the 1950s he wrote several children's
works: "Fantasía de Navidad," and the ballets "El tesoro de
Barba Azul," and "Ballet Folklórico," based on local legends.
Finally his symphonic poem "El libertador." Consult Enrique
Cordero, Julio Mata (1981).

MATINA (canton). Situated in the Matina Valley of *Limón Province.
It was created June 27, 1969. The *cabecera is Matina City
and it has a population of 14,723 and produces *cacao and *bananas along with some *cattle. Most of the inhabitants are Caribbean blacks or of Oriental origin.

MATINA (city). Located in the Matina Valley it received its first
impetus from *cacao culture and was the site of *Fuerte San
Fernando. Matina was opened as a port by *Governor Gregorio
*Sandoval in 1639. Its importance has been eclipsed by Puerto
*Limón. See also: FELONIA DEL TENIENTE DE MATINA;
FERIAS DE MATINA; LIMON; PIRATES.

MAYNARD, Worth J. (b. 1901). Born in Waynesboro, N.C. He
came to Costa Rica in 1944. He helped promote, finance, and
organize Costa Rican baseball teams.

MEAGHER, Tomás Francis (1823-1867). Born in Waterford, Ireland.
After being convicted of sedition, he emigrated to the United
States in 1849 where he studied law. He helped publicize William
*Walker's cause in the United States and even visited Costa
Rica a few times between 1858 and 1861. Finally he wrote a
series of articles for the New Monthly Review called "Holidays
in Costa Rica" (December 1859 to February 1860).

MEAT PRODUCTION. See: CATTLE; LIVESTOCK.

MEDIA ANNATA. A colonial tax paid on the part of the first year's wages of those who obtained some noble or ecclesiastical title.

MEDINA, Crisanto. See: BANCO DE MEDINA.

MEIGGS, Henry (1811-1877). Yankee engineer-financier who built railways in Chile and Peru. When Costa Rica consulted him about building a *railroad to the Atlantic he referred the work to his nephews, especially Minor C. *Keith. [G.K.]

MENDEZ, Oscar (b. 1943). Considered one of the more important *Arte Nuevo artists. He studied in New York and Costa Rica and has had several exhibitions of his oil paintings. In 1982 he shared a collective *Ancora Prize for excellence in the plastic arts.

MENDOZA Y MEDRANO, Juan. *Governor of Costa Rica 1613-19. Accused of mistreating the *Indians of *Talamanca he was sent to Guatemala, where he was tried.

MENTOR COSTARRICENCE. Newspaper founded in 1842.

MERCOMUN (MERCADO COMUN CENTROAMERICANO). A regional trade alliance drafted in 1958, signed in Managua (Nicaragua) December 13, 1960. It went into effect in 1963 after Costa Rica's ratification April 1962. This alliance seeks the ultimate creation of a customs union between the five Central American countries. It has a complex mechanism of specialized agencies which watch over various aspects of the economy. These institutions are: Consejo Económico Centroamericano, composed of the five foreign ministers and constituting the highest authority in the Common Market organization; Consejo Consultivo del Tratado General (with headquarters in Guatemala City); BCIE/Banco Centroamericano de Integración Económica (headquarters in Tegucigalpa, Honduras); and the Unión Monetaria Centroamericana. As a result of the El Salvador-Honduras war of 1969 and other monetary problems, Honduras withdrew from the Common Market. The chaotic political situation in the rest of the isthmus plus lack of cash to balance accounts has further debilitated it. There have been several meetings to try to restructure the Common Market, but to little avail. SIECA/Secretaría Permanente del Tratado General de Integración Económica Centroamericana (headquarters in Guatemala City), has superseded the Consejo Consultivo (above) as the basic bureaucratic entity. See also: FOREIGN TRADE.

MERRERO, Floria (b. 1943). An *Arte Nuevo painter who specializes in semi-abstract oil paintings.

MESETA CENTRAL. The highland valleys of central Costa Rica where most of the population has always lived. A moderate climate and fertile soil exist here. [G.K.]

MESON DE GUERRA. Building in the town plaza of Rivas, Nicaragua, which served as a fortress for William *Walker's forces in the Battle of *Rivas (1856). In this battle Juan *Santamaría became a Costa Rican national hero, by helping to dislodge the filibusters by throwing a flaming torch at the building.

MESTIZOES. The offspring of a European and an American Indian, or the descendants of such persons. Mestizoes in modern day Costa Rica are found mostly in *Guanacaste Province and share some cultural traits with the *Chorotega Indians. Many are immigrants from Nicaragua and other Central American countries. See also: PARDOS. [L.H.]

METATE. Small stone bench used for grinding corn, but also used in pre-Columbian sacrificial ceremonies. In Costa Rica the metates were usually three-legged and ranged from one to four feet long. Sometimes they had elaborate animal or human carvings. *Huetar metates usually had human forms whereas the *Brunkas tended to make metates with animal or jaguar figures.

METRIC SYSTEM. Adopted by Costa Rica officially in 1884. See also: WEIGHTS AND MEASURES.

MEXICAN EMBASSY, Pact of. See: PACT OF THE MEXICAN EMBASSY.

MIER CEBALLOS, José de (1670-1756). Notary public, judge of *Cartago, an official of the *Inquisition. He served as acting *governor of the province February-June 1710.

MILITIA. A colonial militia was organized around the time of the invasion of the *pirates in 1666; however, it never was very effective. In 1673 it numbered 445 men and in 1718 was reported to have consisted of one company of cavalry and ten companies of infantry with a total strength of 1,218 men. In 1787 it was said to have 767 rifles, of which only 94 were in good condition. In 1812 the Provincial Militia under Juan Manuel *Cañas de Trujillo was sent to Nicaragua to put down a rebellion that had begun the year before. For this service the Cortes of Cádiz gave *Cartago the title of "Muy Noble y Leal Ciudad de Cartago." See: ARMED FORCES.

MILPA. A corn field.

MINAS DE TISINGAL. The legend of these rich gold mines probably came from a confusion of two distinct discoveries: a corruption of the name Tegucigalpa (Honduras), where rich silver mines were discovered in 1579; and exaggerations coming out of the fact that Diego *Caro de Mesa on his expedition to *Talamanca in 1579 successfully panned some gold from the Estrella River. Gradually these two facts were fused in the popular mind and a new El Dorado myth evolved about rich gold deposits in the Talamanca region.

MINIMUM WAGE. The first minimum salary was fixed Nov. 22, 1933, as a result of the "Ley de Salarios Mínimos" of the same year. At the present time a tripartite government commission periodically reviews wages and fixes salaries according to various categories of both domestic, agricultural, and industrial labor.

MINISTRIES. See: GOVERNMENT MINISTRIES.

MINT. See: REAL CUNO DE GUATEMALA.

MISKITO INDIANS. Amerindian nation of the Caribbean coast of Nicaragua and Honduras. Also known as Mosquitos. Those living in the southern part of their range interbred with *Blacks and were known as *Zambo-Mosquitos. Great Britain established a protectorate over them but was forced by United States pressure to renounce this in 1894, after having already conceded sovereignty over its southern section (down to the San Juan River) by a 1860 treaty with Nicaragua. See also: CLAYTON-BULWER TREATY. [L.H.]

MITA. A word of Quechua origin. A system whereby *Indians were chosen by turns to work in the mines for certain periods of time. In Costa Rica the mita was also used to work in agriculture. The Indians were paid very low wages, lived in poor conditions, and often were obliged to work all their lives. Some privileged Indians were exempt from this work.

MITOTE. A religious ceremony where *chicha and *cacao were drunk, usually ending in a bacchanal. It was also associated at times with funeral rites for a chief.

MOAS, Manuel (b. 1924). An *Arte Nuevo painter who was born in Argentina, but later became a Costa Rican citizen. He specializes in semi-realistic character studies in oils. He has had his works exhibited in various Central American countries.

MODERNISM. A school of poetry and writing which began in 1907 with Roberto *Brenes Mesén. It was a type of writing in which the writer wrote subjectively of personal themes. Other modernist writers of note were: Rafael *Cardona, Rafael *Estrada, and Julián *Marchena. The latter is perhaps the most important Costa Rican modernist poet.

MOIN. Now a section of the central *canton of *Limón, and seat of the *RECOPE Oil Refinery. Until 1867 it was the official port of the Atlantic region. To forestall Colombian claims to this part of the Atlantic coast Moín was declared the capital of the Comarca of Limón (1870).

MOKO. A disease that affects *bananas.

MOLINA, Pedro (1797-1854). Guatemalan leader of the independence
movement in Central America. Editor of El *Editor Constitucional.
He was part of the three-man temporary council that ruled Central
America in 1823 and its first president. He ran against Francisco
*Morazán in 1830, but was defeated. See also: CENTRAL AMER-
ICAN FEDERATION.

MOLINA BEDOYA, Felipe (1812-1855). Diplomat, born in Guatemala
and son of Dr. Pedro *Molina. He served as Central American
representative in Europe and in 1848 was appointed Costa Rica's
first ambassador to Europe. For this reason he is said to have
been the founder of the Costa Rican diplomatic corps. Molina
suggested that Costa Rica become a British protectorate to prevent the U.S. from swallowing it. He was also involved in preliminary talks that led to the *Clayton-Bulwer Treaty (1850).
He wrote Bosquejo de la República de Costa Rica, which was
one of the first histories of the country. See also: FRONTIER
QUESTIONS (NICARAGUA).

MOLINA BEDOYA, Luis (1820-1873). Diplomat, born and educated
in Guatemala. A member of the distinguished Molina family he
was a leading advocate of Central American unionism and represented Costa Rica in Washington in 1855-1866. Molina conducted
most of the negotiations settling the 1856-57 war.

MONESTEL, Alejandro (1865-1950). Composer and organist who
lived a large portion of his life in New York. He has written
14 masses and five cantatas. Among his most interesting works
are: "Rapsodia Costarricense" and "Rapsodias Guanacastecas"
nos. 1 and 2.

MONETARY REFORM OF 1863. Introduced decimal system. See:
COINAGE.

MONETARY REFORM OF 1900. Actually this reform was enacted in
1896, but went into effect in 1900. It established the gold coin
as the standard unit of currency. See: COLON; GOLD STAN-
DARD.

MONEY. See: BANKS AND BANKING; BI-METALLISM; COINAGE;
EXCHANGE RATE; GOLD STANDARD.

MONGE, Carlos Francisco (b. 1951). Poet who combines romantic
and revolutionary themes in his writing. His most important
works to date are: A los pies de la tiniebla (1972), Astro y
labio (1972), Población del asombro (1975), and Reino de latido
(1978).

MONGE ALFARO, Carlos (1905-1979). Historian and educator.

He was a member of the Asociación Cultural de Estudiantes de
Leyes in the 1930s and of the *Centro para el Estudio de Problemas Nacionales and the *Figueres Ferrer revolution. He served
as rector of the *Universidad de Costa Rica 1961-1970. During
his term of office he supervised academic reforms and the great
growth of the university. He was a prolific writer and after
his death he was declared *Benemérito de la Enseñanza. His
most important works are: Geografía social y humana de Costa
Rica (1943), El universitario ante la patria (1962), Educación
para la democracia en un mundo convulso (1963), La Universidad
y el desafío de la década de 1970-1980, La Educación fragua
de nuestra democracia (1978), and his Historia de Costa Rica,
which has become a standard history of the country.

MONGE ALVAREZ, Luis Alberto (b. 1926). President 1982-1986.
Monge was *deputy at the Constituent Assembly of 1949. He
served as deputy and president of the *Legislative Assembly.
During his long political career he was active working with labor
unions internationally and in the National Liberation Party (*Partido Liberación Nacional). He ran unsuccessfully for the presidency in 1978, but won in 1982. Monge came to power at a
critical time. With help from the International Monetary Fund
and the United States, his administration alleviated Costa Rica's
grave financial crisis. During his administration there were
problems with Nicaragua, including armed incidents and the
intermittent use of northern Costa Rica as an anti-Sandinista
base. Monge traveled abroad more than any other sitting president, trying to present a positive image of Costa Rica. In 1983
he declared Costa Rica's perpetual neutrality. See: NEUTRALI-
DAD, Estatuto de. On his role as General Secretary of ORIT
(Inter-American Regional Organization of Workers), consult Sera-
fino Romualdi, President and peons (1967).

MONGE ZAMORA, Jorge Arturo (b. 1928). Physician and politician.
President of the Christian Democratic Party (*Partido Demócrata
Cristiano) and its candidate for the presidency in 1970 and 1974,
and *deputy 1962-1966.

MONTE DE AGUACATE. A mountain in the province of *Alajuela.
Gold was discovered here in 1820 and caused a minor gold rush.
There are still mining operations in this area.

MONTEALEGRE, Mariano (1782-1843). Guatemalan-born diplomat
and politician and Costa Rica's first "coffee baron." He negotiated a treaty with the government of Nicaragua (Granada,
Aug. 16, 1823 and León, Sept. 9) in which Nicaragua seemed
to accept in principle the annexation of *Guanacaste by Costa
Rica. This treaty also had mutual assistance clauses, and stated
that Costa Rica would be neutral in the civil wars between the
two cities. In the 1824 elections Montealegre opposed Juan *Mora
Fernández for chief of state but was not elected.

MONTEALEGRE FERNANDEZ, José María (1815-1887). Physician and the first Costa Rican to have studied medicine in Europe. A member of the *Cámara de Representantes (1844-46), and of the Senate (1863-68), where he served as its president. The movement that overthrew Juan Rafael *Mora Porras brought Montealegre to the presidency in 1859 after which he was elected to a full term of office 1860-63. While in office he canceled many of the contracts that had been imposed during the William *Walker period. Also during his administration Costa Rica issued its first postage stamps. Because of political pressures, he left the country in April 1872. He died in California, September 26, 1887. His remains were buried in Costa Rica in 1978.

MONTERO BARRANTES, Francisco (1864-1925). Professor of history. He wrote Geografía de Costa Rica (1892) and Elementos de historia de Costa Rica, a two-volume work published in 1892 which should be considered the first real history of the country. He also wrote a still-unpublished "Compendio de Historia de Costa Rica" (1894), which used the new scientific principles then becoming popular.

MONTERO PADILLA, Alvaro (1916). Physician and politician. He studied in El Salvador and served as *deputy in 1958-62 and president of the Legislative Assembly in 1958-59 and 1959-60.

MONTERO VEGA, Arturo (b. 1924). Poet. His most important works are: Vesperal (1951), Poemas de la revolución (1961), Le digo al hombre (1971), Rosa y espada (1972), Poemas escogidos (1975), and Poemas para sembrar los sueños (1977).

MONTES DE OCA. *Canton in *San José Province, whose *cabecera is San Pedro, about two miles from San José. It was chartered (Aug. 1, 1915), and has a population of 39,065. In addition to being the seat of the *Universidad de Costa Rica this canton produces *coffee and vegetables. It is increasingly becoming a bedroom community for the nearby capital.

MONTES DE OCA NUVERRAN, Alberto (1912-1952). He was a strong promoter of Costa Rican folklore. Because of his efforts the "*Punto Guanacasteco" was named the "National Dance."

MONTEVERDE. Cloud forest nature preserve northwest of *San José in the Tilarán range. The rare and spectacular quetzal is a bird found in such high-altitude woods. During the 1950s, Quaker religious colonies established dairy farms here, which as the road system developed provided cheese to urban areas. National Geographic, July 1981, gives several pages to Monteverde. [G.K.]

MONTUFAR, Lorenzo (1823-1898). Lawyer and politician. Born in Guatemala where he received his law degree in 1848. He is

considered one of the liberal leaders of the time, and left the
country because of those beliefs. In Costa Rica he was magistrate of the Supreme Court, and a close friend of Dr. *Castro
Madriz. He had to leave the country after the fall of President
Juan *Mora Fernández but he returned in 1861 and served as
rector of the *Universidad de Santo Tomás. Through his membership in the Masonic Lodge he became involved in a dispute
with Bishop *Llorente y Lafuente, and left the country again
for a short period of time, briefly serving in 1862-63 as El Salvador's European representative. Returning in 1870, he became
minister of education and of foreign relations (see: MONTUFAR-
CORREOSO TREATY). Montúfar was later involved in another
dispute with the Church and returned to his native Guatemala
where he was an unsuccessful candidate for the presidency.
He became rector of the University of San Carlos and died in
his native land in 1898.

MONTUFAR-CORREOSO TREATY (1873). Treaty with Colombia
which would have awarded Costa Rica most of the land in the
disputed Almirante area. This treaty was never ratified. See
also: FRONTIER QUESTIONS (SOUTH).

MORA. *Canton in *San José Province located about 16 miles from
*San José. Originally founded May 25, 1883 as *canton of Pacaca.
Its name was changed (July 3, 1886) to honor President Mora.
Its *cabecera is Ciudad Colón and its population is 12,679. The
chief products are rice, *coffee, cereals, and *sugar.

MORA, Marco (b. 1950). An *Arte Nuevo painter who specializes
in abstract semi-geometric oil paintings.

MORA FERNANDEZ, Joaquín (1787-1862). Member of the Consejo
Representativo 1829-31 and 1836-38, and president of that body
June-Dec. 1836. Because of an electoral dispute he occupied
the post of acting president of the Republic March 1 to April 17,
1837. Mora was involved subsequently in a plot against the
government of Braulio *Carrillo Colina, who exiled him for his
complicity in it. However, he was allowed to return to the country in a few years.

MORA FERNANDEZ, Juan (1784-1854). Lawyer and chief of state
(1824-29) and (1829-33). Studied in León, Nicaragua. Returning to Costa Rica he served as principal of an elementary school
in *San José and then became judge of a lower court. He was
elected provisional chief of state on September 8, 1824, and
then subsequently elected to a regular four-year term in 1825.
During his first term of office he declared the *Virgin of the
Angels to be the patron saint of Costa Rica, established *San
José as the seat of Congress, pardoned those involved in the
*Cartago uprising (see: CIVIL WAR, 1823), decreed a coat
of arms for the new country, and granted titles of incorporation

to various cities and towns. During his second term of office
(1829-33) he encouraged the *Casa de Enseñanza de Santo Tomás,
brought a printing press to the country, and founded a newspaper in 1830. In addition to this he established a mint (see:
CASA DE LA MONEDA), tried to develop *Puntarenas, and brought
machinery to exploit the gold mines of *Monte de Aguacate.

MORA FERNANDEZ, Manuel (1800-1865). Jurist. One of the first
students to study at the *Casa de Enseñanza de Santo Tomás.
*Alcalde of *Cartago in 1832, president of the Cámara de Justicia
1842. Defeated for presidency in 1860 and 1863.

MORA PORRAS, José Joaquín (1818-1860). Brother of President
*Mora Porras. He was in charge of the Costa Rican army during
the William *Walker war and rose to the rank of general. He
led the Costa Rican forces in the capture of the *Transit Route
(Vía del Tránsito) and personally participated in the assaults
on Fort *San Carlos and *Castillo Viejo. General Mora also participated in the Battle of *Rivas (April 10, 1857) and was
commander-in-chief of the allied forces for a short period.

MORA PORRAS, Juan Rafael (1814-1860). Merchant and politician.
President of the Republic 1849-53 and 1853-59. After making a
successful career in commerce he entered politics and served
as minister in the cabinet of Dr. *Castro Madriz, president of
Congress 1856-57, and *deputy to the Constituent Assembly
1846-47. He was elected president in 1846 and during his first
term of office he built the state *liquor factory, established
the *Universidad de Santo Tomás, and helped establish the first
archdiocese in Costa Rica. He was reelected in 1853 and during
his second term of office he organized Costa Rican forces for
the war against William *Walker (1856-57). Shortly after the
war his enemies deposed him from office Aug. 14, 1859. The
next year he landed with a force at *Puntarenas and tried to
recapture the government. This attempt failed and he was executed by a firing squad in that Pacific port (Sept. 30, 1860).
"Juanito" Mora is remembered primarily for his leadership against
*Walker's filibusters in the *National Campaign (Campaña Nacional).

MORA PORRAS, Miguel (1816-1887). President of the Congress
1856 and acting president of the Republic briefly Nov. 15 to
26, 1849 and March 22 to April 6, 1850. Held office as trusted
ally of his brother, Juan Rafael *Mora Porras.

MORA VALVERDE, Manuel (1910-   ). Lawyer and politician. One
of the principal founders of the Costa Rican Communist Party
(*Partido Comunista) in 1929 which became the *Partido Vanguardia Popular after 1943. Candidate for the presidency 1940 and
1974. He served as *deputy in 1934-48 and 1970-74. Under
his leadership the Costa Rican Communist Party had generally
followed a moderate line. After a bitter factional struggle

(1983-84) Mora was deposed as head of the Party. He formed
a new group called "El *Partido del Pueblo." See also: COM-
MUNIST PARTY; SOCIAL GUARANTEES; VARGAS CARBONEL,
Humberto.

MORACIA. The name used for *Guanacaste Province between 1854
and 1860. This name was adopted for political reasons to honor
President Juan Rafael *Mora Porras. See also: GUANACASTE;
LIBERIA; MORA PORRAS, Juan Rafael.

MORALES, Gonzalo (b. 1945). One of the better known *Arte
Nuevo painters. His style combines a realistic background with
a series of dreamy figures evoking a feeling of mysterious nos-
talgia for houses and people of the past. He shared the *Ancora Prize for excellence in the plastic arts in 1982.

MORALES, Raúl (b. 1931). Poet born in Zarcero (*Alajuela Province). Most important works to date: La aguja and Trans-
parencia.

MORALES, Ricardo (b. 1935). An *Arte Nuevo artist. He studied
in Mexico and Costa Rica. He specializes in landscapes in oils,
but also has done etchings and lithographs. He has had his
works shown in the United States and several Central American
countries.

MORALES CERVANTES, Braulio (1824-1898). An *Heredia coffee
farmer who served as secretary in various government ministries. He was a member of the Tertulia Patriótica, *deputy
in 1859 and second vice-president of the country in 1876. He
helped finance the war of 1856 (*Campaña del Tránsito) and
helped expand coffee production in Heredia Province.

MORAVIA. *Canton located on the slopes of Volcano *Irazú about
six miles from *San José. Its *cabecera is San Vicente and
the *canton has a total population of 33,038. Moravia is also
the seat of several exclusive private high schools. It produces
*coffee, grains, dairy *cattle and vegetables. It has been grow-
ing rapidly as a bedroom community for the neighboring capital
city, and can boast of some very exclusive neighborhoods.

MORAZAN, Francisco (1792-1842). Born in Tegucigalpa, (Honduras),
and elected president of the Central American Federal Republic
in 1830. Morazán tried to unify Central America, but was finally
overthrown by Rafael *Carrera in 1840. After making contact
with the enemies of President Braulio *Carrillo Colina, Morazán
landed with a military force at *Caldera in April 1842. The
government sent a force to stop him, headed by General Vicente
*Villaseñor, but instead of fighting, Villaseñor made a pact with
Morazán (see: PACTO DEL JOCOTE) after which Morazán was
proclaimed chief of state. He then declared Costa Rica back in

the *Central American Federation and began to levy taxes and draft an army to forcibly reestablish the federation. He was overthrown in a revolt (September 1842), and captured in *Cartago. He was later shot in the central square of *San José September 15, 1842.

MORAZAN PARK. *San José city park constructed by President *Soto Alfaro.

MOREL DE SANTA CRUZ, Pedro Agustín (d. 1768). Born in Santiago de los Caballeros, Panama, he was bishop of Nicaragua and Costa Rica in 1751-53. He made an extensive visit to the province of Costa Rica in 1751 and wrote a famous report on the conditions of the colony at that time. He also founded schools in *Heredia and Santa Cruz (*Guanacaste Province). He was transferred to Cuba in 1753.

MORENO CANAS, Ricardo (1890-1938). Physician. He studied medicine in Switzerland and became director of surgery at the *San Juan de Dios Hospital, where his great skill as a physician sparked legends of supernatural powers. Elected *deputy in 1932, Dr. Moreno became a leading spokesman for restricting concessions which had been granted to foreign companies, especially the *United Fruit Company. He was talked of as a leading candidate for the presidency in 1940 when, on August 23, 1938, a crazed mental patient, Beltrán *Cortés Carvajal, shot and killed him and several others. Moreno Cañas is important today as a spiritist and curandero's talisman. His picture is still sold in the markets and is said to have supernatural qualities. He was declared *Benemérito de la Patria in 1949.

MORERA, Rosibel (b. 1959). Poet born in *Alajuela. She was affiliated with the *Círculo de Escritores Costarricenses and has written Cartas a mi Señor (1973).

MORERA, Timoleón. A young man from *Alajuela who was shot by authorities on the night of the February 1944 election in Sabanilla de Alajuela as he was trying to bring electoral documents that were legally in his possession to Alajuela City. He has become a symbol to the National Liberation Party (*Partido Liberación Nacional) of alleged oppression during the *Calderón Guardia years.

MORTALITY. See: BIRTH AND DEATH RATES.

MOSQUITO INDIANS. See: MISKITO INDIANS; ZAMBO-MOSQUITOS.

MOULAERT, Jean. A theatrical director who came to Costa Rica to try to improve the theatre. He was associated with the "Teatro Arlequín." He set the tone for a more professional theatre by presenting more organized and better performed productions. See: THEATRE.

MOVIMIENTO SOLIDARISTA. See: SOLIDARISTA MOVEMENT.

MOYA, Carlos (b. 1925). A painter born in *Cartago. He studied
in the Academia de Bellas Artes. His paintings are usually
landscapes and local scenes. He uses a combination of abstraction and impressionism. He has also done engravings with Indian
motifs.

MOYA MURILLO, Rafael (1800-1864). Politician, agriculturist, and
merchant. Governor of *Heredia Province, and magistrate of
the Supreme Court. In 1835 he was involved in a plot against
the *Carrillo Colina government. He continued in politics and
was a member of the Constituent Assemblies in 1838 and 1842;
deputy and president of the Senate 1844; and, after the resignation of Francisco *Oreamuno Bonilla, acting president of the
Republic December 17, 1844 to April 30, 1845.

MULE TRAIL. See: CAMINO DE MULAS.

MUMMIES. It was reported by Bartholomew *Columbus that the
*Huétares had a system of mummification which consisted of
embalming bodies in a solution of *caraña and then wrapping
the bodies in woven blankets. They were then buried with
effigies of the dead, gold, jewels, and necklaces of beads that
the *Indians considered valuable. See also: CARANA; HUETARES.

MUNOZ, Francisco. Merchant and Costa Rican minister in New York
in 1860-84. He promoted Costa Rican trade with the United
States by writing informative articles about Costa Rica in American newspapers and magazines.

MURCIELAGO, El. (1) Place in *Guanacaste Province near the
Nicaraguan border where *Calderonista forces launched their
unsuccessful counterrevolution in December 1948. Several people were killed by the invaders, even though they were clearly
marked as Red Cross workers. See also: CODO DEL DIABLO;
CIVIL WARS (1948).

(2) Estate of the late Nicaraguan dictator Anastasio Somoza,
which was confiscated by Costa Rican authorities after the Sandinista victory in 1979.

(3) A flat area in San Juan de Tibas where President
Braulio *Carrillo Colina tried to establish the capital of Costa
Rica in 1835. This action was practically responsible for the
War of the League (*Guerra de la Liga), but despite the defeat
of the League, the idea of a capital at El Murcielago was aban-
doned by Dr. Manuel *Aguilar Chacón. See also: CARRILLO
COLINA, Braulio; CIVIL WARS (1835); and consult Rafael Obre-
gón Loria, Hechos militares y políticos (1981).

MURRAY, Alexander. Born in Scotland and migrated to Costa Rica
in the late 1880s. He established the "Botica Francesa" drugstore

in *San José. He later helped found the Pharmacy School of
what is now the *Universidad de Costa Rica.

MURRAY, Alexander. Canadian citizen raised in Costa Rica. Because of his experience with the British forces in the Second
World War, he was of great help to José *Figueres in the planning and successful execution of the 1948 *civil war.

MURILLO GUTIERREZ, Pío (1795-1863). Delegado in the Junta
Gubernativa in 1821 and one of the signers of the *Pacto de
Concordia. He was mayor of *Barva in 1826 and 1836, and be-
cause of his many works there he has sometimes been called the
"Father of Barva." In 1835 he used his good efforts to avoid a
civil war, and also helped open a trail to the *Sarapiquí region.

MUSEO DE ARTE COSTARRICENSE. Museum of Costa Rican Art
located in what had been the terminal building of La *Sabana
airport. Since 1975 the museum has been financed by its right
to a tenth of the receipts of the 6% entertainment tax.

MUSIC. See: CONSERVATORIO DE CASTELLA; CORO DE LA
ORQUESTA NACIONAL; DUSI, Marco; ESCUELA DE ARTES
MUSICALES; ESCUELA DE MUSICA SANTA CECILIA; FLORES,
Bernal; GUTIERREZ, Benjamín; GUTIERREZ, Manuel María; HER-
RERA, Arnoldo; HERRERA, Luis Diego; INSTITUCION DE LAS
BANDAS; LOOTS DEBLAES, Juan; MARIANI, Hugo; MATA,
Julio; MONESTEL, Alejandro; NATIONAL ANTHEM; ORQUESTA
SINFONICA NACIONAL; PORRAS, William; RETRETAS; SAENZ,
Rocío; VARGAS, Carlos Enrique; VARGAS CALVO, José Joaquín.

- N -

NABORIA. A type of labor where *Indians worked on land for
very low wages. A local adaptation of the *encomienda system,
but without the rigors of the *mita.

NACAOME MEETINGS. In October 1847 at Nacaome (Honduras),
Nicaragua, El Salvador, and Honduras met to form a federal
government which was ratified the next year. Costa Rica did
not join in this federation, nor were they present at the meetings. This is an example of Costa Rica reluctance to join any
federation after the breakup of the Central American Federation
in 1838.

NACION, La. Costa Rica's best known newspaper, a conservative
daily with the largest circulation in the country (c. 120,000),
founded in 1946, and generally representing the views of the
*Asociación Nacional de Fomento Económico. From 1968 to 1980
its editor was Avido *Fernández. [L.H.]

NAHUAS. A tribe originally from Mexico, they had some small colonies in *Bagaces and in the Sixalóa River valley, and are said to have numbered about 400 at the time of the conquest. They spoke Nahuatl and are believed to have brought *cacao from Mexico, which they kept as a tribal monopoly. Nahuas worshipped the cult of *Huitzilopochtli, the pot-bellied Mexican war god. They engaged in human sacrifice and occasionally practiced ritual cannibalism. Upon the death of a woman, slaves were immolated to serve their mistress in the new world. Their religious festivals were at the times of the corn and bean harvests. Their priests were also a combination of soothsayers, witchdoctors, and physicians.

NAMBI. A *Chorotega Indian *cacique or chief who ruled in the Nicoya Peninsula at the time of the Spanish conquest.

NANDAYURE. (1) A *Chorotega Indian chief.
(2) A *canton in the southern part of the *Nicoya Peninsula in *Guanacaste Province. Created October 15, 1961, its *cabecera is Carmona. Its chief product is *cattle, but it also produces some *coffee. Its population at present is 9,604.

NARANJO. City and *canton located in *Alajuela Province about 20 miles from *Alajuela City. The canton was established March 9, 1886, and Naranjo was declared a city July 24, 1918. The population of the canton is 23,588 and of Naranjo City, 11,600. The canton produces *coffee, *tobacco, corn, *rice, beans, and *sugar.

NARANJO COTO, Carmen (b. 1930). Poet and novelist. She was born in *Cartago and is considered in the tradition of Yolanda *Oreamuno. Carmen Naranjo was minister of culture for several years and won the National Prize for Literature in 1966. Her most important works are: Los perros no ladraron (1966), Camino a mediodía (1967), Memorias de un hombre palabra, and various books of poetry such as: América (1961), Canción de ternura (1964), Hacia tu isla (1966), Misa a oscuras (1967), and Idioma del invierno (1971). Consult Ivette Martínez Santiago, Carmen Naranjo y la narrativa femenina en Costa Rica (EDUCA, 1987).

NARCOTICS. See: DRUGS.

NARRATIVE LITERATURE. Around 1940 national writers began to abandon the then prevalent *costumbrista style and started to concentrate more on social problems. The leaders of this so-called *Generation of 1940 style of narrative literature were: Carlos Luis *Fallas Sibaja, Fabián *Dobles, José *Marín Cañas, Yolanda *Oreamuno, and Abelardo Bonilla. See: individual entries. Consult Abelardo Bonilla, Historia de la literature costarricense.

NATIONAL ANTHEM (Himno Nacional). The music of the national
anthem of Costa Rica was written by Manuel María *Gutiérrez in
June 1852. At an official ceremony for visitors from Great Britain
and the United States, the various national anthems were to
be played, but it was discovered that Costa Rica did not have
any national anthem. Therefore the minister in charge of the
ceremonies (José Joaquín *Mora Porras) commissioned Gutiérrez
to write the music. In 1903 a national contest was held for
the words to this music. This contest was won by José M.
"Billo" Zeledón. (See: ZELEDON BRENES, José María.)
      The words and music were used unofficially until they
were declared the official national anthem on June 1, 1949.

      HIMNO NACIONAL DE COSTA RICA
      Lyrics by José María Zeledón B.
      Music by Manuel María Gutiérrez

      Noble patria, tu hermosa bandera
      expresión de tu vida nos da:
      bajo el límpido azul de tu cielo
      blanca y pura descansa la paz.

      En la lucha tenaz de fecunda labor
      que enrojece del hombre la faz,
      conquistaron tus hijos--labriegos sencillos--
      eterno prestigio, estima y honor.

      ¡Salve, oh tierra gentil!
      ¡Salve, oh madre de amor!
      Cuando alguno pretenda tu gloria manchar,
      verás a tu pueblo, valiente y viril,
      la tosca herramienta en arma trocar.

      ¡Salve, oh patria!, tu pródigo suelo,
      dulce abrigo y sustento nos da;
      bajo el límpido azul de tu cielo,
      ¡vivan siempre el trabajo y la paz!

NATIONAL ARCHIVES. Consult: Kenneth Grieb, ed., Research
      Guide to Central America and the Caribbean (Madison: 1985),
      p. 134.

NATIONAL BIBLIOGRAPHY. Costa Rica's first attempt at a national
      bibliography seems to have been the Catálogo de periódicos, an
      1897 listing of newspapers by Bernabé Quirós. The first attempt
      at a comprehensive bibliography to cover both works published
      in Costa Rica and works about the country published abroad,
      was Luis Dobles Segreda's Indice bibliográfico de Costa Rica,
      whose publication, begun in 1927, took nearly forty years. In-
      tended to be in eleven volumes, by subject, with a twelfth volume
      author index, the extent of its coverage varies by subject,
      beginning in some cases in the 1820s, and extending generally
      to 1926, but occasionally to 1935 or 1936. The 1830s and 1840s

are also covered in Jorge Lines' Libros y folletos publicados en Costa Rica, durante los años 1830-1849, published in 1944. The official current national bibliography began with the *National Library's Boletín bibliográfico, 1946-1955. This then became the Anuario bibliográfico costarricense [L.H.].

NATIONAL CAMPAIGN (Campaña Nacional). One of the names used to denote the Transit Campaign (*Campaña del Tránsito) against William *Walker and his group of filibusters (1856-57). Also known as the War of National Independence.

NATIONAL DANCE. See: PUNTO GUANACASTECO.

NATIONAL EMERGENCY LAW. Passed in 1969 to enable the executive to decree prompt financial response to problems. Relief to *Guanacaste during the drought of 1982-3 was accomplished under the law. But improper use of the law and funds for less-than emergencies has occurred. [G.K.]

NATIONAL FLAG. The national flag of Costa Rica was designed by Pacífica Fernández in partial imitation of the French tricolor. It consists of five horizontal stripes. The outer stripes are blue, the center stripe is double the size of the others and is red, with the national coat of arms placed in the center. The two other center stripes are white. It was officially declared the national flag in 1848. Nine various earlier flags contained the blue and white to symbolize the unity aspired to for Central America. The red stands for liberty.

NATIONAL FLOWER. The national flower is the *Guaria Morada (Cattleya skinner). It is deep purple in color and blooms during the dry season (January-March).

NATIONAL HOLIDAYS. See: HOLIDAYS.

NATIONAL LIBERATION ARMY (Ejército de Liberación Nacional). The name given to the forces of José *Figueres Ferrer that successfully fought the 1948 *civil war.

NATIONAL LIBERATION MOVEMENT (Movimiento de Liberación Nacional). (1) Name used by the group closest to José *Figueres Ferrer that planned and executed the 1948 *civil war.
(2) A political organization in which membership was by invitation only, composed of veterans of the National Liberation Army. This organization served as a cadre in organizing the *Partido Liberación Nacional.

NATIONAL LIBERATION PARTY. See: PARTIDO LIBERACION NACIONAL.

NATIONAL LIBRARY (Biblioteca Nacional). Established 1887, based on the remains of the library of the *Universidad de Santo Tomás. By 1970 it held 150,000 volumes. Since 1945 it has produced the annual national bibliography entitled, since the 1956 volume, Anuario bibliográfico costarricense.

NATIONAL LITERATURE AWARDS. Prizes are awarded each year for outstanding works in various fields of writing. Among the most important are: The Aquileo J. Echeverría Prize for the leading work in short story, novel, essay, poetry, history, or sometimes any other art form; the Magón Prize, awarded to an outstanding national writer for contributions in the field of national literature; and the García Monge award for journalism and criticism.

NATIONAL MUSEUM. Established in 1887 and moved to its present location in *Bellavista fort after 1948. A variety of private collections have been donated to it. Consult Christian Kandler, Ana L. Báez and Lorena San Román, National Museum of Costa Rica; Over One Hundred Years of History (1987). [G.K.]

NATIONAL PARKS. Created since 1971 in an effort to preserve portions of the ecological diversity, fourteen now exist covering more than eight percent of the national territory. (There are also various National Refuge areas, Biological Reserves, etc.) The four most accessible and most visited are: *Poás Volcano; *Irazú Volcano; *Cahuita, beach on Atlantic Coast; and *Manuel Antonio, beach on Pacific Coast. Others are: *Santa Rosa; *Rincón de la Vieja; *Barra Honda; *Palo Verde; *Braulio Carrillo; *Chirripó; *Amistad; *Corcovado; *Cocos Island; and *Tortuguero. [G.K.]

NATIONAL REPRESENTATION OF CENTRAL AMERICA. A scheme for Central American unification drawn up at a conference in León, Nicaragua, in 1849. The states were to have a common diplomatic representation and enter into a loose federation. Great Britain and the United States did not recognize it and Costa Rica refused to join. The National Representation was ultimately replaced by the Republic of Central America. See: REPUBLIC OF CENTRAL AMERICA.

NATIONAL SEAL. Basic design adopted in 1906, showing two oceans and three mountain peaks between. Military symbols of earlier emblems were dropped. In 1964, two additional stars were added above, making a totla of seven to represent the provinces.

NATIONAL THEATRE. See: TEATRO NACIONAL.

NATIONAL THEATRE COMPANY. See: COMPANIA NACIONAL DE TEATRO.

NATIONAL TREE. A large umbrella-shaped tree native to the lowlands of the northern province, called the *Guanacaste tree (Enteralogum cyclocarpum).

NATIONAL UNIVERSITY. In 1973 the national legislature authorized the creation of a second university on the country. *Heredia City was selected as its seat and the then existing normal school of Heredia (Escuela Normal Superior) was transformed into the *Universidad Nacional de Costa Rica.

NATIONALIZED BANKING SYSTEM (SISTEMA BANCARIO NACIONAL). Under a decree by the ruling junta, on June 21, 1948, all banks were nationalized and placed under the general direction of the central bank (*Banco Central de Costa Rica). Stockholders were compensated at the market value of their stock. Under the *Trejos Fernández administration, private banks were permitted to open offices in the country, but were not allowed to lend money or accumulate capital. The system was effectively abolished late in 1988. See: BANKS AND BANKING.

NAVA, José Joaquín de. *Governor of the province 1764-73. During his administration he arranged a treaty with the *Zambo Mosquito Indians and secured a monopoly of *tobacco production for Costa Rica for all of the Kingdom of Guatemala. In addition he supervised the construction of the present church in *Orosí.

NAVE, La. A periodical published in *Heredia by Jorge *Volio Jiménez in 1911 with a social Christian philosophy.

NAVY. See: ARMED FORCES.

NEGRITA, La. See: VIRGIN OF THE ANGELS.

NEGROES. See: BLACKS.

NEILY, Ricardo. Immigrant Lebanese merchant who came to Costa Rica in 1928; founder of *Ciudad Neily.

NEUTRALIDAD, Estatuto de. It was declared by President Luis Alberto *Monge Alvarez, September 15, 1983. It stated that Costa Rica will be neutral forever in all warlike conflicts. However it qualified this by stating that they would not be impartial in ideological conflicts, would support the western democracies and continue to honor their treaty obligations under the United Nations and Organization of American States (see: TIAR). The act went on to reaffirm national sovereignty and restate Costa Rica's desires to keep from reestablishing their ARMED FORCES, q.v.

NEW ART. See: PAINTING (ARTE NUEVO).

NEWSPAPERS. The first newspaper published in the country was
probably Relación de los Negocios Despachados por el Consejo
in 1832. Although it consisted mostly of official decrees there
was also some general news. The second newspaper was published
by Joaquín Bernardo *Calvo Rosales in 1833, called El *Noticioso
Universal and it published 115 editions. This was followed by
La tertulia, published by Father Vicente *Castro Ramírez (also
known as Padre Arista) on February 21, 1834. However, the
modern era of journalism started with the appearance of El *Diario
de Costa Rica (1885). It was closely followed by El Heraldo
de Costa Rica, published by Pío *Víquez. Today there are
several daily newspapers published in the country and many
weeklies, representing various points of view. Costa Rica has
a free press. Only over the matter of licensing journalists has
the country been criticized. See: COLEGIO DE PERIODISTAS;
EXCELSIOR; NACION, La; PRENSA LIBRE, La; TICO TIMES,
and consult: Juan Rafael Quesada Camacho, Periodicos en Costa
Rica, 1833-1986. San José, Centro de Investigaciones Historicas
de la Universidad de Costa Rica, 1986.

NICARAGUA. See: FRONTIER QUESTIONS (NICARAGUA).

NICOYA. City and *canton in *Guanacaste. Located on the Nicoya
Peninsula, it was the principal settlement of the *Chorotega
Indians and one of the most important towns during the colonial
period. It is the oldest parish in the country and has a famous
colonial church, built in 1634 and reconstructed ten years later.
The *canton was established December 7, 1848, and Nicoya was
declared a city July 24, 1918. The canton has a population of
36,626 and the city, 21,455. Both are the most populous in
the province.

NICOYA, Partido de. The area of the *Nicoya Peninsula which
is now mainly in the province of *Guanacaste was considered a
*corregimiento or semi-independent from the province of Nicaragua
in the colonial period. In 1665 *Governor Juan *López de la
Flor asked that this territory be made part of Costa Rica, but
to no avail. In 1787 it was given the name "Partido de Nicoya"
and in 1812 the *Cortes de Cádiz in order to give Costa Rica
the necessary population to elect a member included the Partido
de Nicoya with Costa Rica. This area always had more connec-
tions with Costa Rica than with Nicaragua. Finally as a result
of constant civil wars within Nicaragua, the populace of the
area voted annexation to Costa Rica in a *cabildo abierto in
Nicoya City on July 25, 1824. This act was confirmed by the
Central American Federal Congress in December 1825 and finally
agreed to by Nicaragua in the *Cañas-Jerez Treaty of 1858.
See also: FRONTIER QUESTIONS (NICARAGUA).

NICUESA, Diego de. Spanish explorer and conquistador. *Governor of *Veragua 1508-11 and a favorite of King Ferdinand of Aragon, having been brought up in the king's palace. In 1510 Nicuesa explored the Atlantic coast of Costa Rica and ultimately reached as far north as Cape Gracias a Dios (Honduras). During this difficult expedition many members of his party perished and he almost lost his life. Nicuesa returned to Spain in 1511, after having lost most of his wealth on these ill-fated expeditions.

NIEHAUS FAMILY. Before Second World War this German family owned 80 percent of the country's sugar mills plus land which was said to be worth $9 million. As a result of the *Alien Property Law and the actions of the *Junta de Custodia de la Propiedad Enemiga this property was confiscated by the state, paying an indemnity of only $2,019,033. The matter was in litigation for a long period of time and the family finally recuperated some of its property. See also: JUNTA DE CUSTODIA DE LA PROPIEDAD ENEMIGA; and consult T. Creedman, The Political Development of Costa Rica, 1936-1944 (1971), and Victor Guardia Quirós and Gastón Guardia V. Aspectos de una demanda inverosímil: una sentencia inverosímil (1955).

NINO, Andrés. Spanish explorer who accompanied Gil *González de Avila on his expedition to the *Nicoya Peninsula in 1522-23. He also is considered the codiscoverer of the Gulf of Fonseca.

NOMBRE DE DIOS. City in Panama at 9°34'N, 79°26'W, founded by the Costa Rican explorer Juan de *Cardenas. It was the main Spanish settlement on the Caribbean coast of Central America until eclipsed by Portobello. [L.H.]

NORTH (Norte). Used in some contexts to refer to the Caribbean shore of Central America, in contrast to sur (south) for the Pacific shore. The usage originated in Panama, where *Nuñez de Balboa, first discovering the Pacific Ocean on the southern side of the Isthmus, christened it the Mar del Sur (South Seas). Hence San Juan del Norte (even though it is actually further south than the Pacific San Juan), Northern Railroad, etc. [L.H.]

NORTHERN RAILWAY. See: FERROCARRIL DEL NORTE.

NOTICIOSO UNIVERSAL. The second newspaper published in the country (1833) by Joaquín Bernardo *Calvo Rosales. It published 115 issues. See: NEWSPAPERS.

NOVOA SALGADO, Benito de. *Oídor of the *Audiencia de Guatemala. In 1675 he tried to improve the condition of the *Indians by decreeing better treatment, especially in matters of the *encomienda and in restraining ultradoctrinaire priests who were abusing the Indians.

NUNEZ DE BALBOA, Vasco (1474-1519). Led the expedition that

discovered the Pacific Ocean. Also cofounder of the city of
Panama and de facto *governor of *Veragua (1511-14). He organized expeditions to Nicaragua and Costa Rica. Unfortunately
he became involved in a rivalry with *Pedrarias Dávila and was
executed by him. See also: VERAGUA.

NUNEZ GUTIERREZ, Daniel (1848-1928). Physician and politician.
Studied medicine in England and was superintendent of the *San
Juan de Dios Hospital. Member of the Constituent Assembly
of 1917, senator (1917-19), and president of the Senate (1917-18).

NUNEZ MONGE, Francisco María (1892-). Journalist and historian.
In addition to many articles in El *Diario de Costa Rica, he
wrote La evolución del periodismo en Costa Rica (1921).

NUNEZ SAGREDO, Fernando (d. 1639). Member of the Trinitarian
Order and bishop of Nicaragua and Costa Rica in 1635-39. He
visited Costa Rica in 1637, being only the third bishop to do
so. Bishop Núñez tried to defend the *Indians against the abuses
of the corregidores de indios and during his term of office the
*Virgin of the Angels appeared in *Cartago. See also: VIRGIN
OF THE ANGELS.

NUNEZ VARGAS, Benjamín (1915-). Priest, labor leader, politician.
While studying in the United States he was called back to Costa
Rica by Bishop *Sanabria to establish a new non-communist labor
union in 1943, which was called the *Confederación Costarricense
de Trabajo "Rerum Novarum." Later Núñez became associated
with José *Figueres Ferrer's revolutionary movement and helped
negotiate the surrender terms at the height of *Ochomogo. He
was a member of the revolutionary *Junta Fundadora de la Segunda
República and later served as ambassador to Israel and as the
first rector of the *Universidad Nacional. Next he was Costa
Rican representative to UNESCO.

- O -

OBREGON LIZANO, Miguel (1861-1935). Educator and geographer
and one of the principal founders of the *National Library. He
wrote many works on geography and natural history. His most
important work is Nociones de geografía patria (1921). He was
declared *Benemérito de la Patria in 1959.

OCAMPO Y GOLFIN, Francisco de [Capt.] (1570-1625 [or 1638]).
Spanish explorer; from a noble family of Castile. He was acting
*governor of the province for short periods of time in 1601,
1619, and 1622, and *alcalde ordinario in the *cabildo of *Cartago.
He led local defense forces against various *pirate invasions,
and later became procurador general (attorney general) of the
province.

OCHOMOGO. A point on the continental divide roughly two-thirds
of the way between *San José and *Cartago City at an elevation
of more than 4,000 feet above sea level. On April 5, 1823,
in a three-and-a-half-hour battle, forces from San José and
*Alajuela defeated the forces of Cartago at a place on the heights
called La Laguna (a now non-existent lake). There were 16
republicans and four *imperialists wounded. As a result of
this battle, San José established its supremacy over Cartago
and Costa Rica joined the *Central American Federation. In
the 1948 *civil war the fate of the government's cause was sealed
when the insurgent forces of José Figueres took these heights
(April 12, 1948) and thus exposed the capital to direct bombard-
ment. Rather than risking the destruction of San José the government sent representatives to Ochomogo where the terms of surrender were arranged. Consult J. P. Bell, Crisis in Costa
Rica (1971), Alberto Cañas, "Sangre, sudor y lágrimas" (1951),
and Jacobo Schifter, La fase oculta de la Guerra Civil en Costa
Rica (1981).

OCON Y TRILLO, Juan de (b. 1559). *Governor of the province
of Costa Rica 1604-13. During his administration economic conditions were so bad that the royal treasury had to contribute
part of his salary, since the colony could not pay enough taxes
to cover it. Ocón y Trillo sent Diego de *Sojo on an expedition
to *Talamanca in 1605. During his administration, Governor
Ocón y Trillo became embroiled in a violent controversy with
the bishop of Nicaragua and Costa Rica, Pedro *Villarreal, and
was almost excommunicated.

ODECA. See: ORGANIZATION OF CENTRAL AMERICAN STATES.

ODIO, Eunice (1922-1974). A poet who wrote in an ironic style.
She lived most of her life in Mexico and Guatemala. Odio's most
important works are: Los elementos terrestres (1947), Zona
en territorio de alba (1953), and El tránsito del fuego (1957),
which is considered her best work. A collection of her works
was published in 1975 under the title: Territorio de alba y
otros poemas.

ODUBER QUIROS, Daniel (1921-). Lawyer and politician. Studied
in Canada and Costa Rica. One of the founders of the *Centro
para el Estudio de Problemas Nacionales. He helped plan and
execute the 1948 revolution and served *Figueres Ferrer's *Junta
Fundadora de la Segunda República as a roving ambassador.
He was *deputy in 1958-62 and 1970-74; president of the Legislative Assembly 1970-73; presidential candidate 1966 and elected
president of the Republic 1974-78.

OFICINA DE CAFE. Originally created July 24, 1933 as the "Instituto de Defensa del Café." It acted as a regularizing agency
for the production and sale of coffee. It sets prices and sets

quotas for each beneficio and supervises internal coffee consumption by storing coffee and then selling it at public auctions. See also: BENEFICIO; COFFEE.

OFICINA DE CONTROL. Created in 1922 to control and supervise government spending. See: LEY ORGANICA DE LA CONTRALORIA GENERAL DE LA REPUBLICA, which largely superseded this office.

OFICINA DE ESTADISTICA Y CENSOS. Created in 1864 to undertake the first real census of the country. In addition to supervising *censuses, this office, now entitled the Dirección General de Estadística y Censos, also gathers vital statistics of the country. The most recent is the Eighth National Census of Population, June 1984. For details on how historians are now utilizing older census data, consult the Bibliography (pp. 179-86) in Lowell Gudmundson, Costa Rica before Coffee (1986).

OFICINA DE PLANIFICACION Y POLITICA ECONOMIC (OFIPLAN). It was organized in 1963 as Oficina de Planificación Nacional. It is charged with planning a policy and program of development of the national economy with coparticipation of the state and private sectors. Consult Jorge Rovira Mas, Estado y Política Económica en Costa Rica.

OFIPLAN. See: OFICINA DE PLANIFICACION Y POLITICA ECONOMICA.

OIDOR. A judge of the Real *Audiencia or some other court. They were usually traveling judges that would hear cases on the spot and had the power to suspend functionaries or send them to be tried by the audiencia in Guatemala.

OIL PALM. See: AFRICAN PLAM OIL.

OLEACHA, Francisco de. Interim *governor of Costa Rica in 1739-40. He was also *alcalde mayor de *Nicoya and captain general of the Guatemalan province of Soconusco.

OLIMPICOS (Olympians). Usually referring to the leaders of the liberal period and especially *Jiménez Oreamuno and Cleto *Gonzalez Víquez. This term originated because these leaders were considered almost beyond reproach.

OLIVERA, Antonio (b. ca. 1533). Accompanied Juan de *Cavallón as a surgeon. He was also with Antonio Alvarez Pereira on his expedition to the Atlantic coast and in 1568 he served as the *alcalde of the Santa Hermandad in *Cartago.

ONCE DE ABRIL. A supply boat, a brigantine, used in the war against William *Walker. It engaged in battle off the Nicaraguan

port of San Juan del Sur (November 22, 1856) where it was
sunk. See: VALLE RIESTRA, Antonio.

ONZA. A *doblón.

OPERA. The first opera performed in Costa Rica was the "Barber
of Seville" at the *Teatro Municipal in San José on January 3,
1862. Costa Rica's most famous opera singer was Manuel ("Melico")
*Salazar. Operas are put on occasionally at the *Teatro Nacional,
but as yet there is no resident opera company.

OPUS DEI. A Catholic action group founded in 1928 and first established in Costa Rica in 1959. Their objective is to make
human beings more saintlike through creative and practical work.
They work with youth and student groups. They have opened
a dormitory for college students in San Pedro, called Centro
Estudiantil Miravalles.

ORCHIDS. See: GUARIA MORADA; RODRIGUEZ CABALLERO,
Rafael Luis.

ORDONEZ DE VILLAQUIRAN, Pedro. Born in Salamanca, Spain.
He came to the colonies in 1559 and undertook military missions
to the north to force the submission of the caciques Chomes
and Abangar, who were allied with the *Huétares. In 1556 he
had a church built at *Chomes (now a town near *Puntarenas
City), which was the second church built in Costa Rica.

OREAMUNO. *Canton founded August 17, 1914. It is located
about three miles from *Cartago City on the slopes of *Irazú Volcano and has a population of 24,145. Its *cabecera is San Rafael.
This canton produces potatoes, corn and because of its cold
climate is excellent for *cattle and truck farming. Archbishop
*Sanabria was born here.

OREAMUNO, Salvador. A leading *imperialist of *Cartago. As
captain in the Cartago forces he was second in command at the
Battle of *Ochomogo (March 29, 1823), for which he was also
imprisoned for a few months.

OREAMUNO, Yolanda (1916-1956). Novelist and writer who specialized in introspective and experimental writing. Her most
important works are: La ruta de su evasión (1949), El negro
sentido de la alegría (1956), A lo largo del corto camino (1961),
and a collected anthology of her works titled: Relatos escogidos
(1977).

OREAMUNO BONILLA, Francisco María (1801-1856). Served as
chief of state November 29 to December 17, 1844. He was elected
but was reluctant to serve, and finally resigned against the
wishes of the Congress. He was also administrator of customs

in *Puntarenas, member of the Constituent Assemblies of 1823
and 1843-44, a *deputy 1825-28, and in his capacity as vice-
president of the country, he served as president of the Congress
1850-56. Oreamuno filled in for President *Mora Porras when
the latter was directing war against William *Walker. He died
of *cholera which he contracted fighting in this war.

OREAMUNO JIMENEZ, Félix (1793-1830). Son of Joaquín de Oreamuno and an ardent *imperialist. It was he who actually broke
into the armory in *Cartago in 1823 to steal the arms which
were used in the uprising of that year. He was one of the
few officials who actually pledged allegiance to Agustín de
*Iturbide. At the battle of *Ochomogo, Félix Oreamuno was
one of the most valiant officers and stood his ground until the
situation became hopeless, then helped negotiate the surrender
to the forces of José Gregorio *Ramírez Castro. He was imprisoned for a few months for his part in the rebellion. Finally
Oreamuno was a member of the *Junta de Legados, served in
the Constituent Assembly of 1822, and was in the Congress
of 1825. See also: CIVIL WAR (1823).

OREAMUNO ORTIZ, Nicolás (1866-1945). Jurist. Deputy in various congresses; judge of the Court of Appeals; minister of war
in 1910. He represented Costa Rica as its second magistrate
(1913-18) on the Central American Court of Justice (*Corte de
Justicia Centroamericana). Oreamuno Ortiz went into voluntary
exile during the *Tinoco Granados presidency and when he returned
in 1920 he served as president of the Supreme Court, a post he
held until 1934.

ORGANIZACION DE ESTADOS CENTROAMERICANOS (ODECA) (Organization of Central American States). Created in 1951 and
started to function in 1955 as a regional peace-keeping organization under the charter of the United Nations. In theory it has
the power to stop fighting, but it proved ineffective in the
El Salvador-Honduras war of 1969, and in 1973 with most of
the countries in arrears in their annual contributions, this organization was reduced to little more than a small office staff.
Recently there have been attempts to revitalize ODECA as a
partial solution to current problems of Central America.

ORGANIZATION OF AMERICAN STATES (Organización de Estados
Americanos). Since 1948 the name of the international body
representing all the sovereign states of the Americas except
Canada. Its earlier name of Pan American Union is now the
name of its Washington-based secretariat. It intervened in Costa
Rica in December 1948 to secure the withdrawal of pro-*Calderón
Guardia forces who had invaded the country from Nicaragua.
[L.H.]
      See also: INTER-AMERICAN COMMISSION ON HUMAN
RIGHTS; INTER-AMERICAN COURT OF HUMAN RIGHTS.

ORIAMUNO ALVARADO, Gregorio (b. 1733). Acting *governor
December-May 1788 during the sickness and after the death
of Governor *Perié Barros.

ORIAMUNO VASQUEZ, Francisco Javier de (1707-1762). Acting
*governor November-December 1747 and governor 1760-62. Dur-
ing his administration he had to contend with an uprising of
the *Indians in *Talamanca and the two invasions of the *Zambo-
Mosquitos in the *Matina Valley.

ORIAMUNO VASQUEZ, José Antonio de (1710-1785). Interim *governor 1762-64 after the death of his brother, Francisco Javier
de *Oriamuno Vásquez. He was also acting governor July 1756
to October 1757, and finally a *regidor and *alguacil mayor of
*Cartago.

ORLICH BOLAMACICH, Francisco José (1907-1969). Merchant,
*coffee grower, and politician. President of the Republic 1962-
66. Educated partly in the United States. President of the
municipal council of his native *San Ramón (*Alajuela Province)
1938-40 and *deputy 1940-44 and 1946-48. He was one of José
*Figueres Ferrer's closest collaborators during the 1948 *civil
war, being in command of the forces of the *National Liberation
Army on the northern front. Orlich was one of the members
of the National Liberation movement (movimiento de Liberación
Nacional). He was unsuccessful candidate for the presidency
in 1958, but won the *election of 1962. During his administration Costa Rica entered the Central American Common Market
(*MERCOMUN); new buildings for the children's hospital, *Banco
Central and Supreme Court were constructed; and the first
section of the autopista (superhighway) to the north was built.
He also had to face the problem of the eruption of *Irazú and
floods along the *Reventazón River near the city of *Cartago.
In 1963 President Orlich was host to meetings of the presidents
of Central America and the United States.

OROSI. A district in the *canton of *Paraíso located in the valley
of the same name. It was an important town in colonial times,
but is now known for its colonial church and museum as well
as some thermal baths. This district's present population is
5,705.

OROTINA. *Canton in *Alajuela Province located about 40 miles
from Alajuela City, along the route of the Pacific Railroad (*Ferrocarril Eléctrico del Pacífico). Its name is derived from the *Chorotega Indians. Its *cabecera is Orotina and it produces lumber,
many *fruits and grains. The canton was created August 1,
1908 and at present has a population of 10,494.

OROZCO CASORLA, José María (1884-1971). Educator and agrono-
mist. He was educated in Chile. Orozco helped establish

coeducational classes in the "Liceo de Heredia" and encouraged a program of adult education. In 1941 he founded the Faculty of Agronomy in the *Universidad de Costa Rica. For all these efforts in furthering national education he was declared *Bene-mérito de la Patria.

OROZCO GONZALEZ, Rafael (1843-1897). After being educated in Honduras, he returned to Costa Rica and filled many positions in governmental administration while pursuing his law practice. Director of the National Archives in 1887 and president of the Supreme Court in 1880-86, Dr. Orozco also wrote some law trea-tises, the most important of which is Elementos de derecho penal en Costa Rica (1881); this work was adopted as a textbook in the *Universidad de Santo Tomás.

ORQUESTA SINFONICA DE COSTA RICA. See: LOOTS DEBLAES, Juan; ORQUESTA SINFONICA NACIONAL.

ORQUESTA SINFONICA NACIONAL. Originally founded in 1926 by the Belgian flutist Juan *Loots Deblaes, it disbanded the follow-ing year after returning from a disastrous trip to Central America and Mexico. The orchestra was reestablished in 1950 by the Italian Hugo *Mariani who also served as its director for many years. In 1971 the orchestra was again reorganized under the aegis of Guido *Sáenz González, the vice-minister in the new Ministry of Culture, Youth, and Sports. They tried to attract foreign musicians and professionalize the orchestra by providing full time jobs for the musicians. An American, Gerald Brown, served as its director for the next ten years. Recently the orchestra has been beset with serious financial problems. Since 1975, the OSN has received ten percent of receipts from a six percent entertainment tax. The orchestra gives over a dozen concerts during its season (April to November), occasionally performs in the provinces, and serves as a sort of school of music. Consult Ricardo Pérez, Orquesta Sinfónica Nacional (San José: Ministerio de Educación pública, 1965).

ORTEGA VICENZI, Dina (b. 1947). Poet born in San José. Her works to date include: Lluvia de enero (1971) and Huellas (1978).

ORTUNO, Gaspar. One of the principal founders of the *Banco de la Unión in 1877.

OSA. *Canton that comprises the peninsula of the same name in the southwestern part of *Puntarenas Province. It is sparsely populated jungle area with resources of *gold and hardwoods. It was originally part of the canton of *Dota until 1925 when it was combined with the canton of *Buenos Aires. It became a canton in its own right August 13, 1940. Its *cabecera is Puerto Cortés and its total population is 26,294.

OSEJO, Rafael Francisco (ca. 1790-1848). Born in Nicaragua, he received his bachelor's degree at the University of León. A *mestizo or mulatto, he came to Costa Rica in 1814 at the behest of the municipal government of *San José to be the first head of the newly formed *Casa de Enseñanza de Santo Tomás. He taught law, mathematics, and philosophy. His defense of the rights of the *Indians and his democratic sentiments displeased *Governor *Cañas de Trujillo. Osejo supported independence and subsequently was elected to be a member of the *Junta de Legados de los Pueblos, secretary of the first Constituent Assembly in 1822, and in 1823 one of the *Triumvirate. Osejo was an ardent republican and opposed joining Agustín de *Iturbide's Mexican Empire. He aligned himself with José Gregorio *Ramírez Castro to fight against the *imperialists in the 1823 *civil war. After the war Osejo served as *deputy 1829-32 and president of Congress 1830-31. He authored the first law of public instruction of May 4, 1832. Later he left the country for Nicaragua where he was a senator for a brief period. He then went to Honduras. Osejo was one of the most important persons in the formation of Costa Rican liberalism. He was declared *Benemérito de la Patria on July 30, 1823, the first person to be so honored in Costa Rica. Consult Chester Zelaya G., El bachiller Osejo (2 vols., 1971).

OSSA, Carlos de la (b. 1946). Poet who studied in Mexico. His works include: Aliosha (1969), Imprimátur I (1970), Fundación de silencios (1970), Imprimátur II (1971), Canciones para la luna roja (1974), Imprimátur III, Imprimátur IV (1979), Nocturnal (Imprimátur V) (1983), and Sonata arriarilla (Imprimátur VI) (1983).

OXCARTS. Symbol of Costa Rica is the colorful design, as traditionally painted on the large wooden wheels of what from the nineteenth century until recently was the principal national vehicle. The circular emblem can be seen on tourist literature and the tail fin of the national airline, LACSA. See: CHAVERRI, Fructuoso; and consult Mary Louise Wilkinson, "The Colorful Carts of Sarchí" in Américas, May-June 1986. [G.K.]

- P -

PACHECO, Abel (b. 1933). Short story writer and novelist. His most celebrated work is Más abajo de la piel which won the Aquileo *Echeverría prize in 1972. It deals with life in the *Limón Province. He has also written Paso de tropa (169) and Una muchacha (1978).

PACHECO, Fausto (1899-1966). Painter. He specialized in watercolors and oil paintings of scenes of the central valley and highland regions. In many ways he could be classified as a *costumbrista painter.

PACHECO, León (1902-1980). Professor of literature, essayist, literary critic, and novelist. Pacheco was a very respected writer who through his newspaper columns served as a sort of alter ego of Costa Rican society. He won two Aquileo *Echeverría prizes for books of essays: El hilo de Ariadne (1965) and Tres ensayos apasionados (1968). Another important work is his novel, Los pantanos del infierno (1974), which deals with the *banana strike in the 1930s.

PACHECO BERTORA, Luis. At the Battle of *Rivas in 1856 he was the person originally designated to carry the torch that set fire to the "*Mesón de Guerra," the strong point of William *Walker's forces. However, he was wounded and the task went to Juan *Santamaría. Pacheco later became a lieutenant colonel and served in the campaign along the San Juan River. See also: SANTAMARIA, Juan; MESON DE GUERRA; RIVAS, Battles of.

PACHECO CABEZAS, Leónidas (1866-1934). Diplomat and politician. He was *deputy 1894-96 and 1914-17, president of the 1917 Constituent Assembly, and foreign minister in various administrations. In 1897 he settled the frontier dispute with Nicaragua by negotiating the *Pacheco-Matus Treaty. He was declared *Benemérito de la Patria in 1963. See also: FRONTIER QUESTIONS (NICARAGUA); FRONTIER QUESTIONS (SOUTH).

PACHECO-DE LA GUARDIA CONVENTION. A treaty with Panama that was never ratified. It would have given Costa Rica acquiescence to the *Loubet Decision. See: FRONTIER QUESTIONS (SOUTH).

PACHECO-MATUS TREATY, 1896. Settled most of the major disputes with Nicaragua over the northern frontier. See: FRONTIER QUESTIONS (NICARAGUA).

PACHUCO. A term of derision usually applied to lower class juveniles. Literally it means "too ripe or too fresh." This term also implies a lack of social status and possible delinquency. There was also a type of street argot called "pachuquismo" which included colorful expressions for everyday things. Some examples are: cruz (a shirt); lengua (a tie); tuánis (very nice); torta (problem); and finally is valocha (O.K. man), a linguistic trick of reversing the syllables of the words. The cultural centers of "pachuquismo" were probably the Central Park and market areas.

PACIFIC RAILROAD. See: FERROCARRIL ELECTRICO DEL PACIFICO.

PACT OF THE MEXICAN EMBASSY, 1948. A treaty arranged by the diplomatic corps and signed (April 19, 1948), by Teodoro *Picado Michalski for the government and Father Benjamin *Núñez

Vargas for the insurgents. This treaty ended the 1948 *civil war and provided for an interim government headed by Santos *León Herrera. It guaranteed lives and property of the losing side, prohibited reprisals, stated that a general amnesty would be granted and that the social guarantees of the *Calderón Guardia era would be maintained. This pact was later dissolved unilaterally by the revolutionary *Junta Fundadora de la Segunda República (June 1948).

PACTO DE CHINANDEGA. See: CONFEDERACION CENTROAMERICANA.

PACTO DE CONCORDIA. Also known as the Pacto Fundamental Interino de Costa Rica. Proclaimed December 1, 1821, it was Costa Rica's first constitution. It was drafted by a committee of the *Junta de Legados de los Pueblos so that the country would have a temporary government while it was deciding whether to join Mexico or the Central American Federation. The Pacto de Concordia declared absolute independence from Spain, but had no provision for religious liberty. It established a legislature called the *Junta Superior Gubernativa de Costa Rica, Costa Rica's second form of government, and remained in effect until March 1823.

PACTO DE CORINTO. See: TRIBUNAL OF CENTRAL AMERICAN ARBITRATION.

PACTO DE HONOR. An agreement signed August 3, 1947, which put an end to the *Huelga de Brazos Caídos. The government promised free elections and an impartial electoral tribunal for the 1948 elections. See: CIVIL WAR; ULATE BLANCO, Otilio.

PACTO DE LA UNION, January 19, 1921. See: FEDERACION DE CENTRO AMERICA.

PACTO DEL CARIBE. A pact signed December 16, 1947, by José *Figueres Ferrer, Rosendo Argüello (Nicaragua), and other exiles from Caribbean countries. It formalized a plan in which the dictatorships of the Caribbean area were to be overthrown and some sort of Caribbean federation established. Its first objective was the overthrow of the Teodoro *Picado Michalski government in Costa Rica, considered the weakest of these governments. After Picado was overthrown, they planned to use Costa Rica as a base for operations against the Somoza government of Nicaragua. See also: CARIBBEAN LEGION.

PACTO DEL JOCOTE. Signed April 1842 between General Vicente *Villaseñor and Francisco *Morazán at El Jocote (*Alajuela Province). General Villaseñor, who had been sent by the government to fight Morazán, agreed to join the Honduran in overthrowing the government of Braulio *Carrillo Colina so that they could

install Morazán as president of the Republic. See also: CARRIL-
LO COLINA, Braulio; MORAZAN, Francisco; VILLASENOR, Vicente.

PACTO SOCIAL FUNDAMENTAL INTERINO DE COSTA RICA. See:
PACTO DE CONCORDIA.

PACTO ULATE-FIGUERES. An agreement between Otilio *Ulate
Blanco and José *Figueres Ferrer signed May 1, 1948, in which
Ulate agreed that the Figueres junta would rule the country
for 18 months; elections for a Constituent Assembly would be
held December 8, 1948; the presidential elections (but not the
congressional elections) of 1948 would be declared valid; and
Ulate would assume the presidency after the junta's period had
expired.

PADILLA CASTRO, Guillermo (1899-   ). Lawyer. In 1921 he participated with the Costa Rican forces in the Coto campaign (see:
COTO WAR). He later went to Chile to study their social security
system and wrote the first draft of the Social Security Law in
1941. In the 1960s he was one of the principal members of a
commission that drafted a new model penal law stressing pro-
rated fines based on daily wages, rather than fixed fines.

PADRE ARISTA. See: CASTRO RAMIREZ, Vicente.

PAINTING. While some type of primitive painting had existed in
the country from pre-Columbian times, most of it had been by
untrained artists. The first serious attempt at training artists
was in 1897, when under the directorship of Tomás *Povedano
the *Escuela Nacional de Bellas Artes was founded. This coincided with the return of Enrique *Echandi, the first Costa Rican
to have studied painting in Europe. Provedano and Echandi
could be considered the founders of the so-called Academic Generation of Costa Rican painting. They painted along classical
lines, sometimes incorporating local scenes with romantic overtones. Other leaders of this movement were: Lolita *Zeller
de Peralta, and later Teodorico *Quirós. In the 1930s a new
group of painters emerged: the so-called *Nationalist Generation. Their technique was more plastic and they sought a more
psychological and naturalistic style. This movement was somewhat related to the *costumbrista literature then in vogue. The
most important leaders in the movement were: Teodorico Quirós,
Fausto *Pacheco (watercolors), Luisa *González de Sáenz, Francisco *Amighetti, and Margarita *Bertheau. In the 1960s the
so-called Arte Nuevo came to the forefront. This movement
sought to establish a new artistic tradition. It became dominated
by abstract and expressionistic works. The leaders of this
movement were Max *Jiménez (although he died before the movement took hold), and Manuel de la *Cruz González. Other important painters in the *Arte Nuevo movement were: Rafael
A. *García, Lola *Fernández, Juan Luis *Rodríquez, and Rafael

*Fernández. Since 1971 and largely because of Costa Rica's lack of success in the 1972 Biennial exposition, abstract painting has declined in importance. Rafael A. García changed his style and is doing local scenes. In 1977 Manuel de la Cruz González presented his mural "La serenata," which shows country people with guitars. Lately there has been a trend toward primitive and religious paintings. Consult Ricardo Ulloa Barrenecha, "La Artes" in Chester Zelaya (ed.) Costa Rica Contemporánea, Tomo II (1979) and by the same author, Pintadores de Costa Rica (1975). A new movement is CONVERGENCIA q.v.

PALENQUE. (1) A house with a thatched roof used by the *Indians. Among the *Chorotegas it was rectangular and in *Huetar tribes usually round. In this house were found stone benches resembling hammocks.

(2) A type of fort used by the Indians; built at the edge of a settlement and sometimes large enough to house a few hundred people.

(3) In modern times a palenque is a structure with a thatched roof of wooden or concrete construction which houses a dance hall and/or a restaurant.

PALM OIL. See: AFRICAN PALM OIL.

PALMA, Gonzalo de. Interim *governor of the province of Costa Rica 1592-95.

PALMAR SUR. Town where the *Inter American Highway crosses the Rio Grande de *Térraba, at 8°57'N, 83°28'W.

PALMARES. *Canton located in *Alajuela Province about 23 miles from Alajuela City. Its *cabecera is Palmares and it produces *coffee and *tobacco. In addition it has some cigarette factories. This canton was established July 30, 1988, and has a population of 17,815.

PALO VERDE. National Park along Tempisque River in Guanacaste Province. An irrigation project funded by the Interamerican Development Bank may threaten the bird species in this marshy wetland. [G.K.]

PAN AMERICAN AIRWAYS. See: AVIATION.

PAN AMERICAN HIGHWAY. Costa Rica's section of the Pan American Highway has been important in opening up previously isolated parts of the national territory but construction, begun in the late 1930s was very slow: a major obstacle was the Cerro de la Muerte region between *San José and San Isidro el General. Although 114 km between *Cartago and *San Isidro in the South, and 184 km between San Ramón and Tempisque were finished by 1951, there was still an unpaved stretch near the Panama border twenty years later. [L.H.]

PANAMA DISEASE. A disease that destroys the *banana plant. It first affected the banana crops in *Limón Province in the 1930s and was one of the main causes for transferring operations to the Pacific zone, with resulting distress among Jamaican-born banana workers forbidden to migrate from the Limón area (see: BLACKS).

PARAISO. *Canton about four miles from *Cartago City, formed December 7, 1848. Its *cabecera is Paraíso. This canton produces *coffee and *sugar and has a population of 27,823. In this canton are located *Orosí and *Ujarrás, both tourist attractions because of the colonial church and museum in Orosí, and the ruins of the church in Ujarrás.

PARDOS. A mixture of Indian and Negro races. This group was formed in the colonial period when slaves were brought to work on *cacao plantations. Pardos first came to *Cartago in the seventeenth century, and lived in a special sector called "La Gotera," the area where the Virgin of the Angels later appeared. Consult Quince Duncan and Carlos Meléndez, El negro en Costa Rica.

PARIS STEFFENS, Rafael (1920-). *Deputy 1953-58 and 1962-66, and president of the Legislative Assembly 1963-64, and 1965-66.

PARRA, Mario (1950-). A sculptor considered part of the *Heredia generation of sculptors even though he was born in *San José. Parra specializes in miniature works which combine a social and sometimes political theme with an occasional touch of eroticism. For these reasons his style is considered particularly distinctive. See: SCULPTURE.

PARRITA. *Canton on the Pacific coast which was carved out of the canton of Quepos July 15, 1971. Its *cabecera is Parrita. The population is 9,774, and it is a center of *banana production and *cattle.

PARTIDO AGRICOLA. See: ECHANDI MONTERO, Alberto.

PARTIDO CIVIL. See: PARTIDO UNION NACIONAL.

PARTIDO COMUNISTA. Organized in 1929, but officially founded June 16, 1931. The party participated for the first time in the elections of 1932 under the name *Bloque de Obreros y Campesinos. It kept that name until 1943 when it was changed to *Partido Vanguardia Popular because of an agreement with the Catholic Church and President *Calderón Guardia. The party gained adherents during the 1934 banana strike and from its part in securing the social legislation of the early 1940s. With the coming of the cold war and the 1948 revolution the party lost prestige. It was illegal from 1948 until allowed to present candidates for the 1970 elections. The Costa Rican Communist

Party generally has followed the conservative Moscow line, and has most of its strength in the banana zone of *Puntarenas Province, the poor neighborhoods of *San José, and in the ports of *Limón and *Puntarenas. Its founder, Manuel Mora Valverde was its president until December 1983. After that time a bitter factional dispute removed him from office. This internal fight is still going on. See: BANANA STRIKE; MORA VALVERDE, Manuel; SOCIAL GUARANTEES; VARGAS CARBONELL, Humberto.

PARTIDO CONFRATERNIDAD. A political party created in 1940 from elements of the *Partido Confraternidad Guanacasteco. Its main purpose was to give opposition to Dr. Rafael Angel *Calderón Guardia. It proposed Virgilio *Salazar Leiva for the presidency. Although this party was on the ballot in several provinces it only received 6,300 votes.

PARTIDO CONFRATERNIDAD GUANACASTECO. Founded by Dr. Francisco *Vargas Vargas in 1937 to give voice to grievances of the province of *Guanacaste. Vargas was elected to Congress in 1938. The party existed until 1942. It was briefly revived in 1948 to run candidates for the Constituent Assembly. This party is important because it was one of the first successful regional parties. See also: LLANO GRANDE DE SAN MIGUEL DE LIBERIA; VARGAS VARGAS, Francisco.

PARTIDO CONSTITUCIONAL (Constitutional Party). Organized by Julio *Acosta García for the 1919 elections. It had the support of the electorate. Acosta, riding the crest of his popularity as the hero of the *Sapoá revolution, easily defeated his opposition, José María Soto Alfaro, by 45,000 to 5,000 votes.

PARTIDO DE NICOYA. See: NICOYA, Partido de.

PARTIDO DEL PUEBLO. See: MORA VALVERDE, Manuel.

PARTIDO DEMOCRATA (Democratic Party). A political party appearing from time to time under the same name, but with completely different purposes.
(1) The first of these parties put up by José María Soto Alfaro for the presidency in 1919.
(2) A party founded by Eladio Trejos and Fernando *Lara Bustamante in December 1941 to oppose Rafael Angel *Calderón Guardia and put forward their candidacy in the 1942 congressional elections. The same party name was then used by León *Cortés Castro in his unsuccessful campaign to return to the presidency in 1944.
(3) In 1953 Fernando *Castro Cervantes opposed José *Figueres Ferrer, also using the name Democratic Party, but it had no connection with that of the 1940s.
(4) A minor party which participated in the elections of 1966, 1970, 1974, 1978, and 1982.

PARTIDO DEMOCRATA CRISTIANO (Christian Democratic Party).
This group was founded (September 15, 1962) by a group of
intellectuals headed by professor of philosophy Luis *Barahona
Jiménez. They first participated in a cantonal election in 1966
in *Coto Brus, and for the first time on a national level in 1970.
They were successful in electing their first member to Congress.
In 1978 the Christian Democrats entered into an alliance with
the Unity Party (*Partido Unidad) and although they did not
run as a separate slate have elected some members to the Congress in 1978 and 1982 as part of a formula worked out with
the Unity Party Coalition. In late 1983 they entered a new
political grouping called Social Christian Unity Party (*Partido
Unidad Social Cristiano), a broader based coalition than the
Partido Unidad.

PARTIDO INDEPENDIENTE (Independent Party). (1) Name of the
party of Julio *Acosta García when he successfully ran for a
congressional seat in the 1938 elections.
        (2) Party founded by Jorge *Rossi Chavarría when he
ran unsuccessfully for the presidency in 1958. The party was
formed as a result of internal problems within the National Liberation Party (*Partido Liberación Nacional). Rossi later returned to the National Liberation Party and served as vice-
president under *Figueres 1970-74.
        (3) Unsuccessfully used by Edwin *Chacón in the 1982
elections.

PARTIDO LIBERACION NACIONAL (National Liberation Party).
Officially founded (October 12, 1951) at the *finca La Paz in
*San Ramón (*Alajuela Province). It is primarily the party
of José Figueres and has its antecedents in the Centro para el
Estudio de Problemas Nacionales, the Social Democratic Party
(Partido Social Demócrata), the *National Liberation movement,
and with those who fought with Figueres in the 1948 *civil war.
It claims to be an idealistic party eschewing the cult of personality and claims to be in the tradition of Latin American people's
parties, especially the *Aprista Movement of Peru. It has controlled the Legislative Assembly (in 1963-74) and was successful
in the presidential elections of 1953, 1962, 1974, and 1982. See
also: CENTRO PARA EL ESTUDIO DE PROBLEMAS NACIONALES;
PARTIDO SOCIAL DEMOCRATA; ODUBER QUIROS, Daniel; OR-
LICH BOLMACICH, Francisco José; FIGUERES FERRER, José;
and consult Carlos Araya Pochet, Historia de los partidos políticos;
Patrick Bell, Crisis in Costa Rica; Theodore S. Creedman, "The
Crisis in Costa Rican Politics," and "The 1970 Costa Rican Elec-
tions"; Burt English, The National Liberation Party of Costa Rica;
Harry Kantor, The Costa Rican Election of 1953; and Henry
Wells, Costa Rican Election Factbook (1970).

PARTIDO NACIONAL (National Party). A political party with a
strong liberal philosophy organized in the early 1890s by former

followers of President *Rodríquez Zeledón who could no longer
support him because of his dictatorial methods. This party
participated in several elections, but only won some congressional seats, never having achieved much on the presidential
level. It disappeared during the administration of Rafael *Yglesias
Castro.

PARTIDO NACIONAL INDEPENDIENTE (National Independent Party).
A right-wing political party founded by millionaire Jorge González
Martén. It participated in the 1974 and 1978 elections, but
only won some congressional seats in the legislature, and some
local representation in national elections. It has disappeared.

PARTIDO REFORMISTA (Reformist Party). Founded by Jorge
*Volio Jiménez so he could participate in the 1924 elections.
It was organized with a social Christian philosophy and had
planks in the party platform supporting workmen's compensation,
wage and hours laws and other social reforms. Thus it was
the first party to advocate social change. Volio received about
14,000 votes, but because no candidate had the required majority,
Congress had to choose the president. Volio agreed to support
Ricardo *Jiménez Oreamuno for the presidency with Volio being
elected vice-president. In addition the Jiménez forces agreed
to enact some social legislation and turn over $100,000 to Volio
to help pay campaign expenses. In 1928 the Reformista Party
elected a few *deputies but aligned themselves with the forces
of Cleto *González Víquez. The party seemed to have started
to disintegrate after the deal of 1924.

PARTIDO REGENERACION NACIONAL. Founded by León *Cortés
Castro in 1930 to launch his candidacy for the presidency in
1932. This party was disbanded after Cortés gave his support
to Ricardo *Jiménez Oreamuno.

PARTIDO RENOVACION DEMOCRATICA. See: CARAZO ODIO,
Rodrigo.

PARTIDO REPUBLICANO (Republican Party). The original Republican Party was founded by Máximo *Fernández Alvarado in 1897.
It had a strong liberal (anti-clerical) outlook and was almost
wholly associated with the personality of its founder. In 1909
and 1923 Ricardo *Jiménez Oreamuno used the party as his vehicle
to win the presidency. During the rest of the 1920s the party
was controlled by Carlos María Jiménez Ortiz and it became less
liberal. The name was resurrected after the 1948 *civil war
by Dr. Rafael A. *Calderón Guardia, who ran under this name
in his unsuccessful effort to regain the presidency in 1962.
Calderón chose this name because someone had already registered
the title to his former party, the National Republican Party
(Partido Republicano Nacional). In 1965 the Republican Party
agreed to join the National Unification Party (*Partido Unificación

Nacional) to run Professor José Joaquín *Trejos Fernández
for the presidency. The current Republican Party backed
Rodrigo *Carazo Odio in 1978 and Rafael *Calderón Fournier in 1982. It was part of the Unity Party (*Partido
Unidad) and claims to be the only legitimate Calderonist
party.

PARTIDO REPUBLICANO INDEPENDIENTE (Independent Republican
Party). Party founded by Julio *Acosta García to run for Congress in 1938 after his Independent Party (*Partido Independiente)
had been disbanded. It was personalist and anti-León *Cortés
Castro.

PARTIDO REPUBLICANO NACIONAL. (1) The first group using
the name National Republican Party was headed by Ricardo *Jiménez Oreamuno for the 1932 election. Jiménez used the name
because his former Republican Party was controlled by his rival
in that election, Carlos María *Jiménez Ortiz. This party was
successful in electing presidents in 1936, 1940, and 1944.
    (2) In the 1974 elections this party was resurrected and
using its traditional colors--red, yellow and blue presented candidates for Congress, but elected only one.
    It claimed to be the only legitimate Calderonist party.

PARTIDO SOCIAL DEMOCRATA (Social Democratic Party). Precursor of the National Liberation Party (*Partido Liberación Nacional),
this party was officially founded (March 10, 1944) by a merger
of the *Centro para el Estudio de Problemas Nacionales and *Acción
Demócrata. However the actual planning and organization occurred
in November 1943. The party was progressive and favored
social legislation similar to that of the Doctrine of *Social Christianity, but with a secular base. It was anti-*Calderonist and
in 1948 backed the candidacy of Otilio *Ulate. Later they elected
some candidates to the Constituent Assembly of 1949. Most
of this group later went on and established the National Liberation
Party (*Partido Liberación Nacional) (October 12, 1951). See
also: FIGUERES FERRER, José; ODUBER QUIROS, Daniel. Consult: Carlos Araya, Historia de los partidos políticos (1963),
Burt English, Liberación Nacional de Costa Rica (1970), and
Jorge Romero, La Social Democracia en Costa Rica (1982).

PARTIDO UNIDAD (Unity Party). A party founded to support
Rodrigo *Carazo Odio for the presidency in 1982. It was com-
posed principally of a coalition of the Democratic Regeneration
Party (Partido Renovación Democrática), the Republican Party
(*Partido Republicano), and the Christian Democratic Party (*Par-
tido Demócrata Cristiano). In December 1983 it merged with
several anti-liberationist parties to form the Social Christian
Unity Party (*Partido Unidad Social Cristiano, PUSC).

PARTIDO UNIDAD SOCIAL CRISTIANO (Social Christian Unity Party, PUSC). A fusion of the Christian Democratic Party (*Partido Demócrata Cristiano, PDC), the Democratic Regeneration Party (*Partido Renovación Democrática, PRD), and the Republican Calderonist Party (*Partido Republicano Calderonista, RC). It was founded (Dec. 17, 1983) to offer unified opposition to the National Liberation Party (*Partido Liberación Nacional). It takes its inspiration from the works of Dr. Rafael Angel *Calderón Guardia and the doctrine of *Social Christianity. However, there is also a conservative element in the party's composition. Its first president was Rafael Angel *Calderón Fournier (son of *Calderón Guardia). He ran unsuccessfully for the presidency in 1982 and 1986 but was elected in 1990. One of his first measures in office was to go ahead with privatizing the banking system.

PARTIDO UNIFICACION NACIONAL (National Unification Party). Founded (October 1965) when long-time political rivals Otilio *Ulate Blanco and Rafael *Calderón Guardia agreed to support common candidates for the 1966 elections. This new party elected José Joaquín *Trejos Fernández to the presidency. In the 1970 election the party unsuccessfully ran ex-President Mario *Echandi Jiménez and had the support of Frank *Marshall Jiménez and his *Partido Unión Cívica Revolucionaria. Otilio Ulate withdrew support of his National Union Party (*Partido Unión Nacional) but many of its members stayed in the Unification Party. In 1974 after an open primary in which the various factions of the party put forth candidates the party chose Dr. Fernando Trejos Escalante for its candidate. He ran a generally weak campaign and received only about one-third of the vote. In 1978 Lic. Guillermo Villalobos ran under the party's banner, but the vast majority of the Unification Party was backing Rodrigo *Carazo Odio. Villalobos received only 13,832 votes. The party has disappeared.

PARTIDO UNION CATOLICA (Catholic Union Party). As a result of the *liberal laws of the 1880s Bishop Bernardo *Thiel felt that the Church should organize a political force to fight for the repeal of these laws and to reverse the trend of liberalism (anti-clericalism) in the country. Under his inspiration and partly in response to the strongarm methods of President José Joaquín *Rodríguez Zeledón, this party was established in 1891. It first participated in the municipal election of that year and surprised the liberals by making a strong showing. This party actively campaigned in the 1894 elections, nominating José Gregorio *Trejos Gutiérrez for the presidency. Despite government harassment and probably outright fraud they won a plurality of the electoral vote, but not a majority. Therefore Congress had to select the president. There was great unrest and an attempt was made--by some priests in *Grecia (*Alajuela Province) --to overthrow the government. The ring-leaders of this revolt, plus the leadership of the Catholic Union Party including its candidate were arrested. All except two of these people were eventually pardoned. The extreme actions of this Church-related party frightened the people and since then there has not been another large Church-oriented political party.

PARTIDO UNION CIVICA REVOLUCIONARIA (Revolutionary Civic Union Party). A rightist paramilitary political organization organized by Francisco (Frank) *Marshall Jiménez in 1957 to oppose what he considered Communist tendencies and repressive measures of his former comrades in arms, the National Liberation Party (*Partido Liberación Nacional). Marshall was successful in winning a seat in Congress and also served another term in Congress (1966-70). However his party lost prestige when he was convicted of smuggling whiskey while still serving in Congress. His party associated itself with the National Unification Party (*Partido Unificación Nacional) for the elections of 1970 and has not participated in other elections.

PARTIDO UNION DEMOCRATA (Democratic Union Party). Founded by Carlos María Jiménez Ortiz and Dr. Rafael *Calderón Muñoz in the 1920s. It was pro-Church and advocated the repeal of the *liberal laws of the 1880s, but they also favored enactment of some progressive social legislation.

PARTIDO UNION NACIONAL (National Union Party). This party has existed at different times under the same name but with no relation between its purposes.

(1) Formed in 1901 from a coalition of the Civil Party (Partido Civil) and members of the "Olimpians" (*Olímpicos). They elected Asención *Esquivel Ibarra in 1902 and Celto *González Víquez in 1906.

(2) Founded in 1913 to foster the candidacy of Dr. Carlos *Durán Cartin for the presidency, it was disbanded by the *Tinoco Granados dictatorship.

(3) The vehicle in which Cleto González Víquez was elected in 1928.

(4) A party founded in 1947 as an amalgam of the opposition parties to run a candidate against Dr. Rafael *Calderón Guardia. It had an open convention and nominated Otilio *Ulate Blanco, who was declared winner of the 1948 presidential *elections after the conclusion of the *civil war of that year. The party unsuccessfully ran Ulate in 1962. In 1966 it supported the ticket of the National Unification Party (*Partido Unificación Nacional), and in 1970, after officially withdrawing from that group, ran its own slate of congressional candidates, but with very poor results. With the death of Ulate in 1973 the party disappeared.

PARTIDO VANGUARDIA POPULAR. The official name of the Costa Rican Communist Party (*Partido Comunista) after 1943. See also: MORA VALVERDE, Manuel.

PASSENGER TRANSIT. See: PUBLIC TRANSPORT.

PASTORA GOMEZ, Edén (1936?-). "Comandante Cero," Nicaraguan
guerrilla leader, who became a Costa Rican citizen in 1978. An active guerrillero against the Somoza regime since the 1960s, he
became deputy defense minister in the Sandinista government
but resigned July 7, 1981 to lead an anti-Sandinista guerrilla
campaign from Costa Rica. After the attempt on his life at La
PENCA (q.v.), for which he blamed the C.I.A. (supposedly
unwilling to tolerate an anti-Sandinista army independent of
the right-wing contras in Honduras), he was offered political
asylum in Venezuela. Instead, on May 16, 1986, he turned
in his weapons to the Costa Rican authorities and the following
day requested political asylum in Costa Rica. He now resides
in suburban San José. [G.K., L.H.]

PATRIOTA, El. The ship in which Captain Gregorio J. *Ramírez
Castro took coffee to Panama in 1822. This was probably the
first commercial exportation of coffee.

PATRON DE ORO. See: GOLD STANDARD.

PATRONATO. The prerogative of the state to intervene in non-
religious aspects of Church business, including the right to
approve of ecclesiastical appointments, known under Spanish
rule as the Real Patronato (royal patronage) and presumed to
have been inherited by the governments of the successor republics. The gradual separation of Church and State was begun
in the 1830s by President Braulio *Carrillo Colina. See: CHURCH-
STATE RELATIONS. [L.H.]

PAVAS. An archaeological site on the outskirts of *San José, and
a key site in the chronology of the *Meseta Central: it was
occupied from c. 200 B.C. to 400 A.D. Characteristic of Pavas
and related sites are pottery decorated with an orange slip and
maroon paint, chipped and ground stone tools, and bell-shaped
storage pits. [G.K.]

PAVON, Francisco. Acting *governor in 1581 who later led an
expedition to explore the *Sarapiquí region.

PEDRARIAS (Pedro Arias de Avila or Pedrarias Dávila) (1443-1531).
Named *governor of Darién (Panama) in July 1513 and arrived
in the New World in the following year. He was one of the
cruelest of the colonial governors. His harsh treatment of the
*Indians earned him the name of Furor Domini. He jealously
guarded his domain which he said included Panama, Costa Rica,
and part of Nicaragua. He was challenged by Vasco *Núñez
de Balboa, the discoverer of the Pacific, whom he ordered be-
headed (1519), and Francisco *Fernández de Córdoba (founder
of the cities of León and Granada, Nicaragua), whom he also

had executed (1526). He was removed as governor of Panama in 1527 but remained as governor of Nicaragua until his death. See also: GONZALEZ DE AVILA, Gil.

PEJIBAYE (Guliebna utilis). (1) An edible palmnut cultivated by the *Indians and said to have originated in the Orinoco Valley (Venezuela). It is cultivated extensively and sold on the streets, usually from the straw baskets.

(2) There are two towns with this name: a) in *Pérez Zeledón canton (population 7,916), and b) in *Jiménez canton (population 3,175).

PENARANDA, Juan de (b. 1537-). Acting *governor of the province of Costa Rica (1589-90).

PENCA, La. Site of May 30, 1984 bombing at press conference of Nicaraguan rebel Edén *Pastora. Several Costa Rican correspondents were killed or injured. Unresolved and controversial remained the question of blame; contra groups opposed to the Nicaraguan government were accused by some. [G.K.]

PENINSULAR. A name used for the Spaniards during the colonial period denoting that they came from the Iberian Peninsula, in contrast to the native born CREOLE, q.v.

PENSIONADO. Legal status for foreigners retired in Costa Rica, originating in Law 4812 of July 28, 1971. Assured income from a pension or other sources (rentista status) provides an initial waiver of customs duties for household goods. In 1985 there were 7,200 families, many being North Americans. [G.K.]

PENTECOSTAL SECTS. See: EVANGELICALS.

PERAFAN DE RIBERA (1492-ca. 1577). Conquistador. *Governor of Costa Rica 1569-1573. He founded the city of Trujillo in Honduras. After it was sacked by *pirates he was named *governor of Costa Rica. In 1568 he had to combat an uprising of the *Indians in *Talamanca. In the process of suppressing the rebellion he brought prisoners to *Cartago to be divided among the colonists, even though this *repartamiento was completely illegal. In 1572 he organized an expedition along the *Reventazón River and Atlantic coast area. This expedition was going badly because of poor planning. Perafán feared a revolt and accused one Vicente del *Castillo of plotting a mutiny. The governor executed del Castillo on the spot, without even granting him the statutory right of appeal. Perafán was censured for this by the *Audiencia de Guatemala. He wound up his days in Mexico.

PERALTA, Antonio de [Captain]. Spanish soldier. He was involved with Gonzalo *Pizarro's rebellion in Peru and sentenced to serve in the galleys for a short while. He came to Costa Rica and helped in the pacification of the *Garabito and *Voto Indian towns. Because of his rebellious character and difficulties with Juan *Vásquez de Coronado and *Governor Fernando de la *Cueva he was obliged to return to Spain.

PERALTA, Hernán G. (1892-1981). Historian, diplomat, lawyer, and university professor. Peralta was a member of various learned societies including the *Academia de Geografía e Historia de Costa Rica. His chief works include the detailed Agustín de Iturbide y Costa Rica (1944), Costa Rica y la fundación de la república (1948), and El pacto de la concordia (1955).

PERALTA DEL CORRAL, José Francisco [Father] (1786-1844). Elected Costa Rica's representative to the Constituent Congress in Mexico in 1822. He and his family were among the most ardent *imperialists of the independence period. Father Peralta also served as *deputy 1828-29, 1838, 1844-45. He was president of the 1842 Constituent Assembly and had been implicated in a plot against President Braulio *Carrillo in 1835.

PERALTA DE LA VEGA, José María (1763-1836). Born in Jaén, Spain, he came to Costa Rica in 1782. He served as *alcalde and *regidor of the municipal government of *Cartago. He was a member of the first *Junta Superior Gubernativa of Costa Rica in July 1822, *jefe político del estado, member of the *Triumvirate, member of the Junta de Electores (Second Constituent Assembly) in 1822, president of the Third Constituent Assembly, 1824-25, and member of Congress in 1825-26 and 1828-34. He served as president of Congress in 1829, 1832, and 1833. He was a liberal and one of the most influential politicians of his time.

PERALTA LOPEZ DEL CORRAL, Manuel María (1791-1837). A leader of the *imperialist forces in *Cartago. He was a member of the *Diputación Provincial, *alcalde of Cartago, and involved in the 1823 *civil war, for which he was admonished by the national government. Peralta was also a member of the Constituent Assembly of 1823 and served as a senator from Costa Rica in the Federal Congress in Guatemala in 1831. He was representative to several sessions of the National Congress and served as its president, 1829-30. Later because of his participation in the War of the League (*Guerra de la Liga) he had to flee to Nicaragua, where he died in León, October 1837.

PERALTA Y ALFARO, Manuel María (1847-1930). Diplomat and historian. Costa Rican minister to Europe off and on from 1871 to 1876 and 1878-79. He negotiated the last stage of the railroad loans in 1878-79. Peralta y Alfaro was resident minister of Costa Rica in Washington 1876-78, 1885-87. In addition he was involved in attempts to settle the question of the southern

frontier. (See: FRONTIER QUESTIONS [SOUTH].) In order
to justify the Costa Rican claims he did a great deal of investigation and wrote many volumes on the boundary questions. His
most important works are: Costa Rica, Nicaragua y Panamá en
el siglo XVI (su historia y sus límites según los documentos del
archivo de Sevilla y del de Simances) (1883) and Costa Rica y
Colombia de 1573 a 1881 (1886). See: Bibliography in this
volume.

PEREIRA, Juana. See: VIRGIN OF THE ANGELS.

PEREZ, Hernán (b. 1951). An *Arte Nuevo painter. He specializes
in local scenes from a modern rather than folklorist point of
view. He has had shows of his works in Central America and
Europe.

PEREZ, Rodrigo [Father]. Franciscan missionary in *Talamanca
whose murder by rebellious Indians c. 1615 led to Alonso del
*Castillo y Guzmán's punitive expedition.

PEREZ ZELEDON. A *canton located in the extreme south-western
part of *San José Province, created October 9, 1931, Its *cabecera is San Isidro. It is a center of agricultural production.
The present population is 82,370. This canton was named in
honor of Pedro *Pérez Zeledón.

PEREZ ZELEDON, Pedro (1854-1930). Lawyer and diplomat. He
studied at the *Universidad de Santo Tomás and was Costa Rican
minister in Washington in 1914. In addition he prepared several
briefs defending Costa Rican interest in the dispute over the
Nicaraguan boundary. See: FRONTIER QUESTIONS (NICARAGUA).

PERIE BARROS, José (d. 1789). *Governor of the province of
Costa Rica in 1778-89. He was a strong-willed man and had
innumerable problems with the residents of *Cartago. These
led to his suspension from office for four years. He was cleared
by the *Audiencia in Guatemala and returned to his post, where
he served until his death in 1789.

PESO ("weight"). In early colonial times an amount of uncoined
silver or gold worth eight *reales used to make up for the chronic
shortage of actual coins. First actual peso coins produced in
the Americas were minted in Potosí (Upper Peru, now Bolivia)
and contained 28.50 grams of gold. The peso continued as the
unit of currency of Costa Rica after independence and was about
on a par with the dollar; it was originally the same coin and
used the same "$" symbol. The peso was withdrawn in 1900
when the new gold *colón was put into circulation; its value
had by then fallen to 2.15 to the U.S. dollar. See also:
COINAGE, COLON, EXCHANGE RATE, GOLD STANDARD. [L.H.]

PESO FUERTE. See: DURO.

PETACA. A colonial unit of weight equivalent to about 100 pounds.

PETROLEUM. So far commercial quantities of oil have not been
found, despite some exploration: (1) There was a British-
American rivalry for oil concessions, 1913-21. See: TINOCO
GRANADOS, Federico; and consult Dana G. Munro, Intervention
and Dollar Diplomacy in the Caribbean 1900-1921.
(2) There was exploration in the early 1960s at extreme
opposite ends of the country. Union Oil drilled several wells
in the southeast, adjacent to Panama; meanwhile, a small Cuban-
U.S. group soon after (1962-64) explored the *Guanacaste region
in the northwest.
(3) By 1980, as the cost of imported oil had soared, the
Mexican national company, PEMEX, provided assistance during
several years of unsuccessful search. [G.K.]

PICADO MICHALSKI, René (1902-1960). Brother of Teodoro *Picado
Michalski. He occupied the post of minister of public security in
his brother's government. In his capacity of vice president
he served for his brother as acting president of the Republic
September 18-19, 1944. He was active in politics and in promoting the 1948 campaign of Rafael A. *Calderón Guardia.

PICADO MICHALSKI, Teodoro (1900-1960). President of the Republic 1944-48. *Deputy 1936-44. President of Congress 1941-
44. He was elected in 1944 with the aid of the Communist Party
(*Partido Comunista) and Dr. *Calderón Guardia. During his
term of office there were constant street fights and attempts
at coups d'état, climaxed by a disputed *election and a *civil
war which forced him out of office and into exile in Nicaragua
where he died. During his administration he signed the law
enacting an *income tax and signed the final treaty ending the
centuries-old dispute on the southern frontier. See also:
ALMATICAZO; CIVIL WAR (1948); FRONTIER QUESTIONS (SOUTH);
HUELGA DE BRAZOS CAIDOS.

PICADO TWIGHT, Clodomiro (1887-1944). Scientist born in Nicaragua.
He received a doctorate from the Sorbonne. Picado lived in
Costa Rica after 1914 where he did research on anti-snake bite
serums and genetics. He is also said to have been a precursor
to the discovery of penicillin. He was declared *Benemérito
de la Patria in 1943.

PICADO UMANA, Mario (b. 1928). Poet born in San José. Some
of his most important works include: Noche (1953), Hondo gris
(1953), Tierra del hombre (1964), the prize-winning Serena
longitud (1967), Poemas de piedra y polvo (1972), La piel de
los signos (1974), and Absurdo asombro (1982).

PINTO, Floria (b. 1923). An *Arte Nuevo artist who specializes in semi-Greek-looking oil paintings.

PINTO, Julieta (b. 1931). Writer and poet. She wrote narrative novels which deal with the frustration of everyday life and its problems, all of which are put into a local setting. Her leading works are: Cuentos de la tierra (1963), Si se oyera el silencio (1967), Los marginados (1970), La estación que sigue al verano (1969), A la vuelta de la esquina (1975), David (1979), and El Eco de los pasos (1979).

PINTO, Oscar. He studied in England and was impressed by the caliber of English *soccer. When he returned to Costa Rica in 1897 he organized what amounted to the first organized soccer team in the country. He even provided them with a ball and uniforms from his own funds. He is considered the founder of organized soccer in Costa Rica and was so honored on a postage stamp.

PINTO CASTRO, José Antonio (1817-1887). Son of General Antonio *Pinto Suárez. He studied law in Guatemala and was a judge of a magistrates court and governor of *San José Province. He was acting head of state while General Tomás *Guardia Gutiérrez visited Europe, June 16, 1872, to January 26, 1873, and later became president of the Supreme Court in 1886-87.

PINTO SUAREZ, Antonio [General] (1780-1865). Born in Oporto, Portugal, he came to Costa Rica in 1810 and entered politics. As commander-in-chief of the armed forces he controlled the nation September 11-27, 1842, because the country was temporarily left without a government after the overthrow of *Morazán.

PIRATES. The constant threat of pirate invasions was a major problem during colonial times and continued until about 1850. Invasions were particularly troublesome during the seventeenth and eighteenth centuries and forced the near abandonment of flourishing settlements along both coasts, especially at *Matina (on the Atlantic) and *Esparza (on the Pacific). These attacks exacerbated the tendency of the population to concentrate in the highlands which still remain the population center of the country. Pirates were particularly troublesome in this part of the world because of the Isthmian location; constant warfare between Spain, France, and England; Spain's restrictive mercantilistic policy, which invited illegal trade; and England's use of the *Zambo-Mosquito tribes of the Bluefields region of Nicaragua to foster her expansionist plans in Central America. Although all were "pirates" to the Spanish authorities, many (e.g. Drake) were privateers operating against their countries' enemies, under licence from their home governments. These are some of the major pirate and privateer attacks:

1579:	Sir Francis Drake attacks ships coming from Panama near the Island of Cano.
1604:	First pirate invasion sacks settlements at *Suerre.
1666:	Pirate band under the command of Captain Mansfield and his Lieutenant Henry Morgan lands with a band of about 600 men at Portete and starts to march on *Cartago. They are stopped by a hastily organized colonial militia at Quebrada Honda, aided by the VIRGIN OF UJARRAS, q.v.
1670:	French pirates land on the Pacific coast and sack *Esparza.
1676:	Pirate band of about 800 men capture the *Matina Valley and are finally driven out by a combined Spanish-Indian force under *Governor Juan Francisco *Sáenz Vásquez.
1680:	Band of pirates burns Esparza, forcing the inhabitants to leave temporarily.
1681:	Ships under pirates Dampier and Sharp attack settlements on the Gulf of *Nicoya while other bands of pirates sack Matina and advance on *Cartago but are stopped again at Quebrada Honda. As a result the *Audiencia sends a force of a hundred paid soldiers to be stationed in Costa Rica.
1684:	Pirates under Captain Cook attack settlements on the Gulf of *Nicoya after having attacked settlements in Peru. Other pirates under Dampier are repulsed in Nicoya.
1684-86:	Esparza is sacked twice and temporarily abandoned.
1687:	Pirates under Lorencillo sack Matina.
1702:	Pirates and a band of Zambo-Mosquito Indians from Nicaragua capture and sack Matina.
1724:	Zambo-Mosquitos with English help attack settlements in Matina Valley.
1726:	Zambo-Mosquitos invade Matina and take 25 prisoners.
1740:	Matina is attacked again by Zambo-Mosquitos.
1741:	In an effort to forestall more attacks *Fuerte de San Fernando is built.
1742:	In a surprise attack the poorly manned *Fuerte de San Fernando is taken and burned.

PITTIER, Henry Francois (1857-1950). Most famous among Swiss and other European teachers recruited in Europe to modernize education under the *liberal reforms of the 1880s. A Swiss geographer, Pittier eventually founded the National Meteorological Observatory after teaching many years and writing several books on Costa Rican natural science. [G.K.]

PIZARRO, Juan [Father] (d. ca. 1581). Father Pizarro went on a Christianizing mission to the Quepos region and became involved in a dispute with the *Indians over the manner in which they were celebrating one of their traditional festivals. The Indians set upon his party and killed Father Pizarro.

PLAN NACIONAL DE DESARROLLO EDUCATIVO 1971. This was an integrated plan for developing all levels of education in the 1970s. It sought to incorporate all sections into the educational process, provide at least nine years of universal education especially in the rural areas, and improve educational facilities. It made promotion almost automatic and set goals of libraries in all schools. On the secondary level this plan called for more technological and practical subjects and better training and utilization of personnel. Finally it changed the primary school curriculum to a basic nine-year cycle.

"PLAN SUNDAY." A plan of José *Figueres Ferrer to import arms through the Pacific port of *Dominical to start his revolution. This plan was only moderately successful because a large cache of arms was confiscated by the Mexican authorities in August 1947.

PLATA QUINTADA. Bullion that had paid the tax to the crown of one-fifth.

POAS. (1) Active volcano more than 7,000 feet above sea level located in *Alajuela Province. National park, 35 km N.W. of *San José.
(2) *Canton located on the slopes of the volcano Poás. Its *cabecera is San Pedro and it was formed October 15, 1901. This canton produces *sugar, *coffee, and grains and is popular as a summer resort because of its cool mountain climate. Its present population is 13,939.

POCOCI. *Canton in the area called "*Línea Vieja" in *Limón Province. Its *cabecera is Guapiles and it was created September 19, 1911. The southern part of this canton is the center for *banana plantations. The northern part is the Tortuguero region, a largely uninhabited swamp. There is a great reserve of hardwoods in this region but poor transportation has inhibited the region's development. The canton's present population is 44,187. See also: LINEA VIEJA.

POESIA PARA TODOS. See: CIRCULO DE POETAS COSTARRICENSES.

POLITICAL PARTIES. See: ELECTIONS; entries under PARTIDO....

POMAR Y BURGOS, Juan. Parish priest in *Cubujuquí in the mid-eighteenth century. After an order had been given by the bishop, Isidro Marin de *Bullón y Figuero, to have people move closer to the churches so they could attend mass, Father Pomar y Burgos supervised the systematic burning of several houses in the *La Lajuela region, thus forcing people to move into the towns. It is debatable whether thie action was of religious or economic motivation. See also: BULLON Y FIGUERO, Isidro Marin de.

PONCE DE LEON, Hernán. Spanish explorer. Better known for his exploits in seeking the fountain of youth in Florida and as first Governor of Puerto Rico, but he also explored part of Costa Rica. In 1519 *Pedrarias Dávila sent him and Juan de *Castañada on an expedition to the Golfo Dulce and Gulf of *Nicoya area.

POPULATION. The population of Costa Rica according to the June 1984 census was 2,460,226. During the colonial period there are no accurate census statistics available. Most of what has been estimated was by Archbishop Thiel in Monografía de la población de Costa Rica en el siglo XIX. See: CENSUSES.

YEAR	POPULATION
1522	27,200
1569	17,479
1611	15,538
1700	19,293
1720	19,437
1741	24,126
1751	24,022
1778	34,212
1801	52,591
1824	65,383
1844	93,871
1864 (census)	120,499
1875	156,634
1883	182,073
1888	205,731
1892 (census)	243,205
1900	303,762
1927	471,524
1941	656,129
1942	672,129
1943	687,354
1944	706,596
1945	725,149
1946	746,535
1947	771,503
1948	803,084
1949	825,378
1950 (census of May 22)	800,875
1951	812,056
1952	838,084
1953	868,741
1954	898,329
1955	933,033
1956	969,640
1957	1,014,200
1958	1,052,474
1959	1,099,962
1960	1,149,537

1961	1,199,116
1962	1,251,397
1963 (census)	1,336,274
1964	1,369,659
1965	1,413,531
1966	1,515,292
1967	1,567,230
1968	1,615,480
1969	1,664,581
1970	1,710,083
1971	1,762,462
1972	1,811,290
1973 (census)	1,871,780
1974	1,905,338
1975	1,945,594
1976	1,993,784
1977	2,044,237
1978	2,098,531
1979	2,156,312
1980	2,216,117
1981	2,307,290
1982	2,371,519
1983	2,403,789
1984 (census)	2,416,809
1985	2,488,749
1986	2,529,560
1987	2,781,418
1988	2,851,085
1989	3,054,000
1990	3,260,000

Racially 97% of the population is of European or *Mestizo descent, 2% African (see: BLACKS) and 0.5% American *Indian. A few East European *Jews immigrated in the 1920s. See also: BIRTH AND DEATH RATES; CANTONS OF COSTA RICA; SUBURBANIZA-TION and names of individual localities. [L.H.]

PORRAS, María. Proprietor of a colonial brothel. It was finally closed by order of the *governor in 1807 and Porras was ex-pelled from the colony.

PORRAS, Teresita (b. 1934). Artist. Studied in Costa Rica, then visited Europe. She specializes in oil paintings of local scenes and which touch on social themes.

PORRAS, William. Composer. He studied in the *Conservatorio de Castella and paid for his education by writing "jingles" for radio and television commercials. His most important serious works are: "El canario" (an overture), "Cultivo una rosa blanca" (a choral piece), "Sonata para violín," and various short piano pieces.

PORTETE. Early name for LIMON (q.v.).

PORTOBELO. A port in Panama where the convoys left for Spain every year. It also served as a point of departure for expeditions coming to Costa Rica. [G.K.]

POSITIVISM. Political philosophy of the latter nineteenth century calling for modernization via "scientific" reforms. *Liberal laws of the 1880s were inspired by such ideas, deriving from the French philosopher Auguste Comte (1798-1857).

POSTAGE STAMPS. First issued in 1863 in denominations of 1/2, 2, and 4 reales. These stamps were on sale for over 20 years. In general Costa Rica has had a conservative policy in issuing new postage stamps and has had relatively few scandals involving special issues. Consult various issues of The Oxcart and Carlos Sáenz (ed.), Catálago de sellos postales de Costa Rica (especializado).

POVEDANO, Tomás. Founder of the ESCUELA NACIONAL DE BELLAS ARTES, q.v.

PRENSA LIBRE, La. "The Free Press," Costa Rica's oldest surviving daily newspaper, and for almost all its life the nation's leading afternoon paper. It first appeared June 11, 1889. One of its earliest editors was the Nicaraguan poet Rubén Darío. After various ownership changes it was acquired in 1929 by José Borrase, who ran it until he retired in 1975. Since then it has been managed by his son Andrés Borrase. Current circulation is upwards of 45,000 copies. [L.H.]
    See also: NEWSPAPERS.

PRESBERE, Pablo. Leader of Indian revolt in TALAMANCA, q.v.

PRESIDENTS AND CHIEFS OF STATE. The heads of government were called jefes del estado (or chiefs of state) until the proclamation of the Republic in 1848. After that they have been called "President." Persons who have been acting president for short periods of time are not included on this list. For more details see separate entries.

Juan *Mora Fernández (September 8, 1824 to April 14, 1825) (provisional); (April 14, 1825 to March 9, 1833); (Dec. 19, 1837 to Feb. 19, 1838)
José Rafael *Gallegos y Alvarado (March 9, 1833, to March 5, 1835) (resigned)
Juan José *Lara Arias (March 4-17, 1835) (interim)
Manuel *Fernández Chacón (March 17, 1835 to May 5, 1835)
Braulio *Carrillo Colina (May 5, 1835 to March 1, 1837); (May 27, 1838 to April 5, 1842)
Joaquín *Mora Fernández (March 1, 1837 to April 17, 1837) (interim)

Manuel *Aguilar Chacón (April 17, 1837 to Dec. 19, 1837);
    (Feb. 19, 1838 to May 27, 1838) (overthrown)
Manuel Antonio *Bonilla Nava (April 5, 1842 to April 12, 1842)
Francisco *Morazán (April 12, 1842 to Sept. 11, 1842)
Antonio *Pino Suárez (Sept. 11, 1842 to Sept. 27, 1842);
    Jefe Supremo de las Armas (June 25, 1872 to Jan. 26,
    1873) (acting)
José María *Alfaro Zamora (Sept. 27, 1842 to Nov. 29, 1844);
    (June 7, 1846 to May 8, 1847)
Francisco María *Oreamuno Bonilla (Nov. 29, 1844 to Dec. 17,
    1844) (resigned)
Rafael *Moya Murillo (Dec. 17, 1844 to April 30, 1845)
José María *Castro Madriz (May 8, 1847 to Nov. 15, 1849)
    (resigned): (May 8, 1866 to Nov. 1, 1868) (overthrown)
Juan Rafael *Mora Porras (March 1, 1848 to April 4, 1848)
    (acting); June 9, 1848 to June 16, 1848) (acting); (Nov.
    26, 1849 to May 8, 1853); (May 8, 1853 to Aug. 14, 1859)
    (overthrown)
Miguel *Mora Porras (Nov. 15, 1849 to Nov. 26, 1849) (acting)
José María *Montealegre (Aug. 14, 1859 to May 8, 1860) (interim);
    (May 8, 1860 to May 8, 1863)
Jesús de *Jiménez Zamora (May 8, 1863 to May 8, 1866); (Nov. 1,
    1868 to April 27, 1870) (overthrown)
Eusebio *Figueroa Oreamuno (April 26, 1870 to April 27, 1870)
    (acting)
Bruno *Carranza Ramírez (April 27, 1870 to Aug. 8, 1870)
Tomás *Guardia Gutiérrez (Aug. 10, 1870 to May 8, 1876)
Aniceto *Esquivel Sáenz (May 8, 1866 to July 30, 1886 (overthrown)
Vicente *Herrera Zeledón (July 30, 1876 to Sept. 11, 1877)
Salvador *Lara Zamora (June 10, 1881 to July 20, 1882) (acting)
Saturnino *Lizano Gutiérrez (June 17, 1882 to July 20, 1882)
    (acting)
Próspero *Fernández Oreamuno (July 20, 1882 to May 12, 1885)
Bernardo *Soto Alfaro (May 12, 1885 to Nov. 7, 1889) (resigned)
Carlos *Durán Cartin (Nov. 7, 1889 to May 8, 1890)
José Joaquín *Rodríguez Zeledón (May 8, 1890 to May 8, 1894)
Rafael *Yglesias Castro (May 8, 1894 to May 8, 1898) (May 8,
    1898 to May 8, 1902)
Ascensión *Esquivel Ibarra (May 8, 1902 to May 8, 1906)
Cleto *González Víquez (May 8, 1906 to May 8, 1910) (May 8,
    1928 to May 8, 1932)
Ricardo *Jiménez Oreamuno (May 8, 1910 to May 8, 1914) (May 8,
    1924 to May 8, 1928) (May 8, 1932 to May 8, 1936)
Alfredo *González Flores (May 8, 1914 to Jan. 27, 1917) (over-
    thrown)
Federico *Tinoco Granados (Jan. 27, 1917 to Aug. 12, 1919)
    (resigned)
Juan Bautista *Quirós Segura (Aug. 12, 1919 to Sept. 2, 1919)
    (forced to resign)
Francisco *Aguilar Barquero (Sept. 2, 1919 to May 8, 1920)
Julio *Acosta García (May 8, 1920 to May 8, 1924)

León *Cortés Castro (May 8, 1936 to May 8, 1940)
Rafael Angel *Calderón Guardia (May 8, 1940 to May 8, 1944)
Teodoro *Picado Michalski (May 8, 1944 to April 20, 1948) (over-
    thrown)
Santos *León Herrera (April 20, 1948 to May 8, 1948)
José María Hipólito *Figueres Ferrer (May 8, 1948 to Nov. 8,
    1948) (Chief of Junta) (May 8, 1953 to May 8, 1958)
    (May 8, 1970 to May 8, 1974)
Otilio *Ulate Blanco (Nov. 8, 1949 to May 8, 1953)
Mario *Echandi Jiménez (May 8, 1958 to May 8, 1962)
Francisco J. *Orlich Bolmarcich (May 8, 1962 to May 8, 1966)
José Joaquín *Trejos Fernández (May 8, 1966 to May 8, 1870)
Daniel *Oduber Quirós (May 8, 1974 to May 8, 1978)
Rodrigo *Carazo Odio (May 8, 1978 to May 8, 1982)
Luis Alberto *Monge Alvarez (May 8, 1982 to May 8, 1986)
Oscar *Arias Sánchez (May 8, 1986 to May 8, 1990)
Rafael *Calderón Fournier (May 8, 1990–   )

Presidents of the Legislative Branch:

For most of the Republican Period Costa Rica has had a unicameral legislature, called the Asamblea Legislativa. However,
at times it had different names and was bicameral. Most of
the following men are also listed under separate headings.

President of the *Junta de Delegados de los Pueblos
    Nicholás *Carrillo Aguirre (1821)

President of the Junta de Electores
    Rafael *Barroeta Castilla (1822)

Presidents of the Poder Conservador (Fourth Power) (1823-24)
    José Rafael *Gallegos y Alvarado
    Manuel *Fernández Chacón
    Juan *Mora Fernández

Presidents of the Cámara de Sanadores (Senate)
    Rafael *Moya Murillo (1844)
    Juan *Mora Fernández
    José Rafael *Gallegos y Alvarado
    Manuel José *Carazo Bonilla (1860-61), (1862-63)
    Rafael *Ramírez Hidalgo (1862), (1863)
    José María *Montealegre Fernández
    Joaquín Bernardo *Calvo Rosales (1864-65)
    Francisco María *Iglesias Llorente (1868)
    Manuel Antonio *Bonilla Nava (1917-18)
    Daniel *Núñez Gutiérrez (1919)
    Rafael *Calderón Muñoz (1919)
    José *Astúa Aguilar (1919)

Presidents of the Legislative Branch
    Joaquín Rivas (in 1820s)
    Cecilio Urenas Fallas (1825)
    Félix Romero (Nov. 1825 to Jan. 1826)

Braulio *Carrillo Colina (1828)
Manuel *Aguilar Chacón
Manuel María *Peralta López del Corral (1829-30)
Rafael Francisco *Osejo (1830-31)
José Gabriel del *Campo Guerrero
Joaquín de *Iglesias
José Francisco Peralta López del Corral (1832)
Nicolás *Ulloa (1833)
Juan Diego *Bonilla Nava (May-July 1833) (May-July 1834)
José Andrés *Rivera (1834)
J. J. *Blanco Z. (1837)
Félix *Sancho Alvarado
José María *Castro Madriz (1845)
Juan R. *Reyes Frutos (1845-46)
Manuel José Carazo Bonilla (1848-49)
José María Alfaro Zamora
Juan Rafael *Mora Porras (1846-47)
Francisco María *Oreamuno Bonilla (1850-56)
Rafael G. García *Escalante Navas (1857-59)
Julián *Volio Llorente
Napoleón *Escalante Navas (Aug. 1863)
Francisco *Echeverría Alvarado (1869-70)
Manuel Antonio *Bonilla Nava (1872-74), (1874-76)
Víctor *Guardia Gutiérrez (1882-83)
Juan M. *Carazo Peralta (1883-86)
Aniceto *Esquivel Sáenz (1886-89) (March-June 1891)
Manuel *Aragón Quesada (1889-90)
Francisco María *Iglesias Llorente (1890-92) (1900-03)
Carlos *Durán Cartin
Pedro María *León-Páez Brown (1894-1900)
Ricardo *Jiménez Oreamuno (1903-04)
Mauro *Fernández Acuña
Federico *Tinoco Iglesias (1905-08)
Juan Bautista *Quirós Segura (1908-09)
Ezequiel *Gutiérrez Iglesias (1910-13)
Máximo *Fernández Alvarado
Leondias *Pacheco Cabezas (1914-16)
José *Astua Aguilar
Francisco *Faerrón Suárez (1918-19)
Arturo *Volio Jiménez (1920-25), (1928-29)
León *Cortés Castro (1925-26)
Alejandro *Alvarado Quirós (1929-30)
Oscar F. *Rohormoser Carranza (1930-31)
Ricardo *Castro Beeche (1935-36)
Juan Rafael *Arias Bonilla (1936-38)
Rafael Angel *Calderón Guardia (1938-40)
Otto *Cortés Fernández (1940-41)
Teodoro *Picado Michalski (1941-44)
José *Albertazzi Avendaño
Rafael Angel *Grillo Ocampo
Marcial *Fonseca Von-Charmier (1946-48)

Abelardo *Bonilla Baldares (1952-53)
Gonzalo *Facio Segreda (1953-58)
Alvaro *Montero Padilla (1958-59) (1959-60)
Fernando *Lara Bustamante (1960-61)
Mario *Leiva Quirós (1961-62)
Carlos *Espinach Escalante (1962)
Rafael *París Steffens (1963-64) (1965-66)
Rodolfo *Solano Orfilia (1964-65)
Rodrigo *Carazo Odio (1966-67)
Hernán *Garrón Salazar (1967-68) (1982-83)
Fernando *Volio Jiménez (1968-69)
José Luis Molina Quesada (1969-70)
Manuel *Oduber Quirós (1970-73)
Luis Alberto *Monge Alvarez (1973-74)
Alfonso Carro Zúñiga (1974-77)
Elías Soley Soler (1977-78)
Rodrigo *Madrigal Nieto (1978-79)
Ramón Aguilar Facio (1979-1980)
Rafael Alberto Grillo Rivera (1980-81)
Cristian Tatenbach Iglesias (1981-1982)
José Luis Villanueva Badillo (1983-84) (1984-85)
Rosemary Karpinski (1986-87)
Fernando Volio Jiménez (1987-   )

PRESS, The. See: NEWSPAPERS.

PRESTACIONES PARROQUIALES. A colonial custom in which the local parish provided a number of servants for the local casa cural (priest's house).

PRIETO RUIZ, José Eusebio (b. ca. 1808). Jurist. President of the Supreme Court 1846-47.

PRIMER ESTATUTO POLITICO DE COSTA RICA. Constitution of the country from March 17, 1823 to April 4, 1823.

PRINCIPAL. An *Indian chief but with a rank lower than *cacique.

PRINTING PRESS. The first printing press was brought to Costa Rica by Miguel Carranza Fernández in 1830. See also: NEWS-PAPERS; PUBLISHING.

PROCESO DE ARARIBA. See: CASTILLO, Vicente del; PERAFAN DE RIBERA.

PROFECIA. A decree issued by José Cecilio del Valle as "Supreme Executive Power" of Central America (May 20, 1824). Del Valle spelled out the problems of Central America and said that if these faults were not corrected Central America would become nothing more than a group of small squabbling nations.

PROTESTANTS. Religious toleration was achieved in the nineteenth
century, the first church group being organized in 1848, with
the Good Shepherd Church erected in 1865. The original pre-
fabricated building was replaced in 1937. The early Protestants
were foreign miners (at *Aguacate) and business men whose
religious freedom was guaranteed by commercial treaties Costa
Rica signed. Later, Jamaican laborers brought Protestantism
to the *Limón area (see: BLACKS). The first missionary was
the Presbyterian William McConnell, arriving in 1891. Fewer
Costa Ricans have become protestant than in other Central American republics. See also: BREALEY, Richard; EVANGELICALS;
LE LACHEUR, William; MONTEVERDE.

PROVINCES. See: CANTONS OF COSTA RICA.

PROVINCIA DE ARA. The name given to *Talamanca during the
early colonial period. This is a corruption of the name of the
River Lari.

PROVINCIAS UNIDAS DEL CENTRO DE AMERICA. The official
name of the Central American Federation July 1, 1823 to November 22, 1824. During the turbulence of the independence period
a Congress met in Guatemala June-July 1823 and declared Central
America "independent from all powers" and adopted the name
"Provincias Unidas del Centro de América." On July 2, 1823,
it constituted itself a national Constituent Assembly and started
deliberations on a constitution. After Mexican troops evacuated
Guatemala (August 3, 1823) a triumvirate of Pedro *Molina, Juan
Vicente *Villacorta, and Antonio *Rivera Cabezas ruled the new
country until the inauguration of the first president of the Central
American Republic (José Manuel *Arce) in 1825. Costa Rica
declared itself part of this "REPUBLICA FEDERAL DE CENTRO-
AMERICA" (q.v.) August 3, 1823, and the public swore allegiance
on April 19, 1824. The clergy and *imperialists, mostly concentrated in *Cartago and *Heredia, were opposed to Costa Rica's
entrance into this federation. See also: CIVIL WAR of 1823,
and consult Ricardo Fernández Guardia, Historia de Costa Rica:
la independencia (1941).

PUBLIC HEALTH. Diseases brought by the Spanish (smallpox,
measles, tuberculosis, etc.) were a significant factor in the
reduction of the aboriginal population, in Costa Rica as elsewhere in the Americas. During the 18th century the colony
suffered from leprosy. In the late 1850s there was an outbreak
of CHOLERA (q.v.) which killed a tenth of the population. Tropical diseases endemic in the lowlands, particularly on the humid
Atlantic coast contributed to the general migration to the central
meseta in colonial times and persisted as serious health problems
until the mid 20th century. Malaria remained the chief cause of
death in *Limón and *Puntarenas provinces until the widespread

use of DDT against mosquitoes in 1943-49. The last serious yellow fever outbreak was in 1950. Parasitic infections have long been a problem in rural areas. In 1948 it was found that 88% of countryfolk were so infected. The fact that 77% of farmers still worked barefoot accounted for a high incidence of hookworm. Leading causes of death in the 1950s were diarrhea and enteritis: only 4% of milk was pasteurized, and house-to-house distribution by ladling from a churn was still almost universal. Tuberculosis deaths fell by half in the late 1940s, but the disease remains common in *San Jose's overcrowded shanty-towns (*tugurios). Living standards are still low (despite being the highest in Central America), and malnutrition is widespread. In the 1970s some 3,000 or so children died annually of hunger. Official policy until relatively recently has been against family limitation, making abortion the preferred means of birth control. In 1966 it was estimated that there were 111 abortions per thousand pregnancies, and the complications of illegal abortion constituted the third major cause of hospital admission (after childbirth and gastro-intestinal disease). See: BIRTH AND DEATH RATES; HIGHWAY ACCIDENTS. [L.H.]

PUBLIC HOLIDAYS. See: HOLIDAYS.

PUBLIC TRANSPORT. Anthony *Trollope reports there being an omnibus service already in 1858 between the main meseta cities. After their introduction in the 1870s, the railroads provided the principal long-distance means of passenger transport. Interurban motor bus services began in the 1920s, but were hampered by the lack of good *highways. In 1933 there were still only 90 motor buses in the whole country. By the outbreak of Second World War, however, buses were already effectively competing with rail between *San José and *Puntarenas: Costa Rica had 464 buses in 1941. The terrain and the weather long delayed the completion of a satisfactory highway alternative to the railway between San José and *Limón: even the rail service was occasionally washed out (e.g., in 1928-29 and for a week in 1971). Nowadays, however, bus is the cheapest and most widely used form of intercity travel throughout the country. By 1960 Costa Rica had 942 buses and jitneys serving 351 routes.

President *Yglesias Castro gave San José its first electric streetcar lines. Urban rapid transit in San José was exclusively by streetcar until 1936: the first city buses were called autotranvías. The Compañía Nacional de Fuerza y Luz, the private electric power company which ran the streetcars suddenly withdrew the service in 1950 because government price control refused it sufficient fare hike to make it profitable. Since then San José has had buses only. [L.H.]

PUBLISHING AND BOOKSELLING. Costa Rica's first printing press was the Imprenta La Paz of Miguel Carranza Fernández, established in 1830, responsible for both the country's first newspaper,

El noticioso universal of 1833 and its first book, Rafael Francisco
Osejo's Breves lecciones de artimética para uso de los alunos de
la Casa de Santo Tomás, also 1833. But the absence of book-
stores led President Bruno *Carranza Ramírez in 1870 into import-
ing books himself for his friends. A Spanish immigrant opened
what is reputedly Costa Rica's first bookshop, the Librería Española, in 1885. The first regular commercial book publishing is
attributed to the Librería de Lectura Barata circa 1900. It favored
progressive and radical political viewpoints, and in 1915 its
owner, Joaquín *García Monge was made director of the *National
Library, only to be dismissed in 1935 for his outspoken attacks
on Mussolini and the invasion of Ethiopia. Other firms followed
over the years, many run by Spanish or German immigrants.
Two important publisher-booksellers were the Imprenta de las
Américas and the longest running of all, the still existing Librería
Lehmann. By the early 1960s there were over fifty presses, but
almost all publishing was done on the author's commission. Editions were small--500 copies or less--and the number of new
titles derisory--only 13 in 1963. Production costs were high:
for labor, materials (paper is all imported and taxed at 4%),
and equipment (taxed 10%). Local costs were three times those
of New York.

There has been some improvement since, and there are
currently about half a dozen major publishing efforts going on.
These include a few commercial publishers, of whom the most
important are the bookseller-publishers Librería Lehmann and
Librería Trejos Hermanos; their output mixes commercially produced trade books, and author-commissioned or subsidized publications of the "vanity press" type. Government itself publishes
little. Many agencies, including the Dirección General de Estadística, cannot lawfully charge for what they produce, but lack
the funding to publish much for free. Paragovernmental houses,
on the other hand, constitute the most significant sector of
Costa Rican publishing. Their growth may be said to have
begun with Rodrigo Facio Herrera's 1959 foundation of the Editorial Universitaria de Costa Rica. This publishes mostly textbooks and works by the faculty of the *Universidad de Costa
Rica. In the field of history it has issued many monographs
and articles of very high quality, but its editions are small
and go rapidly out of print. The most important house is the
Editorial Costa Rica, founded expressly to publish works by
national authors and secure them better distribution. Its consejo directivo includes representatives of the authors, of the
two state-supported universities, and of government. In practice its policies have, at times, been greatly influenced by the
*Partido Liberación Nacional. It has republished many of the
more important works listed in the bibliographic appendix to
this Dictionary. Second in importance is EDUCA (Editorial Universitaria Centroamericana), founded in 1961 as a cooperative
venture of the universities of all Central American countries,
largely on the initiative of Costa Rican Sergio Ramírez. Its

headquarters are in San Pedro, near the *Universidad de Costa
Rica campus. In terms of overall quality, this has been outstanding, but in recent years its objectivity has been somewhat under-
mined by a preference for leftist works. In this same league,
but on a much smaller scale is the press of the Juricentro of
the *Universidad Autónoma de Centro América, which has only
recently begun to publish, specializing in legal works, but also
producing some good historical studies. Porvenir, a new small
press with an office in San Pedro has also started publishing
worthwhile scholarly works by both new and established authors.
These have been clinically analytical of Costa Rica. Financial
problems make Porvenir's future uncertain. Possibly the most
prolific publisher is EUNED (Editorial Universidad Estatal a Distancia), the press of the "Open" (correspondence degree) university. To satisfy the demand for home study material, it has
published hundreds of books on a myriad of subjects. Its history
output has included reprints of many older works and scores
of new ones. Another important government publisher is the
Ministerio de Cultura, Juventud y Deportes (Ministry of Culture,
Youth and Sport). Over the last decade, this ministry has
published about a hundred books in the history field alone.
Some have been reissues of older titles, but most have been
biographical, covering most of the country's outstanding people.
Even though, as government publications, they are distributed
free of charge to the general public, many are of high quality.
The ideological chasm of the 1980s is reflected in the Liberation
Theology of the highly regarded Editorial DEI (Departamento
Ecuménico de Investigaciones) and the anti-marxist Libro Libre,
which publishes literature and classic political writing, in addition to its analyses of the current Central American situation.
Total output of the nation's publishers varies greatly from year
to year, plunging from 186 titles in 1975 to only 24 in 1978.
In 1982, 650,000 copies of 240 titles were issued. Normal edition size is nowadays around 3,000 copies. An export tax dis-
courages publishing for anything beyond the national market.
The writer Alfonso *Chase campaigned for a government agency
to foster reading and promote the booktrade, on the lines of
Cuba's Instituto del Libro, Brazil's Instituto Nacional do Livro
and Venezuela's Banco del Libro. Costa Rica's Instituto del
Libro was set up, with Chase as director, in 1978, although
it only began to function in early 1983. It has surveyed the
industry (discovering great inefficiencies in the public sector),
begun a campaign to promote reading, and is encouraging the
publishing of textbooks (hitherto Costa Rican education has
depended almost entirely on imported material, mostly from Spain).
[T.C., G.K., L.H.]

PUEBLOS DE INDIOS. See: INDIAN TOWNS.

PUERTO LIMON. See: LIMON (city).

PULPERIA. A small general store that sells basic needs in small quantities. Becoming fewer due to supermarkets.

PUNTARENAS (canton). Territory which comprises the city of Puntarenas and some of the outlying territory. It was created July 24, 1867, and has a population of 74,619. Its main industries are the port facilities, tourism, and a fish cannery.

PUNTARENAS (city). The principal port of the Pacific Ocean at 10°N, 84°50'W. It was opened in 1814 by royal decree, but had been functioning as a port for a decade. It achieved prominence in the 1840s after the decline of *Caldera, which had been the principal port. Steamships on the route between Panama and San Francisco stopped regularly. This was the main travel route between Costa Rica and other Central American countries until the 1930s. Puntarenas remained an open roadstead until a pier was built in 1927. Recently because of anchorage problems at Puntarenas, Caldera is being revived as the chief Pacific port. Puntarenas is connected to the capital by an electric railroad (see: FERROCARRIL ELECTRICO DEL PACIFICO). Its chief industry is tourism and it has deteriorating port facilities. The population of the city has grown from 2,538 in 1892, 3,569 in 1904, 7,790 in 1927, 19,582 in 1963 to 29,224 in 1982. It was chartered as a city September 17, 1858. [T.C., G.K., L.H.]

PUNTARENAS (province). The province extending from the southern part of the Gulf of *Nicoya along the Pacific litoral to the Panamanian border. It was originally created as a comarca in 1848 and then made a province July 1909. Its total population was 32,989 in 1910, 29,008 in 1984. Most of this province consists of a hot coastal plain, but it also has some cool mountainous regions. For this reason the province produces a variety of products. In the lowlands there are huge plantations of *bananas and *African palm. There are some industries such as extracting sea salt, *gold in the *Osa Peninsula, and fishing. In addition there are hardwoods and a growing number of beach resorts.

PUNTO GUANACASTECO. A regional dance which is typically accompanied by marimba and guitar, in which the dancers dance in circles and make up short piquant poems called "bombas." The Punto Guanacasteco is the national dance of Costa Rica.

PURISCAL. *Canton in the province of *San José created August 17, 1868. Its *cabecera is Santiago located about 23 miles west of the city of San José. This canton produces rice, corn, *coffee, and *tobacco among other crops. Its present population is 23,123.

- Q -

QUAKERS. Members from Alabama of the Society of Friends, with religious objection to the draft, and attracted by Costa Rica's abolition of its *armed forces, migrated in the early 1950s to MONTEVERDE (q.v.), becoming ecologically concerned dairy farmers. [L.H.]

QUESADA SALAZAR, Napoleón (1873-1938). Educator, poet, and grammarian. He was minister of education, and was influential in introducing reforms into the traditional curriculum.

QUETZAL. A small green bird. The male has long tail feathers which were worn by some *Indian chiefs as a symbol of royalty. Although the quetzal is the national symbol of Guatemala, it is also found elsewhere in the highlands of Mexico and Central America. It is one of the endangered species of the region. *Monteverde is a mecca for those seeking a glimpse of the quetzal.

QUIJANO, Manuel. Artillery expert and strong supporter of asso- ciating with *Iturbide's Mexican Empire. In March 1823 he helped in the assault on the Plaza of *Cartago and participated in the Battle of *Ochomogo. Later *Quijano was involved in a conspiracy (December 1835) to give arms to *imperialist forces in Cartago, but the plot was discovered and he was exiled. The next June (1836) he invaded Costa Rica with a force of about 150 men and fought several battles in and around *Liberia before his forces were finally repulsed.

QUIJONGO. A folk instrument particular to *Guanacaste province. It is a one-string instrument with a gourd on the end of a shaft which supports the cord. The use of this instrument had been dying out but with a reemphasis on folklore it has made a partial comeback.

QUINTAL. In traditional measure, 46 kg., but the "metric quintal is 100 kg., and quintal is also used for a 46 kg. sack of coffee. [L.H.]

QUINTO REAL. The right of the Spanish crown to a fifth of the value of all extractions of *gold, silver, pearls and precious stones in the Indies. [L.H.]

QUIROS, Teodorico (1897-1977). One of the most important Costa Rican architects and artists of this century. He studied archi- tecture at the Massachusetts Institute of Technology and designed the churches of San Isidro de Coronado, *Curridabat, *Barva de Heredia, and *San Ramón (*Alajuela Province). In painting he was always an important figure, being one of the leaders in the *Academic Generation and one of the principal innovators who helped usher in the Generación Nacionalista in the 1930s.

He specialized in both oils and watercolors of landscapes with
a Costa Rican backdrop. He has also done some expressionist
paintings. His works have been shown in Europe and the United
States. See also: PAINTING.

QUIROS SANABRIA, Rodrigo (b. 1944). Poet and writer born
in *San José. He was a member of the *Círculo de Poetas Costarricenses. Among his works are: Después de nacer (1967),
Abismo sitiado (1973), En defensa del tiempo (1977) and Del
sueño a la jornada (1979).

QUIROS SEGURA, Juan Bautista (1853-1934). Soldier and politician.
Studied in England and was administrator of the Pacific Railroad
(*Ferrocarril Eléctrico del Pacífico), military commander in *San
José, *deputy 1908-12, and president of the Assembly 1908-
09. He was vice-president of the country under *Tinoco Granados
and when Tinoco resigned he turned the government over to
Quirós. But at the strong insistence of the American consul,
Valentine Chase, who brought a note saying that the United
States government would not accept Quirós and that the cruiser
Denver was standing in *Puntarenas harbor, Quirós was obliged
to resign. The government was then turned over to Francisco
*Aguilar Barquero, who had been third vice-president in the
*González Flores government.

- R -

RACES. See: BLACKS; IMMIGRATION LAWS; INDIANS; JEWS;
MESTIZOES; PARDOS; POPULATION.

RAILROADS. Costa Rica's first railroad was a mule-hauled line
running nine miles from Barranca de *Puntarenas city, opened
in 1857. The first substantial route was that of the Atlantic
Railroad (see: FERROCARRIL DEL NORTE), begun in 1871
which provided the only transportation link between the capital
and the eastern seaboard until a modern all weather road was
opened in the 1950s. The Pacific Railroad (see: FERROCARRIL
ELECTRICO DEL PACIFICO) linking *San José to Puntarenas
was not begun until 1897. These two lines are both 3'6" (1,067
m) gauge. They were merged in 1972 as the government-owned
FECOSA (Ferrocarriles de Costa Rica) and carry most of the
country's rail traffic. There are also lines in both Pacific and
Atlantic coastal areas owned by the *banana companies built
for their own needs, but which do provide some passenger services. Declining banana production and a developing highway
network are making the railroad obsolete. See also: LEY
GENERAL DE FERROCARRILES, and consult Joaquín Fernández
Montuar, Historia ferrovial de Costa Rica (1934) and Watt Stewart's
Keith and Costa Rica (1964). [L.H.]

RAMIREZ, Alejandro (1774-1821). Secretary to the Captain General of Guatemala and editor of the Gaceta de Guatemala. He is credited with introducing cinnamon, peppers, camphor, and breadfruit into Central America.

RAMIREZ, Gilbert (b. 1941). Born in *Limón, he is one of the few Costa Rican art photographers. His photographs have naturalistic qualities usually with a background of the Costa Rican landscape. Many times his photos show people working or in contemplative poses. Ramírez' use of black and white contrasts is particularly striking.

RAMIREZ CASTRO, Gregorio José (1796-1823). A ship's captain who also served in the second *Junta Superior Gubernativa in 1831 and then retired to his farm in *Alajuela. When *Cartago started an uprising in 1823 he was asked to form an army to stop them. He hastily organized this force and on April 5, 1823, defeated the insurgents at the heights of *Ochomogo. Since all government had disappeared, by default he became the supreme power in the country. But he had no interest in being a dictator and after calling elections turned his power over to a Constituent Assembly (April 16, 1823) and retired again to private life. See also: CIVIL WARS (1823).

RAMIREZ HIDALGO, Rafael (1805-1875). Member of the Constituent Assemblies of 1838, 1859, 1869, 1870, and 1871. President of the Congress, 1844-45, and of the Senate, 1862 and 1963. He was also president of the Supreme Court, 1847 and 1854.

RAMOS, Domingo (b. 1947). Sculptor. Although born in *San Ramón (*Alajuela Province), he is considered part of the Heredia *Generation of 1980 sculptors. His works are a bit classical in nature, probably because of his formal academic training. See: SCULPTURE.

RAMOS, Lilia (1903-). Specialist in early childhood education, and author. Studied in Chile and the United States. She became interested in existentialist psychology and employed the ideas of Charles Baudoin and Harry J. Sullivan. In addition she published the first thematic anthology of Costa Rican poetry: La voz enternecida (1963), Fulgones en mi ocaso (1978), and Luz y bambalinas (1981).

RAPID TRANSIT. See: PUBLIC TRANSPORT.

RAZON, La. An anti-Catholic Church newspaper published in 1875 by students of Lorenzo *Montúfar. It ceased publication after being condemned by the Church as "ultra-rationalistic."

REAL. A basic unit of Spanish colonial currency. When first established in 1369 the real consisted of 1 part silver (.355

grams) and 3 parts of copper. Later it was also called "antiguo
castellano de plata." At the time of Ferdinand and Isabel its
silver content was reduced to 1/67 part. In colonial times eight
reales were worth a *peso, two reales were worth a peseta,
four reales were worth a tostón, and eight reales were worth
a *doblón (also called piece-of-eight because it was worth eight
reales). Much of this colonial terminology lingered in Costa
Rica. It was common to refer to a coin of 25 céntimos as dos
reales (two reales). The smallest coin before decimalization in
1863 was half a real.

REAL AUDIENCIA. See: AUDIENCIA REAL.

REAL CUNO DE GUATEMALA (The Royal Mint of Guatemala). Established in 1733 with machinery brought from Mexico. It used
silver mined principally in Honduras, but because of the limited
amount of silver available the mint could not produce enough
to greatly relieve the coin shortage in Central America. Many
different types of money continued to circulate. But in spite
of these problems the mint did manage to coin over four million
doubloons (*doblones). See also: COINAGE.

REAL HACIENDA. A colonial governmental agency that supervised
the collection of taxes, served as public treasury, and served
as an accounting agency.

REAL QUINTO. See: QUINTO REAL.

REALEJO. Small port on the Nicaraguan Pacific coast where William
*Walker landed June 13, 1855, to start his Central American
career.

REBULLIDA, Pablo de [Fray] (d. 1709). Spanish missionary who
went to *Talamanca in 1695 and learned seven *Indian languages.
In order to control the Indians more effectively many of them
were taken from Talamanca to Térraba on the Pacific coast.
Father Rebullida was put in charge of this project. This move
gave rise to the settlement of San Francisco de Térraba. In
1709 Rebullida was killed in an Indian uprising.

RECOPE. See: REFINADORA COSTARRICENSE DE PETROLEO,
SOCIEDAD ANONIMA.

RECOPILACION DE LAS LEYES DE LAS INDIAS. See: LEYES DE
LAS INDIAS.

RECREO. (1) A concert played during the day (usually a holiday
or a Sunday) by the local (semi) military band in the main square
of a town. It was an excuse for socializing and showing off
new clothes. Although this custom has died out, it still exists
in altered form in a few places.
    (2) The recess period in a school.

REFINADORA COSTARRICENSE DE PETROLEO, SOCIEDAD ANONIMA.
(RECOPE). A refinery which produces gasoline, kerosene,
diesel, bunker, and fuel oil. It was established in 1963 under
the joint ownership of Standard Oil Company, Allied Chemical
Company, Union-Texas Petroleum Company and the government
of Costa Rica. Although heralded as an advance, its products
have tended to be of poor quality and have not benefitted the
consumer much. The refinery at Moín near *Limón was nationalized in 1974.

REFUGEES. A considerable number of refugees have entered Costa
Rica over the last decade, mainly from Nicaragua, propelled
by both political and economic reasons, see: FRONTIER QUES-
TIONS (NICARAGUA). Costa Rica's humanitarian traditions
have made it difficult to deny them entry or continued residence,
and by mid-1989 there were about 200,000 of them, many living
precariously in *tugurios. [L.H.]
See also: IMMIGRATION LAWS.

REGIDOR. In colonial times, an alderman or councilman in the
*cabildo, elected by the townsmen to represent them. But as
early as the seventeenth century, the whole municipal system
was honeycombed with patronage and graft. As a result, local
officials came to be appointed rather than elected, and the office
of a regidor usually went to the highest bidder.

REGISTRO DE MAR. A dependency of the *Casa de Contratación.
It kept a record of all merchandise that was transported between Spain and the Indies and in addition kept a list of all
passengers and prices of commodities.

REINA, Carlos Roberto. Honduran lawyer and a leader of the
Honduran Liberal Party. He was elected as second judge of
the Inter American *Human Rights Court in 1981.

REINO DE GUATEMALA. See: KINGDOM OF GUATEMALA.

RELACION DE LOS NEGOCIOS DESPACHOS POR EL CONSEJO.
This was tantamount to the first newspaper issued in the country. Although it carried mostly official decrees, it also had
some general news. It was first published May 30, 1832 and
ceased publication June 1, 1835, having published 55 issues.

REPARTIMIENTO. A system by which *Indian labor was provided
to certain of the *conquistadors and later Spanish settlers under
the pretense that the Indians would be educated in return for
working for the Spaniards. The first repartimiento in Costa
Rica probably took place in 1524 at *Villa de Bruselas. However,
the first substantiated record was in *Cartago on January 12,
1569, when 9,800 Indians were said to have been parceled out
to 85 Spaniards. A total of 23,250 Indians were supposedly

distributed during the colonial period. This relatively small number may be attributed to the lack of a large indigenous population and the strong resistance the Spanish incurred in the mountains of *Talamanca. This scarcity of labor may have been one of the reasons why class divisions were not so sharp in the early colonial period in Costa Rica as they were in other colonies. Consult: Ralph Lee Woodward, Central America (a nation divided) (1976).

REPUBLIC OF CENTRAL AMERICA. See: REPUBLICA DE AMERICA CENTRAL.

REPUBLICA, La. After La *Nación, Costa Rica's largest circulation daily (c. 50,000 copies), founded 1950 as the voice of the National Liberation Party (*Partido Liberación Nacional) and reformist politics. In the early 1970s it adopted a less political policy, encouraging José *Figueres Ferrer's supporters to start the short-lived *Excelsior. [L.H.]

REPUBLICA DE AMERICA CENTRAL. (1) In October 1852 President Trinidad Cabañas of Honduras tried to strengthen the national representation of Central America by summoning the states to a conference. The plan fell through because of a war between Honduras and Guatemala.
(2) In a meeting in San Salvador (October 1889) and in Managua in November of that same year, all states agreed to common foreign representatives and an eventual integration of all countries. Costa Rica refused to ratify this agreement. Consult Thomas Karnes, The Failure of Union: Central America, 1824-1960 (1961).

REPUBLICA FEDERAL DE CENTRO-AMERICA. Official name for the government of Central America after November 22, 1824. It was a federal republic of the five current Central American republics, plus Los Altos, and for a time most of it was governed by a Congress of Representatives (one for each 30,000 inhabitants), a Senate (two senators from each state), and a President elected for a four-year term. Every member state was expected to have its own constitution and its own head of state (or jefe supremo, as he was called in Costa Rica). From the beginning the federation failed to solve basic problems such as the permanent location of the capital, the rivalry between *serviles (proclerical conservatives) and the anti-clerical liberals. It was further plagued by foreign domination (mostly British), and chronic lack of funds. Its faltering economy forced it to go into debt, and finally local *civil wars broke out. It was officially dissolved after a *cholera epidemic and a civil war between Francisco *Morazón and Rafael *Carrera devastated Guatemala. Costa Rica had withdrawn in 1829, but then returned, to withdraw definitively November 14, 1838. Costa Rica was saddled with its share of the Federation's debts, which made it wary of joining any further unification projects.

REPUBLICA MAYOR DE AMERICA CENTRAL (Greater Republic of
Central America). A brief attempt at reunification, the initiative
of Policarpo Bonilla, recently Honduras minister in Washington
DC, who brought about a meeting at Ampala, June 1895, which
led to the Pact of AMPALA, q.v. An attempt to strengthen
the union led to the short-lived ESTADOS UNIDOS DE CENTRO-
AMERICA, q.v.

REPUBLICANS. (1) Those people in 1821-1823 who favored the
*Pacto de Concordia and association with the *Provincias Unidas
del Centro de América. They were opposed by the *Imperialists,
mostly in the cities of *Cartago and *Heredia. This clash of
opinions led to the first civil war in April 1823 (see: CIVIL
WAR OF 1823), which was won by the Republicans.
    (2) Those who have belonged to the subsequent republican
parties; but this term has no connection with the first. See:
PARTIDO REPUBLICANO; PARTIDO REPUBLICANO NACIONAL.

RESGUARDO. Popular name for the customs-force (*guardia fiscal)
that operated principally in rural areas. It was in charge of
finding illegal liquor distilleries and illegal plantings of marijuana,
and uncovering smuggling operations. It was superseded in
1970 by the Guardia de Asistencia Rural.

RESIDENCIA, Juicio de. A type of broad review of all the viceroys'
or *governors' actions while they were in office, conducted by a
special court appointed in Spain. They could hear any evidence
and take measures to punish the official if they found that any
regulation had been violated.

RETANA, Marco (b. 1938). Writer and educator. He was a member
of the *Círculo de Poetas Costarricenses, and in addition has
served on various cultural, historical, and educational commissions.
His most important works to date are: El manicomio de los niños
dioses (1972), La noche de los Amadores (1975), La Chocola
(poetry) (1979), De orates y semejantes (1982). In addition
he has published various articles.

RETRETAS. A concert played at night in the main square of a
town by the local (semi) military band (see: INSTITUCION
DE LAS BANDAS). It provided an opportunity for young people
to make social contacts. It was a formal affair with groups
of young men walking in the opposite direction. Contact between
the two sexes was made in a highly controlled almost ritualistic
way. This custom has largely died out, except in a few places
where it exists in a modified form.

REVENTAZON. River which has flooded parts of *Cartago Province.
As it flows eastward down toward the sea, it becomes one of
the rivers environmentalists and sport-tourism groups hope to
conserve (as well as the Pacuare River) for white-water rafting.
See: SUERRE. [G.K.]

REVOLUCION. A newspaper published for about a year after March 15, 1930, by a group of law students headed by Manuel *Mora Valverde.

REVOLUTIONS, WARS, CIVIL WARS, AND MAJOR UPRISINGS. Costa Rica, when compared to the rest of Central America, has had relatively few uprisings and revolutions. But they have had more than is popularly believed. For the most part these disturbances were limited affairs with small numbers of people taking part. Generally they were bloodless, and failed. The culprits were either exiled temporarily or jailed for short periods of time, usually ending up with full pardons. However, there have been some sanguine clashes with many deaths, especially in 1823, 1918, and 1948. The most important uprisings can be found with a fuller explanation under separate headings. This list is not complete since many of the plots were insignificant affairs, but these will give some indication of the development of the country.

April 1823:	First *Civil War
Jan. 1826:	Attempt of José *Zamora
March 1835:	Resignation of José Rafael *Gallegos y Alvarado under military pressure
Sept. 1835:	Second *Civil War
Dec. 1835:	Conspiracy of Manuel *Quijano to arm imperialists
June 1836:	Quijano Invasion
Aug. 1837:	Attempted overthrow of Manuel *Aguilar Chacón
May 1838:	Overthrow of Manuel Aguilar
Jan. 1840:	Conspiracy of Joaquín *Mora to assassinate Braulio *Carrillo Colina
Feb. 1840:	Conspiracy against Carrillo
March 1840:	Conspiracy of Manuel Acosta
April 1842:	*Morazán's invasion and overthrow of Carrillo
May 1842:	Conspiracy of Major Mercedes Jiménez against Morazán
Aug. 1842:	Colonel Manuel Angel Molina took the arsenal in *Liberia in an attempt to overthrow Morazán
Sept. 1842:	Overthrow and execution of General Morazán
June 1846:	Second overthrow of the *Gallegos y Alvarado government
Oct. 1847:	Failure of revolution of Francisco Emigdio Aqueche in *Alajuela
March, June, July, Aug., and Oct. 1848:	Various conspiracies
Oct. 1849:	Conspiracy in *Alajuela
Nov. 1849:	Army forces the resignation of Dr. *Castro Madriz
Jan. 1852:	Revolution of General José Manuel Quirós
March-April 1856; Nov. 1856 to May 1857:	War against the *filibusters of William *Walker
June 1856:	Conspiracy against the government of Juan

	Rafael *Mora Porras
Aug. 1859:	Overthrow of Mora by Generals *Salazar Herrera and *Blanco Rodríguez
Dec. 1859:	Mora's intent to take back government, invasion of *Puntarenas
Dec. 1859:	Uprising in favor of *Mora Porras in San Ramón
Jan. 1860:	Revolution in *Guanacaste
Jan., Sept. 1860:	Frustrated invasions and execution of Mora
April 1860:	Conspiracy of La Soledad
Nov. 1868:	Second overthrow of Dr. Castro Madriz by generals Salazar and Blanco
Feb. 1869:	Failure of a revolution by General Salazar
April 1870:	Revolution of General Tomás *Guardia Gutiérrez, overthrow of the government of Jesús de Jiménez Zamora
May 1871:	Conspiracy against Tomás Guardia
May 1874:	Conspiracy in *Desamparados
Oct. 1874:	Revolution of Joaquín Fernández
May 1875:	Attempted revolution of *Alajuela
July 1876:	Frustrated attempt on the government of Tomás Guardia
July 1876:	Overthrow of the government of Aniceto *Esquivel Sáenz by the forces of General Tomás Guardia
Jan. 1878:	Invasion of Federico Mora
Jan. 1881, May 1882:	Failure of revolutionary movements by Joaquín Fernández
Sept. 1884:	Revolution of Father Víctor Ortiz
March 1885:	Declaration of war on Guatemala
June 1885:	Conspiracy of General Gutiérrez
Nov. 1889:	The night of November, 1889 (electoral disorders) and the resignation of Bernardo *Soto Alfaro
Feb. 1894:	Rebellion of the *Partido Unión Católica
Sept. 1894:	Attempt against President Rafael *Yglesias Castro
Sept. 1897:	Frustrated revolution by Father Joaquín Hernández
Feb. 1899:	Revolution of General Federico Valverde
Feb. 1900, Feb. 1901:	Intent of an invasion of F. Mora
May 1902:	Insurrection against Rafael Yglesias following the elections
May 1906:	Conspiracy against Cleto *González Víquez
Jan. 1917:	Overthrow of Alfredo *González Flores
Feb., April 1918:	Uprisings against the *Tinoco Granados government
May 1918:	Declaration of war on Germany
May 1919:	Revolution of *Sapoá
Aug. 1919:	Assassination of José Joaquín Tinoco, Minister of War, and resignation of Federico Tinoco

Sept. 1919:	Forced resignation of General Juan B. *Quirós Segura because of the threat of United States intervention
March 1921:	War with Panama
Sept. 1926:	General Jorge *Volio Jiménez attacks arsenal in *Liberia
June 1931:	Frustrated attempt to start uprising in *San Ramón
Feb. 1932:	The *Bellavistazo
Dec. 1941:	Declaration of war on Germany, Italy, and Japan
June 1946:	The *Almaticazo
March–April 1948:	Third *Civil War (War of National Liberation)
Dec. 1948:	Calderonista counterrevolution
April 1949:	The Cardonazo (see: CARDONA QUIROS, Edgar)
1955:	Calderonista Invasion

Consult R. Obregón, Hechos militares y políticos, Alajuela, 1981.

REYES FRUTOS, Rafael (1799-1854). Father Reyes was *Deputy on various occasions, president of the *Cámara de Representantes 1845-46, and senator 1846.

RICE. This old-world cereal has long been grown in Costa Rica, even by partly acculturated Indians, but until the Second World War it was chiefly a crop grown in small quantities by small farmers for their subsistence. Market demand was supplied almost wholly by imported rice. Cultivation expanded as the Pacific coast became more populated and farmed. The area under rice doubled between 1950 and 1967; by the mid-1970s five times as much farmland was devoted to rice as in 1950, mostly in *Guanacaste and the *Nicoya peninsula, but not all of it in climatically suitable areas. Almost half the rice farms were large mechanized plantations. By 1970 production was sufficient for domestic demand, and Costa Rica became for a few years a rice exporter. This, however, did not prove profitable, production was cut back, and by the early 1980s rice had once more to be imported. It remains a major food crop, and the largest crop by weight after *sugar and *bananas. The 1983 production was 212,000 tons, compared with 2,500,000 tons of sugar, 1,021,000 tons of bananas and only 113,000 tons of corn. [L.H.]

RIEGO, Juan Rafael (1799-1823). Spanish army officer who started a revolution in 1820 to oblige Ferdinand VII to restore the liberal constitution and summon another Cortes. This started a chain reaction in the New World and accelerated the independence movement, which was largely conservative in nature. See also: INDEPENDENCE.

RINCON DE LA VIEJA. National Park in remote northwest known

for its geysers. Its volcano (of the same name) has erupted
four times since 1984.

RIOS, Pedro de los. De facto *governor of Costa Rica after the
removal of *Pedrarias Dávila 1527-1529.

RIVAS, Battles of. (1) On April 11, 1856, Costa Rican forces
captured the city after a hard fought battle climaxed by Juan
*Santamaría's throwing a torch into the filibusters' stronghold.
(2) A second Battle of Rivas took place a year later in
which 1,000 Central American soldiers surrounded the city and
forced the surrender of William *Walker May 1, 1857. Walker
was then escorted to the port of *San Juan del Sur and taken
to Panama.

RIVAS, Domingo (1836-1900). Received doctorate in canon law
from the *Universidad de Santo Tomás and was considered one
of the leaders of the pro-Church forces. He was anti-liberal
and anti-Mason. In addition to being rector of the *Universidad
de Santo Tomás he was de facto head of Costa Rican Catholic
Church after the death of Mgr. *Llorente. Rivas was also president of the Catholic Union Party (*Partido Unión Católica), and
was exiled with Archbishop *Thiel. During his term of office
work was started on the cathedral in *San José.

RIVAS, Joaquín (d. 1843). Born in Nicaragua. Administrator of
customs in *San José. He served as general minister in the
government of Braulio *Carrillo Colina. Member of the 1823
and 1842 Constituent Assemblies. *Deputy 1825-31 and president of Congress twice.

RIVAS Y CONTRERAS, Francisco Antonio de. Interim *governor
of Costa Rica March-September 1678. He was sent to investi-
gate Governor *Sáenz Vázquez, whom he suspended from office.

RIVERA, Amparo (b. 1919). An *Arte Nuevo painter who has
had her works exhibited in the United States as well as in Costa
Rica.

RIVERA, José Andrés [Father]. Father Rivera served as *deputy
1831-35 and was president of Congress in 1834.

ROAD ACCIDENTS. See: HIGHWAY ACCIDENTS.

ROADS. See: HIGHWAYS.

ROCHWERGER, Susana (b. 1946). An *Arte Nuevo painter specializing in oil paintings.

RODRIGUEZ, Juan Luis (b. 1934). Artist and metal engraver.
He studied in Costa Rica and also lived and studied in Europe

for twelve years. He was considered one of the leaders of the
*Arte Nuevo movement. His paintings are mostly symbolic in an
abstract style with the colors having a pulverized look. Rodríguez has also done wood and metal forms which he puts in frames.
He was director of the literary page of La República for several
years.

RODRIGUEZ, Rebeca (b. 1950). An *Arte Nuevo artist who specializes in metallic collages. She has had her works exhibited
in Costa Rica and Finland.

RODRIGUEZ CABALLERO, Rafael Lucas (1915-1981). Illustrator
and botanist. Born in *San Ramón (*Alajuela Province) he received the doctorate from the University of California at Berkeley.
He worked with the propagation of local varieties of orchids
and founded the Revista de biología tropical. In addition to
this he did illustrations for various books.

RODRIGUEZ CASTRO, Floryluz (b. 1950). Poet whose poems deal
with love and her intimate thoughts and feelings. Most important
works are: Aquí nacen los ríos (1972), El lenguaje del vacío
(1973), and Estancias del silencio (1975).

RODRIGUEZ, CONEJO, Marcial (1892-   ). Physician and politician.
He studied medicine in El Salvador and served various posts
of beneficent institutions; he was *deputy in 1940-42 and 1946-
48; member of the Constituent Assembly of 1949, where he served
as its vice-president; reelected *deputy in 1949-53; and president
of the Legislative Assembly in 1949-52.

RODRIGUEZ DE FONSECA, Juan (d. 1524). Named superintendent
of the Indies by Queen Isabella in 1492, an office he held until
his death. He was in charge of planning expeditions and served
as assistant to the controller general and treasurer of the kingdom.

RODRIGUEZ QUIROS, Carlos Humberto (1910-1986). Archbishop
(1960-1979). A member of the Costa Rican aristocracy, educated
in Europe. His conservatism led to tension with Church groups
affected by new ideas of social activism. [G.K.]

RODRIGUEZ VEGA, Eugenio (b. 1925). Professor of economics and
rector of the *Universidad de Costa Rica. He was comptroller
general of the country during the *Trejos Fernández administration. He is author of Apuntes para una sociología costarricense,
which was the first attempt to treat the sociology of Costa Rica.

RODRIGUEZ ZELEDON, José Joaquín (1838-1917). Lawyer. President of the Supreme Court 1887-90, President of the Republic
1890-94. He suspended constitutional guarantees and postponed
the Congress before the end of his first year in power and

then ruled by decree. During his administration he signed
the first contracts to bring *telephone service to Costa Rica
and started construction of the ornate *Teatro Nacional.

ROHRMOSER CARRANZA, Oscar F. (1870-1931). (1) Agriculturalist
and merchant. He held ministries in the *Tinoco Granados and
*González Víquez governments and was president of Congress,
1930-31.

 (2) A prosperous neighborhood on the western edge of
*San José, where the family once grew coffee, is called Rohr-
moser.

ROMERO, Félix. Father Romero studied in Nicaragua and was a
member of the Constituent Assemblies of 1823 and 1824-25. He
was a *deputy in 1825-26 and president of the Congress November 1825 to January 1826.

ROMERO, Sonia (b. 1929). Artist who works in oils, pen and ink
drawings, and water colors. She does landscapes and human
figures. Her work has been shown in Costa Rica and Mexico.

RONDON. A stew usually made with fish and tubular vegetables
with a coconut milk base. It is typical of the *Blacks in the
Atlantic zone.

ROSS, Marjorie (b. 1945). Poet born in *San José. She wrote
Agua fuerte (1969).

ROSSI CHAVARRIA, Jorge (b. 1920). Lawyer, businessman, and
politician. Minister of economics 1953-58. In 1957 he split with
the National Liberation Party (*Partido Liberación Nacional) because of what he considered dictatorial control of the party
by its leaders. He formed his own *Partido Independiente to
run for the presidency the following year. Although he did
not win, he split the National Liberation Party vote and thus
assured Mario *Echandi Jiménez the victory. He was chosen
to run on the PLN ticket by José *Figueres Ferrer in 1970 to
demonstrate that the old feud had been patched up. Thus he
served as vice president 1970-74.

ROTHE DE VALLBONA, Rima (b. 1931). A writer who uses the
narrative and at times autobiographic style. Most of her works
deal with family relations. Her most important works are: La
espuma perenne, Noche en vela (1967), Polvo del camino (1971)
(which won a national prize), Una rosa al viento, La obra de
prosa de Eunice Odio (1980), Las sombras que perseguimos (1983).
She has resided since 1964 in Houston, Texas, where she teaches
literature at St. Thomas University.

ROVINSKI, Samuel (b. 1932). Engineer and writer. Rovinski is
the first Jewish person to rise to national literary prominence.

His novels include Cuarto creciente (1964), La pagoda (1968),
La ceremonia de casta (1976), and La política cultural en Costa
Rica (1977). His subjects deal with social problems, the Jewish
community and its problems, philosophical speculations, and
some eroticism. Rovinski has also been successful in writing
plays. Some of them are: "Gobierno de alcoba," which deals
with dictatorships in Latin America; "Las fisgonas de Paso Ancho"
(1971), which treats the subject of life in a poor neighborhood
of the capital; "Un modelo para Rosaura," which is concerned
with interpersonal problems among various couples over the
years; and "El martirio del pastor," which concerns the 1980
assassination in El Salvador of Archbishop Romero. Rovinski
has won national prizes several times and is one of the most
important Costa Rican playwrights.

RUBIO DE AUNON, Diego Morcill [Fray] (d. 1730). A Trinitarian
brother and bishop of Nicaragua and Costa Rica 1701-08. Named
protector of the *Indians in 1706 and supervised the building
of the first Hermitage in El Barreal (*Heredia), which served as
a nucleus for the foundation of the city of *Heredia. See:
HEREDIA (city).

RUIZ DE BUSTAMANTE, Pedro. Interim *governor 1717-18. He
was sent to the province after the former governor, *Lacayo de
Briones, was suspended for illicit commerce with the *Zambo-
Mosquito Indians. Ruiz became involved in several disputes.
One involved the vicar of *Cartago who excommunicated him.
This act was ultimately annulled by the *Cabildo of León. The
second dispute was over his harsh treatment of Governor Lacayo.
Because of these actions Ruiz was fined and deprived of his
rank.

RUIZ DE MENDOZA, Esteban (d. 1773). Acting *governor for a
brief period in 1745.

- S -

SABANA, La. A common for cattle, donated by *Chapui de Torres,
then, 1930-70, San José's main airfield. When Juan *Santamaría
International Airport opened at *Alajuela, La Sabana became the
main recreational area for western San José. The old terminal
building is now the Museo de Arte Costarricense.

SACASA, José. Lawyer. He was born in Guatemala and served as
the president of the Ruling Junta of the short-lived state of
Los Altos. He came to Costa Rica where he became secretary
of the Supreme Court in 1827 and then president of that body
in 1830.

SAENZ, Carlos Luis (1899-1984). Poet, novelist, and professor in the *Universidad de Costa Rica. As a member of the Communist Party (*Partido Comunista) he ran for Congress in 1938 but was deprived of election by fraud. Sáenz was a candidate for the presidency in 1936 and also wrote novels, volumes of poetry, and textbooks for primary schools. His most important works are: Mulita mayor (1952), Raíces de esperanza (1940), and Memorias de alegría (1951).

SAENZ, Rocío. See: SANZ, Rocío.

SAENZ, Vicente (1896-1963). Journalist, socialist, and strong critic of dictatorships and imperialist penetration. During his stormy life he tried to organize a socialist party in Costa Rica, fought against *Tinoco Granados, and participated in other struggles in his own country. For these reasons he spent most of his life outside Costa Rica, mostly in Mexico where he died in voluntary exile. Among his most prominent works are Hispano-américa contra el colonaje, Rompiendo cadenas, and Opiniones y comentario de 1943.

SAENZ GONZALEZ, Guido (b. 1929). Author and leading intellectual. While serving as assistant minister of culture he helped reorganize the *Orquesta Sinfónica Nacional and establish the National Theatre Company and the *Orquesta Nacional Juvenil (National Youth Symphony). He has written a book of essays called Egipto con la visión dilatada (1979).

SAENZ HERRERA, Carlos, Dr. (1910-1980). Physician educated in Belgium. He pioneered pediatric medicine and was minister of health, and vice-president of the Republic 1966-70. The National Children's Hospital is named in his honor.

SAENZ LLORENTE, Vicente (1832-1895). Lawyer and jurist. Studied in Guatemala and occupied many posts in public administration and the courts. He was a delegate to the 1869 Constituent Assembly and President of the Supreme Court on and off from 1874 to 1889.

SAENZ PATERSON, Guillermo (b. 1944). Writer and poet. Most of his works are still unpublished. In addition to writing occasional newspaper articles, he has published the following works: El caminante y otros soles (1972), De lluvia y sol (1974), and De luz y de eternidad (1982).

SAENZ VAZQUEZ, Juan Francisco (1620-1686). *Governor of the province of Costa Rica 1674-81. Under his leadership a *pirate invasion was stopped at Quebrada Honda in 1676. He also fortified *Esparza and *Caldera in an effort to stop further pirate incursions. He was accused of illegal trade with an English ship, but the *Audiencia de Guatemala finally acquitted him of the charges. See also: PIRATES.

SALAS, Félix Angel (1908-1948). Poet whose most important works are: Abre el surco (1940), "Juan Santamaría," and "Tomás Guardia," which appeared in Costa Rica de ayer y hoy (1950).

SALAS, Germán. See: CIRCULO DE POETAS COSTARRICENSES.

SALAZAR, Carlos (b. 1954). An *Arte Nuevo painter. His works combine realism with a sort of subconscious dreamlike quality. The effect is like a fantasy.

SALAZAR, Fernando de (1610-1680). Treasurer (of the Royal Treasury, caja real) of the province and *alcalde ordinario of *Cartago. He also served as acting *governor in 1662-63, while the governor was leading a military campaign in *Talamanca.

SALAZAR, José Francisco (1892-1968). Painter and architect who studied in the United States. He designed the Temple of Music in Morazán Park and the *Club Unión. He served as dean of the Academia de Bellas Artes of the *Universidad de Costa Rica 1945-48.

SALAZAR, Manuel ("Melico") (b. 1887). Operatic tenor famous in Europe and the United States. The recently restored Raventos Theater has been named for him. [G.K.]

SALAZAR HERRERA, Lorenzo (1813-1871). Army officer and politician. After becoming a national hero during the war against William *Walker, General Salazar turned to politics. Working in conjunction with General Máximo *Blanco Rodríguez, he became the dominant political figure in the country, imposing and deposing several presidents. The power of these two men was finally curtailed by Tomás *Guardia Gutiérrez. Consult Cleto González Víquez, El sufragio en Costa Rica ante la historia y la legislación.

SALAZAR LEIVA, Virgilio. Teacher and politician. He was active in the *Partido Confraternidad Guanacasteco in the 1930s. In 1940 he ran for the presidency on the *Partido Confraternidad ticket and was on the ballot in several provinces, although he received only 6,300 votes.

SALAZAR SOLORZANO, Rodolfo (1908-1982). Poet born in *Guanacaste Province. He served as a teacher, *deputy in the National Congress, and governor of his native province. But he is chiefly remembered for his poetry glorifying his province. His most important poems are: "Despertar guanacasteco," "Del espeque al tractor," "Los amores del Cholo Juan," "Filadelfia," "Liberia," and "Sabanero."

SALES TAX. A national sales tax originally ranging from 5 to 25 percent on most non-food items was enacted July 17, 1967. It has since been modified to a straight 10 percent, with some basic items excluded.

SALINAS ALMENGOLAS, Mauricio (d. 1847). Military commander of the forces of *Heredia city, which during the first *civil war attacked and captured *Alajuela city. He was also involved in the War of the League (*Guerra de la Liga) for which he was fined and exiled to *Esparza for a short time. See: CIVIL WARS.

SAN CARLOS (Fort). A strong point on the San Juan River held by the *filibusters. Captured by the Costa Rican forces in December 1856.

SAN CARLOS. *Canton in *Alajuela Province founded September 26, 1911. Its *cabecera is Ciudad Quesada. It is a developing area of varied agricultural produce. Its main products are hardwoods, *bananas, *cattle, and tropical fruits. It is one of the richest agricultural zones, but poor transportation and a long rainy season have inhibited its growth. The present population is 75,576.

SAN FERNANDO (Fort). See: FUERTE DE SAN FERNANDO.

SAN ISIDRO. *Canton chartered July 18, 1981, in the province of *Heredia. Its *cabecera is San Isidro and its principal product is *coffee. The present population is 8,528. See also: PEREZ ZELEDON (canton); and CORONADO, cabecera of *Coronado canton.

SAN JOSE (city). City in Central Costa Rica at 9°59'N, 84°04'W, 1,161 meters above sea level. Settlers from *Cartago started to flow into the Asserí Valley and in 1736 a parroquia was set up at Villa Nueva de la Boca del Monte under the patronage of St. Joseph (San José). For a long while it was called Villanueva to distinguish it from *Cubujuquí (*Heredia), which was called Villa Vieja. The *San José area began to grow toward the end of the colonial period because of *tobacco plantings and its role as a commercial center. It was reported in 1783 to have eclipsed *Cartago. After the 1823 *civil war the capital was moved to San José (May 1, 1823). But there was still considerable rivalry among the four cities of the central valley leading to another civil war and the *Ley de Ambulancia. San José was finally accepted as the capital of the country in 1835. It had 19,326 inhabitants in 1892, 24,500 by 1904 and 51,000 by 1930. Despite much growth since the Second World War, San José has as yet few tugurios (shanties). This may now change. San José's population was 87,000 in 1950, 101,162 in 1963, 223,300 in 1975, and 215,000 in 1985. This is misleading because it takes into account only the central canton, and does not include the surrounding towns and territories which are practically part of the

city. Greater San José attained 150,000 population by 1950
and 395,000 by 1970. Official districts within the canton include:
Zapote, where the presidential offices are located; La Uruca,
a north side industrial zone; Hatillo, a poor area to the south;
Pavas, an affluent area on the west; Mata Redonda; San Sebastián;
San Francisco de Dos Ríos; Catedral; Hospital; Carmen; and
Merced. See also: SUBURBANIZATION. [T.C.; G.K.]

SAN JOSE (province). The central province of the country. It
was created December 7, 1848, had a population of 118,497 in
1910 and 893,254 in 1984. In addition to containing the administrative capital it is also the center of manufacturing, distribution, communication, and transportation. The province is mountainous and has a cool climate with rainfall roughly from May
to December. Besides *coffee, it produces *sugar, fruits, vegetables, and dairy products.

SAN JUAN DE DIOS. Since 1852, the main hospital in San José.
Funds yielded by a *hacienda created in 1815 by the bishop
were before then used for a leprosarium in Cartago. See also:
TRISTAN, Esteban Lorenzo de; CHAPUI DE TORRES, Manuel
Antonio.

SAN JUAN DEL NORTE. Nicaraguan port on the Caribbean, just
north of the mouth of the San Juan River at 10°58'N, 83°40'W,
and until 1858 in *Miskito territory, and known as Greytown.
Before *Limón was opened, San Juan del Norte was Costa Rica's
chief access to the Atlantic, although the difficult journey down
the torrential *Serapiquí made it accessible only for the mail
and for individual travelers. [L.H.]

SAN JUAN DEL SUR. A small port on the Pacific coast of Nicaragua.
It was the terminus for the *Transit Route Company's ships
going to California. During the 1856-67 war (*Transit Campaign)
it was the scene of several battles and changed hands several
times. After the surrender, *Walker and his army embarked
at this port.

SAN JUAN RIVER. Half of the troubled northern boundary. See:
FRONTIER QUESTIONS (NICARAGUA).

SAN MATEO. A *canton of *Alajuela Province created August 7,
1868. It consists mostly of broken terrain on the slopes of
*Monte de Aguacate about 25 miles from Alajuela city. Its *cabe-
cera is San Mateo and the total population is 3,783. Some *gold
mining is still carried out in this canton although on a limited
scale (see: MONTES DE AGUACATE). In addition San Mateo
produces *rice, corn, beans, *sugar, and fruits.

SAN MATEO DE CHIRIPO. See: CHACON DE LUNA, Sebastián;
TALAMANCA.

SAN PABLO. A *canton of *Heredia Province, chartered July 18,
1961. Its *cabecera is San Pablo and it has a population of
11,802. *Coffee is the main crop.

SAN PABLO, S.S. A United Fruit Company ship which was tor-
pedoed by a German submarine in Puerto *Limón July 2, 1942,
with about 26 people killed.

SAN RAFAEL. A *canton located about four miles from *Heredia
City. It was founded May 28, 1885, and has a present popula-
tion of 22,871. Its chief crops are *coffee, corn, and hardwoods.
Its *cabecera is San Rafael.

SAN RAMON. City and *canton in *Alajuela Province about 25
miles northwest of Alajuela City. This canton produces *coffee,
potatoes, *tobacco, corn, beans, and *sugar. It prides itself
on having a regional center of the *Universidad de Costa Rica
and on being known as the "city of poets." Recently it has
given the country two presidents (*Orlich Bolamacich and *Figueres Ferrer). The present population of the canton is 39,963
and of the city, 9,624.

SAN VITO. See: COTO BRUS; SOCIEDAD ITALIANA DE
COLONIZACION AGRICOLA.

SANABRIA MARTINEZ, Víctor (1890-1952). Bishop of Costa Rica
1940-52. He studied in Rome where he received a doctorate
in both civil and canon law. In the 1940s he was influential
in securing the passage of the *Social Guarantees and also sponsored the formation of noncommunist *labor unions. He differed
from his predecessors in that he believed that the Church had
to foster temporal as well as spiritual well-being. This attitude
and dedication to *Social Christianity caused some resentment in
the more conservative elements of the Church. In 1943 he gave
Catholics permission to join the *Partido Vanguardia Popular,
which was the Costa Rican Communist Party. By this action
he indirectly helped the *Bloque de la Victoria elect Teodoro
*Picado Michalski president. In addition Sanabria wrote several
volumes on Church history and a multi-volume work on the gene-
alogy of *Cartago, which many people wanted suppressed as
it exposed too many skeletons in the closet. Sanabria was declared *Benemérito de la Patria in 1959. See: SOCIAL GUARAN-
TEES, and consult James Backer, La Iglesia y el sindicalismo en
Costa Rica (1978) and Ricardo Blanco Segura, Monseñor Sanabria
(apuntes biográficos) (1962).

SANCHEZ, Juan Manuel (b. 1907). Sculptor. Considered one
of the so-called *Generation of 1930 sculptors. His style is
somewhat expressionist with geometric overtones. Two of his
most interesting works are: "Amantes" (wood, 1934) and "San
Francisco de Asís" (stone, 1963).

SANCHEZ DE BADAJOZ, Hernán (1489-1546). *Adelantado and captain general of Costa Rica, 1539-41. He came to the New World in 1514 and spent time in Peru where he made his fortune in military campaigns. In 1540 he led an expedition to the *Sixaola River region and also accompanied Martín *Estete in explorations of the *San Juan River region. In that same year he built the fortress of Marabella near the present-day city of Almirante, Panama. The construction of this fortress brought about a bitter controversy with Rodrigo de *Contreras, who claimed that Marabella was located within his territory. Sánchez was ultimately taken to Spain as a prisoner, lost his wealth, and died in jail in Valladolid.

SANCHEZ DE GUIDO, Miguel (b. 1528). Accompanied *Cavallón on his expedition and also served as *alcalde ordinario of *Garcimuñoz. He was also interim governor of Costa Rica in 1564-66. During this period he had to contend with a major *Indian uprising and the tendency of many settlers to abandon the colony.

SANCHO, Alfredo (b. 1924). Mexican playwright and theatrical person who resided in Costa Rica (1950-67). He directed the "Teatro Experimental" (1953) and "El Instituto Nacional de Artes Dramáticas" (1961). He tried to organize a universal type of theatre and teach elemental theatrical techniques. Sancho wrote several plays, most of them touching on biblical themes and contemporary problems. His most important works are: "Débora" (1955), "Taller de reparaciones (se repara seres humanos)" (1956), "Las Alomeónidas" (1961), and "Volumen repartido" (1976). In addition some of his poems were published in Brecha (1958).

SANCHO, Mario (1899-1948). Essayist and social critic. He was a student of Valeriano *Fernández Ferraz and was exiled to Nicaragua during the *Tinoco Granados dictatorship. He spent most of the time until 1930 in the United States where he taught at Simmons College and Brown University. He was always a sharp critic of the faults in Costa Rican society and his most important work remains Costa Rica, Suiza centroamericana (1935), which takes to task many of the myths of Costa Rican democracy.

SANCHO ALVARADO, Féliz (1813-1856). *Alcalde of *Cartago. He was part of the Consultive Council in the government of Braulio *Carrillo Colina. Sancho was also a delegate to the Constituent Assemblies of 1842, 1843-44, 1846-47; *deputy on several occasions; and three times president of Congress.

SANDERS, Edward J. [Lt. Col.]. Filibuster commander in the 1856-57 war. He was second in command to General *Henningsen at San Jorge, February 1857.

SANDOVAL, Gregorio. *Governor 1636-44. Through his efforts the port of *Matina was opened. This brought some prosperity to the colony for a brief period.

SANSA. See: AVIATION.

SANTA ANA. *Canton in *San José Province located about six miles from the capital. The canton was established August 31, 1907. It produces *sugar, *rice, beans, and fruits. Because it has a warmer climate and less rainfall it is a favorite summer place for people from the capital. It is also developing into a favorite spot for *pensionados. Its present population is 19,605. Its *cabecera is Santa Ana.

SANTA ANA CONVENTION, 1921. See: UNIONIST PARTY.

SANTA BARBARA. *Canton located about four miles from *Heredia City. This canton was founded September 29, 1882, and it has a population of 16,643. Its chief products are *sugar, *coffee and cereals. Its *cabecera is Santa Barbara.

SANTA CRUZ. *Canton and city in *Guanacaste Province roughly in the center of the *Nicoya Peninsula. The canton was chartered December 7, 1848, and is a center for agriculture and *cattle ranching. It is a stop en route to several beach resorts. The city was chartered August 31, 1917. The population of the canton is 31,133 and of the city, 12,866.

SANTA ROSA. (1) A ranch located north of *Liberia, Guanacaste. It has been the scene of some important battles. The first battle occurred March 20, 1846, when a force of *filibusters under Colonel Louis *Schlesinger were surprised by a larger force of Costa Rican troops. The battle lasted for 15 minutes and the filibusters were forced to retreat. This battle ended the threat of a filibuster invasion of Costa Rica. Nineteen of the prisoners taken at Santa Rosa were executed five days later in *Liberia. This battle has become a symbol of the national struggle against the forces of William *Walker. See: WALKER, William; and consult Rafael Obregón Loria, La campaña del tránsito (1956).
   (2) In January 1955 Santa Rosa was the site of a skirmish in which a small army of *Calderonista forces were repelled in an attempt to invade the country from Nicaragua.
   (3) In 1968 Santa Rosa was declared a national park, the first national park to be established in the country. It is a beach and lowland forest area.

SANTAMARIA, Juan (1831-1856). An illiterate, mulatto drummer boy from *Alajuela who became a national hero at the Battle of *Rivas (1856). He volunteered to carry a torch through a hail of bullets to set fire to the *Mesón de Guerra, the stronghold of William *Walker's forces. He was killed in this assault but his setting fire to the building ensured the victory for the Central Americans and has made him a national hero. The International Airport is named in his honor.

SANTAMARIA DE DOTA. The *cabecera of the *canton of *Dota. It was important during the 1948 *civil war because it served as the general headquarters of the *Figueres forces. The population is 3,324.

SANTIAGO DE TALAMANCA. A settlement established by Diego de *Sojo in October 1605 on the *Tarire River. Sojo treated the *Indians very harshly and introduced the *encomienda system. This led to an uprising in 1610 in which the settlement was destroyed and most of the population was killed.

SANTO CRISTO DE ESQUIPULAS. A small black statue of Christ in the church of *Alajuelita. This town is the site of a picturesque festival highlighted by a special mass on January 15. This is the pilgrimage date to the cult's primary carved statue in Esquipulas, Guatemala. The carnival continues throughout January with picnics, the sale of intoxicating corn and sugar based drinks, popular dances, and games. See also: ALAJUELITA.

SANTO DOMINGO. *Canton located between the cities of *San José and *Heredia. It was founded September 28, 1861, and the *cabecera is Santo Domingo (de Heredia). This canton has a population of 23,985 and its chief crop is *coffee.

SANTO TOMAS, Casa de Enseñanza. See: CASA DE ENSENANZA DE SANTO TOMAS.

SANTO TOMAS, University of. See: UNIVERSIDAD DE SANTO TOMAS.

SANTOS DE ABREU, Ninfa (b. 1916). Poet, who is one of the group of Costa Rican intellectuals who have lived in voluntary exile in Mexico. She wrote Amor quiere que muera (1949). Some of her poems were published in Repertorio Americano.

SANZ, Rocío. Musician who studied in the National Conservatory in *San José and then in the United States. She lived in Mexico after 1953. Her most important works are: "Dos canciones para coro mixto" (1951), which uses the poems of the Chilean Pablo Neruda and was premiered in Mexico in 1959, and "Tres canciones para soprano y piano" (1959). She has also written incidental music for the Mexican theatre and movies. In 1971 she wrote "Cantata a la Independencia de Costa Rica," for the 150th anniversary of independence, where it also won a prize as an outstanding musical work.

SANZ DEL RIO, Julián (1814-1869). Spanish philosopher who popularized *Krausism (a branch of Positivist philosophy) in Costa Rica.

SAPOA, Revolution of. Costa Rican émigrés residing in Nicaragua

under the leadership of Alfredo *Volio Jiménez and encouraged
by the Nicaraguan President Emiliano Chamorra launched an
invasion (May 5, 1919) to overthrow the *Tinoco Granados dictatorship. They crossed the Sapoá River and attacked the frontier posts of Peñas Blancas, Pocitos, *La Cruz, and Zapote,
but the government's forces carried the day. The importance
of the Revolution of Sapoá is that it helped create the climate
for the eventual downfall of the Tinoco dictatorship and also
created a new future political leadership. Julio *Acosta García
who took over the leadership of the revolution after Alfredo
Volio was killed in combat, became the country's president in
1920 and held an honored political position for the rest of his
life. See also: GARCIA FLAMENCO, Marcelino; VOLIO JIMENEZ,
Jorge; and consult Carlos Monge Alfaro, Historia de Costa Rica
(1966 edition), pp. 273-76.

SAPRISSA, Ricardo. Industrialist of Salvadorean origin whose
family has directed several businesses--wine and cider-making
among them--since c. 1910. The Saprissa team is the "Yankees"
of Costa Rican *soccer, with a large following. [G.K.]

SARAPIQUI. A *canton located in the lowlands of *Heredia Province,
25 miles northeast of Heredia City. Its *cabecera is Puerto
Viejo and it has a population of 18,909. *Braulio Carrillo National Park, a large region of jungle, was created here in 1986.
Before the railroad in the latter 19th century, the region was
one of the difficult routes from the central region to the outside
world. Consult Paulino González Villalobos, Ruta-Sarapiqui; Historia socio-política de un camino (UCR 1976, mimeographed).
[G.K.]

SARCHI. *Cabecera of *Valverde Vega *canton. Its best known
inhabitant is Fructuoso CHAVERRI, q.v.

SARGENTO MAYOR. Not "sergeant major," but a colonial commissioned rank, equivalent to a major. [L.H.]

SARSAPARILLA. Aralia nudicaulis, a native American plant found
in swampy terrain such as Costa Rica's Caribbean coastal lowlands. Its root was highly esteemed in 16th-century Europe
for its supposed medicinal qualities: it was drunk as a tea-
like infusion. Gathering it had to be done in the rainy (i.e.
planting) season, prejudicing the ability of those pressed into
its collection to feed themselves and their families, and thereby
contributing to the populational decline of the aboriginal *Indians.
Root extraction killed the plants, which became increasingly
hard to find. Demand in Europe, however, fell steadily from
the 1620s. By 1650 sarsaparilla had ceased to be a significant
Costa Rican export. [L.H., G.K.]
See also: EXPORTS.

SCHLESINGER, Luis [Colonel] (1820-1900). Born in Hungary. One of the chief military and political aides of William *Walker. In February 1856 Schlesinger was sent on a mission to Costa Rica by Walker, but it failed because the Costa Ricans refused to talk to him. Later, Schlesinger was blamed for the defeat at *Santa Rosa and the killing of several people in an invasion at Salinas (Guanacaste). He was court-martialed by the filibuster commander but escaped and then fought against Walker. At the conclusion of the war he went to Guatemala and spent the rest of his life growing coffee.

SCHMIDT, Stephen B. A New York journalist employed by the *Tico Times, who deliberately challenged the journalist licensing law (see: COLEGIO DE PERIODISTAS), and then appealed his conviction (for practicing unlicensed) to the *Inter-American Commission on Human Rights, where on October 3, 1984 it was upheld 5 votes to 1. The dissenting brief, by U.S. representative R. Bruce McColm, was published as To Licence a Journalist? (Washington: University Press of America, 1986). However the *Inter-American Court of Human Rights did agree unanimously in 1985 that such compulsory licencing of journalists was incompatible with Article 13 of the American Convention on Human Rights. [G.K.; L.H.]

SCHRODER, John. A Norwegian who immigrated to Costa Rica and established a farm in the San Carlos region in the 1860s. He later wrote a Directory of the City of San José which was intended to attract European (mostly German) immigrants. His descendants still live in the country and are important coffee growers.

SCOTTISH RITE MASONS. See: ESCOSESES.

SCULPTURE. Although sculptured pieces exist from pre-Columbian times (*Brunka spherical stones are seen on *San José's plazas) this art form has only recently developed in Costa Rica. The first serious movement in sculpture was in the 1930s with the so-called *Generation of 1930. They tried to rebel against the established academic standards of sculpture and did abstract, impressionist works inspired by local themes. The leaders of this movement were: Juan Rafael *Chacón, Juan Manuel *Sánchez, Francisco *Zúñiga, Néstor *Zeledón Varela, and Max *Jiménez. In the 1960s another important movement in sculpture emerged, called the *Generation of 1960. Its leaders were Néstor *Zeledón Guzmán and Hernán *González. It was an eclectic movement with generally softer less harsh figures. In 1980 another movement started. It consisted mostly of young poeple from *Heredia who had studied in Europe. The leaders of this movement were: Emilio *Argüello, Crisanto *Badilla, Miguel Angel Brenes, Fernando *Calvo, Aquiles *Jiménez, Jorge Jiménez, Mario *Parra, Domingo *Ramos, and Carlomagno *Venegas. This movement has two tendencies: expressionism with exaggeration of forms and the other tendency of stylized, abstract or even oversimplified works. Consult Arnoldo Ferreto, La escultura en Costa Rica, and José Sancho, "La escultura costarricense," Tertulia (Revista nacional de la cultura, Número 7, enero 1982) pp. 5-9.

SECCION DE MUSICA DE LA ESCUELA DE BELLAS ARTES. The Music Section of the School of Fine Arts was founded in 1974 as the musical school of the *Universidad Nacional in *Heredia under the directorship of Patricia *Brockman, a Chilean singer who resided in the country for several years.

SECOND REPUBLIC. A name given by José *Figueres Ferrer to the governmental structure that was created following the 1948 *civil war. Many of the ideas had been developed by the *Centro para el Estudio de Problemas Nacionales (Center for the Study of National Problems). See also: CIVIL WARS, 1948.

SECRETARIAS. See: GOVERNMENT MINISTRIES.

SEGREDA ZAMORA, Vicente (1837-1885). Founded the first night school in *Heredia 1870, served as *deputy 1889-1896. He was an important leader in the liberal movement to secularize the cemeteries and in the expulsion of the *Jesuits.

SEGUA, La. (Also spelled ZEGUA.) A folktale-superstition which says that from time to time a beautiful woman appears on lonely roads to men who have drunk too much. When they approach her she suddenly turns around and has the face of a mare (yegua). A movie has been made based on the play, "La Segua," by Alberto *Cañas Escalante.

SEGUNDO ESTATUTO POLITICO DE COSTA RICA. The Constitution of the country from May 16, 1823 to September 6, 1824.

SEGURA MENDEZ, Manuel (b. 1895). Poet and writer born in *San José. His most important works are: Los pájaros de los poche (1936), Doña Adela (1948, a novel), and an anthology of his works which appeared in La Poesía en Costa Rica (1963).

SENATE. During most of its republican life Costa Rica has had a unicameral legislature with the exceptions of the governments under the Constitutions of 1825, 1844, 1859, 1869, and 1917. See: CAMARA DE SENADORES; CONSEJO REPRESENTATIVO.

SERRABA, Juan. *Talamanca Indian *cacique defeated and executed in 1615. Today respected for his courage. [G.K.]

SERRANO BONILLA, Alfredo (b. 1897). Musician and violinist. In the 1920s he organized the "Cuarteto Serrano," a chamber music group. He lived in New York for ten years. On his return to

Costa Rica in 1940 he helped reorganize the *Orquesta Sinfónica Nacional. After a strike by the musicians and other problems he again left to live in the United States.

SERRANO DE REYNA, Francisco (d. 1712). *Governor of the province of Costa Rica (1698-1704). During his administration there occurred an attack of *Zambo Mosquitos. He was convicted of illegal trading with *pirates, removed from office, and taken to Spain as a prisoner.

SERRANO JIMENEZ, Benito (1850-1945). Occupied many posts in public administration. President of the Supreme Court in 1915.

SERVICIO NACIONAL DE ELECTRICIDAD. Created June 1948 by the revolutionary junta as a governmental institution to oversee the country's water and electric supply. It granted concessions and regulated the distribution and sale of electric energy. It was succeeded in 1949 by the *Instituto Costarricense de Electricidad (ICE).

SERVILES. A group, mostly in Guatemala in the 1820s, who were conservatives and opposed the *liberals. They were generally centralists, supporting Guatemalan domination of Central America and a strong central government. They favored maintaining the Catholic Church's established rights. Gradually they emerged as the stronger party in the Confederation.

SIECA. See: CENTRAL AMERICAN COMMON MARKET.

SIEVEKING, Alejandro (b. 1934). Actor and dramatist. He left Chile in 1973 and later settled in Costa Rica. He was part of the group "El Angel." His most important plays are: "Pequeños animales abatidos" (which won a prize in Cuba in 1975) and "La virgen del puño cerrado" (1976). See also: THEATRE.

SIGATOKA. A disease which began to attack the *banana plants in the 1930s. This was one of the chief reasons why the *United Fruit Company moved its operation from *Limón Province on the Atlantic coast to the *Golfito region of the Pacific coast.

SIGUA. A small pre-Columbian settlement of Mayans in or near *Bagaces (*Guanacaste Province) and in the valley of Guaymí (*Talamanca Province). They were called "Tlalpixtli" or tax collectors during the Aztec Empire of Moctezuma II.

SIQUIRRES. *Canton located in *Limón Province midway between Puerto *Limón and *Turrialba. Its *cabecera is Siquirres City and it was established September 19, 1911. Its present population is 29,079 and the chief products are *bananas, *cacao, and *cattle.

SISAL. See: FIBER.

SISTEMA BANCARIO NACIONAL (SBN). See: NATIONALIZED BANKING SYSTEM.

SIXAOLA RIVER. Boundary at Caribbean end of frontier with Panamá.

SLAVERY. Slavery was probably first introduced with the earliest settlers. It is known to have existed in Villa *Castillo de Austria and *Garcimuñoz. However, this institution never was extensive in Costa Rica, probably because the settlers did not have enough capital to buy Negro slaves. Slaves were freed by the *Central American Federation on April 17, 1824, and by Costa Rican law on May 24, 1824. The number of slaves in Costa Rica at the time of emancipation has been estimated at between 50 and 200.

SMUGGLING. See: DRUGS; FERIAS DE MATINA.

SOCCER (Association Football). Futbol was introduced into Costa Rica from Britain at the beginning of the 20th century, and is now the country's most popular sport. Clubs play a long Sunday season to qualify five for a "pentagonal" leading to the national championship. The April 16, 1989 victory of the Costa Rican national team over that of the United States, one goal to nil, was an occasion for national rejoicing unmatched since a Costa Rican woman swimmer had won a silver medal at the Seoul Olympics. [G.K.; L.H.]
    See also: BRENES MORA, Alberto Manuel; PINTO, Oscar; SAPRISSA, Ricardo.

SOCIAL CHRISTIANITY. A doctrine evolved from the papal encyclical Rerum Novarum and the social code of Malines (Belgium), which said that the government had the right to intervene in the economy to guarantee the workers a fair wage and decent living and housing conditions. This idea was the basis of Jorge *Volio Jiménez's Reformist Party (*Partido Reformista) in 1924-28, and was the stated philosophy of the government of Rafael Angel *Calderón Guardia (1940-44). The progressive legislation of this regime was largely based on this philosophy. See also: CALDERON GUARDIA, Rafael Angel; PARTIDO DEMOCRATA CRISTIANO; PARTIDO REFORMISTA; SANABRIA MARTINEZ, Víctor; SOCIAL GUARANTEES.

SOCIAL GUARANTEES. The amendments to the Constitution of 1871 which were passed in 1943. They comprise articles 51 to 65 of this constitution, as adopted July 2, 1943. They guaranteed, among other things, a minimum wage; an eight-hour day; the right to organize unions and strike; the right of employers to the lock-out collective bargaining; equal wages for the same work between men and women; a special labor court; and the institution of the Social Security System. These reforms, although they had no force in themselves, were enabling acts that allowed Congress to pass legislation. These reforms became the battle cry of the *Calderón government and are still the base of the popular appeal of the National Republican Party (*Partido Republicano Nacional). Consult Oscar Aguilar B., Costa Rica y sus hechos políticos de 1948 (1969); Theodore Creedman, "The Political Development of Costa Rica, 1936-44" (1971).

SOCIAL SECURITY. See: CAJA COSTARRICENSE DE SEGURO SOCIAL.

SOCIEDAD COSTARRICENSE DE SEGUROS DE VIDA. A state enterprise formed in 1909 to sell life insurance. It was the antecedent of the later *Instituto Nacional de Seguros.

SOCIEDAD DE ARTES Y OFICIOS. Founded 1889, it was an early attempt to establish an association of workers.

SOCIEDAD DE ARTESANOS. Possibly the first trade union in Costa Rica. It was established in *Puntarenas in 1916 and lasted only a short time.

SOCIEDAD DE GEOGRAFIA E HISTORIA DE COSTA RICA. An organization founded in 1927 by Luis Demetrio *Tinoco Castro, Hernán *Peralta, Francisco María Núñez, Miguel Obregón Lizano and Fidel *Tristán (among others). It was a precursor of the present *Academia de Geografía e Historia de Costa Rica. They published five issues of a journal, but unfortunately disbanded about a year later.

SOCIEDAD ECONOMICA ITINERARIA. A semi-governmental organization founded November 23, 1843 by the leading *coffee growers. It encouraged construction of roads and the betterment of the coffee industry. Between 1844-46 it contributed to the construction of the Puente de Damas, on the Jesús María River, near *Puntarenas. This society also organized the construction of a road between *San José and *Puntarenas. See: HIGHWAYS. Consult Carolyn Hall, El Café y el desarrollo histórico-geográfico de Costa Rica (1976).

SOCIEDAD ITALIANA DE COLONIZACION AGRICOLA. A contract signed with the government in 1951 that allowed Italian immigration to form an agricultural colony in *San Vito de Java (*canton of *Coto Brus). The project was only moderately successful.

SOJO, Diego de. Spanish conquistador. He founded the settlement of Santiago de *Talamanca in 1605. Sojo treated the *Indians in a harsh manner, imposed the *encomienda system, and inflicted harsh punishments. This provoked a revolt in 1610. Sojo and

many settlers were killed in the uprising and the settlement
was abandoned.

SOLANO, Juan (1538-1615). He came to Costa Rica with Juan de
*Cavallón and was wounded slightly in actions against the *Indian
chief, *Garabito. He later went on expeditions with Juan *Vázquez de Coronado and participated in an attack on the *palenque
of Chief *Coto (or Couto). He led several punitive expeditions
after an uprising against the *Governor *Venegas de los Ríos
in *Talamanca. Solano also served as *regidor of *Garcimuñoz,
royal treasurer, first *alcalde of *Cartago, and as acting *governor
1573-74 and 1578-79.

SOLANO ASTABURUAGA, Francisco (d. 1892). Chilean diplomat
and geographer. He was Chilean chargé d'affaires in 1857 and
helped to secure Chilean help in the war against the *filibusters.
He represented Costa Rica and signed its adherence to the Treaty
of American Union in 1857. He wrote Las repúblicas de Centroamérica (1857), which is a combination travel, history, and impressionist geography.

SOLANO ORFILA, Rodolfo (1929-). He studied economics in the
United States and Brazil and filled several positions in public
administration, such as *deputy 1962-66, and president of the
Assembly 1964-65.

SOLER, Manuel. *Governor of the province of Costa Rica, 1758-60.

SOLEY GUELL, Tomás (1875-1943). Important economist in the
laissez-faire liberal school. Educated in Spain. He filled many
government posts. He wrote Historia económica y hacendaria
de Costa Rica (2 vols., 1947 and 1949), which was published
posthumously and is possibly the best economic history of the
country. He also wrote Historia monetaria de Costa Rica (1926)
and was instrumental in the foundation of the governmental insurance monopoly. See: INSTITUTO NACIONAL DE SEGUROS.

SOLIDARISMO. The doctrine of the *Solidarista movement.

SOLIDARISTA MOVEMENT. A movement popularized in Costa Rica
since 1949 by Alberto *Marten. Its central idea is that workers,
through pension contribution by their employers, should be able
to retire with the same amount of money as the executives, and
to have meanwhile their own capital to invest. It is believed
that this will raise the economic level of the workers and create
a "universal capitalism." This compliant approach is criticized
by more militant unions.

SOLORZANO DE GUARDIA, Emilia (1830-1914). As wife of President
Tomás *Guardia Gutiérrez she used her influence to have the
*death penalty abolished. Solórzano de Guardia was declared

*Benemérita de la Patria in 1972, the first woman to be so honored.

SORIA, Cristóbal Ignacio de. He was a lieutenant on a Spanish frigate in Cuba, *corregidor in Nicaragua, and *governor of Costa Rica 1750-54. During his term of office he had to cope with two raids on *Matina by the *Zambo-Mosquitos. He granted settlers in *Aserrí and Villa Nueva de la Boca del Monte (*San José) charters so they could form their own government. This helped encourage more settlements in the area.

SOTELA, Mariamalia (b. 1945). Poet. Her most important works are: Ciudad de Cáñamo (1974) and Memoria del desencuentro (1981).

SOTELA BONILLA, Rogelio (1894-1943). Poet, lawyer and professor. He served as editor of the intellectual review Atenea and founded a radio station which was called "Radio Atenea." He served as *deputy in the national Congress, *governor of the province of *San José, and was a member of the Real Academia de la Lengua. His most important literary works are: Valores literarios de Costa Rica (1923), La senda de Damasco (1918) and El triunfo del ideal (1914) and Sin literatura (1949). Two historical works are: La doctrina de Monroe desde un punto de vista subjetivo (1921) and Crónicas del centernario de Ayacucho (1927).

SOTO, Hernado de. This famous Spanish explorer was sent by *Pedrarias Dávila to reestablish the latter's authority in Nicaragua and Costa Rica. De Soto fought against Francisco *Fernández de Córdoba, and as a result Fernández de Córdoba was taken prisoner and executed on order of Pedrarias.

SOTO ALFARO, Bernardo (1854-1931). President of the Republic (May 12, 1885 to November 7, 1889) and son-in-law of his predecessor, Próspero *Fernández Oreamuno. Soto began his career as a lawyer and then *governor of his native *Alajuela Province. He also served as minister of finance and was made a brigadier general in 1884. He was elected vice-president, and at the death of Próspero Fernández Oreamuno (May 12, 1885) he was chosen to serve out the unexpired term as acting president. Soto Alfaro was then elected in his own right in 1886. During his administration, there were many important measures taken. The most important were the Ley Fundamental de Instrucción Pública and the Ley General de Educación Común (see: EDUCATION LAWS); the opening of several secondary schools; the foundation of the *National Library and *National Museum; and the formation of the Costa Rican Red Cross. A national lottery was also established to provide funds for the *Chapuí Mental Hospital. The city of *San José was enhanced by the construction of Morazán Park, one of the most alluring in Central America.

Towards the end of his administration there were electoral disturbances when it was feared that he might favor one of the
candidates. On the night of November 7, 1889, farmers and
townspeople converged on the presidential palace with hoes and
pitchforks demanding that he accept the electoral results. He
told the crowd that he would and to reinforce his word, resigned
that night, turning the government to Dr. Carlos *Durán Cartim.
This action, although it did not ensure free elections, nevertheless set an idea and example of what the country aspired to
achieve. Democracy is sometimes dated to this event. Soto
was declared *Benemérito de la Patria.

SOTO ALFARO, José María. Unsuccessful candidate in the presidential election of 1919, supported by the Partido Democrata.

SOTO BORBON, Enrique. See: ISTARU, León.

SOTO QUESADA, Apolinar de Jesús [General] (1827-1911). Merchant, soldier, *coffee grower, and acting president of the
Republic November 6 to December 4, 1886, July 7 to August 13,
1887, and November 2, 1888 to March 15, 1889. He fought against
William *Walker and was in the army most of his life. He is
said to be the first man to plant coffee in *Alajuela Province.
In addition he was governor of Alajuela Province and served
as a member of Congress.

SPAN, Emilio (1869-1944). Realist painter born in Germany. He
came to Costa Rica in 1906 and taught in the *Escuela Nacional
de Bellas Artes and had an important influence on the local
art scene. His style was a combination of naturalism and baroque.
Most of his paintings are of flowers, landscapes, or local scenes.

SPANISH. The official language of the Republic, and, except for
a tenuous survival of Jamaican *creole ENGLISH (q.v.) among
older *Blacks in the *Limón area, the universal vernacular.
Historically considered, Costa Rican Spanish occupies an inter-
mediate position between the conservative Spanish of the high
Andes (Bogotá, Peru, Bolivia) and the more innovative lowlands
(Panama, Cuba and the Caribbean coast of South America).
Yeísmo (y for ll) is universal, with some tendency to palataliza-
tion, but the pronunciation of final s is clear and tense. As
in other Central American countries, j is weakened to a sound
like an English h, intervocal y almost disappears, and final n
is velar (like an English ng). A peculiarity that Costa Rica
shares only with Guatemala is a strong, sibilant rr (and final
r) pronounced with the tongue high against the upper tooth
roots. Unique to Costa Rica is the way e, i, o and u become
consonantal immediately before a stressed vowel, so that only
the r distinguishes puerta from poeta. Costa Rica is traditionally a region of voseo (i.e. vos for tu), but the egalitarian nature of Costa Rican society means that the social
range of usted is much greater than in many other Hispanic

countries. Consult the section on Costa Rica (pp. 87-93)
in Rafael Angel Rivas D. et al., Bibliografía sobre el
español del Carbe hispánico. Caracas: Instituto Universitario Pedagógico de Caracas, 1985. [L.H.]
See also: PACHUCO; TICO.

SPENCER, Sylvanus [Captain]. American sailor sent by Cornelius
Vanderbilt to help reclaim the *transit route (vía del Tránsito)
from William *Walker. Captain Spencer helped plan the San
Juan River campaign and fought with Costa Rican troops at
La Trinidad and at the capture of Fort *San Carlos. He was
relieved of his command (January 8, 1857) because of a dispute
over the deposition of ships captured in the campaign. Spencer
wanted the ships returned to the transit company. His object
in helping the Costa Ricans was to secure the transit route
for Vanderbilt's company.

SPORTS. Twentieth-century life facilitates public recreation.
*Baseball is played but hasn't flourished as much as in Nicaragua
or elsewhere around the Caribbean. *Soccer is the primary
sport. A female swimmer won three gold medals among Costa
Rica's ten medals in all at the 10th Pan American Games in 1987;
only a bronze in soccer during the first games in 1951 was previously won. Among traditional pastimes, cock-fighting was
outlawed in 1922, though it still exists; *Tico-style bullfights
by law tease but do not kill the animal. See: BRENES MORA,
Alberto Manuel; GARNIER U., Eduardo; MAYNARD, Worth; PINTO,
Oscar; STAHL, Juan F.; Consult Agustín Salas, Historia del
deporte en Costa Rica (1951). [G.K.]

SQUIER, Ephraim George (1821-1888). American diplomat accredited
to Costa Rica and Nicaragua (1849). Squier opposed *Chatfield's
machinations and represented American interests. He was a
negotiator of the *Clayton-Bulwer Treaty (1850) and seemed
to favor Nicaragua over Costa Rica in the *frontier question.
In addition Squier wrote several works on Central America,
the most important being Notes on Central America (1855), and
The States of Central America (1858 and 1870). See also: CHAT-
FIELD, Frederick; and consult Charles L. Stansifer, The Central
American Career of E. George Squier (1959).

STAHL, Juan F. Born in Puerto Rico. Stahl lived in Costa Rica
(1912-1921). He organized baseball leagues and is called the
father of Costa Rican baseball.

STANDARD FRUIT COMPANY. A large United States-owned company
(since 1964 part of Castle and Cooke). It started operations in
Costa Rica in the 1950s and has largely concentrated its efforts
in the Estrella Valley of *Limón Province, after the United Fruit
Company had withdrawn from the Atlantic coast. It is now re-
ducing operations because of high operating costs. It also owns
some railroad trackage.

STANLEY, Rodolfo (b. 1950). An *Arte Nuevo artist, who specializes in oils. He has had his works shown in Central America and in the United States. In 1982 he was co-winner of the *Ancora Prize for plastic arts.

STATUTE OF NEUTRALITY. See: NEUTRALIDAD, Estatuto de.

STEPHENS, John Lloyd (1805-1852). Lawyer born in Trenton, New Jersey. He came to Central America in 1839 to study pre-Columbian civilizations and also to undertake a diplomatic mission for Martin Van Buren. He wrote Incidents of Travel in Central America, Chiapas, and Yucatan (1841). In the U.S. Stephens was active in politics and wrote similar books on the Middle East and Eastern Europe. He helped organize finance of the *railroad across Panama, which reduced Costa Rica's isolation (via steamboat) when it opened in 1855.

STORK-WORTH, Juan Gaspar (1856-1920). Bishop of Costa Rica (1904-20). Born in Cologne, Germany, he was educated in France, and came to Costa Rica in 1893. He taught in the seminary in *San José until named bishop in 1904, a position he held for the rest of his life. He was conservative and sought to keep the status quo as much as possible.

STRIKE OF THE ITALIANS. When Minor C. Keith built the Atlantic Railroad (*Ferrocarril de Norte) he brought some workers from Italy who found the conditions intolerable. They went on strike in 1888. Some of them went back to Italy, others stayed and founded families in Costa Rica.

STRIKES. See: BANANA STRIKE; HUELGA DE BRAZOS CAIDOS; SOCIAL GUARANTEES.

SUBURBANIZATION. Since the early 1960s, the *cantons of *Desamparados, *Goicochea, *Curridabat, *Escazú, *Moravia, and *Tibás have grown at a faster rate than the central canton of *San José. From 1963 to 1973 San José grew 2.4%, whereas the surrounding cantons had a much higher rate. Most dramatic growth were: Escazú 5.6%, Desamparados 7.8%, Curridabat 4.9%. This process continues, but as late as 1977 the urban population of the country was still only 44.4%. But the rural areas are steadily losing population.

SUERRE. (1) The name of the *Reventazón River in the early part of the colonial period. It was discovered by Martin *Estete in 1529.
(2) The name of a small colonial port situated at the confluence of the Reventazón and Pacuare rivers. It fell into disuse after 1630 because of the opening of *Matina. Suerre was opened again in 1651, but after the establishment of Portete (*Limón) as a major port it declined again in importance.

SUGAR. Sugar was brought to America by *Columbus in 1493 on his second voyage. It was introduced into Costa Rica sometime in the sixteenth century. The first crude sugar mill was established in 1565, but there was little sugar raised at that time. As late as 1632 there were reported to be no sugar mills (*trapiches) in the country. Sugar began to be produced in increased quantity in the beginning of the nineteenth century. It received protection of the State in 1833, but was always subordinate to *coffee. In 1910 sugar was given some tax concessions. The Junta de Producción de la Agricultura Cañera (Committee for the Production of Sugarcane Agriculture) was established in 1940 to protect growers and increase exportation. In 1959 Costa Rica entered the International Sugar Convention and received a quota to sell sugar in the United States. In 1982 Costa Rica exported 54,766,000 kilograms of sugar valued at $14,654,000, and in 1986 $17,600,000 worth.

SUKIA. (1) A medicine man.
(2) Statues made of stone or gold which were replicas of different gods. Usually the *Brunkas and the *Huetar sukias are made of gold, whereas the *Chorotega are stone.

SUPERINTENDENCIA DE INDIAS. See: RODRIGUEZ DE FONSECA, Juan.

SURCO. The monthly publication of the *Centro para el Estudio de Problemas Nacionales. Published between 1940 and 1945. It is important because most of the ideas of the founders of the National Liberation Party (*Partido Liberación Nacional) are discussed in this publication.

- T -

TACA (Transportes Aéreos Centroamericanos). Pioneer Central American airline founded in 1932 by New Zealander Lowell Yerex in Honduras. In 1940 Yerex acquired *ENTA, which thereby became the Compañía de TACA de Costa Rica, and he also acquired *Aerovías Nacionales de Costa Rica. In October 1940 Yerex's attempt to sell the whole TACA concern out to American Export Lines for $2,000,000 was blocked by a legal maneuver by Pan American Airways. In 1952 TACA de Costa Rica was acquired by *LACSA. [L.H.]
See also: AVIATION.

TAFT DECISION, 1923. United States Chief Justice William Howard Taft arbitrated a dispute between Costa Rica and the *United Kingdom, over a loan made to the *Tinoco Granados government by the Royal Bank of Canada, and an oil concession to a Costa Rican subsidiary of British-owned J. M. Amory and Son. Upholding the LEY DE NULIDAD (q.v.), he declared the Tinoco regime to have been illegal in international law, and its contracts therefore void. [L.H.]

TALAMANCA. A mountainous jungle region in the southeastern part of the country which borders on Panama, said to have *petroleum deposits. During colonial times it was the scene of almost constant strife caused by the rugged terrain and the *Indians' fierce opposition to Spanish conquest. The first expeditions to touch on this area were Diego de *Gutiérrez in 1543-44 and *Estrada Rávago in 1560. Juan *Vázquez de Coronado passed through this region in 1564 and one of his lieutenants, Diego *Caro de Mesa, panned some *gold in the Chinguinola River. This gave the region false fame for being rich in gold. (See: MINAS DE TISINGAL.)

*Perafán de Ribera led an expedition to this region in 1570 and tried to start a settlement on the Estrella River. When he arrived he discovered that the Indians had fled, burning everything; therefore he had to abandon the enterprise. There were some Spanish attempts to penetrate the fringes of the region in 1574, 1577, and 1601 but it was not until 1605 that the first real efforts to establish a settlement were made. In that year *Governor *Ocón y Trillo sent Diego de *Sojo to found the city of *Santiago de Talamanca. Sojo treated the Indians harshly, imposing the *encomienda system, and finally provoked an uprising in 1610. Because of this the city of Santiago had to be abandoned. The following year Sojo tried to reconquer the area but failed. In 1619 Governor *Castillo y Guzmán sent some soldiers to Talamanca and brought back 400 Indians to do menial work in *Cartago. In 1662 Rodrigo *Arias Maldonado tried to establish a settlement in this region but also failed.

In 1689 two priests, Antonio Margil and Melchor López, entered the area and baptized many Indians. However, for many years a fort established in the *Chiripó region was considered the boundary between *Cartago and Talamanca. In 1709 the Indians rose up against the missionaries and killed fathers Pablo de *Rebullida and Antonio de *Zamora. This revolt was started by Chief Pablo *Presbere who mistakenly thought a soldier he saw writing a letter was asking that more troops be sent to the region. As a result of the revolt a punitive expedition was sent. Some Indians were executed, among them Chief Pablo Presbere. Others were brought back to Cartago and forced to work in encomiendas.

There were short-lived settlements established in 1742 by two priests, Antonio de *Andrade and José Vela, and in 1761 the Indians revolted on Palm Sunday and burned the Convent of San Francisco de Térraba. Talamanca remained largely isolated until the end of the colonial period, when gradually some small Spanish settlements were established. Even today it is little explored and is largely populated by a few thousand Indians of the *Bribri and *Cabecar tribes living in scattered communities, making a meager living by selling *cacao and livestock.

TALAMANCA (canton). A *canton in *Limón Province established
May 20, 1969; its *cabecera is Bratsi. It is largely mountainous
region populated chiefly by *Indians and some *Blacks. This
canton is largely an Indian reserve. The non-Indians live along
the coastal section. Its chief crop is *cacao and its population
is 11,013.

TAPA DE DULCE. Crude brown sugar cake, in Costa Rica, usually
conical and weighing from one half to two and one half pounds.
In addition to being used as a sweetener it is also used as a
beverage called agua dulce (sweet water).

TAPARRABO. A small cloth garment worn by Indian men in pre-
Columbian times.

TARIACAS. A tribe of Indians of Caribe origin, also called Cariacas. They cordially received *Columbus when he first came
to Costa Rica on his fourth voyage in 1502.

TARIRE. Original name for the *Sixaola River.

TARRAZU. *Canton in *San José Province. Its *cabecera is San
Marcos located about 25 miles from the city of San José. The
canton was chartered August 7, 1868, has a population of 8,845
and produces coffee, hardwoods and dairy cattle.

TAXES. See (colonial): ALMOJARIFAZGO; BULA DE LA CRUZADA;
MEDIA ANNATA; PLATA QUINTADA; TITHES; TRIBUTOS; (mod-
ern): ENTERTAINMENT TAX; GASOLINE MONOPOLY; INCOME
TAX; SALES TAX.

TEATRO GRUPO. A fledgling company operating in 1969 which
served as a theatre of protest and was one of the precursors
of the National Theatre Company (*Compañía Nacional de Teatro).

TEATRO MELICO SALAZAR. Named after Manuel SALAZAR, q.v.

TEATRO MORA. This was the first real theatre built in Costa
Rica. It was opened November 1850 and named for the then
President Juan Rafael *Mora Porras, who gave the project his
support. The opening of the theatre provoked an outcry by
the clergy who considered it prejudicial to public morality. After the overthrow of Mora the name was changed to the Teatro
Municipal and was used until 1988 when it burned down. Consult Fernando Borges, Teatros en Costa Rica (1941).

TEATRO MUNICIPAL. See: TEATRO MORA.

TEATRO NACIONAL. Considered the most beautiful theatre in
Central America, it was constructed in various styles, mostly
Baroque-Rococo. It was built in imitation of the "Teatre Comique"

in Paris. Its construction was begun in 1890 and financed by a
20-centavo tax on each 100 pounds of coffee exported from the
country. It was formally dedicated by President Rafael *Yglesias
October 20, 1897, and was said to have cost over two million
colones. Above the luxurious main floor, "gallinero" ('chicken-
coop') seating was provided for cheaper admission. Although
it was opened as a theatre, it was used mostly for dances by
the *San José aristocracy until this practice was halted in the
1940s. It is now used exclusively as a theatre and is frequently
host to various types of international touring companies as well
as to an increasing number of national companies. The National
Theatre receives fifty percent of funds raised from a six percent
*entertainment tax. See also: YGLESIAS CASTRO, Rafael;
and consult Alfonso Ulloa Zamora, El teatro nacional.

TEATRO RAVENTOS. See: SALAZAR, Manuel.

TEATRO VARIEDADES. The second theatre built in San José.
It was opened in 1891 and is still used today as a motion picture
theatre.

TEJAR, El. Small town on the outskirts of *Cartago City in the
*canton of *Guarco with a population of 11,158. On April 13,
1948, it was the scene of the most severe battle of the 1948
*civil war. The battle was won by the insurgent forces of José
*Figueres Ferrer and thus assured him domination of the Cartago
region. This battle was said to have convinced President *Picado
Michalski that he could not win the war. It is also claimed that
190 of the government forces and 14 of the insurgent troops
were killed, thus making El Tejar the bloodiest battle in the
country's history.

TELEPHONES. The first contract for telephone service was signed
in 1897 with the Compañía de Teléfonos de Costa Rica. A modern direct-dialing, long-distance system was installed by the
Erickson Company of Sweden in 1966. It is run by the *Instituto Costarricense de Electricidad (ICE), a government agency.

TELEVISION. After a proposal by President *Figueres Ferrer to
establish a nationalized television service had been frustrated
by the Supreme Court, Costa Rica's first TV station, Televisora
de Costa Rica, part-owned by the American Broadcasting Company,
began operating in May 1960. There were 25,000 sets in 1965,
122,000 in 1973, and 183,000 in 1983. By then television was
reaching 90% of households in San José and environs, but the
northern third of the country could only receive transmissions
from Nicaragua. Color television was introduced in 1969. The
high proportion of foreign material used has led to protests
that the service is imposing United States and Mexican cultural
values, particularly through the extremely popular Mexican
telenovelas (soap operas). A public educational service began
in 1978. [L.H.]

TEMPISQUE. River in *Guanacaste Province flowing into the Gulf
of Nicoya. See: PALO VERDE; ZAPANDI. [G.K.]

TERRABA. (1) An Indian group inhabiting, at the time of the
Spanish conquest, the Caribbean shore of western Panama and
eastern Costa Rica.
   (2) The plains along the Rio Grande de Térraba (also
called the Rio Diquís), a river formed south-east of *Buenos
Aires by the confluence of the rivers General and Brus, and
flowing past El Palamar Sur and Puerto Cortés into Coronado
Bay.
   (3) A small village on the banks of the Rio General.
   (4) The Rio Grande de Térraba itself.
   See also: BRUNKAS.

TERRITORIAL DIVISION. The first formal geographical division
in Costa Rica was in 1848. The country was divided into provinces, *cantons, *distritos, and barrios. There were five original
provinces: *San José, *Alajuela, *Cartago, *Heredia, and *Guanacaste. Before being made into provinces, *Puntarenas and *Limón
were called comarcas. There are now 7 provinces, 81 cantons,
and over 400 districts in the country.

TERRITORIAL EXTENSION. After Costa Rica's boundary with
Nicaragua had been established in 1858 (see: FRONTIER QUES-
TIONS, NICARAGUA), the country had an area of 51,760 square
kilometers (20,704 square miles): a fifth more than the Switzerland to which it has so often been compared, or about the same
as West Virginia. But loss of territory to Panama (definitively
conceded in 1941; see: FRONTIER QUESTIONS, SOUTH) reduced
the area to its present 51,011 square kilometers (19,695 square
miles). It stretches 484 km. from NW to SE, with a maximum
width of 274 k., and a minimum of 119 km. The only noteworthy
island is COCOS ISLAND, q.v. [L.H.]

TERTULIA, La. The second newspaper published in the country,
beginning in 1834.

THEATRE. The theatre in Costa Rica has been rudimentary until
recently. The first production supposedly took place in the
garden of the *governor's house. From then on there were
occasional theatrical productions. The first theatre built in
San José was the *Teatro Mora in 1850. Organized theatre companies were sporadic and short lived. The *Teatro Nacional
was built in the 1890s. Most of its productions were by visiting
companies, mostly of Italian opera or Spanish zarzuela (Spanish
operetta). During the two world wars some of the leading solo-
ists appeared in the Teatro Nacional. The first attempt to write
local plays began at the beginning of this century with Ricardo
*Fernández Guardia's "Magdalena." Among the first pioneers
in Costa Rican playwriting are Carlos *Gagini, Carlos Orozco,

and Eduardo Casamiglia. The first real theatre company was the Compañía Lope de Vega organized under José Tamayo in the 1860s. It was formed by a group of Spanish actors stranded for lack of funds. At about this time the Teatro Universitario was founded under the Italian director Lucio Ranucci. Ranucci was also important in founding another company, Teatro Las Máscaras, the first privately established local company. They performed works by Sartre, Anouilh, and other contemporaries. With the arrival of Jean Moulaert, theatre productions began to be more professional. This company did plays by such authors as Ionesco and Ugo Betti. During this period some local play-wrights emerged and began to have their works performed. The most important of these were Daniel *Gallegos, Samuel *Rovinski, and Alberto *Cañas Escalante. In the 1970s the arrival of the Catania family from Argentina helped to improve further the theatre. This practically coincided with the University of Costa Rica's establishing the Facultad de Artes Dramá-ticas, and under the guidance of the new Ministry of Culture the Compañía Nacional de Teatro was formed. The latest influ-ence and stimulus fór Costa Rican theatre was from a group of South Americans, mostly Chilean political refugees who came to Costa Rica in the mid and late 1970s. There are about a half dozen theatre companies operating in the country, and at times there are international theatre festivals. See also: Guido Fernández, Los caminos del teatro en Costa Rica (1977) and the various issues of Escena (a local theatre magazine).

THIEL, Bernardo Augusto (1850-1901). Born in Eberfield, Germany, he came to Costa Rica in 1877. He was a leader of the anti-liberal forces and was appointed bishop of Costa Rica in 1880. Bishop Thiel led an attack on the *liberal laws of 1884 and as a result was expelled from the country, but he was allowed to come back in 1886. Thiel strongly supported the Catholic Union Party (*Partido Unión Católica). He traveled to many remote parts of the country, one of the few high churchmen to do this. He wrote several volumes on the history of the Church in Costa Rica and on the indigenous populations. He was declared *Benemérito de la Patria in 1921. See: Víctor Sanabria, Bernardo Thiel, segundo obispo de Costa Rica: Apuntamientos Históricos (1941).

THIERRIAT, Charles. See: GENIE, Le.

TIANGUEZ. (1) A *Chorotega marketplace where business was conducted by the barter system.
    (2) Sometimes this expression is used today to refer to any open-air market.

TIAR. See: TRATADO INTERAMERICANO DE ASISTENCIA RECIPROCA.

TIBAS. *Canton created July 27, 1914, and located about two miles from *San José. At one time it served as the capital of the country. Today Tibás is largely a bedroom community for the capital, but it does produce *coffee, truck farming crops, and flowers. Its *cabecera is San Juan and it has a population of 57,693. The central section of this canton was known as el Llano de Murciélago, and in 1835 President Braulio *Carrillo Colina declared it the capital of the country. However, this project was forgotten in the same year during the *Civil War of the League.

TICO. A nickname applied to the Costa Ricans. Supposedly it comes from the use of the diminutive tico that they add to words, like "un momentico" instead of the standard "un momentito" (a little moment).

TICO TIMES, The. English language newspaper established by the Dyer family in 1956. More than half its circulation is airmailed abroad, particularly to occasional visitors to Costa Rica. Long active in promoting charity and community service, the Tico Times became important by 1980 in regional reporting. One of its reporters was killed in 1984 at La *Penca. The paper has taken a case to the Interamerican Court of *Human Rights over a Costa Rican law requiring licensing of journalists (see: SCHMIDT, Stephen B.). It claims continual harassment by the COLEGIO DE PERIODISTAS (q.v.) going back twenty years, even though Colegio officials admit to being unable to supply the newspaper with qualified journalists.
  Until recently the Tico Times was published on Tuesdays (with a circulation of 2,500 copies) and on Fridays (6,500 copies), but it is now a weekly. [G.K., L.H.]

TIERRA ADENTRO. The name generally applied to the unconquered regions of *Talamanca during colonial times.

TILARAN. *Canton and city in *Guanacaste, located on the western side of the cordillera about ten miles from the city of *Cañas. Tilarán was formed August 21, 1923, and is a center of *coffee, *cattle, and some cereal production. *Gold was mined in the area during the nineteenth century. During the 1980s a refugee camp for Salvadorans was located here. Its population is 14,586.

TIMBER. See: FORESTS AND FORESTRY.

TIME ZONE. Costa Rica is on Central Time: six hours behind Greenwich Mean Time, one hour behind Panama. Being in the tropics, it has no summer daylight saving time.

TINOCO GRANADOS, Federico [General] (1870-1931). President, January 1917 to August 1919. As secretary of war in the cabinet

of Alfredo *González Flores he disapproved of a proposed *income
tax and the refusal of the President to sign some *petroleum
contracts. Tinoco overthrew President González January 27,
1917, and established himself in the presidency. At first he
was popular with the people, but discontent grew and there
was a series of revolts (see: SAPOA; ACOSTA GARCIA, Julio).
His brother José Joaquín, the minister of war, was assassinated
and Tinoco, convinced by the diplomatic corps that his government would fall, resigned August 12, 1919, and left the country.
He died in exile in Paris.

The Tinoco regime had failed to achieve international recognition. This provided the successor government with grounds
to repudiate Tinoco government contracts, notably those with
the Royal Bank of Canada (a loan to the government of ₡998,000)
and the Delaware-registered, but British-owned, firm of J. M.
*Amory and Son (oilfield exploration concessions to its subsidiary
the Central Costa Rica Petroleum Company). The resultant
protest by the United Kingdom government (then still responsible
for Canada's external affairs) led to arbitration by the United
States (see: TAFT DECISION). [T.C., L.H.]

TINOCO IGLESIAS, Federico (1840-1915). Vice-president of the
Republic, *deputy on various occasions, and president of the
Congress, 1905-08.

TIRIBI. A dialect of Térraba, spoken by Térraba Indians. Also
a small river south of the capital.

TISINGAL MINES. See: MINAS DE TISINGAL.

TITHES (Diezmos). The Biblical ten percent tax on agricultural
income to support the Church was universal in medieval Europe.
The close relationship between Church and State in Spain (see:
PATRONATO) resulted in its being collected by the secular
authorities. *Indians were exempt until 1565 and again after
1802. In 1815 the bishop of Nicaragua and Costa Rica decreed
excommunication for those who failed to pay. The diezmos were
abolished by President Braulio *Carrillo Colina, creating a serious
problem in Church-State relations.

TOBACCO. Native American plant. It was grown during colonial
times chiefly in the Aserrí, Tiribí, and Varilla valleys. The
cultivation of this plant was responsible for the growth of *San
José in the late colonial period. In 1787 Costa Rica was granted
a monopoly (*estanco) on the sale of tobacco in the *Kingdom
of Guatemala, partially to help raise its poor standard of living.
But its quality was so bad that the monopoly was abolished in
1792. During various times in the nineteenth century the government reimposed the unpopular tobacco monopoly. It was finally
abolished by President Jesus de Jiménez Zamora. Today tobacco
is grown commercially around *Palmares (*Alajuela Province)
and near *Puriscal in *San José Province.

TOLEDO MURGA, Nazario (1821-1887). Physician born in Guatemala. He came to Costa Rica in 1836 and served as rector of the *Universidad de Santo Tomas, 1850-59, president of the Constituent Assemblies of 1838 and 1846-47, and *deputy, 1849-58. He was a minister in the government of Juan Rafael *Mora Porras and after Mora's overthrow went back to Guatemala. He did much to introduce *positivism into Costa Rica when he taught philosophy at Santo Tomás. He also represented Costa Rica in Chile where he helped secure a loan in 1856 and served as Costa Rican ambassador to Guatemala, one of the first ambassadors that Costa Rica sent to another Central American country.

TOMA DE LIMON. The taking of Puerto *Limón during the 1948 *civil war by the *Figueres Ferrer forces. In this operation the so-called *Caribbean Legion distinguished itself.

TORRES, Río. One of the rivers running through *San José. Named after Margarita Torres, daughter of Salvador Torres, a large land holder in Mata Redonda (original site of San José).

TORTUGUERO. National Park along Atlantic coast. Famed as the nesting area of the giant green sea turtle. Tourist excursions go to this remote area along a natural canal of the same name. [G.K.]

TOYOPAN, Altar of. A type of pre-Columbian altar found in San Isidro de Coronado and also in *Heredia. They are about 89 centimeters long and contain carvings of the god of rain and an alligator. This is supposed to signify the world and a serpent, symbols popular with the *Huétares.

TRABAJO. Weekly newspaper published by the Costa Rican Communist Party (*Partido Comunista) from July 14, 1931, until the 1948 civil war. After the war it was superseded by another newspaper, Libertad.

TRADE UNIONS. See: LABOR UNIONS.

TRAFFIC ACCIDENTS. See: HIGHWAY ACCIDENTS.

TRAMS (tranvías). See: PUBLIC TRANSPORT.

TRANSIT CAMPAIGN. See: CAMPANA DEL TRANSITO.

TRANSIT ROUTE (Vía del Tránsito). The route across the Central American isthmus used prior to the opening of the Panama Canal. This route consisted of water travel up the *San Juan River, a boat trip across Lake Nicaragua, and then a portage across the isthmus of *Rivas to the port of *San Juan del Sur. The discovery of gold in California made this route lucrative and intensified the border dispute between Nicaragua and Costa Rica. [See: FRONTIER QUESTIONS (NICARAGUA).] The

American financier Cornelius Vanderbilt secured concessions from Nicaragua and set up a profitable Transit Company, but the operation became menaced by the appearance of William *Walker and his *filibusters. Vanderbilt, to secure his interests, encouraged Costa Rican President Juan Rafael *Mora Porras to declare war on Walker. Costa Rica was eventually joined by other Central American forces. In a war which lasted two years (1856-57), Walker's forces were expelled from Central America (see: CAMPANA DEL TRANSITO). After the war both Costa Rica and Nicaragua were guaranteed free navigation of the San Juan River. Since the opening of the Panama Canal this route has lost its importance, but there is still talk about constructing a sea level canal along this route. For more details consult Manuel María Alfaro, El Río San Juan de Nicaragua (derechos históricos de sus ribereños) (1882); Carlos Meléndez, Dr. José Mara Montealegre (1968); Rafael Obregón Loria, La Campaña del Tránsito (1956); and Armando Rodríguez, Juan Rafael Mora Porras y la guerra contra los filibusteros (1955); William O. Scroggs, Filibusters and Financiers (1916); Paul Woodbridge, Los contratos Webster-Mora (1968).

TRAPICHE. Mechanism on a farm where sugarcane juice is extracted and made into crude *sugar. See also: TAPA DE DULCE.

TRATADO DE CANAL INTEROCEANICO (1870). The treaty which gave Costa Rica the same rights as Nicaragua in dealing with the French, who at the time had concessions to build a canal along the San Juan route.

TRATADO INTERAMERICANO DE ASISTENCIA RECIPROCA (TIAR). The Rio Pact of 1949, the inter-American security alliance which pro-Western Costa Rica signed just after abolishing its army and to which it continues to adhere despite its declared *neutralidad. [G.K.]

TREATIES OF CENTRAL AMERICAN INTEGRATION. A series of treaties signed in 1963 which established the Central American Common Market (see: MERCOMUN).

TREJO, Diego de [Captain] (b. 1538). He came to Nicaragua in 1560 and then accompanied *Cavallón in his explorations. He was one of the leaders of the expedition that discovered the Estrella River in 1564 (see: MINAS DE TISINGAL). He also served in such posts as *alcalde ordinario, chief justice of *Cartago in 1567, and lieutenant governor. See also: CARO DE MESA, Diego; and consult José Francisco Trejos, Los conquistadores.

TREJOS, Eladio. Founder of the PARTIDO DEMOCRATA (q.v.), 1941.

TREJOS, Gerardo. Lawyer and professor of law, dean of the law faculty of the *Universidad Autónoma de Centroamérica. Founder of the Editora Juriscentro. He has written several treatises dealing with family, divorce, and adoption laws.

TREJOS, Juan de Dios (1853-1912). A leader of conservative Catholic opinion who, through various newspaper polemics with such persons as Mauro *Fernández Acuña and the Nicaraguan poet Rubén Darío, helped mold public opinion and establish the tradition of discussing public issues in the newspapers.

TREJOS ESCALANTE, Fernando. See: PARTIDO UNIFICACION NACIONAL.

TREJOS FERNANDEZ, José Joaquín (b. 1916). Economics professor and president of the Republic 1966-70. With little previous political experience he was elected by the newly organized National Unification Party (*Partido Unificación Nacional). He conducted a generally conservative administration, trying to reduce spending, increasing taxes, establishing the country's first *sales tax, and entering into a general Central American Common Market (see: MERCOMUN) agreement to put a surtax on imported goods. During the Trejos administration Congress chartered the *Banco Popular y de Desarrollo Comunal. A proposed contract to give ALCOA (*Aluminum Company of America) strip mining concessions in the *canton of *Pérez Zeledón sparked disorders. There was also some persecution of hippies. Trejos prides himself most on his financial successes.

TREJOS GUTIERREZ, José Gregorio (1830-1903). Lawyer. He held various judgeships in the lower courts. He was president of the Constituent Assembly in 1870 and a member of the Constituent Assembly of 1880. Trejos served for a while as rector of the *Universidad de Santo Tomás and was president of the Supreme Court in 1868.

TREJOS QUIROS, Juan (1884-1970). Lawyer, book dealer, and academic writer. Founder of the Librería Trejos. He served as delegate to the Constituent Assembly and as Secretary of the Academia Costarricense de la Lengua. He opposed government intervention in business and always defended traditional ways. His most important works are: Resumen de psicología, Cuestiones de psicología racional, Principios de economía política, Los principales problemas económicos que tiene planteados el país.

TREVITHICK, Richard (1771-1833). English engineer. The son of a Cornish mine manager, his work on improving mine pumping engines led to his inventing the high-pressure steam engine (1800) and the steam railroad locomotive (1804). In 1816 he emigrated to Peru to superintend the silver mines at Cerro de Pasco. He made a fortune but lost everything in the fighting there and moved to Costa Rica to prospect for minerals. He had a contract with the government to buy mercury from the mines of *Monte de Aguacate. In 1822-1827 he proposed building a railroad across the country to link the Caribbean with the Pacific, but nothing came of it. When there was a threat of a Spanish invasion, he helped secure 600 rifles from Peru. His fortunes failed to prosper and he arrived back in Falmouth, England, penniless in October 1827. [T.C., L.H.]

TREXO, Diego de. See: TREJO, Diego de.

TRIBUNA, La. The newspaper published by José María Pinaud which during the 1940s served as the semi-official spokesman for the *Calderón-*Picado governments. It ceased publication when its presses were damaged during the *civil war of 1948.

TRIBUNAL DE RESIDENCIA A judicial body which functioned under the *Pacto de Concordia to judge infractions of the constitution, principally by public officials. It was seemingly copied from the colonial Juicio de *Residencia.

TRIBUNAL OF ADMINISTRATIVE PROPERTY. A special court created in 1948 by the revolutionary *Junta Fundadora de la Segunda República to prosecute people suspected of illegal income during the *Calderón-*Picado era. It operated outside of the regular legal system and there was no right of appeal.

TRIBUNAL OF CENTRAL AMERICAN ARBITRATION. In 1902 President José Santos Zelaya of Nicaragua invited the rest of the presidents of Central America to a meeting in Corinto, Nicaragua, to talk about international boundary questions. Out of this meeting, in which all the Isthmian chief executives participated save that of Guatemala, came the Pact of *Corinto. It established the Tribunal of Central American Arbitration which was supposed to provide a mechanism for settling disputes between countries. Its structure was modified in conferences in San Salvador (1903) and in Corinto (Nicaragua, 1904). It was replaced by the Central American Court (*Corte de Justicia Centroamericana) in 1907. The tribunal was in reality more ceremonial than practical since it did not judge any major cases. Ultimately, this was one more failed effort at Central American unity. Costa Rica, geographically isolated from the other republics, was not much affected.

TRIBUNAL SUPERIOR DE JUSTICIA. A group of three men and two substitutes which functioned as a court in the latter stages of the colonial period. See also: DIPUTACION DE COSTA RICA.

TRIBUNAL SUPREMO DE ELECCIONES. This so-called "fourth

power" of the government was established by Article 99 of the Constitution of 1949. This body consists of three magistrates elected by the legislature for staggered six-year terms. The Tribunal Supremo de Elecciones is in charge of all aspects of the electoral process and within a six-month period before and after the elections can order the public forces (police) to take any action it deems necessary. The electoral tribunal has the last word in electoral matters and is highly respected for its impartiality.

TRIBUTOS. A tax that the *Indians had to pay either in money (which they usually did not have) or a certain number of days in public works. This system lent itself to many abuses and in reality was a system of conscript labor.

TRINIDAD, La. A strategic port located on the confluence of the San Juan and Sarpiquí Rivers. It was a strong point of the William *Walker forces on the *Transit Route. It was taken by Costa Rican forces December 22, 1856.

TRISTAN, Fidel (1874-1932). Scientist. He studied seismic actions of the volcanoes of Costa Rica, especially *Irazú and *Rincón de la Vieja. A prolific writer, his most important works are: Fenómenos sísmicos en Costa Rica, 1608-1910; Las hornillas del volcán Miravalles (1903); and Telefotografía del volcán Irazú (1917).

TRISTAN, Lorenzo de (d. 1794). Bishop of Nicaragua and Costa Rica (1777-83). He was possibly the most notable person to occupy this post. During his administration he improved the training and made the selection of new priests more rigorous. Tristán issued new standards for the administration of the sacraments and helped to establish a congregation in La *Lajuela (1782) which eventually became the city of *Alajuela. In addition Bishop Tristán established the first *San Juan de Dios Hospital (1874) which at that time was located in a convent in *Cartago. He also gave 700 *pesos for its maintenance. Tristán made an extended pastoral visit to Costa Rica and went to many out-of-the-way places that had never been visited by any previous bishop. It was Bishop Tristán who declared the *Virgin of the Angels the Patron Saint of Cartago.

TRIUMVIRATE. Also known as the *Diputación de Costa Rica, José María *Peralta, Rafael Francisco *Osejo and Hermenegildo *Bonilla were formally in charge (March 20-29, 1823) as Costa Rica rapidly changed tentative political forms in the first years of independence. [G.K.]

TROLLOPE, Anthony (1815-1882). English writer and post office official who visited Costa Rica in April 1859 to inspect routes proposed for an inter-oceanic ship canal and to negotiate international postal agreements. H.M.S. Vixen took him from Panama

to *Puntarenas, whence he traveled on mule back to spend Holy
Week in *San José. After visiting *Cartago and the crater of
*Irazú, he took a canoe down the precipitous *Sarapiquí River
and the San Juan River to the sea at Greytown (*San Juan del
Norte) in *Misquito Indian territory, where he was picked up
by H.M.S. Trent and returned to England. He considered his
resultant travelogue, The West Indies and the Spanish Main
(1858), the best thing he ever wrote. [L.H.]

TROPICAL TRADING COMPANY. See: KEITH, Minor C.; UNITED
FRUIT COMPANY.

TROYO, Rafael Angel (1875-1910). Novelist and poet. His most
important works are Terracotas, a series of short stories; Corazón
joven, a psychological novel; and Poemas del alma. He was
killed in the 1910 *earthquake.

TUGURIO. Costa Rican term for an urban shanty-town.

TUNA FISHING. Costa Rica signed in 1949 the Inter-American
Tropical Tuna Convention (CIAT) but withdrew in 1977. Within
the claimed (by laws of 1948 and 1972) 200-mile territorial limit
is a prime tuna fishery near *Cocos Island. Disputes with the
U.S. over tuna fishing were constant in the 1970s and 1980s.
[G.K.]

TURICHIQUI. A *Chorotega chief. In 1568 because of the harsh
rule of *Governor *Venega de los Ríos he led an attack on *Ujarrás. Turichiquí's forces were within a few miles of *Cartago
when the arrival of *Perafán de Ribera saved the city.

TURNO. A parochial festival held for the purpose of raising
money for a church and its activities. The term had its origin
in colonial times, when each *cofradía prepared a festival for
its patron saint, and the poor people would wait their "turn"
in line for the distribution of charity, thus the term turno or
turn originated. The expression has come to denote this type
of festival, which no longer distributes charity but is usually
an affair with gambling, carnival attractions, dances, local food,
marimba music, fireworks, and sometimes religious services.

TURRABARES. *Canton in San José Province chartered July 31,
1920. Its *cabecera is San Pablo, which is connected to the
capital by a road passing through *Puriscal. It produces corn,
beans, rice, and *sugar. The population is 4,471.

TURRIALBA. (1) *Canton comprising the city of Turrialba and
some of the surrounding territory. Founded as a canton August
19, 1903. It produces *sugar, some lumber, and *cattle. In
addition it is the seat of the Inter American Institute of Agricultural Sciences (*Instituto Interamericano de Ciencias

Agropecuarias/IICA), established in 1942 on land confiscated
from Axis nationals. No longer a half-way point between the
*Meseta Central and *Limon since the new (1987) highway,
Turrialba has compensated economically through kayakers using
the *Reventazon River. The population of the canton is 50,567
and of the city 23,705.
    (2) An active volcano in Cartago province.

- U -

UJARRAS. An important town in the colonial period. In 1725
    during a flood the people prayed to the Virgin to save them
    and miraculously the church bells rang spontaneously three
    times and the town was saved. An image of the Virgin of
    Ujarrás was also used in the battle with the *pirates in 1666.
    The image of the Virgin of Ujarrás was transferred to the church
    in *Paraíso in 1832. Today the ruins of the colonial church
    of Ujarrás are a popular tourist attraction. See also: PIRATES;
    VIRGIN OF UJARRAS.

ULATE BLANCO, Otilio (1892-1973). Conservative newsman and
    politician. President of the Republic 1949-53. He served several
    times in Congress and came to the forefront of politics by using
    his newspaper El *Diario de Costa Rica to attack the government
    of Calderón Guardia. In 1947 he was chosen by the united
    opposition in an open convention to be the candidate of the
    National Union Party (*Partido Unión Nacional) for the 1948
    elections. After a disputed election, *civil war, and rule by
    a Revolutionary *Junta Fundadora de la República he became
    President of the country November 8, 1949. During his term
    of office a rudimentary civil service system was started and
    the International Airport in *Alajuela Province was begun, as
    were some hydroelectric plants. He conducted a frugal govern-
    ment and somewhat reduced the national debt. Ulate became
    a leader of the anti-*Figueres Ferrer forces and ran unsuccess-
    fully for the presidency in 1962. In 1965 he entered into an
    arrangement with his long-time enemy, Dr. Calderón Guardia,
    to form the National Unification Party (*Partido Unificación Na-
    cional) to back professor José Joaquín *Trejos Fernández for
    the presidency. Ulate withdrew from the National Unification
    during the 1970 elections and unsuccessfully ran a slate of can-
    didates for congressional and municipal posts. He served for
    a few years as ambassador to Spain and continued to be important
    as an elder statesman until the time of his death. He was later
    declared *Benemérito de la Patria.

ULLOA, Nicolás (1799-1864). Politician and lawyer. *Deputy,
    1832-33, president of Congress 1833, president of the Supreme
    Court 1842, and Senator 1845. He was a *Yorkino mason and
    was proposed unsuccessfully for the presidency in 1835. During

the uprising of *Alajuela, *Heredia, and *Cartago against *San José (see: CIVIL WAR OF THE LEAGUE) he was selected as president of the League of Cities and is sometimes referred to as "Dictator of the League." Consult Ricardo Fernández Guardia, La guerra de la Liga y la invasión de Quijano (1950).

ULLOA BARRENCHEA, Ricardo (b. 1938). Artist, writer, and musician. Born in *San José, he studied in Costa Rica and Spain. He has worked in oils, pastels, and water colors having had exhibitions locally and in Europe. He is also involved with the "Nueva Pintura" having contributed landscapes to a national exhibition of Nueva Pintura in August 1983.

ULLOA GARAY, Ricardo. Poet. His latest work is Como nacer a tiempo (1983).

ULLOA SOLARES, Juan José (1827-1888). Studied law in Guatemala. Judge of lower courts and special representative of President Juan Rafael *Mora Porras in Guatemala in 1856. He was president of the Constituent Assembly of 1869 and also president of the Supreme Court in that same year. He later served as administrator of the *Banco Nacional 1874-77, and rector of the *Universidad de Santo Tomás.

ULLOA ZAMORA, Alfonso (b. 1914). Poet and writer. His works include: Alto sentir, presistencia de ti y otros poemas (1953), Lograd conmigo el canto (1954), Suma de claridades y los sonetos del beso (1955), Amerilis (1966), El Teatro Nacional (1974), and Lo cancionel y 3 odas para un hermoso pasado (1981).

ULLOA ZAMORA DE FERNANDEZ, María del Rosario (d. 1935). A pioneer in children's literature. As an elementary school teacher she wrote dramatic works for children. Her works include: Dramatizacions infantiles (1924), Nuevas dramatizaciones infantiles (1928), and Teatro infantil moderno (1933).

UMANA FALLAS, Cecilio (1794-1871). Father Umaña was first president of the Asamblea Ordinaria del Estado, which started to function April 14, 1825. In addition he owned some land in San Vicente de Moravia which he donated to help finance the *San Juan de Dios Hospital.

UNION, La. *Cantón in *Cartago province, founded December 7, 1848, and whose *cabecera is Tres Rios. The chief crop is *coffee, but *cattle and timber are also important. The population at the June 1984 *census was 41,005, and the cantonal area only 44.83 km^2.

UNION, Pacto de la. See: FEDERACION DE CENTRO AMERICA.

UNION CATOLICA. See: PARTIDO UNION CATOLICA.

UNION CATOLICA DEL CLERO DE COSTA RICA. An organization
founded by Bishop *Stork in 1907 to organize the clergy to
intervene politically and fight liberal legislation. It also pronounced on moral issues.

UNION GENERAL DE TRABAJADORES. A *banana workers union
organized in the early 1930s by the newly formed Costa Rican
Communist Party (*Partido Comunista).

UNION PATRIOTICA CENTRO-AMERICANISTA. See: UNIONIST
PARTY.

UNIONIST PARTY. Originally a group favoring Central American
unity, it started functioning in 1899 under the leadership of
the Nicaraguan, Dr. Salvador Mendieta. The party was formally
organized in Guatemala July 14, 1904, and advocated abolishing
frontiers in Central America and the creation of a unified country
with 19 districts and a federal district. They organized parties
in the various countries and largely through their efforts the
second Washington Conference (1922-23) took place. In 1921
they held a conference in Santa Ana, El Salvador, in which
they proposed the ratification of the Pact of San José of the
previous year and the perfection of the Federation of Central
America. In 1942 to mark the centennial of the execution of
Francisco *Morazán they held another conference in San José.
At that time the unionists proposed the restoration of political
democracy (Costa Rica was the only country with a freely elected
president), a common currency, flag, and customs union, a
joint army, and a federal congress. This congress marks the
shift of the party to a more anti-totalitarian position. In 1944
the party changed its name to Unión Patriótica Centro-Americanista.
They held talks with President Arévalo of Guatemala and President
Salvador Castañeda of El Salvador, which led to a federal union
between these two countries. But this union disappeared with
the fall of Castañeda in 1948. The remnants of this party later
supported the Central American Common Market (*MERCOMUN)
and *ODECA. Consult H. Karnes, The Failure of Union, Central
America, 1824-1960 (1961).

UNITED BRANDS COMPANY. Acquired United Fruit in 1969.

UNITED FRUIT COMPANY. It was founded in 1899 by Minor C.
*Keith when he merged the Tropical Trading Company, which
he had founded, with the Boston Fruit Company. This company
(referred to as the bananera) had a virtual monopoly on the
cultivation of *bananas for export in the Atlantic zone. During
the 1930s various diseases (especially *sigatoka) began to attack
the bananas and the serious *Banana Strike of 1934 occurred,
so contracts were secured from the Costa Rican government
to transfer operations to the *Coto Valley near *Golfito on the
Pacific coast. Today the bulk of their operations are in this

area and the *Parrita-Quepos area. However, the company, which was acquired in 1969 by United Brands, is in the process of divesting itself of banana lands, preferring to buy the crop from individual growers. Even after its partial diversification into palm oil production, high production costs led the company to abandon banana production in Costa Rica in 1985; its Numar Division continues to produce margarine and other products for the local market. Consult Stacy May and Galo Plaza, The United Fruit Company in Latin America (1958).

UNITED NATIONS. Costa Rica is one of the charter members of the United Nations, having declared war on the Axis Powers in December 1941. It was represented at the San Francisco Conference of 1945 by ex-President Julio *Acosta García.

UNITED STATES INVESTMENT. As elsewhere in Latin America, U.S. direct investment became important at the turn of the century, and displaced the *United Kingdom as the main source of foreign investment capital during the 1920s and 1930s. The Pacific Railroad (the future *Ferrocarril Eléctrico del Pacífico) was begun with American capital. Although British finance was crucial in the case of the *Ferrocarril del Norte, the line was built by an American, Minor C. Keith, and he was responsible for the development of *banana growing on railroad lands which led to the *United Fruit Company (now *United Brands). The Costa Rican pattern of land ownership has, however, limited the spread of widescale foreign-owned agribusiness so characteristic of some neighbor countries. United States investment has also been limited by the direct involvement of the Costa Rican government in the economy. The *Instituto Nacional de Seguros made insurance a state monopoly in 1924, the electricity supply industry was taken over in 1949 (see: INSTITUTO COSTARRICENSE DE ELECTRICIDAD), and for the forty years from 1948, banking was the domain of the NATIONALIZED BANKING SYSTEM (q.v.). [L.H.]

UNIVERSIDAD AUTONOMA DE CENTRO AMERICA (UACA). The first private university in Costa Rica. It was chartered December 23, 1975, by the Ministry of Education. The school was organized with a conservative orientation. It has fifteen faculties offering undergraduate degrees, masters, and doctorates in law. Its best known faculties are law, medicine, and several schools specializing in business and commerce. It also has faculties in liberal and fine arts. The university maintains a university press and the law faculty has published several works. This university does not have a central campus as such. Instead it has buildings in various parts of the capital area. During the 1981 academic year it had a total enrollment of 4,500 students in all its affiliated faculties. See: Universidad Autónoma de Centro América, Ordenanzas y anuario universitario (1982).

UNIVERSIDAD DE COSTA RICA. In 1935 a commission headed
by the Chilean Luis Galdames started to formulate plans for
the re-opening of a university in Costa Rica (see: UNIVERSI-
DAD DE SANTO TOMAS, closed in 1886). A law was passed
August 20, 1941, creating this university, and the first classes
began in March 1942. This new university incorporated the
existing schools of law and pharmacy. It now has its own campus in suburban San Pedro de Montes de Oca and has an enrollment of over 30,000 students in about one dozen faculties.

UNIVERSIDAD DE SANTO TOMAS. The University of Santo Tomás
was founded in *San José (March 3, 1843). However, it had
existed earlier as the *Casa de Enseñanza de Santo Tomás, which
was in reality a secondary institution. The Universidad de
Santo Tomás was divided into faculties of medicine, law, philosophy, humanities, mathematics, physics, and ecclesiastical sciences.
It was governed by a rector and a Directorate of Studies (Dirección de Estudios), the latter making the basic decisions. Between
1844 and 1888 it granted the bachelor of philosophy and the
bachelor of law degrees after three years of study. Eighty
baccalaureates in philosophy and 213 bachelors of law degrees
were granted during this period. The university also granted
doctorates and licenciatures, but they were something of a rarity.
Between 1870 and 1874 the university was in a state of crisis,
caused in part by the lack of adequately prepared secondary
school graduates. After 1874 the university dissolved into a
de facto secondary school, with only the law faculty pretending
to offer higher education. In 1888 Minister of Education Mauro
*Fernández Acuña decided that the university was not fulfilling
its function and it would be better for the country to concentrate
its meager resources on primary education. Mostly for this
reason the university was closed in that year, except to its
Faculty of Law. The following year, 1889 the Faculty of Pharmacy was also reestablished, and the remains of the university
library was reopened as the *National Library in 1890. The
country was without a university until the Universidad de Costa
Rica was opened in 1942. See also: UNIVERSIDAD DE COSTA
RICA.

UNIVERSIDAD NACIONAL DE COSTA RICA. It was organized in
the city of *Heredia using the Escuela Normal de Heredia as
its nucleus. It still specializes in teacher education but also
offers other subjects including liberal arts and agriculture.
See: NATIONAL UNIVERSITY.

UNIVERSITY FOR PEACE (Universidad para la Paz). Not an undergraduate institution for general study by local students, but
seminars are held for international groups. Located several
miles west of San José, adjacent to a protected highland forest.
For its establishment by the United Nationals during the *Carazo

administration, consult Margaret A. Laughlin, "An Emerging
Institution: The University for Peace in Costa Rica" (Milwau-
kee: University of Wisconsin). [G.K.]

UPALA. A large isolated *canton in the north of *Alajuela Province
which lies along the plains of Upala on the Zapote River. It
has better communications with Nicaragua than with the rest
of Costa Rica partly because of a lack of roads. It produces
grains and its *cabecera is Upala. This *canton was founded
March 17, 1970, and has a population of 26,061.

URBANA, Victoria (b. 1926). Novelist and short story writer.
She has spent most of her life living in Mexico. Her most important works are: El Marfil (1951), Los nueve círculos (1970),
and Y era otra vez hoy (1978).

URENA, Daniel (1876-1933). He was one of the first people to
write plays in the country. Most of his works deal with problems of interpersonal relations and their resultant social problems. His most important works are: "María del Rosario" (1906),
"Luz y sombra" (a play in verse), "Los huérfanos" (1910), and
"Muñequerías."

URENA, José (b. 1941). A primitive painter of local folk scenes.
Many of his paintings are found in the Guayabos Restaurant
in San Sebastián.

USEKARA. High priests of the *Huetar and *Brunkas who performed human sacrifices. They usually used small stone statues
and a flint knife to sever the victim's head.

UVITA, La. Columbus landed at this island off Puerto *Limón on
his fourth voyage (September 1502). "La Huerta" was the name
he bestowed, owing to the lush "garden" vegetation. Declared
a national monument. See also: CARIARI. [G.K.]

- V -

VALDERRAMA, Baltasar Francisco de. *Governor of the Province
of Costa Rica 1727-1736. This governor had many problems
with the Church. When he assumed the governorship a priest
tried to stab him for his anti-Catholicism. Valderrama tried
to limit the Church's power and at one point had another priest
arrested. In turn he was excommunicated by Bishop Villavicencio,
but the *Audiencia of Guatemala ordered this excommunication
lifted.

VALDIVIESO, Antonio de (d. 1550). First Bishop of Nicaragua
and Costa Rica in a new bishopric created by a cedula real in
1545. Before that date Costa Rica had been under the ecclesiastical

jurisdiction of Panama. Bishop Valdivieso tried to help the Indians by attacking the abuses of the *encomienda system. In return he attracted the enmity of the Contreras family, who decided to eliminate the bishop. The *governor's brother, Hernando de Contreras, was the chief culprit when several people stabbed the bishop to death in his own house February 26, 1550. As a result of this death, the bishopric remained vacant until 1557. Consult Ricardo Blanco Segura, Historia eclesiástica de Costa Rica (1967).

VALLBONA, Rima de. See: RIMA ROTHE DE BALLBONA.

VALLE RIESTRA, Antonio (1835-1856). Commander of the Costa Rican brigantine Once de abril, which fought a battle with the *filibuster ship Granada November 23, 1856. During this battle the Costa Rican ship blew up and Valle was killed. He is remembered as one of the heroes of the war.

VALVERDE, César (b. 1928). Artist who studied in Costa Rica, Italy, and the United States. He was a cofounder of the *Grupo Ocho. His style is both abstract and modern. One of his works was selected in a contest to appear on a postage stamp in 1970.

VALVERDE VEGA. *Canton in *Alajuela Province formed October 12, 1949, and named in honor of Dr. Carlos Luis *Valverde Vega. Its *cabecera is Sarchí, famous for *oxcarts and tourist souvenirs. But in addition this canton produces *coffee and lumber. Total population is 10,716.

VALVERDE VEGA, Carlos Luis (1903-1948). Physician. He studied in France and was a leader of the opposition to *Calderón Guardia. He was killed in a demonstration March 3, 1948. He was declared *Benemérito de la Patria by the Constituent Assembly in 1949.

VALVERDE VEGA, Fernando (d. 1981). Vice-president and minister of public security in the 1948 *junta. He also served as minister of the interior in 1970-74. He was one of the more controversial elements during the *civil war and was an important power in the National Liberation Party (*Partido Liberacion Nacional).

VAN PATTERN, Charles, Doctor (1814-1889). Dentist and physician. Born in Schenectady, New York, of Dutch descent. He studied dentistry and medicine at Harvard. Van Pattern came to Costa Rica in 1859 and finally settled in San José in 1865. A widower, he married the widow of Dr. James *Hogan, Catalina Guardia. The Van Patterns merged with the Escalante family and have since distinguished themselves in public service.

VANGUARDIA COSTARRICENSE. Name given to the army raised to fight the *filibusters in 1856-67.

VANGUARDISTAS. (1) An art movement of the late 1950s which stressed abstract painting. Its chief members were Manuel de la *Cruz González, Rafael Angel *García, and Lola Fernández.
(2) Members or followers of the Costa Rican Communist Party, called *Partido Vanguardia Popular (PVP).

VARA. Pre-metric measure of length: 1 foot, 8.9 inches.

VARGAS, Carlos Enrique (b. 1919). Composer and pianist. He studied music in Costa Rica and also in the Santa Cecelia conservatory in Rome. His most important works are "Sinfonía y concierto para el piano" (the first such work written by a Costa Rican), "Lieder de amor, soledad y tierra" (1960; this is in the form of a lieder). He has been conductor of the *Orquesta Sinfónica Nacional.

VARGAS CALVO, José Joaquín (1881-1956). Musician. He was director of the faculty of music for fifty years and a music teacher for 62 years. He founded several short-lived musical companies and wrote several marches for local colegios. He was most influential in the development of musical education.

VARGAS CARBONELL, Humberto. Leader of a militant faction of the Costa Rican Communist Party (*Partido Comunista). He studied in Moscow and served as Deputy. Vargas challenged the leadership of Manuel *Mora Valverde as being too accommodating to capitalism. After a bitter factional dispute in 1983-84 and many legal battles Vargas unseated Mora. The latter founded a new group (Partido del Pueblo). This dispute still goes on. Consult Rumbo Centroamericano. Año I, No. 8 (13 al 19 de diciembre de 1984).

VARGAS COTO, Joaquín (1895-1939). Journalist. He constantly wrote public letters and articles in the newspapers criticizing the vanity of the Costa Rican people and the actions of its public figures. Many of these articles appeared under the pseudonym "El Husar Blanco." Some of his works also appeared in a pamphlet published in 1969: Cartas de don Camilo Galagarza. Vargas represents the custom of public debate prevalent in the country through newspapers.

VARGAS DENGO, Carlos Alonso (b. 1954). Poet. His most important work to date is Vientos, cirros y febrero (1972).

VARGAS MOLINA, Balvanero (d. 1905). Captain of infantry in Puerto *Limón. Vargas is responsible for much of the early progress of Limón. He helped improve the city by filling in the land and persuading the government and Minor C. *Keith to build the sea wall. Vargas Park in Limón is named in his honor.

VARGAS PACHECO, José María (1878-1956). Jurist and professor
of law. He was governor of the province of *San José, minister,
and vice minister in three governments. In 1946 he was named
by the Supreme Court as its representative on the electoral
commission for the turbulent 1948 *elections. He also served
as president of the Supreme Court for a few months in 1948.
In 1949 Licenciado Vargas was elected president of the Constituent Assembly, but because of illness he never presided over
any session.

VARGAS VARGAS, Francisco. See: PARTIDO CONFRATERNIDAD
GUANACASTECO.

VASQUEZ DE CORONADO. New name of the *canton of CORONADO,
q.v.

VAZQUEZ DE CORONADO, Gonzalo (1552-1613). Second *adelantado
and interim *governor of Costa Rica 1600-04. During his administration the *Camino de Mulas (Mule Road) to Panama was opened.
His father, Juan *Vázquez de Coronado, had lost a great part of
his fortune in exploratory ventures. To compensate the family,
Gonzalo was named governor of the new Province in *Talamanca
called *"Duy y Mexicanos" (1610-13). But he too failed to conquer this region.

VAZQUEZ DE CORONADO, Juan (1523-1565). Conquistador and
*governor of the province of Costa Rica 1562-65. He had par-
ticipated in expeditions in the New World since 1540 including
the famous search led by his brother Francisco for the Seven
Cities of Cibola in what is now the southwest of the United States.
Vázquez de Coronado then served as alcalde mayor of Honduras
and El Salvador and in 1562 became *alcalde mayor of Nicaragua.
He decided to go to Costa Rica to continue the work of Juan de
*Cavallón. He landed near *Nicoya and started to pacify the
*Indians. Things went rather smoothly except for the strong
resistance of *Garabito. After this, Vázquez led an expedition
to the central valleys and Quepos. It was on this expedition
that he first saw the Guarco Valley and decided that it would
be an ideal place for a permanent settlement. Thus, Vázquez
de Coronado founded the city of *Cartago and in March 1564
he moved the settlers from *Garcimuñoz to this new city (see:
CARTAGO; CIUDAD DE LODO). In that same year he led an
expedition to *Talamanca where he was well received by the
Indians. Pressing his good fortune he went to Spain to secure
the title of *Adelantado de Costa Rica; however, he died in
a shipwreck in 1565 on the return journey. It is said that he
lost 20,000 *pesos in his colonizing ventures. The Crown tried
to reimburse the family by making his son governor of the new
province of Duy y Mexicanos. See also: VAZQUEZ DE CORO-
NADO, Gonzalo; TALAMANCA; DUY Y MEXICANOS.

VAZQUEZ DE LA QUADRA, Antonio (d. 1736). *Governor of Costa Rica April-July 1736. He was one of the few colonial governors to die in office. During his short administration the Parish of *San José was established as an independent entity from that of *Cubujuquí, thus helping in the development of the region of the Aserrí Valley, which ultimately became the capital city.

VAZQUEZ MENDEZ, Bernarda. The first woman actually to have voted in a Costa Rican election. She voted in a *canton election July 30, 1950. Women's suffrage had been approved by a Constituent Assembly June 20, 1949.

VECINO ("neighbor"). A colonial term which designated a household; on the average, this would be five Spanish settlers. Thus, a town with 20 vecinos would have had 100 inhabitants (not counting the *Indians).

VELAZQUEZ RAMIRO, Juan. Interim *governor 1590-91.

VENEGAS, Carlomagno (b. 1946). Sculptor born in Santa Ana. He first worked in several styles, but of late he has concentrated on a totemic style with creole themes which have social and political overtones.

VENEGAS DE LOS RIOS, Pedro. Interim *governor 1566-68. He also served as treasurer of Nicaragua and alcalde mayor of Costa Rica (1567) until the arrival of *Perafán de Ribera. Under his administration the *Indians of *Ujarrás led by Chief *Turichiquí rebelled and marched on *Cartago.

VERAGUA. A name generally applied to the Isthmian region from the Gulf of Darién to Cape Gracias a Dios beginning in 1508 when Diego de *Nicuesa received a land grant to this area from the Queen of Castile. The name was later changed to *Castilla del Oro. Costa Rica was separated from this area in 1539 and made a separate province. The name is still used for one of the provinces of Panama but is spelled Veraguas.

VERDAD, La. A newspaper published at the end of the nineteenth century. It was run by Rafael *Yglesias Castro and expressed his political point of view.

VESCO, Robert. Fugitive financier who enjoyed asylum in Costa Rica 1972-78. In the United States he was accused of embezzlement of over $200 million in mutual funds and of an illegal Nixon campaign contribution of $200,000. Critics of Costa Rica's venerable José *Figueres Ferrer charge that funds lent to the president's enterprises such as the newspaper *Excelsior assured Vesco refuge. His lavish above-the-law lifestyle was unpopular among Costa Ricans and the promise by the opposition to expel Vesco was one reason the National Liberation Party (*Partido

Liberación Nacional) lost the election of 1978. Subsequently, a more effective extradition treaty with the United States was negotiated. Costa Rica feared becoming a refuge for criminals. [G.K.]

VICEITAS. An *Indian tribe living along the Atlantic coast, roughly in the *Matina region.

VICENZI, Alfredo (b. 1928). Poet, writer, and scientist. His most important works are: Los mundos olvidados y otros poemas (1962), L.S.D. composición y ensayo poético (1967), Un cyborg en el espacio (1972), and Peces lacustres y fluviales de Costa Rica.

VICENZI PACHECO, Moisés (1895-). Novelist, essayist, biographer, and professor of philosophy. He served in several posts such as director of the National Archives and of the *National Library. His most important works, aside from his regular newspaper column called "La Bandera Blanca" which appeared in La Prensa Libre, are: Atlante (1924), La rosalía (1931), Elvira (1940), Filosofía de educación (1940), El conocimiento (1941), and El Hombre y el cosmos (1961). He was declared *Benemérito de la Patria in 1964.

VICEROY. Viceroys were the chiefs of the larger Spanish colonies. This office was first created in New Spain (Mexico) in 1535. Viceroys were considered the direct representative of the king and therefore were accorded the same respect as if they were the king. The viceroy exercised vast political and military authority. During most of the colonial period Costa Rica was subject, although indirectly, to the authority of the Viceroy in Mexico City. Technically during this period Costa Rica was a province of the Captaincy General of Guatemala, which in turn was a subdivision of the Kingdom of New Spain. In 1790 the system of viceroys was changed to that of *intendents. See also: AUDIENCIA REAL; INTENDENTS; RESIDENCIA.

VILCHES, Rosario (b. 1935). An *Arte Nuevo painter born in Ocotal, Nicaragua, who later became a Costa Rican citizen. She specializes in oil paintings of flowers.

VILCHEZ Y CABRERA, Carlos (d. 1774). Bishop of Nicaragua and Costa Rica 1765-74. During his regime the Church in *Orosí was completed (1766). However, most of his work was taken up with trying to correct certain excesses in the *cofradías and in restraining exuberances in religious festivals, such as public bloodletting. He also tried to encourage education by recommending that each parish establish an elementary school.

VILLA DE AUSTRIA. See: CASTILLO DE SAN CARLOS DE AUSTRIA, (VILLA).

VILLA DE BADAJOZ. A short-lived settlement located on the At-
lantic coast. It was founded by Hernán *Sánchez de Badajóz
April 25, 1540, but had to be abandoned shortly thereafter.
See also: TALAMANCA.

VILLA DE BRUSELAS. The first settlement founded by the Spaniards in Costa Rica. It was established by Francisco *Fernández
de Córdoba in 1524 near *Orotina. But because of a jurisdictional dispute between Fernández de Córdoba and *Pedrarias
Dávila the city was abandoned in 1525. It was resettled shortly
afterwards but finally destroyed by Diego *López de Salcedo,
then *governor of Honduras, in 1527 in another jurisdictional
dispute.

VILLA HERMOSA. People from the Barva and Aserrí valleys in
the second half of the eighteenth century began to move into
the Río Segundo area where they raised *sugar and set up small
sugar mills (*trapiches) in five settlements (called La *Lajuela,
Ciruelas, Targuas, *Poás, and Río Grande). When there were
finally enough people in the area (1784), Bishop Tristán gave
permission for the construction of a small church, which was
called Villa Hermosa. This ultimately developed into what is
now *Alajuela City. See also: ALAJUELA.

VILLA NUEVA (DE LA BOCA DEL MONTE). See: SAN JOSE.

VILLA VIEJA. Toward the end of the seventeenth century a colony
began to grow in the *Barva Valley, north of the Virilla River.
In 1705 there were enough colonists in that region to justify
building a church. In 1706 the church was built at a place
called *Lagunilla. It was then moved to *Cubujuquí or the present site of the city of *Heredia. In 1763 the name was changed
to Heredia, although it continued to be called Villa Vieja for
some time. One of the reasons was to differentiate it from *San
José, which was called Villa Nueva. See also: CUBUJUQUI;
HEREDIA; SAN JOSE.

VILLALOBOS, Guillermo. See: PARTIDO UNIFICACION NACIONAL.

VILLALOBOS BRENES, Asdrúbal (b. 1893). Modernist poet, lawyer,
and orator. His most important works are: Frutos Caídos (1929),
El Cuento de Aquileo (1913), and Nocturno en gris (1953). He
was also a *deputy from 1925 to 1936.

VILLALTA, Juan de (d. 1634). Career soldier who served as
*governor from 1630 until his death in office in 1634.

VILLARREAL, Pedro de (d. 1619). Bishop of Nicaragua and Costa
Rica, 1603-19. He made the first pastoral visit of any bishop
to Costa Rica in 1608-09. During this visit he administered
the sacrament of confirmation for the first time in the colony.

However, he had serious problems with *Governor *Ocón y Trillo.
Ostensibly the problem centered around the position of the bishop's
chair in the Church, but it was in reality a struggle between
the authority of the Church and State. One day Governor Ocón
y Trillo actually attacked Bishop Villarreal physically during
a religious celebration. The governor was brought to trial for
his actions but was acquitted. Later Bishop Villarreal ordered
that the old church in *Cartago be rebuilt. The governor refused to help. Consult Ricardo Blanco Segura, Historia eclesiástica de Costa Rica (1967), Chapter VIII.

VILLASENOR, Vicente (d. 1842). A Salvadoran general who fled
his country after unsuccessfully trying to defeat Francisco
*Morazán's invasion of the country. Instead, Villaseñor made
an agreement with Morazán (see: PACTO DEL JOCOTE) to help
the latter overthrow Carrillo. After Morazán was defeated and
executed, Villaseñor was declared a traitor and met the same
fate.

VILLAVICENCIO, Dionisio (d. 1735). Bishop of Nicaragua and
Costa Rica, 1730-35. During his administration a new church
in *Cubujuquí was inaugurated (1734). A dispute ensued between Bishop Villavicencio and *governor *Valderrama over who
would be named as first priest of this new church. The bishop
named Father Juan de la *Cruz Zumbado, who excommunicated
the governor. The matter was ultimately decided by the *Audiencia in Guatemala. They lifted the excommunication of the
*governor and relieved several priests of their duties. Consult
Ricardo Blanco Segura, Historia eclesiástica de Costa Rica (1967
ed.).

VILLEGAS, Jerónimo. Provided arms for the expedition of *Cavallón
and one of the founders of the port of *Landocho and the city
of *Garcimuñoz. He also participated in several expeditions
against the *Indians. Later Villegas represented Costa Rican
interests before the *Audiencia in Guatemala and protested against
some of the abuses of the *repartamiento that were perpetrated
by *Perafán de Ribera.

VILLEGAS, Olger (b. 1934). Considered one of the new school of
sculptors. He tries to use themes inspired by "Indoamerican"
art. Some of his statues are "Madre Indoamérica" (1971), "Madre
Negra" (1971), and two bronze heads, "Retrato de Melico [Manuel]
*Salazar" (1971) and "Retrato de Juan Rafael Chacón."

VILLEGAS, Wilbert (b. 1941). Painter born in San Ramón (Alajuela)
and educated in Costa Rica. His paintings are in an abstract
geometric style.

VIQUEZ, Pío (1850-1899). Journalist, lyric poet, and liberal leader.
Pío Víquez worked on La Gaceta (the official newspaper of the

government) and later founded El *Heraldo de Costa Rica (1889) which fought against the Catholic Union Party (*Partido Unión Católica). His most important works include such poems as "El Apache," "La Camelia," and "Tercaz."

VIQUEZ, Rosa María (b. 1939). An *Arte Nuevo artist who specializes in oils showing ornamental plants growing near buildings.

VIRGEN, La. A small port on Lake Nicaragua, which was a critical point on the *transit route (vía del tránsito) and the site of several skirmishes during the war against William *Walker.

VIRGIN OF THE ANGELS (Virgen de los Angeles). The patron saint of Costa Rica. According to tradition (which has very little documentation), one day in August 1635 a small black statue ("La Negrita") of the Virgin Mary appeared to a woman (Juana *Pereira) as she was gathering wood in the black section (Barrio de los *Pardos) in *Cartago. She took this statue home with her, only to find that it disappeared and miraculously reappeared at the same spot where she had originally found it. She took it to the parish priest and the same thing happened. This incident was repeated several more times and other miracles began to be attributed to the statue. Finally it was decided to build a church in honor of this figure. Aside from religious reasons, it has been argued that building a church in honor of a black Madonna and in the pardos section of Cartago would tend to keep the blacks from moving to other parts of the city. Other churches were built on this same spot in 1675, 1722, 1790-1805, 1822, 1849, and 1921. All except the last one were destroyed or nearly so by earthquakes. The Virgin of the Angels was declared the patron saint of Costa Rica in 1782. On the night of August 1 it is a tradition for people to walk to *Cartago from the *San José area to fulfill various religious promises. It is called a romería and initiates a fiesta of the Virgin. Consult José Fil Zúñiga, "El Culto de la Virgen de los Angeles (1824-1938)."

VIRGIN OF UJARRAS. Named from the now ruined hermitage in the Valley of *Ujarrás, the Virgin of Ujarrás was the Patron Saint of Costa Rica until she was replaced by the *Virgin of the Angels in 1824. The major miracle attributed to her was that of April 16, 1666 when English *pirates led by Morgan and Mansfield fled on being confronted by a vision of the avenging Virgin, who is now, by law, the "Captain of the Costa Rican security forces."

VIRILLA, Treaty of (1935). Ended the *civil war of the League (*Guerra de la Liga). This agreement was signed by Braulio *Carrillo Colina and Nicolás *Ulloa and promised no retributions in return for the surrender of the cities of the League. However, it was not ratified by the Congress and several of the leaders of the League were exiled or imprisoned for short periods of time.

VISITADOR. A high functionary sent by the King of Spain to resolve conflicts between the highest authorities. He also had the power to hear complaints and accusations against these authorities.

VITERI Y UNGO, Jorge (1802-1853). The last bishop of the combined bishopric of Nicaragua and Costa Rica, 1849-53. He had been previously expelled from El Salvador because of a Church-State controversy.

VOLCANOES. Costa Rica, located in an unstable zone, has many volcanoes. Some are relatively active and have caused trouble from time to time. Geothermal power is a potential asset; Miravalles is the first Costa Rican project. The main volcanoes are:

*Orosí	inactive
*Rincón de la Vieja	active (National Park)
Miravalles	active
Tenorio	inactive
*Arenal	active
Barva	inactive
*Irazú	active (National Park)
*Turrialba	active
*Poás	active (National Park)

VOLIO JIMENEZ, Alfredo (1879-1919). Delegate to the Pan American Conference of 1910. He was the first leader of the *Sapoá Revolution but was killed in a skirmish. He was succeeded by Julio *Acosta Garcia, who effectively took over leadership of the revolt.

VOLIO JIMENEZ, Arturo (1886-1962). *Deputy on various occasions and president of the Congress 1920-25, 1928-29.

VOLIO JIMENEZ, Fernando (1924-). Minister of foreign affairs 1982-83; president of Legislative Assembly 1987-88; law professor. Has served on several United Nations human rights commissions and has made U.N. human rights investigatory trips to many countries. [G.K.]

VOLIO JIMENEZ, Jorge (1882-1955). Soldier, philosopher, Catholic priest, university professor, vice president of the country 1924-28, and *deputy 1922-26, 1932-36, and 1953-55. Volio is one of the most interesting people Costa Rica has produced. He was born in *Cartago and studied at the *Colegio San Luis Gonzaga where he became acquainted with the progressive ideas of the Russian writer Tolstoy which were then in vogue in Costa Rica. Volio was cofounder (1902) of a newspaper called *Justicia Social, which was the first periodical to deal with social problems.

He spent 1903-10 in Europe where he studied at the universities of Louvain (Belgium), Paris, and Fribourg (Switzerland), and in Spain.

Probably the most important influence on him was that of Cardinal Mercier. The ideas of *Social Christianity propounded by that Belgian bishop influenced Volio's social attitudes the rest of his life. Volio was ordained a Catholic priest before coming back to Costa Rica. Father Volio then founded another progressive Catholic periodical in *Heredia city called El Nave (1911). The next two years (1912-13) he spent fighting in Nicaragua on the side of the army of León against the American occupational forces. For his valor he was named a general. Meanwhile, back in Costa Rica he was temporarily suspended from his parish. During the *Tinoco Granados dictatorship Volio left the country and taught in both Panama and Honduras. Later he took an active part in the fight against the dictator. His brother, *Alfredo Volio Jimenez, was killed in the *Sapoá Revolution. For his contribution to this cause he was named a brigadier general in the Costa Rican army.

In the early 1920s General Volio founded the Reformist Party (*Partido Reformista), probably his most important contribution. This party was the first to advocate a large-scale program of social legislation. Volio did not win the election, but he was in a position to make a deal in which he was selected as the second vice president and secured a promise that some of his party's program of social legislation would be enacted. In 1926 he was involved in a civil uprising in *Liberia and was sent to Europe by President *Jiménez Oreamuno for a "rest." In 1934 he was defrocked after going personally to Rome to try to patch up things with the Catholic Church. Volio, now economically ruined, spent the next six years (1934-40) trying to farm in the *Osa region. In 1940 he was named director of the National Archives by President *Calderón Guardia. He later served as professor of philosophy and dean of the Faculty of Arts and Philosophy in the newly established *Universidad de Costa Rica. Volio was elected a deputy again in 1953 and was serving in that post at the time of his death. For more details consult Marina Volio Brenes, General Volio y el Partido Reformista (1972). General Volio was declared *Benemérito de la Patria in 1989.

VOLIO LLORENTE, Julián (1827-1889). He studied in Guatemala and in León, Nicaragua, and received the licenciature degree in law. Volio helped push the *Ley Orgánica de Instrucción Pública in 1866 (see: EDUCATION LAWS), which established a national educational system. Volio also served as minister of finance in the government of Dr. *Castro Madriz and in 1868 was sent on a diplomatic mission to the United States and Europe. In Europe he secured a loan to build the Atlantic Railroad (*Ferrocarril del Norte), but the loan was cancelled with the overthrow of the government that same year. Volio made an important

contribution in the 1860s because he was one of the prime forces
in Costa Rica's decision to grant political asylum to Gerardo
*Barrios. This action, although it almost led to war, estab-
lished the Costa Rican tradition of political asylum. He was
an unsuccessful presidential candidate in 1862 and 1868 and
left the country for several years during the dictatorship of
Tomás *Guardia Gutiérrez. Volio was declared *Benemérito de
la Patria in 1961.

VOTOS. A small tribe of *Indians, numbering about 900 at the
time of the conquest.

- W -

WALKER, William (1824-1860). American soldier of fortune born in
Nashville, Tennessee. Walker had a history of stirring up trouble
in Latin America. He tried to provoke a secessionist movement
in the state of Sonora, Mexico, but failed. In June 1855 he
landed at the port of *Realejo, having been brought to Nicaragua
by the *liberals in León to raise an army to defeat conservative
President José María Estrada. Instead, Walker had himself elected
president of Nicaragua and started to take over Cornelius Vanderbilt's *Transit Company and menace Costa Rica. At Vanderbilt's
suggestion and partly to bolster a shaky political base, President
Juan Rafael *Mora Porras declared war and led a Costa Rican
army against Walker. This army became a joint Central American force when the other nations sent troops (see CAMPANA DEL
TRANSITO). Walker's forces were defeated in April 1857 and
he was escorted to the port of *San Juan del Sur where he
was taken on an American ship to Panama. Undaunted, he tried
to return later that year but was arrested by an American captain. In 1860 he attempted a landing in Honduras, but was
forced to surrender to a British sea captain who turned him
over to Honduran authorities who at the port of Trujillo had
him shot. Costa Rican nationalism was strengthened by the
war against William Walker. It gave Costa Ricans national heroes
and myths that the independence period did not (see: SANTA-
MARIA, Juan). This war has other names (see NATIONAL CAM-
PAIGN). See also: FILIBUSTER.

WAR OF NATIONAL INDEPENDENCE. See: WALKER, William.

WAR OF NATIONAL LIBERATION. One of the names given to the
1948 *civil war, usually used by the winning side. See: CAL-
DERON GUARDIA, Rafael Angel; CIVIL WAR (1948); FIGUERES
FERRER, José; PICADO MICHALSKI, Teodoro.

WAR OF THE LEAGUE (1835). See: GUERRA DE LA LIGA.

WARS. See: REVOLUTIONS, WARS, CIVIL WARS AND MAJOR
UPRISINGS.

WASHINGTON CONFERENCE (1907). A conference held November 14
to December 20, 1907, in Washington, D.C. cosponsored by
President Theodore Roosevelt and President Porfirio Díaz of
Mexico. Luis *Anderson Mona, foreign minister of Costa Rica
was its chairman. This conference produced treaties providing
for peace and friendship between the countries, compulsory
arbitration of disputes, neutralization of Honduras, reestablish-
ment of the *International Central American Bureau, the establishment of a *Central American Pedagogical Institute and the
creation of a Central American Court (*Corte de Justicia Centroamericana). See also: AMAPALA CONFERENCE, 1907; CENTRAL
AMERICAN COURT; CENTRAL AMERICAN PEDAGOGICAL INSTI-
TUTE.

WASHINGTON CONFERENCE (1922-23) (Second Washington Conference). At this conference an *International Central American
Tribunal was created. In addition there were treaties of peace
and amity, in which recognition of revolutionary government
was discouraged. The Tribunal created was not very successful
and in 1933 Costa Rica announced that it would not renew its
membership. This was followed by a like decision on the part
of El Salvador. The ten-year agreement expired at the end
of its statutory time and the whole system of arbitration disappeared.

WEBSTER, William Robert Clifford. English adventurer who came
to Costa Rica in 1856 and negotiated a series of contracts with
the Costa Rican government of President Juan Rafael *Mora Porras.
See: WEBSTER-MORA CONTRACTS.

WEBSTER-MORA CONTRACTS. A series of contracts signed between the English adventurer William *Webster and President
Juan Rafael *Mora Porras in 1856. One of the proposals would
have required Costa Rica to relinquish a large part of *Guanacaste in return for a direct cash payment to President Mora.
The purpose was to get the rights to build an interoceanic canal.
In another contract General José María *Cañas proposed setting
up a separate state along the northern border. At one point
President Mora even proposed that Costa Rica become a U.S.
protectorate. Consult Paul Woodbridge, Los contratos Webster-
Mora (1968).

WEIGHTS AND MEASURES. Although Costa Rica has been officially
on the *metric system since 1884, there remains a jumble of
colonial, Spanish, English and assorted measurements which
are still but less frequently used. See: ARROBA; CALENDAR;
FANEGA; LIBRA; MANZANA; QUINTAL; TIME ZONE; VARA.

WEST INDIAN IMMIGRATION. See: BLACKS.

WHEAT. It was probably first brought to Costa Rica and cultivated at Villa *Bruselas in 1524, and then reintroduced in 1561 with Juan *Cavallón's expedition. The first mill was established in *Cartago about 1577. Wheat was the first major export of the colony, having been sent to Panama in the form of hardtack (*bizcocho). Production started to decline around 1824 because of an increased interest in raising *tobacco. Imported flour had a tax on it until 1948. In 1964 a modern flour mill was established in *Alajuela with a capacity of 200 tons a day. Today practically no wheat is grown in Costa Rica. It could be grown again, especially in the central valleys, but profits would be only half as much as those from growing coffee.

WHITE DECISION. An arbitral decision in 1914 by the Chief Justice of the United States, E. Douglas White, in which he awarded some of the disputed territory in the Atlantic region to Costa Rica. Panama did not accept this verdict and the matter was left pending. See: FRONTIER QUESTIONS (SOUTH).

WOMEN'S SUFFRAGE. Women were given the right to vote for the first time in the 1949 Constitution. The first actual election that they participated in was a plebiscite over annexation of two districts in the *canton of *San Carlos (July 30, 1950). The first national election in which women voted was in 1953. Consult Tirza Emilia Rivera, Evolución de los derechos políticos de la mujer en Costa Rica (1981).

WORK FORCE. According to the 1976 estimates by the Ministerio de Trabajo (Ministry of Work) there were 616,799 people in the work force, divided approximately as follows:

	Number of workers	percentages
Agriculture	214,539	34.8
Industry	90,294	14.6
Construction	40,242	6.5
Basic services*	34,349	5.6
Commerce**	100,804	16.3
Professional services	136,560	22.1

*This includes utilities, transportation, and communication.
**This includes commerce, wholesale and retail, restaurants, and financial services.

The most important fact is that the work force, which was overwhelmingly agricultural in the 1940s, has been shifting to industry. Another trend is for the small, independent farmer to abandon his land or become a paid worker. The percentage of people in agriculture declined in the period from 54.3% to 47.2% in 1963 to 34.8% in 1976.

WORLD WARS. The *Tinoco Granados government declared war on Germany in March 1918. The dubious legality of the Tinoco regime (see: TAFT DECISION) in international law makes the validity of the declaration open to argument. Costa Rica's formal declaration of war on Japan after Pearl Harbor (December 7, 1941) anticipated even that of the United States. Declarations of war against Germany and Italy then followed. Later legislation allowed the government to confiscate property owned by Costa Rican residents with Axis (i.e. German, Italian or Japanese) nationalities (see: ALIEN PROPERTY LAW). [L.H.]

See also: BEYER, Karl; EISENACH; FELLA; SAN PABLO, S.S.

- X -

XATRUCH, Florencio. Honduran general who had to seek political asylum in Costa Rica. Later, in December 1856, he led a group of about 200 Hondurans in a battle against William *Walker at Granada, Nicaragua. In January 1857 General Xatruch was named provisional commander of the allied forces. He served in that capacity for a few months, and then became inspector general of the Central American Army.

- Y -

YAPRI, Esteban. An *Indian who escaped from the *pirates in 1666 and warned the authorities that an attack by the same pirates was imminent. His warnings gave the settlers time to get their defenses in order. They eventually repelled the attack at Quebrada Honda. See: PIRATES.

YAZDANI FAMILY. Wealthy Iranians who arrived in Costa Rica as exiles in 1979. Their investments in coffee growing soon rivaled those of established families. They also have important interests in office building investment. [G.K.]

YCAZA, Alberto (b. 1945). An *Arte Nuevo painter born in León, Nicaragua, but now a naturalized Costa Rican. He studied in Italy, Cuba, and in Mexico. Ycaza specializes in abstract oil paintings on canvas and wood, with bright colors and stressing balance. He has had his works shown in Latin America and Italy. Many of his paintings are satirical of political and social problems.

YGLESIAS, Antoni. Playwright. His most important works are: "Las Hormigas," and "Pinocho Rey," both of which focus on the world scene.

YGLESIAS CASTRO, Rafael (1861-1924). President of the Republic 1894-98; 1898-1902. He went into politics as a young man and opposed Tomás *Guardia Gutiérrez for which he was exiled. Later he took a leading part in the campaign of 1889 and was

minister of war under José Joaquín *Rodríguez Zeledón. He
founded the *Partido Civil in 1893 and which featured the revolt of the Catholic Union Party (*Partido Unión Católica).
Yglesias conducted a strong, semi-dictatorial administration.
He was reelected in 1898 after the opposition refused to run,
feeling that the government would not allow free elections. During his two administrations there were substantial material gains.
Yglesias encouraged improvements in Puerto *Limón, inaugurated
the first trolley car line in *San José, had a school complex
called the Edificio Metálico (Metal Edifice) brought over from
Europe, inaugurated the *Teatro Nacional (National Theatre),
started construction of the Pacific Railroad (*Ferrocarril Eléctrico del Pacífico), and had the Parque Nacional (National Park)
built. To solve the chronic monetary crisis he put Costa Rica
on the *gold standard (patrón de oro). After he left office in
1902 he ran unsuccessfully for the presidency a few times and
remained a strong political force until his death.

YORKINOS. A political faction favoring Nicolás *Ulloa in the election of 1833. There is some doubt that this term was actually
used at that time. See also: ESCOCESES.

- Z -

ZAMBO or SAMBO. A term used to describe a person born of an
Indian-Negro union. See also: PARDOS.

ZAMBO-MOSQUITOS. A tribe formed along the Atlantic coast of
Nicaragua after 1641, when some slaves escaped from a Portuguese
ship and intermarried with the native Mosquito Indian tribes.
They began to grow numerous, and in 1693 attacked the cacao
plantations in *Matina. From then on until the mid-nineteenth
century they were a problem to the country. Often in colonial
times they aided the British *pirates. During the nineteenth
century, the British recognized them as a separate nation and
they were used as a ploy to foster British aims in Central America. See also: MISKITO INDIANS; PIRATES.

ZAMBRANA, Antonio (1846-1922). Born in Cuba, he received a
doctorate from the University of Havana but was exiled for political activities. He settled in Costa Rica in 1873 and his liberal
and *positivist ideas exerted a great deal of influence on what
became known as the *Generation of 1889. Zambrana was a
strong advocate of the separation of Church and State. He
founded the Costa Rican Academy of Science in 1876, persuaded
the country to adopt the *metric system, and to create a civil
register, which would handle vital statistics (now known as
the Registro Civil). He lived in Costa Rica intermittently until
1912 when he returned to Cuba for good.

ZAMORA, José. Spanish citizen who on January 29, 1826 led about 200 men in an attempt to take the arsenal of *Alajuela City. Zamora's objective was to overthrow the government and return Costa Rica to Spain. This revolution failed, although it continued as a sporadic guerrilla movement for a while. Finally Zamora was captured and executed.

ZAMORA, José María (1786-1850). Costa Rican delegate to the Cortes de Madrid in 1820. He represented the combined province of Costa Rica-Partido de Nicoya constituency. Zamora strongly advocated the establishment of a separate bishop for Costa Rica. See: NICOYA, Partido de.

ZAMORA ELIZONDO, Hernán (1895-1967). Lawyer, poet, and university professor. He wrote poems glorifying the family, domestic life, and religion. His most important works are: Aguja y ensueño (1927), Las horas vagabundas (1929), Ritmo doliente (1930). In 1968 a collection of his poems was published under the title Poesía.

ZAMORA RODRIGUEZ, Pedro (1787-1835). An extreme *imperialist and principal leader of the *Heredia imperialists. He planned and actually led Heredia's attack on *Alajuela city (April 5, 1823) in the first *civil war. Later he served as a member of the Constituent Assembly of 1823 and as a *deputy (1826-29).

ZAPANDI. The name of the *Tempisque River in colonial times. The river was named after one of the *Chorotega Indian chiefs.

ZATARIN, Domingo de (d. 1741). Bishop of Nicaragua and Costa Rica in 1738-41. He visited Costa Rica during his term of office and declared August 2 the official day of the festival of the Virgin of the Angels. See: VIRGIN OF THE ANGELS.

ZAVALA, José Víctor (1815-1886). Guatemalan general who was named commanding general of the allied forces March 1857. He had become leader of the Guatemalan army after the death by *cholera of General Mariano Paredes. General Zavala fought at Granada in October and December 1856 and escorted William *Walker to *San Juan del Sur after his surrender in May 1857.

ZEGUA. Alternative spelling of SEGUA, q.v.

ZELEDON BRENES, José María (1877-1949). Journalist and poet. He wrote the words to the Costa Rican national anthem. Consult Victoria Garrón, José María Zeledón (1978).

ZELEDON GUZMAN, Néstor (b. 1933). Sculptor and one of the leaders of the so-called *Generation of 1960. His most important works are: "Ondulación marina" (wood, 1967), and a monument to Cleto *González Víquez (granite, 1965).

ZELEDON MORA, Pedro (1802-1870). Studied in León, Nicaragua. A minister in the government of Juan *Mora Porras, magistrate of the Supreme Court 1829-32, *deputy to the Federal Congress of Central America, *deputy to the Costa Rican Congress 1825-29, and president of that body for parts of 1825, 1826, and 1827. He left Costa Rica and served in Nicaragua as deputy and minister in several governments. After 1865 he renounced politics and entered the priesthood.

ZELEDON VARELA, Néstor (b. 1903). Sculptor. One of the leaders of the so-called *Generation of 1930. His works are inspired in the pre-Columbian tradition. Consult Luis Ferrero, La escultura en Costa Rica.

ZELLER DE PERALTA, Lolita (b. 1904). Painter born in *San José. She traveled extensively in Europe and studied the works of El Greco. She specializes in portraits and was one of the leaders of the so-called *Academic School of painting. See: PAINTING.

ZOROBARO. An area where Christopher *Columbus was told he could find a large amount of *gold (the place today is Almirante, Panama). When his brother Bartholomew *Columbus explored it he found some gold, but not nearly the quantity he was led to believe existed.

ZUNIGA, Francisco (b. 1912). Painter and sculptor. He is the son of Manuel *Zúñiga Rodríguez. His work is rooted in the Latin American experience, and shows the hardship of life. His work relies heavily on form, and some paintings seem to have sculptured lines. He has spent a great deal of time in Mexico, and his works have been highly influenced by that culture. Zúñiga's sculptures have been given a great deal of attention, but mostly outside of Costa Rica and he has renounced his Costa Rican citizenship. Zúñiga was important as one of the so-called *Generation of 1930 artists.

ZUNIGA, José Daniel (1899-1981). Musician. He dedicated his life to the collection and writing of Costa Rican music, having written over 300 compositions. His most well-known works are: "Auroral," "Oración de duelo," and "Caña dulce."

ZUNIGA-ESPRIELLA TREATY, 1938. A treaty concluded by the foreign minister of Costa Rica, Tobías Zúñiga, and the government of Panama, which would have settled the long-smoldering frontier question in the south. Essentially it would have accepted Costa Rican claims to the Pacific side, and given Panama most of the territory it claimed in the Almirante area. When the treaty was presented to the Costa Rican Congress it evoked strong opposition. Violent public demonstrations forced President *Cortés Castro to withdraw it. Ironically, the final settlement in 1940 was essentially the same territorial settlement agreed on in 1938, but presented to the Costa Rican people in a different manner. See also: FRONTIER QUESTIONS (SOUTH).

ZUNIGA RODRIGUEZ, Manuel María (b. 1890). Sculptor. He specializes in church statuary. His statues are found in many churches such as La Merced, the Cathedral of *Alajuela and the church of the Sacred Heart of Jesus in *San José. All the statuary in the Basílica de Nuestra Señora de los Angeles (*Virgin of the Angels) in *Cartago were also done by him.

BIBLIOGRAPHY

This bibliography is designed to provide a listing of works relating to the history of Costa Rica, and some general material on Central America. It is divided into historical periods, and one initial catch-all section called "General Works." Some annotative comment is provided to help in the researcher's initial selection. Unfortunately, most of these titles are difficult to find outside of Costa Rica, though some of the more important ones should be available in the larger research centers. With the growing importance of Central America, many of the new books are being acquired by a growing number of libraries.

The fundamental reference for Costa Rica or any of the Central American republics from independence in 1821 until the region's sudden prominence after 1979 is the volume published in 1988 by G. K. Hall of Boston, edited by Kenneth J. Grieb, Central America in the Nineteenth and Twentieth Centuries. This is an author bibliography arranged by country (Costa Rica, pp. 119-227 has 1,139 items) with a subject index (with Costa Rican subjects on pp. 543-547). Mesoamérica. Directorio y bibliografía, 1950-1980, edited by Alfredo Méndez-Domínguez (Guatemala: Universidad del Valle de Guatemala, 1982) is a directory of scholars listing their publications of the period. For writings dealing with the 1980s, there appear elsewhere current bibliographies, often selective with a political bias. Works on the colonial period are included in Sidney David Markman's Colonial Central America, a bibliography (Tempe AZ: Center for Latin American Studies, Arizona State University, 1977), arranged by disciplines and types of material, with a combined author-subject index. More recently published material on colonial Costa Rica, as well as material on the current crisis too recent for Grieb, is listed below.

Kenneth Grieb has also edited a Research Guide to Central America and the Caribbean (Madison, WI: University of Wisconsin Press, 1985) of which the first 193 pages deal with Central America. This gives information in essay form, on archives and libraries in North America and Europe that cover Central America, and on pages 134-139 has a section on the libraries and archives of Costa Rica. Another useful source is Efrain Rojas Rojas' entry "Costa Rica, Libraries in" on pp. 207-214 of volume 6 of the Encyclopedia of Library and Information Science, edited by Allen Kent et al. (New York: Marcel Dekker, 1971).

Most of the works below were published in San José, and if
no place of publication is mentioned it is to be assumed that it
was San José, Costa Rica. In most cases the publisher has been
omitted because until recently the name of the individual press
meant little. So many small shops have printed books and then
disappeared that it would be pointless to mention most of them.
(See: PUBLISHING in the dictionary.)

In the list that follows there are many works cited that despite
their promising titles are only short pamphlets with limited value.
The reason for this is that until well into the twentieth century
most historical tomes written in Costa Rica were short panegyrics
or political tracts.

The first attempts at scientific histories were made by Fernando Montero Barrantes and León Fernández in the 1890s. The
latter's son, Ricardo Fernández Guardia later took up the work
of his father and may be considered the founder of the scientific
school of history in the country. Ricardo Fernández went to Europe,
studied the original documents, and then produced what are still
some of the best works on the development of Costa Rica.

From the time of Ricardo Fernández Guardia until rather
recently few good histories were written in the country. In general, partisan politics, the lack of commercial publishers, the absence
of historical criticism caused by the closing of the university, and
other factors inhibited the production of worthwhile objective historical works.

In the last two decades this has begun to change, because of
several factors. Students began to take doctorates in history abroad--
in France, in the United States, and other countries. This raised
the level of historical research and historical criticism. Secondly,
the founding of schools of history at the Universidad Nacional and
the Universidad de Costa Rica increased emphasis and the quality
of the local training of historians. The establishment of presses
such as EDUCA and the Editorial Costa Rica ensured outlets and
encouraged production of new scholarly works, which heretofore
might not have been published. The writing of scholarly histories
in Costa Rica has improved a great deal in the last decade.

To conclude, a word about abbreviations used in this bibliography. Works published by the Ministerio de Cultura, Juventud
y Deportes are designated MCJD; the San Pedro-based
Editorial Universitaria Centroamericana is designated by EDUCA.
The new books published by the press of the Universidad Estatal
a Distancia are labeled by EUNED, whereas those put out by the
press of the University of Costa Rica are designated by EUCR.

1. GENERAL BIBLIOGRAPHIES, HISTORIOGRAPHIES, AND RESEARCH MATERIALS

The works cited in this section are general histories of Costa Rica or of Central America, as well as some books from related fields. This is a catch-all classification and its object is to give the reader an idea of the range of materials available. This category includes all historical periods.

Acevedo, Jorge Luis. La música en Guanacaste. EUCR. 2d ed., 1986.

Acuña de Chacón, Angela. La mujer costarricense. 2 vols. 1969-70.

Acuña Ortega, Víctor Hugo. El desarrollo del capitalismo en Costa Rica 1821-1970. San Pedro: Universidad de Costa Rica, 1982. Mimeographed.

Aguilar Bulgarelli, Oscar. Breve reseña de algunas ideologías políticas de Costa Rica. San Pedro: Universidad de Costa Rica, Departamento de Historia y Geografía, Seminario de Investigaciones, n.d. (1968?). A pamphlet with a general overview of Costa Rican history; has some interesting insights.

Alfaro, Anastasio, and Manuel M. de Peralta. Etnología centroamericana. Madrid, 1953 edition.

_____. Arqueología criminal americana. 1905. Both of these works are of value in the pre-Columbian period.

Ameringer, Charles D. Don Pepe; A Political Biography of José Figueres of Costa Rica. University of New Mexico Press, 1978.

_____. Democracy in Costa Rica. New York, 1982. Brief survey provides social statistics and description of 1982 elections.

Araya Pochet, Carlos. "La Minería y sus relaciones con la acumulación de capital en Costa Rica." Estudios Sociales Centroamericanos. (año II, no. 5 [mayo/agosto]), 1973.

Araya R., José Rafael. Vida musical de Costa Rica, 1957. A good source of information, although dated.

Baciu, Stefan. Costa Rica en seis espejos. Republished by MCJD, 1976.

Backer, James. La iglesia y el sindicalismo. 1974. A very well-done study of the Catholic Church's part in the labor movement.

Bancroft, Hubert Howe. History of Central America. San Francisco, 1882-87. The still classic history of Central America in the English language.

Barahona Jiménez, Luis. Apuntes para una historia de las estéticas en Costa Rica (1962). Basically a reworking of other commentaries on writers, but with an attempt to focus on Costa Rican conceptions of esthetics.

_____. El gran incógnito: visión interna del campesino costarricense. 1953.

_____. Historia de la política en Costa Rica, 1971. Both these works are wordy, but may give some insights into some aspects of the Costa Rican character.

Biesanz, John, and Mavis Biesanz. Costa Rican Life. New York: Columbia University Press, 1946. This classic pioneer study of Costa Rican society still holds up. Translation published by MCJD in 1976 as La vida en Costa Rica.

Bird, Leonard. Costa Rica; the Unarmed Democracy. London: Sheppard Press, 1984. Centers on the 1948 civil war, but also on the peaceful tradition.

Blanco Segura, Ricardo. Obispos y arzobispos de Costa Rica. 1966. A list of clerical officials with some general information on the church. Updated as Obispos, arzobispos y representantes de la Santa Sede en Costa Rica. 1984.

Bogantes, Oliveth. "La Iglesia Católica de Costa Rica y el desarrollo." Thesis, Université Catolique de Louvain (Belgium). 1971.

Bolaños Villalobos, Rafael Angel. Estudio histórico del Cantón de Mora. 1984.

Bonilla, Abelardo. Historia de la literature costarricense (2 vols.). 1959, reissued 1967. First volume contains a history of Costa Rican literature; the second is an anthology.

Bonilla, H. H. Los presidentes. Reprinted 1979 and 1985. Basic data on all of the chief executives.

Booth, John A. Características sociográficas de las regiones períficas de Costa Rica. 1974.

Borges, Fernando. Teatros en Costa Rica. 1941 (Reissued 1980). A short history of theatre in Costa Rica, 1837-1940.

Bosch, Juan. Apuntes para una interpretación de la historia de Costa Rica. 1963. A pamphlet which generally follows the line of the National Liberation Party, but is interesting for some insights into Costa Rican history.

Busey, James L. Latin America: Political Institutions and Processes. Chapter 3: "Costa Rica and her Neighbors," pp. 50-84. New York: Random House, 1964. By a political scientist who has written many short articles on Costa Rica. See: "The Presidents of Costa Rica" The Americas 18:1 (July 1961).

Bustamante de Rivera, Tirza. "La Ciudad de San José (ensayo)." 1961. A graduate thesis presented at the University of Costa Rica.

Camacho, Daniel. Desarrollo del movimiento sindical en Costa Rica. EUCR, 1981.

Camacho Monge, Daniel. Lecciones de organización económica y social de Costa Rica. San Pedro: UCR, 1967. A basic text used for courses in Costa Rican sociology. It has some good critical essays and useful statistics.

Cañas, José Marín. Yolanda Oreamuno. MCJD, 1973.

Castro, Nils. Cultura Nacional y Liberación. EUCR, 1979.

Castro Rawson, Margarita. El costumbrismo en Costa Rica. 1966. Discusses folklore and traditions.

Cazanga Solar, José. "Las cooperativas de caficultores de Costa Rica en el proceso de desarrollo del capitalismo en el café." Tesis de grado, Escuela de Historia, Universidad de Costa Rica, 1982. Shows that the cooperative movement, although it might have brought economic advantages, still has not eliminated class distinction among agricultural people.

Cersósimo, Gaetano. Los estereotipos del costarricense. EUCR, 1978.

Chacón, Nelson. Alajuela de ayer. 1986.

Chacón Granados, Jaime, and Ligia Estrada Molina. Reseña histórica de Limón. 1967.

Chacón Trejos, Gonzalo. Tradiciones costarricenses. 1964. Deals
with some of the folk legends of the Costa Rican people.

Conejo, Adina. Henry Pittier. MCJD, 1974.

Cordero, José A. El ser de la nacionalidad costarricense. Madrid,
1964; EUNED, 1980. This work deals mostly with aspects of
the colonial period at the Universidad de Santo Tomás. Unfortunately it does not live up to the promise of its title.

Cordero, Rodrigo. Moisés Vicenza. MCJD, 1975.

Costa Rica. Secretaría de Gobernación. Costa Rica en el siglo XIX.
1902. A collection of essays, memories, pictures, and miscellane-
ous information which is valuable for studies of this period.

_____. Guanacaste: libro conmemorativo del centenario de la
incorporación del Partido de Nicoya a Costa Rica. 1924. A
survey of life in the northern province of Guanacaste.

Costenla, Rodolfo, and Espíritu Santo Maroto. Leyendas y tradiciones borucas. EUCR, [19--?]. Has some information on the
Indians who live in the south of Puntarenas Province.

Cruz, Wladimir de la, ed. Historia general de Costa Rica.
Euroamérica de Ediciones Costa Rica, 1988- . To be completed
in 5 vols. of 500pp. each.

Dammers, Kim. "An Introduction to the Labor Union Movement
of Costa Rica." San Pedro, Costa Rica, Associated Colleges of
the Midwest, 1965. 78 pp. An undergraduate research paper.

Dengo, Gabriel. Bibliografía de la geología de Costa Rica. San
Pedro: Universidad de Costa Rica, 1959.

Diccionario de la literatura latinoamericana. (América Central,
Tomo I, Costa Rica, El Salvador y Guatemala). Washington,
D.C.: Pan American Union, 1963.

Dobles Segreda, Luis. Indice bibliográfico de Costa Rica. 1927-65?,
10 vols. A more or less complete bibliography of works on Costa
Rica, conveniently listed by topic. An excellent place to start
research.

_____. Documentos históricos posteriores a la independencia,
1923.

_____. La provincia de Heredia. 1934.

Downing, Theodore, and Jean Matteson. "Squatters: A form of
Spontaneous Colonization in Costa Rica." San Pedro: Associated

Colleges of the Midwest, 1955. An undergraduate research paper.

Facio, Rodrigo. La moneda y la banca central en Costa Rica. Mexico, 1947. A good monetary history concentrating on the 1930-45 period.

Fernández B., León. Documentos para la historia de Costa Rica. 10 vols. Paris, 1886, Vols. 1-5; Barcelona, 1907 vols. 6-10. Excellent collection of documents dealing principally with the colonial and independence periods.

Fernández Guardia, Ricardo. Cartilla histórica de Costa Rica. 1964 and other years. Basically a good high school text, but one of the few complete histories of the country available.

_____. Cosas y gentes de antaño. 1939; EUNED, 1980. Short vignettes of historical incidents.

_____. Costa Rica en el siglo XIX: tradiciones, datos biográficos y notas. 1929; reissued 1970.

_____. Reseña histórica de Talamanca. 1918.

Fernández Montúfar, Joaquín. Historia ferrocarril de Costa Rica. 1934. This voluminous book is both a picture gallery and a history of the early days of railroading in Costa Rica.

_____. Costa Rica, precolombina. 1975. A good introduction.

_____. Talamanca, el Espacio y los Hombres. MCJD, 1974.

Flores, Bernal. La Música en Costa Rica. 1978.

Fonseca, Virginia de. Manuel González Zeledón. MCJD, 1974.

Gagini, Carlos. Los aborígines de Costa Rica. 1917.

Gamboa, Francisco. Costa Rica, monografía. Havana, Cuba, 1963. A Marxist history of the country. Excellent for the modern period, giving details of the workers' movement. It has been reissued in Costa Rica.

Garrón de Doryan, Victoria. Anastasio Alfaro. MCJD, 1974.

_____. Joaquín García Monge. MCJD, 1971.

_____. José María Zeledón, "Billo." MCJD, 1978.

Gil Zúñiga, José. "El culto del la Vírgen de los Angeles (1824-1935). Una aproximación a la mentalidad religiosa." Tesis de grado, Escuela de Historia, UCR, 1982. Well done and insightful.

González, Luis Felipe. Historia de la influencia extranjera en el desenvolvimiento educacional y científico de Costa Rica. 1921. In actuality, this is a treatise on foreign influence in Costa Rican culture.

González, Luisa. Carlos Luis Sáenz. MCJD, 1972.

González Flores, Luis Felipe. Benefactores de Heredia. 1930. Brief biographies of prominent Heredians. A good source of information on second-echelon people.

González Truque, Guillermo. Apuntes sobre la economía costarricense. EUCR, 1978.

González Villalobos, Paulino, ed. Desarrollo Institucional de Costa Rica (1523-1914). San Pedro: UCR, Sección Historia de las Instituciones. A textbook for the course in the history of Costa Rican institutions. An anthology. Many of the articles are excellent contributions. There are also some extensive and well done bibliographies.

González Víquez, Cleto. Apuntes sobre geografía histórica de Costa Rica. 1906.

_____. Personal del poder ejecutivo de Costa Rica. This catalogue of chief executives of the country was extensively revised by Ricardo Fernández Peralta in 1958.

_____. El puerto de Puntarenas. 1933.

_____. Reseña histórica del Hospital de San Juan de Dios. 1926.

Guevara de Pérez, Raquel. Pedro Pérez Zeledón. MCJD, 1971.

Gutiérrez, Pedro. La historia del automovilismo en Costa Rica. 1981.

Hall, Carolyn. Cóncavas: formación de una hacienda cafetalera. EUCR, 1978. This complements her earlier general study.

_____. El Café y el desarrollo histórico-geográfico de Costa Rica. 1976. An excellently organized, and thoroughly researched piece of work. Basic to understanding the development of this key industry.

_____. Costa Rica: A Geographical Interpretation in Historical Perspective. Boulder, Westview Press, 1985.

Hamnet, Florence. "A Study of Costa Rican Petroglyphs." San Pedro: Associated Colleges of the Midwest, 1967. An undergraduate research paper.

Hernández de Jaén, Mireya, et al. Monografía del Cantón de Carrillo. EUCR, 1976. A study of one of the most typical cantons on the Guanacastecan pampas.

Hoffman, Carl. Viajes por Costa Rica. Republished 1976 by MCJD.

Jiménez, Manuel de Jesús. Noticas de antaño. 1946 is the latest edition of this selection of historical incidents and anecdotes.

_____. Selecciones. 1964. A selection of his historical writings; both works are good background material.

Jiménez, Mario Alberto. Obras completas. Vol. II (1962), pp. 41-280 contains "Desarrollo constitucional de Costa Rica," possibly the only integrated constitutional history of the country.

Jiménez, Wilburg. Movimientos migratorios internos en Costa Rica y sus causas. 1952.

Jinestra, Ricardo. El Canal de Nicaragua; su historia, baso internacional y participación de Costa Rica. n.d. Reissued by the Ministry of Foreign Relations in 1964.

_____. La evolución penitenciaria de Costa Rica. 1940.

Jones, Chester Lloyd. Costa Rica and Caribbean Civilization. Madison, Wis., 1935; reissued, New York, 1967. Once the best history in English, but unfortunately out of date.

Kohkemper, Mainrad. Historia de la travesías de la Cordillera de Talamanca. 1955.

Lascaris, Constantino. Abelardo Bonilla. MCJD, 1973.

_____. Desarrollo de las ideas filosóficas en Costa Rica. 1964. An extensive effort to detail all the intellectual trends using vignettes of individuals' contributions. Very useful, possibly more as a reference work than for straight reading.

_____. El Costarricense. 1975. An impressionistic and anecdotal introduction to the character of the Costa Rican people.

_____. Historia de las ideas de Centroamérica. San Pedro, Costa Rica: Editorial Universitaria Centroamericana, EDUCA, 1970.

Lizano F., Eduardo. Cambios sociales y económicos en Costa Rica. 1975.

McBride, Dorothy. "Elite Political Culture in Costa Rica." Ph.D. dissertation, Vanderbilt University, 1968.

Martz, John. Central America, the Crisis and the Challenge. Chapel Hill: University of North Carolina Press, 1954. His chapter on Costa Rica has some very good information on the Ulate and first Figueres administrations.

Massing, Ulv. "Foreign Agricultural Colonies in Costa Rica: An Analysis of Foreign Colonization in a Tropical Environment." Ph.D. dissertation, University of Florida, 1964.

May, Stacy, and Galo Plaza. The United Fruit Company in Latin America. Washington, D.C., 1958. Pro-Company, it has some information devoted to Costa Rica.

Meléndez Chaverri, Carlos, ed. Antología de historia de las instituciones de Costa Rica. San Pedro: UCR, Facultad de Ciencias y Letras, 1969. A reader in Costa Rican history. Especially useful for charts dealing with the evolution of the Costa Rican constitution.

_____. "¿A dónde vamos? (Evolución de problemas más destacados)." 1953. A pamphlet written for a museum exhibition, but it contains valuable vignettes of national problems covering everything from chayotes (an ubiquitous squash) to marijuana.

_____. Viajeros por Guanacaste. MCJD. 1974.

_____. "La historia de Costa Rica como proceso e ideología." Argos: Revista cultural, Marzo, 1982.

_____. D. Rafael Moya M.: esbozo de su biografía. 1964.

_____. Historia de Costa Rica. EUNED, various editions from 1979, widely used.

Monge, Carlos Francisco. La imagen separada: modelos ideológicos de la poesía. 1985.

Monge Alfaro, Carlos. Historia de Costa Rica: texto para primeros y quintos años de segunda enseñanza, rev. ed. 1974. This new edition is a complete history of the country up to the present period. It was written for secondary school use.

_____. Nuestra historia y los seguros. 1974. This work concentrates on the Instituto Nacional de Seguros.

Monge Alfaro, Carlos, and Francisco Rivas, Francisco. La Educación: fragua de nuestra democracia. EUCR, 1978.

Montero Barrantes, Francisco. Elementos de historia de Costa Rica. 2 vols., 1894. One of the earliest attempts to write a complete history of the country. It is particularly strong in the earlier period and still worthwhile for background reading.

Mora Valverde, Eduardo. Historia del movimiento obrero internacional. 1969. Marxist view of Latin American labor movements. It contains some specific material on the Costa Rican labor movement.

Mourelo, José Néstor. Bibliografía del Río San Juan. Alajuela: Museo histórico Juan Santamaría, 1983. Deals with the constant dispute over the San Juan River from a Costa Rican point of view. Also reprints some documents relating to the dispute.

Munro, Dana Gardner. The Five Republics of Central America; their political and economic development and their relations with the United States. New York: Oxford University Press for Carnegie Endowment for International Peace, 1918. For a long while the standard introduction to the area. Chapter on Costa Rica still valuable as an introduction.

Murchie, Anita Gregario. Imported Spices. (A study of Anglo-American Settlers in Costa Rica 1821-1900). MCJD, 1981. A valuable study, showing the great contribution of many English and American immigrants to Costa Rica and the subsequent history of their families.

Naylor, Robert A. "British Commercial Relations with Central America." Ph.D. dissertation, Tulane University, 1958.

Nelson, Harold D., ed. Costa Rica: A Country Study, 1983. Prepared for Department of the Army by the American University. Supersedes prior edition, Area Handbook for Costa Rica, 1970.

Noreiga, Félix F. Diccionario geográfico de Costa Rica. 2d ed., 1923.

Núñez, Francisco María. Iniciación y desarrollo de las vías de comunicaciones y empresas de transportes de Costa Rica. 1924. Contains useful information on postal services, railroads, telegraphs, and telephones.

Nunley, Robert E. The Distribution of Population in Costa Rica. Washington, D.C., National Academy of Sciences, 1960.

Obregón Loria, Edgar Arturo. Miguel Obregón. MCJD, 1974.

Obregón Loria, Rafael. Hechos militares y políticos. Alajuela.

1981. Details internal revolutions, plots and golpes de estado. Proves that Costa Rica had problems similar to other Latin American nations. A most valuable contribution. There are other editions of this work, with varying titles.

_____. El poder legislativo en Costa Rica. 1957. A list of all the people who have served in the national legislature, plus short biographies of the men who served as presidents of this body. A source of much valuable information.

_____. Los rectores de la Universidad de Santo Tomás. 1955.

_____, and George F. A. Bowden. La masonería en Costa Rica. 1938.

Olien, M. D. The Negro in Costa Rica: The Role of an Ethnic Minority in a Developing Society. Winston-Salem, N.C., 1970.

Palmer, Frederick. Central America. 1910. A pollyanna traveler's view.

Palmer, Paula. What happen: A Folk History of Costa Rica's Talamanca Coast. 1977. Oral history of fishermen and farmers over several generations.

Parker, Franklin Dallas. The Central American Republics. New York: Oxford University Press, 1964. Best survey of the area.

Partido Vanguardia Popular. Breve esbozo de su historia. 1971.

Peralta, Hernán. Las constituciones de Costa Rica. Madrid, 1961.

_____. La diplomacia en Costa Rica. Pamphlet.

_____. Los Aborígenes de Costa Rica. Paris, 1901.

_____. Atlas histórico-geográfico de la República de Costa Rica, Veragua y Costa de Mosquitos: estudios hechos para la celebración del cuarto centenario del descubrimiento de América. Madrid. 1980.

_____. El canal interoceánico de Nicaragua y Costa Rica en 1620 y 1887. Brussels, Belgium, 1887.

_____. Costa Rica, Nicaragua y Panamá en el siglo XVI: su historia y sus límites. Madrid, 1883.

_____. Costa Rica, su clima, su organización y sus recursos. London, 1873. There is also an English edition.

_____. Costa Rica y Colombia de 1573 a 1881: jurisdicción y límites territoriales. Madrid, 1886.

_____. Costa Rica y Costa de Mosquitos: documentos para jurisdicción territorial de Costa Rica y Colombia. Paris, 1898. Most of the works by this author are pamphlets written to justify Costa Rican boundary claims. Nevertheless, they contain a great deal of valuable data; Peralta was a first-class historian.

_____. Costa Rica y la Costa de Mosquitos. Paris, 1898.

_____. Exposé des droits territoriaux de la république de Costa Rica. Paris, 1898.

_____. Límites de Costa Rica y Colombia. Madrid, 1890.

_____. "La República de Costa Rica." A published paper given at the Geneva Geographic Society. Geneva, Switzerland, 1871.

_____. El Río San Juan de Nicaragua: derechos históricos de sus ribereños. Madrid, 1882.

Pérez Zeledón, Pedro. Cuestión de límites de Costa Rica y Nicaragua, n.d.

Perigay, Le Comte Maurice de. La République de Costa Rica--su avenir économique et le canal de Panama. Paris, 1918.

Picado Chacón, Manuel. Dr. Clodomiro Picado: vida y obra. EUCR, 1980.

Portugues de Belames, Elizabeth. El cuento en Costa Rica. 1964. Half history, half anthology.

Quesada Soto, Alvaro. La formación de la narrativa nacional costarricense. EUCR, 1986.

Ramos, Lilia, and Marianade Silva. Carlos Gagini. MCJD, 1973.

Retana Charpentier, Saddie. "Historia y geografía económica de Costa Rica." n.d. Bachelor's degree thesis. Designed to be used as a source book for elementary teachers lacking sufficient preparation.

Rivera B., Tirza Emilia. Evolución de los Derechos Políticos de la mujer en Costa Rica. MCJD, 1931. A history of the status of women in Costa Rica. A well-documented and valuable study.

Rodríguez, Mario. Central America. Englewood Cliffs, N.J.: Prentice-Hall, 1965 (paper). Emphasis on contemporary problems, but also a good survey of Central American history. Also available in Spanish.

_____, and Vincent C. Peloso. A Guide for the Study of Culture in Central America: Humanities and Social Sciences. Washington, D.C., Pan American Union, 1968.

Rodríguez, Valerio. Turrialba, su desarrollo histórico. Turrialba, Costa Rica, 1953.

Rodríguez Vega, Eugenio. "Apuntes para una sociología costarricense." Tesis de grado, Universidad de Costa Rica, 1953. Good pioneer work in Costa Rican sociology, discusses political, social, and religious problems.

Rodríguez Zamora, José Miguel. "Aspectos ideológicos y estructras de la relación entre la iglesia católica de Costa Rica y el sistema político." Thesis, UCR, 1976.

Sáenz, Adela F. de, and Carlos Meléndez Ch. Nueva historia de Costa Rica (para los grados superiores de la escuela primaria y para colegios de segunda enseñanza), 1970. A combination history and anthology of short readings.

Salas, Agustín. Historia del deporte en Costa Rica. 1951. A bit sketchy, but has some information not found elsewhere.

Sando de Fonseca, Virginia. El Presbítero Don Juan Garita. MCJD, 1977.

Schifter Sikora, Jacobo, Lowell Gudmundson, and Mario Solera Castro. El judio en Costa Rica. Editorial Universidad Estatal a Distancia, 1979 An extensive study of the origins, immigration patterns, and life of the Jewish people in Costa Rica.

Shapiro, Sandra Lee Fichtner. "The Arts in Costa Rica. Honduras, Nicaragua, and El Salvador as Reflected in Travel Literature before the First World War." M.A. thesis at Tulane University, 1956.

Solera R., Guillermo. Beneméritos de la patria. 1964. A filial pietistic work which provides sketches of some of the country's leading historical personages.

Soley Güell, Tomás. Historia económica y hacendaria de Costa Rica. 2 vols., 1947-49. The standard economic history of the country. Very valuable for the wealth of information it contains.

Sotela, Rogelio. Escritores de Costa Rica. 1942.

Soto de Avila, J. V. ¿Quién es quién en Centro América y Panamá? Libro 2. Guatemala, 1954.

Squier, Ephraim George. Notes on Central America. New York,
Harper, 1859. A perceptive traveler's interesting account of
Central America in the mid-nineteenth century.

Stone, Doris Zemurray. "Basic Cultures of Central America."
Smithsonian Institution Bulletin 143, Washington, D.C., 1948,
pp. 169-193.

_____. "The Boruca of Costa Rica." Papers of the Peabody
Museum of American Archeology and Ethnology, vol. 26, no. 2,
Cambridge, MA, 1949.

_____. "Costa Rica: Social Organization of the Cabecare and
Bribri Indians," Boletin indigenista, vol. 20, no. 3, Mexico,
September 1960, pp. 206-211.

_____. "Indians of Costa Rica," Bulletin of the Pan American
Union, vol. 86, Washington, D.C., February 1948, pp. 61-69.

_____. "Una inspección ligera del llano del Río Grande de
Térraba," Publicaciones de la Sociedad de Geografía e Historia
de Costa Rica, no. 4, 1943.

_____. "Synthesis of Lower Costa Rican Ethnohistory," Hand-
book of Middle American Indians. vol. 4, Austin: University
of Texas Press, 1966, pp. 209-233.

Stone, Samuel Z. "Los cafetaleros: une étude des planteurs de
café au Costa Rica." Doctoral dissertation, Faculté des Lettres
et Sciences Humaines, Université de Paris, 1968. This excellent
study demonstrates how certain families tended to dominate the
political life of the country. It has also been published in Spanish
in Costa Rica.

_____. La dinastía de los conquistadores; la crisis del poder en
la Costa Rica contemporánea. San Pedro: EDUCA, 1975. A
very useful study of the ongoing control exerted by certain
families in Costa Rican political life.

Thiel, Bernardo Augusto. Apuntes lexicográficos de las lenguas
de Costa Rica. 1882.

_____. La iglesia católica en Costa Rica durante el siglo XIX.
1902.

_____. Monografía de la población en Costa Rica en el siglo
XIX. Latest edition of this classic study of the development of
Costa Rican population is published in Revista de Estudios y
Estadística No. 8 (octubre, 1967), pp. 77-119.

_____. Viajes a varias partes de la República de Costa Rica,
América Central. 1895.

316 / BIBLIOGRAPHY

Trejos Quirós, José Francisco. Origen y desarrollo de la democracia en Costa Rica. 1939. Impressionistic and in the tradition of the Leyenda Blanca.

Trejos Quirós, Juan. Geografía ilustrada de Costa Rica. 1966;
other editions. A high school text.

Tropical Science Center. Anthropological Bibliography of Aboriginal
Costa Rica. (San José: Tropical Science Center), 1967.

Urrez, Jaimil. "Algunos aspectos del sindicalismo y su desarrollo
en Costa Rica." Thesis, Universidad de Costa Rica, 1966.

Valerio, Juvenal. Turrialba: su desarrollo histórico. 1953.
A well-done local history and geography.

Van Horne, Willard. "An Ethnographic Study of the Huaquero."
San Pedro: Associated Colleges of the Midwest, 1963. An undergraduate research paper.

Vega Carballo, José Luis. "Etapas y procesos de la evolución socio-
política de Costa Rica," Estudios Sociales Centroamericanos,
no. 1, Jan.-April, 1972, pp. 45-73.

_____. "La evolución agroeconómica de Costa Rica: un intento
de periodización y sínteis (1560-1930)." In Revista de Costa
Rica No. 9, abril 1975, pp. 19-70.

Villalobos Vega, Bernardo. Bancos Hipotecarios en Costa Rica
1847-1949. Tesis de grado, UCR, 1968.

Villavicencio, Enrique. La República de Costa Rica. 1886.

Wagner, Phillip L. Nicoya: A Cultural Geography. Berkeley,
California: 1958: A sociological, geographic study of part of
Guanacaste.

Who's Who in Costa Rica. San José and Chicago, 1979-80.

Who is Who in Latin America; A Bibliographical Dictionary of Notable
Living Men and Women. Part II, Central America and Panama.
Palo Alto, Calif.: Stanford University Press, 1945.

Willie, María Eugenia B. de. Bibliografía Costarricense de Ciencias,
no. 2. Facultad de Letras, UCR, 1968. An annotated bibliography dealing mostly with sociology but also contains general
information.

Zelaya, Antonio. Cien años de libertad de prensa en Costa Rica
1843-1943. 1943.

Zeledón, Marco Tulio. Fronteras de Costa Rica. 1946.

Zúñiga Tristán, Virginia. "El anglicismo en el habla costarricense."
Ph.D. dissertation, Tulane University, 1958.

2. THE PRE-COLUMBIAN, CONQUEST, AND
COLONIAL PERIODS (1494-1821)

Baudez, Claude. Recherches Archiologiques dans la vallée du
Tempisque, Guanacaste, Costa Rica. Paris: Institute des Hautes
Etudes de l'Amérique Latine, 1967.

Between Continents/Between Seas: Precolumbian Art of Costa Rica.
New York, 1981. Catalog for art exhibit contains thorough
summation.

Blanco Segura, Ricardo. Historia eclesiástica de Costa Rica. 1967.
Contains good material on life in the colonial period.

Blaños Villalobos, Rafael A. "Contribución al estudio del decimiento
de la población nativa de Costa Rica en el período colonial (1502-
1821)." Thesis, Facultad de Historia, UCR, 1981. This thesis
reiterates the great harm done to the native population by use
of the encomienda, mita and repartimiento.

Castro y Tosi, Norberto. Dos investigaciones históricas: Juan
López de Ortega: ¿primer historiador? and El Pretecelo de Gaspar de Chinchilla de 1607. 1967.

Cockburn, John. The Unfortunate Englishmen; or, A Faithful
Narrative of the Distresses and Adventures of John Cockburn
and Five Other English Mariners ... Containing a Journey over
Land from the Gulf of Honduras to the Great South Sea. London: various editions from 1731. Title varies: first edition
was Distresses and adventures ...; second edition A Journey
over Land from the Gulf of Honduras ...; most subsequent editions have the full title as given. A translation published by
Editorial Costa Rica in 1962 contains also a description of Cocos
island by the 19th century French sailor Daniel Lièvre and is
entitled: Viajes de Cockburn y Lievre por Costa Rica.

Fallas, Marco Antonio. La factoría de tabacos de Costa Rica.
Editorial Costa Rica, 1972.

Fernández B., León. Historia de Costa Rica durante la dominación
española 1502-1821. Madrid, 1889. The best general history of
the colonial period. English edition, New York, 1913.

Fernández Guardia, Ricardo. Crónicas coloniales. 1921, reissued 1968.

_____. El descubrimiento y la conquista. 1924. An excellent and well-documented work.

Floyd, Troy S. The Anglo-Spanish Struggle for Mosquitia. University of New Mexico Press, 1967. A chapter on the seventeenth century Talamanca missions.

Fonseca, Elizabeth. Costa Rica colonial: la tierra y el hombre. 1983. Using comparisons with other countries and quantitiative methods she gives an overview of the colonial period.

Fonseca Zamora, Oscar and Luis Murtado de Mendoza. Algunos resultado de las investigaciones en la región de Guayabo de Turrialba. San Pedro: UCR, Departamento de Antropología, 1982.

Gagini, Carlos. Los aborígenes de Costa Rica. 1917. Part dictionary and part gazetteer.

González, Luis Felipe. El gobierno eclesiástico en Costa Rica y la influencia de los sacerdotes en el desenvolvimiento religioso y cultural del país. 1957.

_____. Historia del desarrollo de la instrucción pública en Costa Rica. Tomo I: La Colonia. 1945. In part an intellectual history of the period. Tomo II: 1961. Covers 1821-84.

Gudmundson, Lowell Kristjanson. Estratificación socio-racial y económica de Costa Rica 1700-1850. EUNED 1978.

Hartman, C. V. Archeological Researches on the Pacific Coast of Costa Rica. Pittsburgh: Carnegie Institute of Technology, 1907.

Liceo de Costa Rica. Dos documentos históricos. 1924. Pamphlet on the 1723 eruption of Irazú volcano.

Lines, Jorge A. Anthropological Bibliography of Aborigianl Costa Rica. San Pedro, Costa Rica: Tropical Science Center, 1967.

_____. El arte aborigen de Costa Rica. 1941.

_____. Cabezas-retrato de los Huetares. Publicación no. 4 de la Sociedad de Geografía e Historia de Costa Rica, 1943.

_____. Colección de documentos para la historia de Costa Rica relativos al cuarto y último viaje de Cristóbal Colón. 1952.

_____. Notes of the Archeology of Costa Rica. 1938.

Lines, Jorge A., and Carlos Meléndez Chaverri. Cavallón en Costa Rica. 1961.

_____. Integración de la Provincia de Costa Rica bajo el reinado de D. Carlos V. 1959.

_____. Notes on the Archeology of Costa Rica. 1939.

Macleod, Murdo J. Spanish Central America: A Socio-economic History 1520-1720. Berkeley, Calif.: University of California Press, 1973.

Markman, Sidney David. Colonial Central America: A Bibliography. Arizona State University, 1977.

Martínez, Eduardo. Historia de Centro América 1502-1821. Tegucigalpa, Honduras, 1907.

Meléndez, Carlos Chaverri. Conquistadores y pobladores. (Orígenes histórico-sociales de los costarricenses). 1982.

_____. Costa Rica vista por Fernández de Oviedo. MCJD, 1978.

Milla, José. Historia de la América Central desde el descubrimiento del país por los Españóles hasta su independencia de la España. Multi-volume. Guatemala 1879- . Very wordy, but detailed description of the period; conveys the feeling of the time; good as reference.

Molina, Felipe. Bosquejo de la República de Costa Rica: seguido de apuntamientos para su historia. 1851. Contains some useful information.

Molina Estrada, Ligia. La Costa Rica de Don Tomás de Acosta. 1965. Good on the late 18th and early 19th centuries; information on government and the economy.

Quesada Pacheco, Miguel Angel. Fuentes documentales para el estudio del español colonial de Costa Rica. 1987.

Rivas Ríos, Francisco. "La Conquista de Costa Rica. Primera Fase (1502-1560)." Tesis, UCR, Departamento de Historia, 1979.

Rojas Rodríguez, María Eugenia and Flor de Marfa Herrera Alfaro. "El Añil en Centroamérica." Tesis de Grado, UCR, Facultad de Historia y Geografía, 1981.

Sanabria Martínez, Víctor [Monseñor]. Reseña histórica de la iglesia en Costa Rica desde 1502 hasta 1850. Editorial DEI (Depto. Ecuménico de Investigación), 1984.

Sherman, William L. Forced Native Labor in Sixteenth Century Central America. Lincoln: University of Nebraska Press, 1979. Considered by many the definitive work on Central American labor in this epoch.

Sibaja, Luis Fernando and Chester Zelaya. La anexión de Nicoya 2d ed., 1980, EUNED. Colonial background to 1824 attachment of Guanacaste region to Costa Rica.

Stone, Doris Zemurray. Pre-Columbian Man in Costa Rica. Peabody Museum, 1977. A well-illustrated survey.

Trejos Quirós, José Francisco, et al. Progenitores de los costarricenses, los conquistadores. 1940. Mostly vignettes of the lives of the conquistadors, and good article on the encomienda and repartimiento system in Costa Rica.

Urbano, Victoria. Juan Vázquez de Coronado y su ética en la conquista de Costa Rica. Madrid, 1968.

Wortman, Miles L. Government and Society in Central America 1680-1840. New York, Columbia University Press, 1982. Examines the economy and changes that the coming of the Bourbons and independence period caused. He says that peonage never existed in Costa Rica.

Zamora Acosta, Elías. "Etnografía histórica de Costa Rica (1561-1615)." Seminario de Antropología Americana, Universidad de Sevilla (Spain), Vol. 16, 1980.

3. THE INDEPENDENCE PERIOD (1821-ca. 1825)

Aguilar, Oscar. José Santos Lombardo. MCJD, 1973.

Cerdas Cruz, Rodolfo. Formación del estado de Costa Rica. 1967. Deals with the independence period and shows how San José came to dominate the country. It also has insight on the formation of the concept of the Costa Rican nation.

Comité Nacional de Sesquicentenario de la Independencia de Centro America. Congreso centroamericano de Historia: ponencias, discursos y resoluciones. San Pedro, Costa Rica, 1971. A collection of papers of varying quality presented at the Central American Historical Congress to commemorate the 150th anniversary of Central American independence.

_____. D. Florencio del Castillo: homenaje a su memoria en ocasión a la traída de sus restos a Costa Rica el 27 de Octubre de 1971. 1972.

_____. El pacto social fundamental interino de Costa Rica o Pacto de Concordia. 1971.

Fernández, León. Documentos relativos a los movimientos de independencia en el reinado de Guatemala. San Salvador, 1929.

Fernández Guardia, Ricardo. Historia de Costa Rica: la independencia. 2nd ed. 1941. The standard and well-done work on the period.

Fonseca, Elizabeth. Juan Manuel de Cañas. MCJD, 1975. Based on 1973 thesis, UCR.

Meléndez, Carlos, and José Hilario Villalobos. Gregorio José Ramírez. MCJD, 1973.

Montúfar, Manuel. Memoria para la historia de la revolución de Centro América. 5 vols. Guatemala, 1853.

Obregón Loria, Rafael. De nuestra historia patria: los primeros días de independencia. 1971.

Peralta, Hernán G. Augustín de Iturbide y Costa Rica. 1944. 2nd ed. revised, Editorial Costa Rica 1968. Very detailed and worthwhile.

_____. Costa Rica y la fundación de la república. 1948.

_____. El pacto de concordia. 1955. Pamphlet.

Zelaya Goodman, Chéster J. Las tres etapas de la independencia de Centroamérica. History Department, UCR, 1967. Pamphlet.

_____. El Bachiller Osejo. 2 vols., 1971.

Zeledón, Marco Tulio. El acto de independencia de Centroamérica a la luz del derecho y la razón. 1967.

4. THE CONFEDERATION PERIOD AND CENTRAL AMERICA IN GENERAL

Batres, Luis. La cuestión de unión Centro-Americana. 1881. A pro-unionist argument.

Baugartner, Louis F. José del Valle of Central America. Durham, N.C., 1963. Biography of an outstanding statesman of the Central American Federation.

Castro Ramírez, Manuel. Cinco años de la Corte de Justicia. 1918. A review of the work of the soon-defunct Central American Court of Justice.

Cerdas, Matilda A. "Costa Rica de la Independencia a la fundación de la República." In Historia de las instituciones de Costa Rica. Lecturas complementarias (No. 1). UCR, 1982.

Chamorro, Pedro Joaquín. Historia de la Federación de la América Central, 1823-1840. Madrid, Ediciones Cultura Hispanica, 1951.

Corrales Briceño, Juan Bautista. La anexión de Guanacaste a Costa Rica. 1962.

Facio Brenes, Rodrigo. La Federación de Centroamérica: sus antecedentes, su vida y su disolución. 1965. Reissue of his Trayectoria (below), but without pages 86-130, the part dealing with Costa Rica's withdrawal from the Confederation.

_____. Trayectoria y crisis de la Federación Centroamericana. 1949. Good history with emphasis on Costa Rican separatism.

Fernández Guardia, Ricardo. La guerra de la liga y la invasión de Quijano. 1950.

Gómez, Carmen Lilia. Juan Mora Fernández. MCJD, 1973.

_____. Los gobiernos constitucionales de don Juan Mora Fernández (1825-1833). San Pedro: Publicaciones de la UCR, Serie Historia y Geografía, No. 16, 1974.

Gómez Carillo, Augustín. Compendio de historia de la América Central. Madrid, 1892.

_____. Elementos de historia de Centro América. 1899.

Gudmundson, Lowell. Costa Rica Before Coffee: Society and Economy on the Eve of Agro-Export Based Expansion. Baton Rouge: Louisiana State University Press, 1986. Originally Ph.D. thesis, University of Minnesota, 1982; Spanish edition projected by Editorial Costa Rica. A revisionist work which says that the growth of coffee stimulated rural growth and that the availability of land and this new cash crop stimulated movement to rural areas, thus creating a more equitable distribution of wealth.

Herrarte, Alberto. La Unión de Centroamérica: tragedia y esperanza. Guatemala, 1964. Very comprehensive and possibly the best work in this area.

Ireland, Gordon. Boundaries, Possessions and Conflicts in Central and North America and the Caribbean. Cambridge: Harvard University Press, 1941.

Karnes, Thomas. The Failure of Union: Central America 1824-1960. Chapel Hill, N.C., 1961. An excellent synthesis of the problems which have bedeviled the many schemes for Central American unity. Revised ed., The Failure of Union: Central America, 1824-1975. Tempe, AZ: Arizona State University, 1976.

La Tertulia, 1834-5. 1977. Facsimile reproduction of this political journal.

Lines, Jorge. Libros y folletos publicados en Costa Rica durante los años 1830-1849. 1944.

Mendieta, Salvador. La enfermedad de Centro América. Barcelona, 1919. An interesting analysis by one of the outstanding leaders of the Central American unionist movement.

Montúfar, Lorenzo. Reseña histórica de Centro América. 7 vols. Guatemala, 1878-88. Very comprehensive.

Montúfar y Coronado, Manuel. Memorias para la historia de la revolución centro americana. San Salvador, 1905.

Moreno, Laudeline. Historia de las relaciones interestatales de Centroamérica. Madrid, 1982. Good coverage of events until the 1920s.

Munro, Dana Gardner. Intervention and Dollar Diplomacy in the Caribbean, 1900-1921. Princeton: Princeton University Press, 1964.

_____. A Student in Central America, 1914-1916. New Orleans, Middle American Research Institute, Tulane University, 1983. Recollections of society, with political insight.

_____. The United States and the Caribbean Republics, 1921-1933. Princeton: Princeton University Press, 1974.

Núñez, Francisco María. Rafael Francisco Osejo. MCJD, 1973.

Obregón, Clotilde. "La primera administración del Dr. José María Castro Madriz 1847-1849." Tesis de Grado, UCR, 1968.

Obregón Loría, Rafael. De nuestra historia patria: (3) Costa Rica en la Federación. 1968.

Pérez, Héctor, and Ciro Cardoso. Centroamérica y la economía occidental. EUCR, 1978. A semi-marxist overview of Central American economics. Interesting but not fully objective.

Richard, Pablo, and Diego Irázbal. Religión y política en América
Central. 1982.

Salvatierra, Sofonías. Compendio de historia de Centro América.
Managua, 1946.

Stansifer, Charles L. "The Central American Career of E. George
Squier." Ph.D. dissertation, Tulane University, 1959. Excellent
study of Great Britain's part in the breakup of the Central
American Confederation.

Torres Rivas, Edilberto. Interpretación del desarrollo social centroamericano. 1971. Defends dependency theory describing the
development of Central American society and economy.

Vega Carballo, José Luis. Orden y progreso: la formación del
estado nacional en Costa Rica. 1981.

Woodward, Ralph Lee. Central America, a Nation Divided. New
York: Oxford University Press, 1976; second edition, 1985.
Widely-used survey textbook.

5. THE PERIOD 1840-1890

Alemán Bolaños, Gustavo. Centenario de la guerra nacional de
Nicaragua contra Walker. Guatemala, 1966.

Argüello Mora, Manuel. Páginas de historia. 1898. A sketch of
the war against William Walker.

Belly, Félix. Atravers l'Amérique centrale. Paris, 1867.

Bielley, Paul. Le Costa Rica et son avenir. English edition,
Washington, 1889.

Blanco Segura, Ricardo. 1884: el estado, la iglesia y las reformas
liberales. 1984.

Calvo, Joaquín Bernardo. República de Costa Rica, 1886. A
largely political pamphlet.

Castro Saborío, Octavio. "Bernardo Augusto Thiel en la historia."
Revista de la Academia Costarricense de la Historia. Año X,
Nos. 24-26 (enero, 1959).

Comisión de Investigaciones Históricas de la Campaña de 1856-1857.
La batalla de Rivas. 1955.

_____. Crónicas y comentarios. 1956. Episodes of the war by various authors.

_____. Documentos relativos a la guerra contra los filibusteros. 1956.

_____. Elementos de historia de Costa Rica. 1955. (Taken from Montero Barrantes, Elementos de historia de Costa Rica. 1897).

_____. Mora: el hombre, el estadista, el héroe, el mártir. 1956.

Dunlop, Robert Glasgow. Travels in Central America. London, Longman, 1847.

Fallas Monge, Carlos Luis. El movimiento obrero en Costa Rica, 1830-1902. EUNED, 1983.

Fernández G., Ricardo. Morazán en Costa Rica. 1942.

Ferrero Acosta, Luis. Manuel de Jesús Jiménez. 1962. A pamphlet and biographic sketch.

Fumero, Alejo. Juan Rafael Mora. MCJD, 1977.

González Víquez, Cleto. "Capítulos de un libro sobre la historia financiera de Costa Rica," 1965. Vol. II. The story of some scandalous loans in the nineteenth century.

_____. "El Sufragio en Costa Rica ante la historia y la legislación," Obras Históricas. Universidad de Costa Rica, 1958. Vol. I. An excellent account of the political developments and pressures from the 1830s to Tomás Guardia (1870s); also contains various documents pertaining to that era.

Guier, Enrique. William Walker. 1971.

Hernández, Edward Dennis. "Modernization and Dependency in Costa Rica during the Decade of the 1880s." Ph.D. dissertation, UCLA, 1975.

Iglesias, Rafael. Apuntes de Rafael Iglesias. 1967. Autobiography of a Costa Rican dictator.

Instituto de Alajuela. Libros del Centenario de Juan Santamaría. Alajuela, 1934. Very filial-pietistic.

Jamison, James Carson. "La segunda batalla de Rivas." Boletín del Museo Nacional (San José), vol. I, no. 1, 1955.

_____. With Walker in Nicaragua. Columbia, Mo., 1909. Personal memoirs of a participant in much of the action.

Jinesta, Carlos. Juan Mora Fernández (1784-1854). 1938. A 43-page laudatory biography.

Joint Commission of the United States and Costa Rica. Case of the Accessory Transit Company (Opinion of the Costa Rican Commissioner, Luis Molina). Washington, D.C.

Masís Rojas, Teresa. Breve introducción para el estudio de la guerra contra los filibusteros 1856-57. 1956. A day-by-day chronology; serves as a splendid introduction.

Meléndez Ch., Carlos. José María Montealegre. 1968. A good biography which also has information on political trends of the times and a new slant on President Juan Rafael Mora.

_____. Manuel María Guitérrez. MCJD, 1979.

Navarro, José D. Páginas olvidadas. 1941. About the Costa Rican soldiers who fought against Guatemalan General Justo Rufino Barrios in 1885.

Obregón Loría, Rafael. El campaña del tránsito: 1856-1857. San Pedro: Editorial Universitaria, 1956. Military account of the war against William Walker; very complete and worthwhile history.

_____. De nuestra historia patria: la caída de Carrillo. San Pedro, 1967.

_____. Dr. José María Castro Madriz. 1949.

Pacheco, León. Mauro Fernández, MCJD, 1973.

Peralta, Hernán. Costa Rica y la fundación de la república. 1948.

_____. El Colegio San Luis Gonzaga. 1941.

_____. El tres de junio de 1850. 1950.

Pinaud, José María. La epopeya del civismo costarricense: el 7 de noviembre de 1889. MCJD, 1979; original edition 1942.

Roche, Jeffrey. Historia de los Filibusteros. MCJD, 1980; original edition 1908.

Rodríguez Porras, Armando. Juan Rafael Mora Porras y la guerra contra los filibusteros. 1955. An interesting example of Costa Rican family history.

Sanabria M., Víctor. Bernardo Agusto Thiel, segundo obispo de Costa Rica. 1941. Some good views of the political events in the 1880s and 1890s, the time the Jesuits were expelled.

Sancho Riba, Eugenio. "Merchant-Planters and Modernization: An Early Liberal Experiment in Costa Rica, 1847-1870." Ph.D. dissertation, University of California at San Diego, 1982.

Scroggs, William Oscar. Filibusters and Financiers. New York, Macmillan, 1916. Still the best thing on William Walker.

Sociedad de Geografía e Historia de Costa Rica. Las verdaderas causas de la caída y muerte del General Don Francisco Morazán. 1941. Pamphlet.

Wagner, Moritz, and Carl Scherzer. La República de Costa Rica en Centro América. Translated from German, 1944. Excellent travel account of life in Costa Rica around the 1850s.

Woodbridge A., Paul. Los contratos Webster-Mora. 1968. Some interesting revelations of the machinations of some of the country's foremost heroes.

6. THE "LIBERAL" PERIOD: 1889-1940

Acuña V., Miguel. Jorge Volio, tribuno de la plebe. 1972.

Aguilar, Marielos. "Carlos Luis Fallas y el Partido Comunista." Tesis de grado, Escuela de Historia, UCR, 1982.

Alonso, Elena Isabel. Antecedentes y primer gobierno de don Ricardo Jiménez. Tesis de grado, UCR, 1971.

Barahona J., Luis. Manuel de Jesús Jiménez. MCJD, 1976.

Botey, Ana María, and Rodolfo Cisneros. "La fundación del Partido Comunista de Costa Rica." Tesis de grado, Escuela de Historia, UCR, 1982.

Brenes Rosales, Raymundo. "Don José Joaquín Rodríguez: un dictador constitucional." Tesis de Grado, UCR, 1972.

Calvo Gamboa, Carlos. Rafael Iglesias Castro. MCJD, 1980.

Casey, Jeffrey. Limón, 1880-1940: un estudio de la industria bananera en Costa Rica. 1979.

Castro, Zenón. Rafael Yglesias ante la historia: carta política. 1903. A short political pamphlet.

Chase, Alfonso. Max Jiménez. MCJD, 1973.

Creedman, Theodore S. "León Cortés y su tiempo." Anales de la Academia de Geografía e Historia de Costa Rica, 1967-1969, pp. 149-167.

_____. "The Political Development of Costa Rica: 1936-1944: Politics of an Emerging Welfare State in a Patriarchal Society." Ph.D. dissertation, University of Maryland, 1971.

Cruz, Vladimir de la. Las luchas sociales en Costa Rica 1870-1930. 1980. Presents many details of the workers' movement which were not previously available. Well documented and organized.

DiLuca, Clara. "El Partido Unión Católica: primer partido ideológico de Costa Rica." Tesis de Grado, UCR, 1973.

Documentos relativas a la transacción (verificados entre los partidos políticos de la República con el fin de elegir un presidente para el período constitucional 1902-1906). 1901. A short but interesting pamphlet.

Fallas, Carlos Luis. Alfredo González Flores. MCJD, 1978.

Fernández, Víctor Hugo. Ricardo Fernández Guardia. MCJD, 1978.

Flores, Bernal. Julio Fonseca. MCJD, 1973.

Frutos V., Juan Bautista. Dr. Salón Núñez. MCJD, 1979.

Gamboa, Emma. Omar Dengo. MCJD, 1972.

Garrón de Doryan, Victoria. Joaquín García Monge. MCJD, 1971.

González, Luis Felipe. Biografía de lic. Cleto González Víquez. 1958.

González, Luisa, and Carlos Luis Sáenz. Carmen Lira. MCJD, 1972.

González Flores, Alfredo. La crisis económica de Costa Rica. 1936.

_____. El petróleo y la política en Costa Rica. 1920. President González's side of the revolution which overthrew him and its aftermath.

Guevara de Pérez, Raquel. Pedro Pérez Zeledón. MCJD, 1971. Biography of a famous jurist.

Jiménez, Carlos María. Historia de la aviación en Costa Rica.
1962.

Jiménez Oreamuno, Ricardo. Artículos originales del Prócer.
1946. A collection of articles written by President Jiménez on
various subjects during his long political career.

Leiva Quirós, Elías. Por nuestras fronteras naturales. 1935.
Pamphlet issued to oppose the then pending border settlement
with Panama.

Lizano, Joaquín. "Colegio San Luis Gonzaga," in Revista de los
Archivos Nacionales, nos. 7-8, 1943.

López, Jacinto. La caída del gobierno constitucional de Costa Rica.
New York, 1919. This was taken from La Reforma Social, vol.
IX, no. 2, 1917. It contains a series of articles and facts on
the Tinoco government. Much of this material is also available
in the New York Herald, November 18-23, 1916.

Martínez, Fernando. El presidente Cortés a través de su corres-
pondencia. 1939. Material selected to cast León Cortés in the
most favorable light.

Murillo Jiménez, Hugo. "Wilson and Tinoco: The United States
and the Policy of Non-Recognition in Costa Rica, 1917-1919."
Ph.D. dissertation, University of California at San Diego, 1978.

Oberdorfer, Richard W. "Wilson and Tinoco: United States Non-
Recognition of Costa Rica, 1917-1919." M.A. thesis, University
of Florida, 1970.

Oconitrillo García, Eduardo. Rogelio Fernández Güell: escritor,
poeta y caballero andante. 1980.

O'Connor, Suzanne. "Costa Rica in the World Community of Nations,
1919-1939." Ph.D. Dissertation, Loyola University (Illinois),
1976. A Case Study in Latin American Internationalism.

Oliva Medina, Mario. Artesanos y obreros costarricenses, 1880-1914.
1985.

Peralta, Hernán. Don Rafael Yglesias (apuntes para su biografía).
1968.

Quirós Berrocal, Ana Cecilia. "Ascensión Esquivel Ibarra: análisis
de la libertad dentro del orden." Tesis de grado, UCR, 1957.

Rodríguez Ruiz, Armando. Administración González Flores. EUCR,
1978.

Rodríguez Vega, Eugenio. Los días de Don Ricardo Jiménez.
1971. A good introduction to the period.

Salazar Mora, Orlando. Máximo Fernández. MCJD, 1975. A
biography of an important political leader.

_____. "Le Systeme politique au Costa Rica: 1889-1919."
Thesis: Université de Paris II (Institut d'Hautes Etudes de
l'Amerique Latine), 1980.

Salisbury, Richard. "Costa Rican Relations with Central America
1920-1936." Ph.D. thesis, Department of History, University
of Kansas, 1969.

_____. Costa Rican Relations with Central America, 1900-1934.
SUNY-Buffalo, 1975.

_____. "Domestic Politics and Foreign Policy. Costa Rica's
Stand on Recognition, 1923-1943." Hispanic American Historical
Review, Vol. 54, Number 3 (August 1974).

Sancho, Mario. Memorias. 1961. An insightful journey through
most of the happenings in the early part of this century.

_____. La Suiza centroamericana. 1935. One of the very few
critical works done by a Costa Rican in this period. It questions some of the myths about the country.

Solís, Manuel A. Notas sobre la agroindustria capitalista en el
período 1900-1930: los ingenios y otras agro-industrias. 1980.
Foreign interest in sugar production.

Stewart, Watt. Keith and Costa Rica: a biographical study of
Minor Cooper Keith. Albuquerque: University of New Mexico
Press, 1964. There is some material on the United Fruit Company in this biography of Minor C. Keith. It deals chiefly with
the construction of the Atlantic Railway.

Tinoco, Luis Demetrio. La Universidad de Costa Rica (Trayectoria
de su creación). 1984. Details the establishment of the university by a good historian who was Minister of Education at that
time.

Ulloa, Ricardo. Enrique Echandi. MCJD, 1973.

Vargas Coto, Joaquín. Biografía del lic. Ricardo Jiménez Oreamuno.
1959.

Volio Brenes, Marina. General Volio y el partido reformista. 1972.

Zeledón, María. "Vicente Sáenz." Tesis de grado, Escuela de
Filosofía, UCR, 1982.

7. THE 1940s

Acuña, Miguel. El 48. 1975. A superficial account of the civil
war; lacks documentation; very controversial.

Aguilar Bulgarelli, Oscar. Costa Rica y sus hechos políticos de
1948. 1969. This is the first objective treatment of this period.
At the end of the volume are printed interviews with some of
the leading figures, but exercise great caution in using them.

Albertazzi Avandaño, José. La tragedia de Costa Rica. Mexico,
1951. A bitter Calderonista view of the period. Written shortly
after the civil war by one of the leading Calderonista political
leaders, while in exile.

Arrieta Quesada, Santiago. El pensamiento político social de Monseñor Sanabria. 1977.

Bell, John Patrick. Crisis in Costa Rica: The 1948 Revolution.
Austin: University of Texas Press, 1971.

Blanco Segura, Ricardo. Monseñor Sanabria (apuntes bibliográficas).
1962. Interesting biography of one of the most important leaders
of the 1940s.

Bravo, Alberto. Tempestad en el Caribe. 1950. Deals with aspects of the legendary Caribbean Legion.

Calvo Gamboa, Carlos. Costa Rica en la Segunda Guerra Mundial
(1939-1945). EUNED, 1985.

Cañas Escalante, Alberto. Los 8 años. 1955. A biased view of
the years 1940-1948 by one of the leaders of the National Liberation party. Reissued 1982.

_____. "Sangre, sudor y lágrimas." La República (March 11,
1951). The closest thing available to a military history of the
1948 civil war.

Castro Esquivel, Arturo. José Figueres, el hombre y su obra:
ensayo de una bibliografía. 1955. A biography written by
Figueres's brother-in-law. Useful for its chronology and some
factual information.

Centro para el Estudio de los Problemas Nacionales. Ideario
costarricense: resultado de una escuela nacional. 1943. The
ideas of the Center and of those who were to become the leaders
of the revolution and the PLN.

Dengo, María Eugenia. Roberto Brenes Mesén. MCJD, 1974.

Estrada Molina, Ligia. Teodoro Picado Michelski: su aporte a la historiografía. 1967. Except for the last 40 pages, which constitute a biography, this volume is a mere compilation of articles written by the ex-president while in exile in Nicaragua.

Fallas, Carlos Luis. Mamita Yunai. Many editions; also in English. Semi-fiction detailing the process of fixing elections in the Talamanca region in 1940 and describing the conditions which Fallas found in the Linia Vieja Region of Limón Province. A very basic book for understanding Costa Rica.

_____. Calderón Guardia, Manuel Mora, etc. 1955. Communist viewpoint of the 1948 period.

Fernández Durán, Ricardo. La huelga de Brazos Caídos. 1955. A very interesting pamphlet about a short general strike which preceded the 1948 Civil War. Published by the National Liberation Party.

Fernández Mora, Carlos. Calderón Guardia, líder y caudillo. 1939. A short campaign bibliography.

Figueres F., José. El espiritú del 48. 1987.

Gardner, John. "The Costa Rican Junta of 1948-49." Ph.D. dissertation, St. John's University, 1971.

Gómez Picón, A. El presidente de Costa Rica. 1950. Pro-Figueres pamphlet.

Gudmundson, Lowell. "Costa Rica and the 1948 Revolution: Rethinking the Social Democratic Paradigm," in Latin American Research Review, Vol. XIX, No. 1 (1984).

Hess E., Raúl. Rodrigo Facio, el economista. 1972.

Krehm, William. Democracia y tiranía en el Caribe. México, 1949. Contains sections on Costa Rica in the 1940s. An exposé type of work. It has good insights and facts. Finally published in English paperback edition in 1984.

Navarro Bolandi, Hugo. La Generación del 48. Mexico, 1957. Good description of the "Olympians" and what led to the 1948 revolution. Pro-Figueres in his treatment of the revolutionary era.

_____. José Figueres en la evolución de Costa Rica. Mexico, 1953.

Oduber, Daniel. Los pagos de la guerra de liberación nacional. Editorial Liberación Nacional, 1953. An accounting of money spent during the Civil War period.

Picado M., Teodoro. El pacto de la Embajada de México: su incumplimiento. Managua, Nicaragua, n.d., Picado's view of the negotiations which ended the civil war.

Rodríguez Méndez, Carlos Francisco. "Otilio Ulate Blanco: algunos aspectos de su participación en la vida nacional." Facultad de Ciencias Sociales, UCR, 1982.

Rojas Bolaños, Manuel. Lucha social y guerra civil en Costa Rica (1940-1948). 1979. Good, well-documented sketch of the period.

Rosenberg, Mark. "Social Reform in Costa Rica: Social Security and the Presidency of Rafael Angel Calderón," Hispanic American Historical Review, Vol. 61, No. 2 (May 1981).

Salazar Mora, Jorge Mario. "El Partido Republicano y la figura del Dr. Calderón Guardia." Tesis de Grado, UCR, 1974.

_____. Política y reforma en Costa Rica, 1914-1958. 1981.

Schifter, Jacobo. Las alianzas conflictivas. 1986. World War II alliance with the U.S. and against local groups with ties to the Axis led to internal political strife.

_____. La fase oculta de la guerra civil en Costa Rica. 1979. An important revisionist work which tries to show that the movement that Figueres led did not have as much popular support as had been thought, nor were their motives as democratic as had also been thought.

_____. Costa Rica 1948 (análisis de documentos confidenciales del Departamento de Estado). 1982. Schifter is the first person to make extensive use of United States government documents for that period. He gives a good portrait of United States intervention.

Ulloa, Frank. Apuntes para historia de la legislación laboral costarricense. Heredia: UCR, 1980. Mimeographed. A perpetuation of the Communist Party myth of the creation of the social reforms of the 1940s.

Vázquez, Secundino. José Figueres: "ciudadano de América" y Costa Rica: símbolo de paz. Montevideo, Uruguay, 1953. Written by the director of the Biblioteca del Poder Legislativo for Figueres's official state visit to Uruguay.

Wolf, John F. "José Figueres of Costa Rica: His Theory and Politics as a Model for Latin American Development and Security." M.A. thesis, University of Florida, 1963.

8. THE POST CIVIL WAR AND CONTEMPORARY PERIOD

Araya Pochet, Carlos. Historia de los partidos políticos. 1968.
A history of the National Liberation Party.

Arias Sánchez, Oscar. Grupos de presión en Costa Rica. 1971.

_____. Significado del movimiento estudiantil en Costa Rica.
San Pedro: UCR, 1970. UENED, 1987.

_____. ¿Quién gobierna en Costa Rica? 1976. An analysis of
the class, age, and general background of political leadership
in that country.

Barahona, Francisco. Reforma agraria y poder político: El caso
de Costa Rica. EUCR, 1980.

Barahona Jiménez, Luis. La Universidad de Costa Rica 1940-1973.
EUCR, 1976.

Bartlett, Peggy F. Agricultural Choice and Change: Decision
Making in a Costa Rican Community. Rutgers, 1982. Shift
to cattle and tobacco; less cheap land for subsistence crops.

Biesanz, Richard, Karen, and Mavis. The Costa Ricans. Englewood Cliffs, N.J.: Prentice Hall, 1982. A sequel to Costa
Rican Life. Although somewhat impressionistic, it is an excellent
introduction to the actualities of the country. A larger version
was published in Spanish in Costa Rica: Hiltunen de Biesanz,
Mavis, Richard Biesanz, and Karen Zubris de Biesanz, Los
costarricenses, EUNED, 1979.

Burnett, Ben G., and Kenneth F. Johnson, eds. Political Forces
in Latin America: Dimensions of the Quest for Stability. Bel-
mont, Calif., 1968. Chapter by Prof. Tomasek on Costa Rican
politics.

Busey, James L. Latin America: Political Institutions and Processes.
New York, Random House, 1964. Includes a chapter on "Costa
Rica and Her Neighbors."

_____. Notes on Costa Rican Democracy. Boulder: University
of Colorado Press, 1962; reissued 1967. A superficial and inaccurate study, but the only one then available in English of
Costa Rican government. Very "Leyenda Blanca."

Cartín Herrera, Sandra, and Ileana Peszk Kalina. "Producción de
granos básicos en Costa Rica: evolución histórica y participación del estado en su desarrollo (con énfasis en el período 1970-
78)." Tesis de Grado, Facultad de Ciencias Sociales, UCR,
1981.

Castro Flores, Gloria Isabel. "Análisis de las funciones administra-
tivas del impuesto sobre la renta." Tesis de Grado, UCR, 1965.

Cerdas Cruz, Rodolfo. La crisis de la democracia liberal en Costa
Rica. EDUCA, 1975.

Cespedes, Victor Hugo, et al., Costa Rica: La economía en 1985.
Academia de Costa Rica, 1986. USAID-sponsored survey. One
of an annual sequence, covering from 1980. The first three,
published by STUDIUM in 1983, were: Problemas económicos
de la década de los 80; Costa Rica, una economía en crisis and
Costa Rica, crisis y empobrecimiento. The Academic covered
1983 in Costa Rica, establidad sin crecimiento (published in
1984), and 1984 in Costa Rica: recuperación sin reactivación
(published 1985).

Delgado Rojas, Jaime. "El pensamiento ideológico: filosofía del
Partido Liberación Nacional: un análisis de la social democracia
costarricense."

Edelman, Marc. "Recent Literature on Costa Rica's Economic Crisis,"
in Latin American Research Review, Vol. XVIII, No. 3, 1983.

English, Burt. Liberación Nacional of Costa Rica: The Development
of a Political Party in a Traditional Society. University of Florida,
Latin American Monographs, Series 2, 1970.

Ernest, Manfred. Costa Rica, die Schweiz Mittelamerikas: Mythos
und Realität; zu den strukturellen Voraussetzungen kapitalisher
Entwicklungsstrategie am Beispeill Costa Ricas seit 1948. Bonn:
Informationstelle Lateinamerikas, 1984?

_____. Demokratie in Costa Rica. Berlin: 1986.

Figueres F., Jose. Cartas a un ciudadano. 1956. A statement of
the philosophy of this important political leader.

Gamboa, Elía María, ed. Los vetos del presidente Echandi: sus
razones y justificación: 1958-1962. 1962.

Garro, Joaquín. La derrota del Partido Liberación Nacional.
1958. Concerns election of 1958.

_____. Veinte años de Historica Chica: notas para una his-
toria costarricense. 1967. A short history of Costa Rica 1948-68.

Gayle, Dennis John. The Small Developing State: Comparing Political Economies in Costa Rica, Singapore and Jamaica. Aldershot:
Gower, 1986.

Hernández Poveda, Rubén. Desde la barra: como se discutió la
constitución política de 1949. 1953. Day-by-day account of
deliberatiois for the 1949 Constitution.

Jacobstein, Helen L. The Process of Economic Development in Costa Rica, 1948-1970: Some Political Factors. New York, Garland, 1987.

Kantor, Harry. The Costa Rican Election of 1953: A Case Study. Gainesville: University of Florida Press, 1958. A pro-Figueres study of the 1953 election. Useful in that this was the first complete study done of an actual election.

Lizano, Eduardo. Cambios sociales y económicos en Costa Rica. 1975.

_____. La crisis del proceso de integración de Centro América. UCR, Serie Económica y Estadistica, no. 4, 1965.

Lombardo, Horacio A. Análisis de una economía agrícola en la meseta central de Costa Rica. 1965.

Loomis, Charles Price, et al. Turrialba: Social Systems and the Introduction of Change. Glencoe, Ill., Free Press, 1953.

McNeill, Helen V. "Teachers in Costa Rican Politics: The Role of Teachers' Associations in the Governmental Policy Process." M.A. thesis, University of Florida, 1970.

Mahar, John. "The Growth of Public Expenditure in Costa Rica, 1936-1964." M.A. thesis, University of Florida, 1967.

Maislinger, Andreas, ed. Costa Rica: Politik, Gesellschaft und Kultur eines Staates mit ständiger aktiver und unbewaffneter Neutralität. Innsbrück: Inn-Verlag, 1986. Contributions in German and English.

Marín, Julian. La crisis de nuestra independencia. 1962. Statement of foreign intervention and foreign control in Costa Rica, from a Marxist viewpoint.

May, Stacey, et al. Costa Rica: A Study in Economic Development. New York, Twentieth Century Fund, 1952, repr. 1967.

Mergener, William. "A Study of Political Patterns of Behavior of the Chinese, White, and Negro in Puerto Rico." San Pedro: Associate Colleges of the Midwest, 1965. An undergraduate research paper.

Milner, Judy Oliver. "Otilio Ulate and the Traditional Response to Contemporary Political Change in Costa Rica." Ph.D. dissertation, Louisiana State University, 1977.

Minkner, Mechthild. Costa Rica: "Entwicklungsmodel" in der Krise. Hamburg: Institut für Iberoamerika-Kunde am Verbund der

Stiftung Deutsches Ubersee-Institut, 1982.

Molina Ch., Guillermo. Integración Centroamericana y dominación internacional. 1971.

Montero Vega, Alvaro. "Necesidad de una verdadera reforma agraria en Costa Rica." Tesis de Grado, UCR, 1961. Written by one of the most important leftist leaders in the Banana Zone.

Movimiento Familiar Cristiano. La situación de la familia en Costa Rica. 1967. A study of the disorganization of the Costa Rican family from a Catholic point of view.

Norris, Thomas L., and Paul C. Morrison. "Coffee Production and Procession on a Large Costa Rican Finca," Papers of the Michigan Academy of Sciences, Arts, and Letters. Vol. 39, 1954.

República de Costa Rica. Tribunal Supremo de Elecciones. Cómputo de votos y declaraciones de elecciones para presidente y vice-presidentes, diputados a la Asamblea Legislativa, regidores, y síndicos municipales, 1969.

Rolbein, Seth. Nobel Costa Rica: A Timely Report on our Peaceful Pro-Yankee Central American Neighbor. New York: St. Martin's Press, 1989. A very light, journalistic account of contemporary Costa Rica.

Sariola, Sakari. Social Class and Social Mobility in a Costa Rican Town. Turrialba, Costa Rica, 1953.

Stephenson, Paul, ed. Costa Rican Factbook (February 6, 1966). Washington, D.C., 1966. Contains many useful statistics and results of past elections.

Stone, William. "The Influence of the United States Agency for International Development upon the Regional Development of the Nicoya Peninsula in the Province of Guanacaste, Costa Rica." M.A. thesis, Tulane University, 1968.

Suñol, Julio C. Roberto Vesco compra una república. 1974.

Trejos Escalante, Fernando. Libertad y seguridad; Libertad económica y seguridad social. 1963. Capitalistic orientation.

Vílchez Vargas, Fernando. "El Presupuesto de la administración central y la planificación." Thesis, Universidad de Costa Rica, 1963.

Wagner, Philip L. Nicoya; a Cultural Geography. Berkeley,

California, University of California Press, 1958. A sociological, geographic study of part of Guanacaste.

Welles, Henry. Costa Rican Factbook. 1970. Washington, D.C., 1970. Very useful and well done.

Worthington, Wayne L. "The Costa Rican Public Security Forces: A Model Armed Force for Emerging Nations?" M.A. thesis, University of Florida, 1966.

Zalazar Solórzano, Joaquín. De una derrota a la victoria de PLN. n.d. Pamphlet explaining why Partido Liberación Nacional won the 1962 elections.

Zeledón, Marco Tulio. Desde la tribuna de la ODECA. San Salvador, 1961.

_____. Historia constitucional de Costa Rica en el bienio 1948-1949. 1950.

_____. La ODECA; Sus antecedentes históricos y sus aporte al derecho internacional americana. 1966. Good historical perspective.

_____. La ODECA en la política centroamericana. San Salvador, 1963. Pamphlet.